The Complete Book
of Arts & Crafts

The Complete Book
of Arts & Crafts

EDITED BY
DAWN CUSICK & MEGAN KIRBY

FALL
RIVER
PRESS

New York

FALL RIVER PRESS

New York

An Imprint of Sterling Publishing
387 Park Avenue South
New York, NY 10016

FALL RIVER PRESS and the distinctive Fall River Press logo are
registered trademarks of Barnes & Noble, Inc.

© 2003 by Lark Books
Originally published as *The Michaels Book of Arts and Crafts*

Editor: Dawn Cusick
Art Director: Megan Kirby
Photography: Steve Mann, Evan Bracken
Contributing Writers: Laura Dover Doran, Cindy Burda,
Kathleen Sheldon, Leda Neal, Jane Laferla
Art Assistance: Lorelei Buckley, Shannon Yokeley

ISBN 978-1-4351-4598-6

Distributed in Canada by Sterling Publishing
c/o Canadian Manda Group, 165 Dufferin Street
Toronto, Ontario, Canada M6K 3H6
Distributed in the United Kingdom by GMC Distribution Services
Castle Place, 166 High Street, Lewes, East Sussex, England BN7 1XU
Distributed in Australia by Capricorn Link (Australia) Pty. Ltd.
P.O. Box 704, Windsor, NSW 2756, Australia

For information about custom editions, special sales, and premium and corporate purchases,
please contact Sterling Special Sales at 800-805-5489 or specialsales@sterlingpublishing.com.

Manufactured in China

2 4 6 8 10 9 7 5 3 1

www.sterlingpublishing.com

CONTENTS

INTRODUCTION

Introduction   8

GLASS CRAFTS

Painting Glass   12
Etching   30

WOOD CRAFTS

Woodburning   52
Clock Making   70
Finishing   84

CRAFT PAINTING

Gilding   102
Stenciling   118
Faux Finishing   136

HOME DECORATING CRAFTS

Decorating Candles   154
Gel Candles   170
Candlescaping   188
Candlemaking   206
Soap Making   224
Mosaics   250

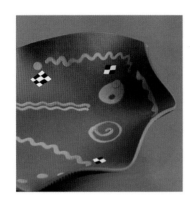

FLORAL CRAFTS

Sachets & Potpourris 272
Dried Flowers 290
Silk Flowers 306

PAPER CRAFTS

Decoupage 324
Card Making 340
Scrapbooking 364
Stamping 382

CLAY CRAFTS

Polymer Clay 400
Bread Dough 424

FABRIC CRAFTS

Tie-Dye 444
Painting on Fabric 458

BEAD CRAFTS

Bead Jewelry 480
Home Beading 496

TEMPLATES, APPENDIX, INDEX

Templates 512
Appendix
  Craft Glues 517
  Tying Great Bows 518
  Picture Framing Made Easy 520
  The ABCs of Custom Lettering 524
Index 527

INTRODUCTION

For most of us, going to a large craft store is a risky proposition. Sure, they'll have the items on our shopping list for our next few projects; that's not the problem. We know exactly where the aisles are that stock them, and we promise ourselves we'll head straight there, pick up what's on our list, and head straight out. Five minutes, tops.

Then, the trouble starts. It's what they have that's not on our list that starts many of us down that slippery—marvelous—slope. What about those sparkling beads on the next aisle? And those rows and rows of bright paints? The wood shapes calling out for decoration? The soap molds that promise to be the start of exquisite handmade gifts? Finally, if we're smart, we simply surrender and wander the aisles, delighting in all the possibilities.

Like a good craft store, this book offers a similar world of possibilities. You'll discover 27 different craft techniques to explore. Each technique will tempt you with a review of the craft's materials, step-by-step general instructions illustrated with four-color photos, a sampling of great projects (each with specific step-by-step instructions), and a gallery of additional projects to stir your imagination. You can replicate the projects exactly as shown in the photos, or vary them in color, style, or materials to suit the artist within you.

As you wander through this book, you'll find an incredible selection of techniques and projects. Look for:

⬧ Glass Crafts (painting glass and etching)
⬧ Wood Crafts (wood burning, clock making, and wood finishing)
⬧ Craft Painting (gilding, stenciling, and faux finishing)
⬧ Home Decorating Crafts (decorating candles, gel candles, candlescaping, candlemaking, soap making, and mosaics)
⬧ Floral Crafts (sachets & potpourris, dried and silk flowers)
⬧ Paper Crafts (decoupage, card making, scrapbooking, and stamping)
⬧ Clay Crafts (polymer clay and bread dough)
⬧ Fabric Crafts (tie dye and painting on fabric)
⬧ Bead Crafts (bead jewelry and bead home decor)

Go ahead, feel free to wander . . . and enjoy . . . and create. Good books, like good craft stores, are indeed a risky proposition. Fortunately, the only danger is that you'll fall in love with one more craft.

GLASS CRAFTS

From wine glasses to windowpanes, glass is everywhere. Why not dress it up a little? Easy-to-use etching creams put the once-esoteric art of glass etching within everyone's reach. And new paints—in a rainbow of hues and translucencies—have finally made glass painting an option, too.

PAINTING GLASS

Take a quick glance around and you'll discover glass objects everywhere, just waiting to be transformed into dazzling works of art. Goblets, plates, bowls, bottles, pitchers, vases, and even light fixtures can be embellished with rich translucent colors and eye-catching designs. Perfect for beginners, the new glass paints are so easy to use that you'll soon find yourself squeezing, sponging, and brushing them onto every available glass surface, with spectacular results!

MATERIALS AND TOOLS

GLASS OBJECTS
Collect old and new glass of all kinds. Don't forget what's in the recycling bin!

ISOPROPYL ALCOHOL AND COTTON BALLS
These are used to condition glass surfaces before painting.

PAINT
Glass paints come in bottles, tubes, pens, and spray cans. Sample different types (and brands) before purchasing an entire collection of colors. The sidebar on pages 14 and 15 has more on paints.

ARTIST'S BRUSHES AND STENCIL BRUSHES
You'll want a variety of shapes and sizes. If you can, spend a bit more for a higher quality brush.

SPONGES
Kitchen sponges (cut into various shapes) or dishcloths, precut sponges in fun designs, or even crumpled paper can all be used to press, rather than brush, paint onto glass.

MIXING PALETTE
Inexpensive plastic palettes are handy for holding and mixing paints while you work. You can also make your own from a flat plastic lid or use a saucer covered with plastic wrap.

PLASTIC APPLICATOR BOTTLES
Pour glass paint into these and you'll be able to squeeze, rather than brush, it onto your glass surface.

CHANGEABLE PAINT TIPS
Used with tube paints or applicator bottles, these plastic or metal tips create special effects when you squeeze paint through them. Be sure the tips will fit your tubes or bottles.

STENCILS
A large variety of stencils can be purchased precut, or you can make your own from heavy paper or acetate.

PAINTER'S TAPE OR MASKING TAPE
Use tape to mask areas of glass you want to keep free from paint. You can also paint between strips of tape to create straight lines.

PEEL-OFF LEADING
These adhesive circles and lines of "leading" press onto glass for a stained glass effect.

COMBING TOOL
Drag this tool through paint to create wavy lines or other special effects. You can also use toothpicks, knitting needles, or dry ballpoint pens to "etch" patterns into paint.

CARBON PAPER
Carbon paper is used to transfer patterns onto the glass surfaces.

RUBBER BANDS
Rubber bands serve to secure patterns and stencils to curved surfaces. They're also useful to mask areas to paint straight lines.

SPRAY ADHESIVE
Spray adhesive is used to temporarily attach a stencil to a glass surface.

13

BASIC TECHNIQUES

GLASS PAINTS

The variety of glass paints is enough to make you dizzy! New products pop up every day, so read the package to find out if that brand will work with your plans to decorate, use, and clean your glassware. Keep the following distinctions in mind when shopping for paint.

AIR-DRYING OR THERMOHARDENING?

Glass paints are either air-drying or thermohardening. Air-drying paints (also called "no-bake") simply sit and dry for a few days after application. Because the finish is less durable than that of thermohardening paints, use these for decorative items that won't be handled or washed often and for objects that won't fit in your oven. Thermohardening paints are baked in a standard oven after they've completely air-dried. This baking makes them wear better than air-dying paints so they can be used on items that will be handled or washed. (Most brands still require hand-washing

THE BASIC PROCESS

As you'll soon discover, the various techniques for applying paint to glass are almost endless, but the essential process can be broken down into three simple steps.

1 To clean and prepare the glass, first remove all stickers and labels, then wash the glass well in warm, soapy water. Rinse the glass with warm water. Once the glass has dried thoroughly, wipe the surface that will be painted with a cotton ball dipped in isopropyl alcohol (this conditions the glass for painting).

2 Prepare your design as described in the following sections.

3 Paint the glass. The simplest way to do this is with glass paint and an artist's brush or with squeeze-type outliner tubes and bottles.

4 Seal your design. Air-dry paints can simply be left to dry for a few days, but you may want to apply a glaze or gloss to your design to give it a more polished appearance. Thermohardening paints will require baking in an oven following the paint manufacturer's instructions.

TRANSFERRING PATTERNS

You don't have to be an accomplished artist to paint intricate designs on glass. Just photocopy your pattern, enlarging or reducing as needed. Then use one of the following three simple methods to transfer patterns onto glass, and painting will be as easy as tracing.

TRACING: Simply place a copied pattern on the back or inside of your object so it shows through to the correct position on the side you'll be painting. If the surface is curved, cut small vertical slits into the paper to help it fit the contours of the glass. Tape the pattern in place, and then trace the pattern as you paint. Containers, such as drinking glasses and vases, can be filled with beans or another substances to help hold the paper tight against the glass.

SILHOUETTING: To transfer simple shapes—such as hearts, circles, and stars—create a template by cutting carefully around the edges of a copied pattern. Tape or hold the shape in position on the glass, and then trace around its edges with a water-based marker.

CARBON PAPER: Place carbon paper (carbonside down) on the glass surface and place the copied pattern on top. Hold these in place with tape or rubber bands. Trace the pattern lines with a ballpoint pen.

rather than the dishwasher.) Because the type of paint will determine the finishing process needed, you should not use both thermohardening and air-dry paints on the same object.

WATER- OR SOLVENT-BASED?

Glass paints are also either water- or solvent-based. Water-based paints are easy. You can squeeze, brush, dab, or spray them on. Mistakes and cleanup are taken care of with water. Simple to mix, water-based glass paints dry to opaque, transparent, translucent, and even textured finishes. A colorless acrylic medium can be added to make water-based glass paint more transparent without thinning its consistency. Solvent-based paints are usually no more durable than water-based paints, but they do require a bit more time for both preparation and cleanup. Brushes and spills need to be cleaned with mineral spirits, and the flammability of solvent-based paints makes proper ventilation a must.

BASIC TECHNIQUES

STENCILING

Here's an easy way to get professional-looking results quickly. Stencils allow you to repeat a pattern and decorate glass quickly, making them perfect for decorating an entire set of dinnerware.

1 Either buy precut stencils or cut your own from heavy weight paper or acetate (acetate will cling to curved surfaces better and can be used over and over). To make your own, first photocopy a template (resizing it if necessary), then use spray adhesive to mount the photocopy to your paper or acetate and allow it to dry for about ten minutes. Once the adhesive has dried, use a craft knife to carefully cut out the stencil.

2 Spray the back of the stencil lightly with spray adhesive and position it onto your glass surface (rubber bands may used to secure stencils to cylindrical objects).

3 Pour a few drops of glass paint onto a palette, plastic lid, or saucer covered with plastic wrap. Dip the tip of a stencil brush into the paint and then blot it on a paper towel to remove any excess paint—an overloaded brush will cause paint to seep under the stencil. Dab paint into the hole of the stencil with a light, circular movement. (You can use a sponge instead of a stencil brush; just make certain the sponge isn't overloaded with paint.) Allow the paint to dry before removing the stencil.

SPONGING

For quick, easy coverage, try sponging glass paint. This low-tech technique creates a soft, luminous effect in minutes.

1 Pour paint onto your palette, a plastic lid, or a saucer covered with plastic wrap for easy cleanup. Dampen your sponge; then squeeze out any excess water.

2 Holding the sponge level, dip it into the paint. Try a test press against an old jar or a piece of plastic wrap. Apply more paint if the pattern is too faint, blot the sponge against an absorbent paper towel if the paint is too heavy.

3 Now simply press the sponge against your glass surface, keeping in mind that heavier pressure will result in more contact with the glass and more uniform coverage, while a lighter touch will create a softer finish. You can use the sponge to "stamp" simple shapes onto the glass or to cover the entire surface. For a graduated effect, use one color and start dabbing paint onto the bottom of your object, then lighten the pressure as you work your way up. For a graduated effect with multiple colors, use several colors, blending one color into the next as you progress.

MASKING

Wondering how to get crisp, straight lines when you lack the steady hand of a neurosurgeon? Learn the simple trick of masking (using tape to keep a section of your glass paint-free), and decorating your glass with parallel stripes and geometric grids will be a snap.

1 Apply painter's tape or masking tape onto glass, remembering that the areas covered with tape will remain free of paint. For instance, to paint a stripe around a drinking glass, place two parallel horizontal strips of tape around the glass, keeping in mind that the distance between the two pieces will determine the width of the stripe.

2 Paint around and over the tape. To make the stripe, paint between and on the lines of tape. Leave the tape in place while the paint dries according to the manufacturer's directions. When the paint has completely dried, remove the tape.

OUTLINING

Outlining paint (also called "relief outliner," "contour paint," or "liquid lead") can enhance your designs with bold lines and borders. This paint comes in tubes or bottles with narrow tips, so applying it is similar to decorating a cake with icing. Make sure your outliner paint is compatible with any other glass paint used on your project. Use thermohardening outliner with thermohardening paint, air-drying outliner with air-drying paint.

Learning to outline can be a bit tricky, so practice first on an old jar, keeping in mind that outliner paint flows best in a warm, dry room. Start off making dots to get a feel for how little pressure is required when using outliner. To make a line, touch the applicator tip against the glass. Then, applying light, consistent pressure, lift the tip just slightly above the glass while moving the tube or bottle. Finish the line by gently pressing the tip back against the glass surface while releasing pressure on the tube or bottle. Wipe the tip with a paper towel and replace the cap after each use.

CITRUS SPLASH LEMONADE SET

As sunny as a summer afternoon, this cheerful lemonade set practically shouts "party time!" The cool design will have your guests chillin' before they even take their first sip.

MATERIALS AND TOOLS

Clear glass pitcher and
  4 clear glasses
Air-drying or thermohardening glass
  paints in 2 yellows (one light, one
  darker) and 2 greens (one light,
  one darker)
Paper

Pen or Pencil
Scissors
Clear tape
Painter's tape
Medium round artist's brush
Small round or flat artist's brush

WHAT TO DO

1 Clean and prepare the glass surfaces.

2 Cut large, medium, and small circles out of the paper (use the project photo as a guide to the size and number of circles).

3 Tape the circles to the inside of the pitcher and glasses in a random pattern. (Use the project photo as a guide for placement, keeping in mind that the circles on the glasses should be placed below where your lips will touch when drinking.)

4 Use the medium brush to fill in the large- and medium-size circles, some with the light yellow paint and some with the darker yellow paint. Don't worry about making perfect circles.

5 Use the medium brush and the lighter green paint to fill in the smaller circles.

6 When the large light yellow circles are dry, use the small artist's brush and the dark yellow paint to paint the fruit segment shapes onto only about one-third of the large light yellow circles.

Real Old-Fashioned Lemonade

Ingredients

3 lemons
6 tablespoons sugar
4 cups (960 mL) water
Ice

Use a reamer to juice the lemons. Remove seeds, then pour the juice into the serving pitcher. Add sugar and let stand until the sugar dissolves. Add water and stir. Serve over ice. Makes 4 glasses.

7 When the large dark yellow circles are dry, use the medium brush and the light yellow paint to paint the fruit segment shapes onto only about one-third of the large dark yellow circles.

8 Once all the circles are dry, use the small brush and the darker green paint to connect some of the yellow and green circles with straight lines and some with wavy lines. (Notice that not every circle is connected by a line.) Use the painter's tape, if needed, to paint the straight lines (see page 17).

9 Once the paint is completely dry, bake or glaze it according to the paint manufacturer's instructions.

Designer: Chris Rankin

TIERED CAKEPLATE AND VOTIVES

Custom design this tower of fun and fanciful glassware for parties, holidays, or whimsical gifts. Glass paint is easy to use and safe for serving. For best results, just make sure you review the manufacturer's instructions before beginning your project. And, for years of enjoyment, follow all instructions for the care of your finished piece.

MATERIALS AND TOOLS

Assorted glasses, glass plates, candle sticks, and votives
Glass paint surface conditioner, air-dry
Brushes - #12 flat , #2 filbert, #1 liner
Glass paint, air-dry enamel in white, yellow, blue, apple green, and fuchsia
Paint palette
Cotton swabs
Sponges for stenciling and stamping
Low tack masking tape
Craft knife
Glass glue

WHAT TO DO

1 Wash and dry all glass pieces. Use the #12 flat brush to apply a coat of surface conditioner to all the glass pieces following label instructions. You will be painting the votives, candlesticks, and plate bases on the outside of the glass. Paint the plates on their backs.

2 Basic instructions for painting the motifs:

Flowers—Use the #2 filbert brush to paint the petals. Use a cotton swab to dab in the centers.

Leaves—Stroke on with the #2 filbert brush. To vary the size of the leaves, use lighter pressure for smaller leaves and heavier pressure for larger ones. Stripes—Use tape to mask off the stripes. Use the sponge to dab color between the tape, then remove the tape. For a clean line, use a craft knife to cut close to the tape before removing it.

Dots—Depending on the size of dot wanted, use the end of the liner brush or a cotton swab.

3 Some of the larger areas will be filled in with stencil sponges. To do this, squeeze glass paint onto the palette. Tap the flat end of the sponge into the paint and tap off any excess. Dab the paint on the surface, making sure to apply an even coat. Let the paint dry to touch, then repeat the step. (A blow dryer will speed up the drying.) Each coat must be dry before applying the next. You may need three or four coats to get the covering you desire.

4 Paint the dots on the center (back) of the plate. Allow to dry, then use a sponge to apply an allover coat of white. Let dry, then repeat as necessary for desired coverage.

5 Using the photo as a reference, and following the basic instructions, paint each piece. Use fuchsia for flowers, stripes, random dots, and rim of votive. Mix the apple green with equal parts of white for a lighter green and use for leaves stripes and dots. Use yellow for the centers of the flowers, rims of votives, dots, and stripes. Light blue is used for wavy lines, the base of the candlestick, stripes and dots. Use white for dots, and checks.

6 Allow the paint to dry thoroughly. The paint must cure for ten days before washing. Be sure to read and follow label instructions for care of the glass.

7 Using the photo as a reference, use the glass glue to glue the pieces together.

DESIGNER TIP

The paint used for this project does not require heat setting. However, some glass paints do. Remember to review all manufacturer's instructions before beginning your project.

FANCIFUL BOTTLE SET

This winsome trio shows the pleasing effect of decorating colored glass with darker shades of the same color. What goes into these playful vessels is entirely up to you.

MATERIALS AND TOOLS

3 glass bottles in solid colors
Air-drying or thermohardening glass paints in shades darker than or in contrast to the bottle colors
Carbon paper and pen
Medium round artist's brush
Fine detail artist's brush

WHAT TO DO

1 Wash and prepare the glass surfaces.

2 Photocopy the templates on page 515, reducing or enlarging as needed. Use the carbon paper and pen to transfer the designs to the bottles, using the photo as a guide for placement. Transfer the leaves, seeds, and berry patterns to one bottle, placing larger leaves toward the bottom of the bottle. Transfer the spiral and star burst patterns to another bottle, varying the direction and size of the spirals. Transfer the star pattern to the last bottle, making the stars a bit larger toward the bottom of the bottle.

3 Paint over the carbon lines in desired colors. (For our bottle with stars, we used silver paint to fill in some stars and to outline others with a shadow effect.)

4 Once the paint is completely dry, bake or glaze it according to the paint manufacturer's instructions.

DESIGNER TIP

Oops! Did you smudge a line of outliner paint? Mistakes can be either wiped away while wet, or, if dried, scraped off carefully with a craft knife.

Designer: Diana Light

Designer: Diana Light

RUBY-&-GOLD WINE GOBLETS

Here's an easy way to add old-world charm to hand-painted stemware. Just a touch of gold transforms everyday glassware into an elegant set perfect for special occasions.

MATERIALS AND TOOLS

2 clear glass wineglasses
8 rubber bands
Water-based, thermohardening transparent glass paint in
  ruby and gold
Medium flat or round artist's brushes with
  natural bristles
Fine detail brush
Craft knife

WHAT TO DO

1 Wash and prepare the wine glasses.

2 To mask off areas for the ruby and gold bands of paint, place two rubber bands on each wineglass. Position the higher rubber band just below where your lips will touch the glass when drinking and the lower one about ⅜ inch (1 cm) below that. Adjust the rubber bands so they are parallel and level with the rim of the glass.

3 Use the medium brush to fill in the area between the rubber bands with the transparent ruby paint, being careful not to allow the paint to pool in one spot. This will be easiest if you rotate the glass slowly with one hand while holding the brush and painting with the other. Allow the paint to dry thoroughly before going on to the next step.

4 Hold your craft knife against the inside edge of the top rubber band and slowly rotate the glass in your left hand to loosen the rubber band. Repeat with the lower rubber band. Gently pull the rubber bands away from the glass. Use the tip of your craft knife to remove any paint that went under the rubber bands.

5 To create an even gold border, place a rubber band above and below the ruby border, spacing it a pleasing distance. Paint the marked area gold with the detail brush. Allow to completley dry, then repeat Step 4 to remove the rubber bands.

6 Photocopy the two leaf and tendril patterns on page 514, reducing or enlarging if needed. Tape the straight leaf and tendril pattern onto the inside of the wineglass, positioned carefully behind the band of ruby paint, so that the photocopied image shows through the ruby paint and can be traced in the next step.

7 Use the detail brush and gold paint to paint the leaf and tendril design following the photocopied image showing through the glass.

8 Tape the curved leaf and tendril pattern onto the bottom of the glass's base so it shows through to the top of the base, then use the detail brush and the gold paint to paint the design.

9 Bake the wineglasses in your oven following the paint manufacturer's instructions.

DESIGNER TIP

Glass paints vary in whether or not they are safe for contact with food. To be safe, always paint on the outside of glassware that will hold food or beverages, and decorate cups and glasses far enough below the rim to avoid mouth contact.

PAINTED CABINET DOORS

Paint plus pattern can turn a utilitarian piece of furniture into a charming work of art. This technique uses the tip of a paint brush handle to dip dots of paint onto your glass cabinet doors—simple, but with sensational results.

MATERIALS AND TOOLS

Cabinet with glass doors
Glass cleaner
Paper towels or a lint-free cloth
Pencil
Transparent tape
Opaque white, air-dry, glass paint
Surface conditioner (if required by
  paint manufacturer)
Medium flat brush (if needed to
  apply surface conditioner)
Artist's brush with small round tip
  on the handle
Plastic paint palette (or a flat
  plastic lid)
Old jar or a scrap piece of glass
  (optional)
Cotton swabs

WHAT TO DO

1 Clean both sides of the glass panes with glass cleaner and a paper towel or lint-free cloth.

2 Photocopy the template on page 514, reducing or enlarging as needed to fit your glass doors. Make as many copies as needed to have the design cover your cabinet's panes.

3 Mark pencil lines lightly on the cabinet doors to indicate where the shelves lie, and then use these lines to help you position the photocopied templates onto the glass. If you prefer to paint the front of the glass (for enhanced texture), tape the photocopies of the templates to interior surface of the glass, making sure the pattern is centered and level. Alternatively, you may tape the templates to the front of the glass and paint the inside pane—you'll lose the textured effect of the paint, but you'll be able to clean the front of the glass more easily.

4 If the paint you are using requires a surface conditioner, use the medium flat brush to apply the conditioner to the side of the glass you'll be painting.

5 Shake or stir the paint, following the manufacturer's instructions, and pour a small amount onto the palette or flat plastic lid. If you like, use an old jar or a scrap piece of glass to practice the technique of applying dots of paint with the tip of the brush handle. Redip the tip of the brush handle into the paint each time you make a dot.

6 Use the same technique to apply dots to the glass door, following the design of the templates. To avoid smearing your work as you paint, begin at the top of the design and work towards the bottom. Use the cotton swabs to wipe any mistakes as you go and the paper towel to clean the tip of the brush as needed.

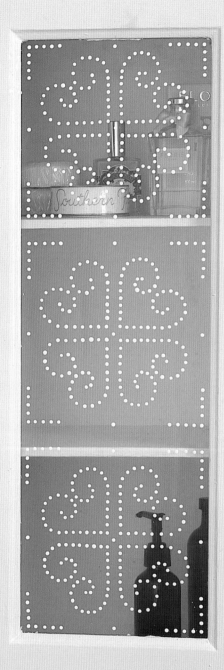

Designer: Diana Light

GLASS PAINTING GALLERY

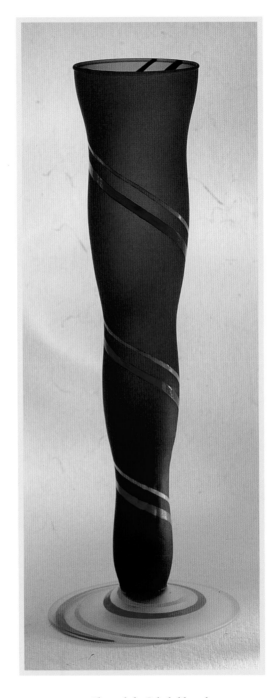

Above, left: Cobalt blue glass creates a lovely background complement to swirls of complementary color. Designer: Diana Light

Above, right: This festive grouping illustrates the versatility of glass paints: blended brush strokes can be as lovely as straight lines. Designer: Chris Rankin

Right: Small glass vials make a great painting surface for translucent colors and designs. Designer: Kelly McMullen

Above, left: White frost paint is a great choice for creating swirling, magical designs that resemble etched glass. Designer: Diana Light

Above, right: Holiday snowflake and star motifs are easy to paint onto glass ornaments and bowls. Designer: Chris Rankin

Left: Think beyond simple geometrics and florals when planning your next glass painting project. Abstract designs offer another whole world of opportunities, especially when you use the transfer techniques on page 15. Designer: Susan Kinney

ETCHING GLASS

It can be your little secret: how easy it is to make unique and functional etched glass items. Though etched glass may conjure images of dangerous, complicated tools and tedious design work, creating fabulous designs on glass is as simple as applying a cream or liquid, then rinsing. The bonus: the results are not only beautiful (think great gifts) but permanent and food- and dishwasher-safe.

MATERIALS AND TOOLS

ETCHING CREAM AND LIQUID
These are the magic potions in glass etching. Ammonium bifluoride, the active ingredient in etching cream and liquid, changes the glass surface to a permanent frosty, matte surface in approximately 15 minutes.

GLASS
Just about any glass surface can be etched. Flat glass or glass with simple curves will prove the easiest surfaces on which to apply the stencil. Glass with many curves or textured glass works best when dipped in etching liquid or when a freehand design is applied with etching cream or resist gel. Colored glass can be etched, as long as the glass is truly colored and not color-coated.

RESISTS
Anything that covers a portion of the glass to prevent etching is called a resist. Stencils are the most commonly used resists, though shapes cut from self-adhesive vinyl, resist gel, and found objects also work very well. Some stencils are sold with adhesive backing, though you can also use spray adhesive to apply to glass surface.

RESIST GEL
Resist gel can be applied with an applicator bottle (see page 36), usually in a freehand manner. Once the gel dries, etching cream or liquid is applied over the gel. Resist gel can also be brushed on to cover a larger area.

SQUEEGEE
Plastic, T-shaped squeegees are the perfect tools for smoothing on adhesive stencils, applying etching cream evenly to the surface of the glass, and scraping excess reusable cream back into the bottle.

PAINTBRUSH
Sometimes you may find it easiest to use a paintbrush to apply etching cream; this technique is particularly useful when etching a freehand design.

APPLICATOR BOTTLE
An applicator bottle makes it possible to apply etching cream or resist gel in a freehand manner. Use an assortment of tips to create lines in a variety of widths.

CRAFT KNIFE/SCISSORS
A craft knife is the best tool for cutting out some stencils; scissors work best for others. A swivel blade works well for rounded shapes.

SAND ETCHER
This technique etches the glass by sandblasting the surface. The materials to do this safely at home are now available in a kit that you can purchase at craft supply stores. A nozzle attached to a bottle of abrasive grit and a can of propellant delivers the sand exactly where you want it.

BASIC TECHNIQUES

MAKING STENCILS

The design and style of the resist are probably the most important decisions you will make in glass etching, and your options are unlimited. Although stencils are widely available in craft stores, it is simple and fun to make your own.

1 You can create a stencil from just about any design, though it's a good idea to choose images with simple lines and shapes, at least at first. Enlarge or reduce images to the desired size.

2 Position a sheet of self-adhesive vinyl on a flat work surface with the adhesive side facing down. Lay a sheet of carbon paper on top of the vinyl, then lay the design on top of the paper. Applying a few strips of double-sided tape between layers is a good idea.

3 Use a ballpoint pen to trace around the design; the carbon will transfer the design on top of the vinyl. Remove the design and the carbon paper.

4 Determine whether you want to cut out the stencil before or after applying it to the glass. This will vary according to the design. For simple designs in which you would like to save the inner portion of the stencil, cut out the design before applying the stencil. For larger or more intricate designs, apply the stencil to the glass first. Use a craft knife to cut out the stencil. Remove the inner pieces of the stencil by lifting them out from the center of the piece with the tip of the craft knife.

APPLYING THE RESIST

Regardless of which type of resist you choose, it is essential that the resist be applied properly to achieve a clean etching. Don't rush through this step.

1 Thoroughly clean and dry the glass surface to be etched. Gather materials and place them on your work surface.

2 Press or apply the resist onto the glass surface. If you are applying the stencil to a curved surface, it helps to use scissors to cut darts or wedges around the edges of the stencil so the stencil will adhere smoothly. If the stencil has an adhesive backing, slowly begin to peel off the backing, then lay the stencil down gradually, smoothing it down as you work from one side to the other. If using an object without backing as a resist, apply spray adhesive to the resist.

3 Rub the resist with a squeegee or your fingers to make sure all areas of the resist are firmly adhered to the glass (using a scrap of vinyl on top of the stencil can provide a buffer that helps keep the stencil from shifting). Pay particular attention to the edges of the resist, making sure there are no wrinkles or air bubbles where etching cream or liquid can seep in.

4 Use a slightly moistened cotton swab or clean rag to wipe off any residual adhesive that may have smeared from the vinyl onto the glass.

BASIC TECHNIQUES

When applying etching cream or liquid, work in a well-ventilated area, and take care to wash tools well immediately after use.

1 If you are etching on a curved surface, cut strips of self-adhesive vinyl and apply strips around the outer edges of the stencil to build up an area where the cream can settle; this will allow you to apply enough etching cream to the glass surface without worrying about seepage.

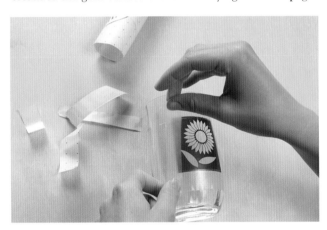

2 Pour or spoon etching cream onto the unexposed area of the resist. If you are etching a drinking glass or other curved surface, steady the glass by nestling it into a towel. Use a squeegee to pull a thick, even layer of etching cream across the exposed area of the glass—or apply cream with a paintbrush for a less even, more textured look. You may also apply cream directly to the glass with an applicator bottle at this point. Work slowly and carefully, as any spilled cream will leave a permanent mark.

3 Let stand 15 minutes or according to manufacturer's instructions. Scrape cream off surface of the glass with a squeegee. (Cream can be scraped back into the original bottle for later reuse.) Rinse off the cream thoroughly with warm water, then remove the resist. Once the glass is completely dry, the etched design will be visible!

DIPPING WITH ETCHING LIQUID

Perhaps the simplest approach to glass etching, dipping is great when you want the entire surface of the glass to be etched or if you're using reverse resists.

1 Determine how much of the glass item you would like to be etched and fill a plastic container with etching liquid to the desired level (see Designer Tip at right). Place the container on a flat, level surface.

2 Carefully place the glass item into the liquid, taking care to avoid any splashing. For small items that are to be completely etched, simply submerge the item in the etching liquid.

3 Let glass sit in liquid for the period of time recommended by the manufacturer. Lift glass out of container, rinse thoroughly, then dry.

DESIGNER TIP

Here's a foolproof way to determine how much etching liquid to use for dipping. First place the item you plan to etch in the middle of a plastic bowl. Add water until the water level just barely exceeds the area you want to etch. Remove your glass item and mark the water level with a marker. Dry the container, then fill it with etching liquid to the level you marked.

OIL AND VINEGAR DECANTERS

Inexpensive decanter tops are widely available and can turn any ordinary glass bottle into a functional dispenser. Add stickers and etching cream and you'll have bottles that are unique and handsome additions to any dinner table.

MATERIALS AND TOOLS

Glass bottles
(with decanter tops)
Glass cleaner
Paper towels
Electrical tape or masking tape
Stickers or decals
(paper or plastic)
Paintbrush or squeegee
Etching cream
Rubber gloves and goggles
(optional)
Ruler (optional)

WHAT TO DO

1 Gather materials together on a flat surface in a well-ventilated, warm workspace (above 70° F, 21° C). Etching creams and liquids will not work properly in cold temperatures. It's a good idea to wear goggles and rubber gloves to protect your eyes and skin. Read and follow all manufacturer instructions.

2 Clean and dry bottles thoroughly with glass cleaner and paper towels.

3 Define the borders of the design by wrapping strips of electrical or masking tape above and below the design area. If necessary, use a ruler to make sure the strips of tape are even. Smooth out any wrinkles or air pockets in the tape.

4 Apply stickers or decals to the surface of the glass in a pleasing design. Use your fingers, a squeegee, or a clean, dry cloth to remove wrinkles or air pockets.

5 Use a paintbrush or a squeegee to carefully apply a thick coat of etching cream to the area of the glass to be etched.

6 Allow the etching cream to set for several minutes, then remove cream by running glass under warm water.

7 Peel off stickers and tape. Clean the glass bottles thoroughly with glass cleaner and paper towels.

DESIGNER TIP

Resist gel can be a lot of fun to work with, especially if you don't want to bother with stencils or more complicated resists. Because it can be washed off easily, resist gel takes the stress out of freehand designing. Apply resist gel, then allow to dry according to the manufacturer's directions. Once gel has set, apply etching cream or liquid, rinse thoroughly, and wipe off gel.

Designer: Megan Kirby

ETCHED TUMBLERS

Colored glassware is widely available at antique markets. Don't worry about looking for sets; collect glasses in an assortment of shapes and sizes and etch each glass with a different design.

MATERIALS AND TOOLS

Glasses
Glass cleaner
Paper towels
Car detailing tape (available at auto supply stores)
Etching cream
Paintbrush or squeegee
Rubber gloves and goggles (optional)
Measuring tape and grease paint pen (optional)

WHAT TO DO

1 Gather materials together on a flat surface in a well-ventilated, warm workspace (above 70° F or 21° C). Etching creams and liquids will not work properly in cold temperatures. It's a good idea to wear goggles and rubber gloves to protect your eyes and skin. Read and follow all manufacturer instructions.

2 Clean and dry glasses thoroughly with glass cleaner and paper towels.

3 Create a pattern on each glass by applying car detailing tape to the outside of the glass surface. You may want to use a measuring tape and a paint pen to mark off sections of the glass. (Make sure you mark the inside of the glass; do not mark areas where you will apply the etching cream.) Smooth out any wrinkles or air pockets in the tape

4 Use a paintbrush or a squeegee to carefully apply a thick coat of etching cream to the area of the glass to be etched.

5 Allow the etching cream to set for several minutes, then remove cream by running glass under warm water.

6 Remove tape. Clean the glass thoroughly with glass cleaner and paper towels.

DESIGNER TIP

Monograms etched in colored glass look particularly distinctive. Blue tumblers, red decanters, or green goblets take on an aristocratic air when etched. Once you've completed several projects etching simple designs, try making a monogram stencil. Tape it to the glass, then follow your etching directions above.

Designer: Megan Kirby

GARDEN LANTERNS

Glass panels with intricate etched designs lend extra character and romance to these garden lanterns. Make sure you purchase lanterns that have removable glass panels.

MATERIALS AND TOOLS

Lanterns with glass panels
Glass cleaner
Paper towels
Precut paper stencils
Scissors
Spray adhesive
Masking tape
Paintbrush or squeegee
Etching cream
Rubber gloves and goggles
  (optional)
Pliers (optional)
Newspaper (optional)

WHAT TO DO

1 Gather materials together on a flat surface in a well-ventilated, warm workspace (above 70° F or 21° C). Etching creams and liquids will not work properly in cold temperatures. It's a good idea to wear goggles and rubber gloves to protect your eyes and skin. Read and follow all manufacturer instructions.

2 Remove glass side panels from the lanterns. (You many need to use pliers to carefully bend the metal prongs that hold panels in place.) Clean panels thoroughly with glass cleaner and paper towels.

3 Trim stencils to fit the surface area of the glass. Lay stencils on a piece of newspaper or any other disposable surface and spray a thin coat of adhesive to one side of the stencils. Apply stencils to the glass with their sticky side down.

4 Use strips of masking tape to create a border around the edges of the stencils. Smooth out any wrinkles or air pockets in the stencils and tape.

5 Use a paintbrush or a squeegee to carefully apply a thick coat of etching cream to the areas of the panels to be etched (inside masking tape borders).

6 Allow the etching cream to set for several minutes, then remove cream by running panels under warm water.

7 Peel off stencils and tape. Clean the surface of the panels thoroughly with glass cleaner and paper towels. Replace glass panels in lanterns.

DESIGNER TIP

There is a bounty of found objects that can be used in glass etching, both for glass surfaces and for resists. Thrift stores are great sources for old glasses, bottles, and other objects to etch, though there may be some treasures in your own garage. A variety of household items make great resists. Masking tape, for example, creates wonderful stripes. Try leaves, flowers, and other natural objects; simply apply the material with spray adhesive and press on glass.

Designer: Megan Kirby

MIRROR

Craft supply stores sell decals designed specifically for use in glass etching. Here, we've used commercial etching decals to transform an ordinary mirror into a charming decorative element and conversation piece.

MATERIALS AND TOOLS

Mirror
Glass cleaner
Paper towels
Rub-and-etch decals
  (designed specifically for etching)
Craft stick
Masking tape
Etching cream
Paintbrush or squeegee
Rubber gloves and goggles
  (optional)

DESIGNER TIP

Since etching creams and liquids make permanent marks on glass, practice with an unimportant glass surface—perhaps a jar or an old glass—before etching a prized antique.

WHAT TO DO

1 Gather materials together on a flat surface in a well-ventilated, warm workspace (above 70° F or 21° C). Etching creams and liquids will not work properly in cold temperatures. It's a good idea to wear goggles and rubber gloves to protect your eyes and skin. Read and follow all manufacturer instructions.

2 Clean and dry mirror thoroughly with glass cleaner and paper towels.

3 Cut the etching decals out, then use a craft stick to transfer and position decals onto the surface of the mirror (with tacky or blue side down); you will notice that the decals will change color. When you are pleased with the design, use masking tape to anchor decals to the surface of the glass. Remove the clear plastic backing, taking care not to tear the decals. (Read and follow any instructions provided with decals.)

4 Use strips of masking tape to create a border around the stencil, overlapping the tape by ⅙ to ⅛ inch (3 to 4 mm). Do not allow tape to overlap decals, as this will disrupt the etched design.

5 Use a paintbrush or a squeegee to carefully apply a thick coat of etching cream to the areas of the mirror to be etched.

6 Allow the etching cream to set for several minutes, then remove cream by running mirror under warm water.

7 Peel off decals and tape. Clean the surface of the mirror thoroughly with glass cleaner and paper towels.

Designer: Megan Kirby

SUNBURST TABLE

This project features a glass tabletop with an appealing etched design reminiscent of the sun's rays. Folding a craft-paper template in half repeatedly is a simple way to create a tabletop with pleasing, elegant symmetry.

MATERIALS AND TOOLS

Table with glass top
Craft paper
Pencil
Scissors
Spray adhesive
Glass cleaner
Paper towels
Masking tape
Paintbrush or a squeegee
Etching cream
Rubber gloves and goggles (optional)

WHAT TO DO

1 Gather materials together on a flat surface in a well-ventilated, warm workspace (above 70° F or 21° C). Etching creams and liquids will not work properly in cold temperatures. It's a good idea to wear goggles and rubber gloves to protect your eyes and skin. Read and follow all manufacturer instructions.

2 Create a template of the tabletop by carefully laying the glass top on a sheet of craft paper and tracing around the edge with a pencil. Remove the tabletop and cut out the template.

3 Fold the template circle in half, then fold in half twice more to create 16 even sections. Unfold the paper and trace over the folds with the pencil.

4 Trace around the cap of the spray adhesive or any other similarly sized circular item (a juice glass works well) on a separate piece of craft paper, then cut out the template.

5 Position the glass tabletop on top of the large template. Clean the surface thoroughly with glass cleaner and paper towels. Spray the back of the small circular template with adhesive spray then apply to the center of the glass top. Smooth out any wrinkles or air pockets and make sure the edges of the template are firmly adhered to the glass.

6 Carefully following the pattern on the template, mask alternate sections of the design with masking tape, pressing tape firmly as you work. (You may want to clean the glass again once tape is applied to remove any fingerprints or adhesive from the exposed sections.)

7 Use a paintbrush or a squeegee to carefully apply a thick coat of etching cream to alternate sections of the tabletop.

8 Allow the etching cream to set for several minutes, then remove cream with warm water.

9 Peel off tape and remove small circular template. Clean the glass thoroughly with glass cleaner and paper towels, then place the tabletop back on table base.

Designer: Megan Kirby

APOTHECARY BOTTLES

These etched designs feature both positive and negative space, which makes for a varied and interesting decorative effect when bottles are displayed together.

MATERIALS AND TOOLS

Glass bottles
Glass cleaner
Paper towels
Plastic containers
Permanent marker or pen
Etching liquid
Electrical tape or masking tape
Vinyl numbers (available at hardware stores)
Etching cream
Paintbrush or squeegee
Rubber gloves and goggles (optional)
Ruler (optional)

DESIGNER TIP

Etched surfaces can be embellished easily with acrylic or oil paint. To paint both etched and unetched surfaces, use paints that are made especially for painting glass. Rubber stamps are also a very effective method of transferring colorful designs to etched glass.

WHAT TO DO

1 Gather materials together on a flat surface in a well-ventilated, warm workspace (above 70° F or 21° C). Etching creams and liquids will not work properly in cold temperatures. It's a good idea to wear goggles and rubber gloves to protect your eyes and skin. Read and follow all manufacturer instructions.

2 Clean and dry bottles thoroughly with glass cleaner and paper towels.

3 Fill a plastic container with the necessary amount of etching liquid. See Designer Tip, page 35, for a quick way to determine the correct amount of etching fluid.

4 Define the borders of the design by wrapping a length of electrical or masking tape above and below the design area. Apply pressure to the tape to smooth out any wrinkles or air pockets. If necessary, use a ruler to make sure pieces of tape are even.

5 Apply vinyl numbers to the lower portion of the bottle, if desired. Smooth out any wrinkles or air pockets in the stencils. Wipe off any residual adhesive that may have smeared from the vinyl onto the glass.

6 Submerge bottle in etching liquid up to taped line and allow to sit for five to ten minutes. Remove bottle, rinse under warm water, then clean and dry thoroughly with glass cleaner and paper towels.

7 To create numbers on top portion of the bottle, peel off vinyl numbers (set aside for another project) and use the vinyl outlines. Cut around the outline, leaving a large

surrounding border. Remove the outline from the backing and apply to bottle. Position strips of tape around edges of stencil. Apply pressure to tape and stencil to smooth out any wrinkles or air pockets.

8 Use a paintbrush or a squeegee to carefully apply a thick coat of etching cream to the inside area of the stencil.

9 Allow the etching cream to set for several minutes, then remove cream by running bottle under warm water.

10 Peel off vinyl and tape. Clean the surface of the bottles thoroughly with glass cleaner and paper towels.

Designer: Megan Kirby

47

ETCHED GLASS GALLERY

Above: These ornaments demonstrate the different effects you can get with the same design. Two of the ornaments were made by drawing the snowflake design with resist cream and then dipping the ornaments in etching liquid, while the other two ornaments were made by applying etching cream only on the snowflake area. Designer: Diana Light

Above, top right: Virtually any glass item is fair game for etching. To create this tabletop design, a pattern was cut from adhesive vinyl that was then applied to the glass to serve as a resist. Designer: Diana Light

Bottom right: Even small items, such as these glass drawer pulls, make great etching surfaces. Designer: Diana Light

Opposite page, far left: Etched checkerboard blocks create a striking effect on large surfaces such as this martini pitcher. Designer: Diana Light

Opposite page, top right: Etching colored glass, even with the simplest designs, can transform inexpensive dishware into customized place settings. Designer: Diana Light

Opposite page, bottom right: Etching half of a martini glass front creates a triangular pattern that echoes the shape of the glass. Designer: Diana Light

49

WOOD CRAFTS

Discover the softer side of woodworking—burning

gorgeous patterns on wooden bowls and fancy gourds,

building custom clocks from precut parts, rescuing a

shabby old yard-sale find with a fresh new finish.

Best of all? No power tools necessary!

Woodburning

Turn plain wood objects into stunning works of art with the centuries-old craft of woodburning. You'll be amazed at how easily a simple woodburning tool creates rich, intricate designs you can color with water-based paints, wax pencils, or gels. With just a little practice, you'll be making home decorations, unique gifts, and handsome heirlooms to pass on to loved ones.

Materials and Tools

Woodburner
A constant temperature, solid shaft electric woodburner that comes with a universal point (or tip) is inexpensive, yet suitable for both beginning and advanced techniques.

Points
The universal point that comes with the woodburner can be difficult for a beginner to get the hang of. Set it aside and use the following three points.

◆ Small, Rounded Point. Similar to the point of a ballpoint pen, this tip is useful for burning details on soft wood.

◆ Large, Rounded Point. This wider point creates a thicker line and is more effective on hard or rough woods.

◆ Shading Point. Use this spade-shaped point to burn backgrounds and to add shading.

Wood
Premade items constructed from basswood, birch, and pine are available at craft and hobby stores. The characteristics of each wood type are described below.

◆ Basswood. The top choice for woodburning, this light, evenly grained wood burns quickly and evenly.

◆ Birch. This wood has a smooth, hard surface that burns lighter than softer woods. Use slow strokes and the large, rounded point for best results.

◆ Pine. The least expensive of woods, pine's distinct grain and knots can make it more difficult to burn lines of consistent width. Use slow, even strokes and the large, rounded point on this wood.

Needle-nose Pliers
Use these to remove heated points from your woodburner. Make sure they have rubber- or plastic-coated handles.

Sandpaper
Use this to sand wood surfaces before burning and also to clean the woodburner's tip.

Masking Tape
This can be used to cover sections of wood you don't want to accidentally burn and also to hold down.

Gray-and-White Eraser
Use the gray end to remove pencil and graphite marks from the wood after burning, then use the white end to finish cleaning the wood.

Graphite Paper
This is used to transfer designs from templates to the wood surface. (Ordinary carbon paper may leave lines that are harder to erase or sand away.)

Nonfusible Interfacing
This material (available at fabric stores) is handy for transferring designs onto curved sections of wood.

Wax-based Oil Pencils
Use these pencils to color your woodburned designs. A variety of effects can be achieved depending on the amount of pressure used.

Transparent Blending Gels
Gels are used to paint rich color onto wood. They can be blended, blotted, or wiped for special effects.

Stains
Premixed, water-based gel stains add

color to objects while allowing the wood grain to show.

PENCIL OR BALLPOINT PEN
Use these to trace over templates and graphite paper to transfer designs onto the wood.

COTTON SWABS AND RAGS
Use these to remove sawdust and

ash from the wood, to blend colors, and to remove mistakes.

METAL RULER
A metal ruler will help you both draw and burn straight lines.

BASIC TECHNIQUES

PRACTICING WOODBURNING STROKES

It takes just a little practice to get the hang of woodburning techniques. Grab some scrap pieces of wood and try your hand at these basic strokes.

LINES

Insert the small or large, rounded point and heat the woodburner. Hold the tool's handle just as you would a pencil, at a normal writing angle, then touch the point to the wood and pull the tool toward you in a smooth, fluid motion. Woodburning designs are created by the speed of your stroke across the wood, not the amount of pressure you apply to the tool. Make fine, light lines with light, quick strokes and dark, deeper lines with slow strokes. Never push or force the burner's tip into the wood. Lift the point from the surface as soon as you finish a line or whenever you need to hesitate; otherwise, it will burn a spot onto the wood. You may find it helpful to use a metal ruler as a guide while you work.

DESIGNER TIP

Easy does it! Remember that you can always make a light line darker, but you can't make dark areas lighter. When you're first learning, burn all areas lightly at first, then reburn to darken them as needed.

DESIGNER TIP

Carbon residue on the woodburner's point is the culprit behind most woodburning problems. These black deposits can cause the point to drag or make lighter-than-desired lines. Check your point often and, if it's dirty, clean it with a piece of sandpaper. Also, tiny ash flakes will accumulate on the wood's surface as you burn your design—stop occasionally and blow or brush these away so your designs will burn deep enough.

STIPPLING OR DOTS

Insert the small or large, rounded point and heat the woodburner. Hold the tool straight above the wood's surface. Touch the point to the wood just long enough to create the size dot desired and then lift quickly. The longer you hold the point to the surface, the larger and deeper the dot will burn.

SHADING

Insert the shading point and heat the woodburner. Hold the point's flattened, spade-shaped part level against the wood while moving the woodburner in small circles. Remember, the length of time the point touches the wood's surface will determine how dark the shading is—don't press the point into the wood.

DESIGNER TIP

Ouch! A woodburner's shaft and point are extremely hot, so be sure to use needle-nose pliers with rubber handles to change points. Also, place both hot points and the pliers on a heat-resistant glass, metal, or ceramic surface when not in use. Your woodburner will come with a bent wire holder to cradle the shaft of the burner when it's not in use. To make sure the hot woodburner doesn't tip over, tape this wire holder to a ceramic tile and then tape the tile to your work surface.

Less than confident in your artistic skills? Don't despair: Easy-to-transfer templates will let you burn just about any design like a pro.

1 Use a photocopy machine to enlarge or reduce the template as needed. If you prefer to work with thinner paper, transfer the template from the copy paper onto tracing paper. Next, cut out the design, leaving a border around all edges.

2 Use masking tape to attach the top of the design to your wood surface; then slip a piece of graphite paper under the design, graphite side to the wood.

BASIC TECHNIQUES

3 Using a pencil or ballpoint pen, press firmly while tracing the lines of the designs to transfer it to the wood. You may need to move the graphite paper around in order to transfer the entire design. When done, lift the graphite paper and template and use a pencil to darken any lines that are too light.

4 Flexible templates (used to transfer designs onto curved areas of wood) can be made from nonfusible interfacing commonly used in sewing (never use fusible, iron-on interfacing for this purpose). To do so, simply place the semitransparent interfacing over the template and trace the design with a ballpoint pen (a pencil may cause the material to tear). If necessary, cut this new interfacing template into sections so it can be taped to the curved portions of wood. Slide graphite paper beneath the interfacing and trace the lines of the design with a ballpoint pen.

Color can add a whole new dimension to your woodburning designs. These simple-to-use pencils, gels, and stains will enhance your work without obscuring the beauty of the woodburning. Be sure to wipe off your woodburned surface well before adding color.

WAX-BASED OIL PENCILS

The wax in these pencils helps their colors adhere to wood. To get light, pastel colors that allow the wood grain to show through, let the pencil just skim the surface as you move it back and forth over the area you want to color. Medium pressure with short back and forth or circular motions will result in more color with less wood showing through. Heavy pressure (press the pencil against the wood as firmly as possible without breaking the point and use short, back and forth strokes) produces bright, deep colors.

56

When you finish coloring your design, use your finger, the tip of a cotton swab, or a pastel blending stick to blend the colors. Mistakes can usually be erased with the gray end of a gray-and-white eraser. Mistakes in very dark colors may need to be sanded off.

WOOD STAINS

Water-based gel stains are available in different colors. Gels don't run like liquid stains, so you can use multiple colors on one piece. Apply them to the wood with a paintbrush, then wipe the area with a clean cloth so the grain of the wood shows through.

DESIGNER TIP

Always use photocopies of templates, so you can use the originals over again. Don't press too hard when tracing the design, or you might tear the paper or dent the wood.

TRANSPARENT BLENDING GELS

These gels remain on the surface of the wood longer than other paints, which allows you to blend, blot, or wipe them for special effects. Apply these gels with a paintbrush, covering all areas of the same color at one time. Use a clean absorbent cloth to blot any excess paint before moving on the the next color. A transparent effect that allows the wood to show through can be achieved by rubbing off more of the gel after blotting. Mistakes can usually be removed with a damp cotton swab if the paint is still wet or erased with a rubber eraser once the gel is dry.

Designer: Shannon Yokeley

EMBELLISHED BUTTONS

These one-of-a-kind wooden buttons make the perfect gift and are a great way to hone your woodburning skills while playing with pattern and design.

MATERIALS AND TOOLS

Wooden buttons
Woodburner with small, rounded
  point
Pencil
Eraser

Fine-grained sandpaper
Clean, soft cloth
Glass head straight pin or 1 finish
  or panel nail
Scrap of wood

WHAT TO DO

1 Lightly sand the buttons with the fine-grained sandpaper and wipe them with cloth.

2 Using the pencil, draw different designs onto the front of the wooden buttons (these can be as simple or as intricate as your drawing and woodburning skills allow).

3 Attach the small, rounded point to your woodburner, cleaning it first with the fine-grained sandpaper if necessary to remove carbon deposits. Plug the woodburner in and wait three to five minutes. Test the woodburner on the back of a button or on the scrap piece of wood.

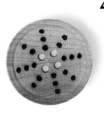

4 Holding small buttons by hand while woodburning will probably result in singed fingers. Instead, push a straight pin or 1-inch (2.5 cm) nail through a button hole and secure it to the scrap of wood.

Then begin burning the pattern into the button, following the pencil lines. Remember to clean the burner's point with sandpaper if the line starts to burn unevenly. (See the techniques on page 54 for tips on using the woodburner and specific woodburning strokes.)

5 Once you've finished all the buttons, remember to unplug the woodburner and leave it resting in its stand until it has completely cooled.

6 Use the eraser to remove any pencil lines that remain.

SAFETY TIP

Wooden buttons can give off fumes when burned, so be sure to work in a well-ventilated area.

OAK-LEAF GOURD VASE

Artists have used burn techniques to decorate gourds for thousands of years. This project uses woodburning and leather dyes to turn a humble cucurbit into an elegant vase. You can grow your own gourds from seed or buy them at roadside stands, farmer's markets, gourd farms, and even on the Internet.

MATERIALS AND TOOLS

Kettle gourd with a narrow top
Dust mask
Basin with warm water
Stainless-steel scouring pad
Clean rag or old towel
Hacksaw
Slip-resistant surface (a block of
   wood or a nonslip rubber mat)
Fine-grained sandpaper
Long-handled screwdriver

Several small pebbles
Scraper tools (serrated utensils,
   grapefruit spoons, sharp seashells,
   and hacksaw blades are all possi-
   bilities)
Painter's tape
Flat black enamel spray paint
Graphite paper
Pencil
Woodburner with small,
   rounded point

Light brown, mahogany, olive
   green, and black leather dyes
2 foam brushes, 1 inch (2.5 cm)
   wide
Cotton swabs
Clear satin lacquer spray finish
Rubber or latex gloves
Hair dryer
Well-ventilated workspace

WHAT TO DO

1 Use the stainless steel scouring pad and warm water to remove the dirt and mold from the surface of the gourd, being careful not to scratch its skin. Dry the gourd with the clean rag or old towel.

2 To cut the gourd, first lay it on its side on a slip-resistant surface, such as a block of wood or a nonslip rubber mat. With one hand holding the gourd firmly and the other holding the hacksaw, make a few short pull strokes to start the cut line, then saw at a slight angle right through the neck of the gourd. Use the fine-grained sandpaper to smooth any rough spots.

3 Because the gourd's opening is narrow, it will be difficult to clean the inside thoroughly. Empty out any seeds and pulp, using the long-handled screwdriver to help break up any stuck areas. Place a few small pebbles in the gourd and shake it gently to help loosen the pulp from the sides. Use your scraper tools to scrape to the extent you can reach, paying attention to the part of the interior that's visible.

4 Once the gourd is clean, use the sandpaper to smooth the inside walls of the opening, again paying attention to the part that's visible. Place painter's tape around the top exterior section of the gourd to pro-

tect it from paint. Then spray the inside opening carefully with the flat black enamel spray paint. Allow the paint to dry thoroughly and then remove the painter's tape.

5 Trace a leaf shape to use as a pattern, then reduce or enlarge it as needed to fit your gourd. If you are photocopying real leaves, remember to also reduce or enlarge them to fit. Transfer the photocopied designs to your gourd, using graphite paper. Place each leaf in a random pattern that's pleasing to you. Add the acorns and branches to the top portion of the gourd.

(continues on page 62)

Designer: Dyan Mai Peterson

6 Attach the small, rounded point to your woodburner, cleaning it first with the fine-grained sandpaper if necessary to remove carbon deposits. Plug the woodburner in and wait three to five minutes; then test the woodburner on the bottom of the gourd (or a scrap from the part you cut) to make sure it is burning a clean, even line.

7 Begin burning the design into the gourd, following the graphite lines. Remember to clean your burner's point with the sandpaper if the line starts to burn unevenly or debris from the gourd skin builds up on the point.

8 Wearing rubber or latex gloves to protect your hands, use one of the foam brushes to coat the entire surface of the gourd's exterior with the light brown leather dye. Don't overload the brush with dye—you'll find that a little goes a long way. Use the hair dryer to dry the gourd completely.

9 Use cotton swabs to apply additional leather dye colors over the light brown dye that's already on the acorns and their caps. Use mahogany dye for the acorns and olive green dye for their caps. Use the hair dryer to dry the dye on the acorns.

10 Use the other foam brush to go over the light brown background of the design with the black leather dye. Use cotton swabs to rub the dye into tight corners of the design. Dry thoroughly with a hair dryer. Apply a second coat of black dye if needed.

11 To seal the gourd and protect your work, apply a fine mist of the clear satin lacquer spray and allow it to dry. Apply two more light coats, allowing plenty of drying time between each coat.

SAFETY TIP

Many people are allergic to the dust created by cleaning and cutting gourds, so always wear a dust mask when doing so. You should also wear a mask when using the woodburning tool and applying the spray lacquer. If you can't work on this project outdoors, be sure to do so in a well-ventilated room.

TIDAL BOWL

The swell and surge of the sea seem the perfect pattern to encircle a bowl. Whether it sits on the dinner table holding the salad or offers snacks at a party, this is one work of art you'll enjoy using and displaying.

MATERIALS AND TOOLS

Unfinished wooden salad bowl
  (make sure it's symmetrical)
Fine-grained sandpaper
Clean, soft cloth
Woodburner with small, rounded point
Pencil and eraser
Graphite paper
Nonfusible interfacing (optional)
Masking tape
Mineral oil

WHAT TO DO

1 Lightly sand the bowl with the fine-grained sandpaper and wipe it clean with the cloth.

2 Photocopy the template on page 513, reducing or enlarging it as needed to fit your bowl. Follow the instructions in Transferring Templates, on pages 55 and 56 to transfer the pattern onto the outside of the bowl, using graphite paper (and nonfusible interfacing, if desired). You may need to repeat the pattern, depending on the size of your bowl.

3 Attach the small, rounded point to your woodburner, cleaning it first with the fine-grained sandpaper if necessary to remove carbon deposits. Plug the woodburner in and wait three to five minutes; then test the woodburner on the bottom of the bowl to make sure it is burning a clean, even line.

Designer: Shannon Yokeley

4 Begin burning the pattern into the bowl, remembering to clean your burner's point with the sandpaper as needed. You'll find it easiest to work by rotating the bowl slowly with one hand while holding the woodburner steadily in the other hand. (Refer to the techniques on pages 54 and 55 for tips on using the woodburner and specific strokes.)

5 Once the pattern is completely burned, unplug the woodburner and leave it resting in its stand until it has cooled completely.

6 Use the eraser to remove any lines remaining from the graphite paper.

7 Rub the bowl (both inside and out) with mineral oil periodically to maintain the quality of the wood. Do not use wood stain.

Designer: Shannon Yokeley

ALPHABET STEP STOOL

We agree: It's way too cute to stand on. In fact, this child's step stool is something that will probably be passed down from generation to generation.

MATERIALS AND TOOLS

Wooden footstool
Fine-grained sandpaper
Clean, soft cloth
Pencil and eraser
Graphite paper

Woodburner with small, rounded
  point
Scrap of same kind of wood
  (optional)
Wax-based oil pencils

Cotton swabs
Clear wood sealer or stain
Foam paintbrush

WHAT TO DO

1 Lightly sand the stool with the fine-grained sandpaper and wipe it with the clean, soft cloth.

2 Photocopy the templates on page 512, reducing or enlarging it as needed to fit the top of your stool. Follow the instructions in Transferring Templates on pages 55 and 56 to transfer the pattern onto the top of the stool, using the graphite paper.

3 Attach the small, rounded point to your woodburner, cleaning it first with the fine-grained sandpaper if necessary to remove carbon deposits. Plug the woodburner in and wait three to five minutes; then test the woodburner on the bottom on the stool or a scrap piece of wood to make sure it is burning a clean, even line.

4 Begin burning the pattern into the stool, following the transferred design. Remember to clean your burner's point with the sandpaper if the line starts to burn unevenly. (Refer to the techniques on pages 54 and 55 for tips on using the woodburner and specific strokes.)

5 Once the pattern is completely burned, remember to unplug the woodburner and leave it resting in its stand until it has completely cooled.

6 Use the eraser to remove any lines remaining from the graphite paper.

7 Use the wax-based oil pencils to color the pattern to your liking. See Adding Color on pages 56 and 57 for information on using these pencils on wood. Use cotton swabs or the eraser to remove any mistakes. (You also may be able to lightly sand away mistakes.)

8 Protect the design by applying a clear wood sealer or a stain, using a foam paintbrush and a very light stroke to avoid smearing the pencil colors.

ROUND KEEPSAKE BOX

Plain, inexpensive wooden boxes are easy to transform into spectacular treasure boxes. Choose a pattern that matches your home's decor, your personality, or a special occasion.

MATERIALS AND TOOLS

Unfinished round wooden box with a flat lid
Fine-grained sandpaper
Clean, soft cloth

Woodburner with small, rounded point
Large, rounded point (optional, see tip)

Pencil
Graphite paper
Eraser
Wood stain (optional)

WHAT TO DO

1 Lightly sand the box and lid with the fine-grained sandpaper and wipe them with the cloth.

2 Photocopy the template on page 513, reducing or enlarging it as needed to fit your box's lid. Follow the instructions in Transferring Templates on pages 56 and 57 to transfer the pattern onto the box lid, using the graphite paper.

3 Attach the small, rounded point to your woodburner, cleaning it first with the fine-grained sandpaper if necessary to remove carbon deposits. Plug the woodburner in and wait three to five minutes; then test the woodburner on the bottom of the box

to make sure it is burning a clean, even line.

4 Begin burning the pattern into the lid, remembering to clean your burner's point with the sandpaper if the line starts to burn unevenly. When woodburning a round object, it's easiest to rotate the object slowly with one hand while holding the woodburner steadily in the other hand. (See the techniques on pages 54 and 55 for tips on using the woodburner and specific woodburning strokes.)

5 Once the pattern is burned, remember to unplug the woodburner and leave it resting in its stand until it has completely cooled.

6 Use the eraser to remove any lines remaining from the graphite paper.

7 You may stain the wooden box or leave it plain.

DESIGNER TIP

If you've become handy with the woodburner, you may want to try using a large, rounded point to burn some of the thicker lines in this pattern. The burning will go faster, but you'll have less control of your line.

WOODBURNING GALLERY

Right: A wood mailbox makes a great canvas for a woodburned landscape created with a shading tool. Designer: Katherine Aimone

Below: The woven plaits of a wood basket are a fun canvas for woodburning designs. Designer: Susan Kieffer

Opposite page, top right: Frame your favorite photos in woodburned motifs. Designer: Susan Kieffer

Opposite page, bottom right: Wood eggs (sold in larger craft supply stores) can be embellished with intricate designs using your wood burner's fine tip. Designer: Susan Kieffer

Opposite page, right: A simple woodburned winding vine pattern creates this stunning effect. The wood boxes are stacked over a plain vase. Designer: Diana Light

CLOCK MAKING

Crafting a clock is a small celebration of the power we have now to affect many moments of our lives. Whether your style is dynamic or restful, whimsical or grand, it's easy to combine a clock's working elements with metal, paper, clay, wood, paint, and familiar objects to create a timepiece you'll treasure. The clock projects in this section will give you an idea of the creative possibilities, but don't stop here. Virtually every technique described in this book can be used to create a one-of-a-kind clock that's both functional and beautiful.

MATERIALS AND TOOLS

CLOCK BASES
Eager to paint and decorate? Purchase a ready-made base in parts or as an assembled whole in one of dozens of availailable styles and shapes.

THE MOVEMENT
Craft suppliers offer packaged, battery-operated quartz movements. Sizes vary, with the largest movements providing best support for big clocks with longer, heavier hands.

THE SHAFT
The shaft is usually included as part of the movement. Measure the depth of your planned clock's face first, to ensure that the one you purchase is long enough to fit through the face and support the hands.

THE DIAL
Precut dials, printed with numbers or symbols and sporting a hole made to fit easily over the shaft, are widely available. Or make your own clock face, using stamps and ink or decorative objects to denote the hours. Modern designs often omit markings of any sort.

HANDS
Find the shape and length you desire in movement sets or packaged separately. Typically made of plastic or metal, hands can be painted or covered for distinctive effects. Lightweight pieces can be drilled and mounted as hands, too.

BEZEL AND PENDULUM MOVEMENTS
A bezel movement contains all the parts of a working clock: the works, a metal frame, a dial, hands, and a glass cover. These units are fitted whole into a prepared base. A pendulum movement is chiefly ornamental, as the battery-powered quartz device moves the gears.

BASIC TECHNIQUES

Once you've chosen a base for your clock, the next step is to decide what type of face you would like. Peel-and-stick clock dials are available in both coated paper and metal, or you can add your own numbers with press type or stencils.

1 To use a peel-and-stick label dial, first hold your chosen dial label against your clock to be sure you are happy with its size and style. Next, remove the adhesive backing from the label, then carefully position it on the clock base, working slowly to prevent bubbles and wrinkling. If you have trouble with bubbles, remove them by inserting the tip of a safety pin into the bubble and then smoothing flat. Severe wrinkling may require removing the label (use a glass scraper if necessary) and starting over.

2 To use a peel-and-stick metal dial, hold the dial against your base to decide on positioning, then remove the adhesive backing and carefully press it in place.

3 There are times when you may prefer the look of press type numbers. You can find them in a variety of styles. Be sure to choose a face that complements the style of your planned clock and the location where you plan to display it. To use press type, first enlarge the numeral positioning guide at right to a size appropriate to your clock, then transfer it onto the clock with graphite paper. Before placing the press type numbers on your clock, practice with a few letters on a scrap of wood. To prevent damaging the numbers, use the lightest touch possible when rubbing them onto the wood, and be sure

to add a few layers of protective sealant to your handsome finished clock.

4 Stenciling provides another way to create a more personalized look. To stencil a clock dial, first transfer the numeral positioning guide onto your clock base as described in the step above, then add the numbers with wood markers or paint and brush. Stenciled numbers can be highlighted with gold or other colors if you like.

ASSEMBLING A CLOCK

1 If you chose to purchase a bezel movement for your clock project, you can skip this step; otherwise, you get the fun of assembling it yourself. If the very idea of self-assembly gives you hives, relax. This is easy—really. The first step is to carefully read the manufacturer's instructions. If you're still confused, look at the nearest clock and try to imagine how the parts may fit together.

2 To start, first stack the washers and hand movements on the front side of the clock. Hold them in place with your left hand, then insert the clock movement into the base's hole from the back side.

3 Twist the movement until you have a secure fit. Turn the clock around and check out the results. If you didn't get it quite right, just untwist the movement and rearrange the front parts.

MARKING TIME

Marking time is a way of measuring life, of describing the dimensions of events and experiences that are important to us. Sometimes we note the length of an experience; sometimes we call attention to the power of each moment. As people have moved from charting seasons and phases of the moon to capturing the closest fraction of a second, the materials we use have also changed. Stones, sundials, springs, and pendulums have led to crystals, magnets, and lasers, the vibrations of which allow us to measure time with an error rate of less than one second every 12 to 18 billion years.

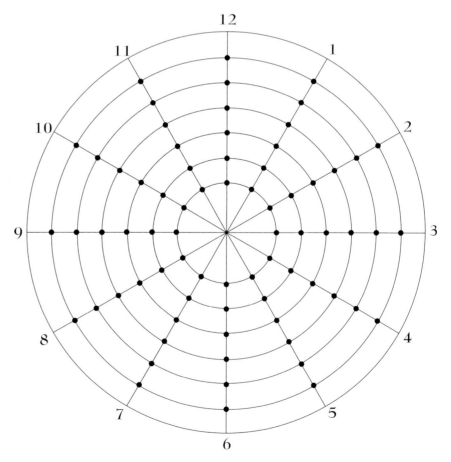

ANTIQUED MANTEL CLOCK

This is an easy way to bring the look of an object from your childhood, or someone else's, into daily use. Experiment with layers of color to find out how rich you want the aging effects to be.

MATERIALS AND TOOLS

Premade wooden mantel clock base
White acrylic paint
Rust color acrylic paint
Dark brown acrylic paint
Yellow acrylic paint
Medium flat paintbrush
Rags
Candle

Ice pick
Hammer
Rough-grade sandpaper
Press-type numbers
Clock movement and hands
Clear, flat acrylic sealant spray

WHAT TO DO

1 Paint clock base with white acrylic. Allow to dry.

2 Roughly cover white coat with rust-colored paint. Streaks add texture, and you don't have to cover the whole thing.

3 Dilute brown paint with water. Wash watered-down brown paint over rust coat and immediately wipe off with a rag. Allow to dry.

4 Rub the candle over areas of the clock base that would be worn over the years, including edges, corners, and places where it might have been handled.

5 Paint the whole clock base yellow. Allow to dry.

6 Using ice pick and hammer, make marks and little holes to create the look of age.

7 Sand clock edges, and any places you have applied candle wax. Sand some areas down farther to show all the layers of color.

8 Following package instructions, position numbers on face of clock. Lightly sand numbers to make them look old.

9 Spray entire clock with two coats of clear flat spray, allowing the first coat to completely dry before adding the second.

10 Insert clock movement, following manufacturer's instructions. See Assembling a Clock on page 73.

Designer: Joan K. Morris

ATOMIC CLOCKS

Wood clock bases are widely available in a great variety of sizes and shapes. The style of this energetic pair inspired the designer to create an atomic clock theme, with the clock's feet resembling atoms and an atomic motif in the background of the clock's face.

MATERIALS AND TOOLS

Unfinished wood clock with clock-
    works
Fine-grit sandpaper
Clean cloth
Computer scanner
Computer with basic graphic design
    software
Printer (color if needed)
High-gloss printer paper
Ruler
Craft knife with sharp blade
Foam brush, 1 inch (2.5 cm) wide
Decoupage medium
Small paintbrush
Assorted acrylic crafts paints in
    molecular colors of your choice
High-gloss spray acrylic varnish
Clock battery

WHAT TO DO

1 Remove the hands from the unfinished wood clock. Remove the face of the clock from its frame. Sand the surface of the clock frame and the clock face with the fine-grit sandpaper as needed. Use a clean cloth to wipe off any sawdust and debris.

2 Scan the template on page 516 onto your computer. Using graphic design software, change the color of the atomic symbol and its background as desired. Print the image on high-gloss paper, using a color printer if needed.

3 Use a ruler and a pencil to find and mark the center of the atomic symbol. Use a sharp craft knife to cut two perpendicular slits in the paper. When opened, the slits should be large enough to accommodate the clockworks.

4 Use a foam brush to apply a thin and even layer of decoupage medium to the clock face. Carefully position the printed atomic symbol on the clock face, feeding the base pin through the slits. Gently smooth the paper down to remove any air bubbles and evenly distribute the glue. Let dry. From the back side of the clock face, use a sharp craft knife to trim all excess paper from around its edge.

5 Select which colors you want to paint which parts of the clock frame. Use a small paintbrush and acrylic craft paints to color the clock. Add as many thin and even coats of paint as needed to reach the level of opacity you desire. Let the paint dry between coats. (In this example, the interior frame surface was painted to match the background color of the clock face. The other elements were painted a variety of bright, contrasting primary tones.)

6 Following the manufacturer's instructions and working in a well-ventilated area, spray a coat of the high-gloss acrylic varnish over the painted clock frame. Repeat as needed to achieve the level of shine you desire, letting the acrylic spray dry fully between coats.

7 Reinstall the clock face into its frame and adjust the orientation of the atomic symbol as desired. Reattach the clock hands and install a proper size battery. Set the time, and enjoy!

Designer: Marthe Le Van

VEGGIE CLOCK

Clock backings come in a variety of shapes and sizes. Though an assortment of charming little veggies makes this clock ideal for a kitchen countertop or windowsill, feel free to vary the decorative motifs to fit your style.

Designer: Irene Semanchuk Dean

MATERIALS AND TOOLS

Wooden clock backing
Heat-resistant PVA glue
Polymer clay, 4 to 6 ounces each
  white and black, small amounts of
  orange, red, purple, green, yellow,
  translucent, and ecru (beige)
Pasta machine, brayer,
  or acrylic roller
Wax paper
Craft knife
Texturing material (such as plastic
  embroidery canvas, lace, or window screen)

Rolling pin
Clock number template
  (see page 73)
Pencil with unused eraser
Black stamp pad
Black-and-white checkerboard cane
Small piece of window screen
Star-shaped cutter (small)
Baking sheet or tile
Cornstarch
Polymer clay cutting

WHAT TO DO

1 Coat the entire surface of the clock backing with PVA glue and allow to dry thoroughly.

2 Roll the white polymer clay into a sheet of medium thickness (about $\frac{1}{16}$ to $\frac{1}{8}$ inch or 1.5 mm to 3 mm) on the pasta machine. You can also use an acrylic roller or a brayer to flatten clay.

3 When glue has dried, position the white polymer sheet on top of the clock backing, then place a sheet of wax paper on top of clay. Smooth the clay onto the base from the center outward. Wrap the clay around the edges of the clock slightly and trim the excess clay with a craft knife.

4 Spray or wipe water (this serves as a mold release) onto the polymer clay (now on the clock backing), then position the textur-ing material on top. Use a rolling pin on the texturing material to create an impression in the clay, then carefully remove the texturing material. Gently dab away excess water with a paper towel. Use a craft knife to cut a circular piece out of the clay in the center for the clock mechanism.

5 Center the clock number tem-plate over the clock, and use a pencil to lightly mark where the numbers (or, in this case, the circles) should go. Remove the template. Press the pencil eraser into the black stamp pad, and stamp circles in the spots you have marked.

6 Roll a snake from the white clay a couple inches (5 cm) shorter than the distance around the clock face. Cut slices from the checker-board cane, then place the slices on the snake until the snake is com-pletely covered, making sure each slice butts against the one before.

(continues on following page)

HOW TO MAKE THE VEGGIES

The carrots are made by shaping orange clay into tapers, then rolling a needle or other tool across the clay to make ridges. Add tiny bits of green to make tops. To make garlic, shape rounded pieces of clay with pointed tops, using translucent clay mixed with a small amount of ecru or beige, then mark as you did the carrots. For asparagus, mix a small amount of black into yellow to make olive green, roll clay into small snakes, then taper the ends. Add small amounts of darker green to cre-ate the tops of each stalk. For corn, roll yellow clay into a short, thick log with one slightly tapered end. Roll the log over win-dow screening to make a kernel impres-sion. Roll a thin sheet of pale green clay and cut several elongated leaf shapes for the husks. Press leaves onto corn, allowing corn to show at top. To make eggplant, mix a small amount of black into purple clay, then form an elongated egg shape. Make tomatoes from orange-red balls of clay. Make green tops for tomatoes and eggplant with a small star cutter.

Smooth the cane slices into the white snake by gently rolling the snake on the work surface. Allow the snake to elongate as you roll, until the snake is long enough to reach around the entire clock face.

7 Wrap the checkerboard snake around the clock face, referring to the photo on page 78. Press firmly but gently, making sure not to distort the checkerboard pattern. Trim excess clay at each end, then set clock aside.

8 Make the veggies (see page 79) and position randomly on the clock face. Bake clock face at the manufacturer's recommended temperature for 20 minutes and allow to cool thoroughly.

9 Make a base for the clock by rolling 3 to 4 ounces (84–112 g) of black polymer clay into a tube slightly longer than the bottom of the clock face. Flatten the tube slightly with a brayer and apply cornstarch liberally to the surface (as a release). Press the clock firmly and evenly into the black clay. Leave clock in place and trim the excess clay edges. Remove the clock face and bake the base at the manufacturer's recommended temperature for 30 minutes.

10 When the base has cooled, clean any remaining cornstarch from the base and the clock face with an alcohol-soaked cotton swab. Apply several drops of PVA glue into the groove in the black clay base and firmly put clock face in base. Allow the glue to dry for several hours or overnight.

11 Assemble the clock mechanism per the manufacturer's instructions.

PAPER BAG MANTEL CLOCK

You see them every day—ordinary brown paper bags. Now you can transform them into a wonderful decorative surface. Choose paper bags from three different sources to create a more interesting, varied appearance.

MATERIALS AND TOOLS

Wooden mantel clock
3 Brown paper bags
PVA glue

Mixing bowl
Spray polyurethane, satin finish

WHAT TO DO

1 Prepare the surface of the clock, as described in the decoupage basic techniques section (page 326). Tear the paper bags into pieces (any shape or size you like). Note: Keep the torn pieces in separate piles (according to bag type), since it may be difficult to distinguish the pieces once they've been torn.

2 In a mixing bowl, combine equal parts PVA glue and water and mix well.

3 Dip a torn piece of paper bag into the mixture. Remove the piece from the bowl, then wrinkle, wad, and squish the paper several times (the more wrinkled, the better).

4 Position the wrinkled, glue-soaked piece of paper anywhere on the front of the clock and smooth the paper with your finger-tips. Repeat this process with additional paper bag pieces—alternating among the three types of paper and overlapping the pieces as you work—until the entire front of the clock is covered. When you reach the edges of the clock, wrap the ends of the paper to the back of the clock. Use a fingernail or a toothpick to push the soaked pieces into any curves or sharp corners.

5 Allow clock to dry for 24 hours, then spray with one or two coats of polyurethane. (Tape plastic wrap over the clock face to protect it when spraying.)

Top left: Woodcarving tools were used to add textured patchwork quilt patterns to a wood clock base. The quilt blocks were painted with acrylic paints, and then a time-telling talisman was created from a foam ball (for the head) and fabric-wrapped wire (for the arms). Designers: Allison and Tracy Page Stilwell

Top right: A mosaic plate forms a clever background for this clock, while a faux fork and spoon mark the hours and minutes. Designers: Allison and Tracy Page Stilwell

Right: An all-over stenciled pattern creates a lovely background for a clock face. Designer: Chris Rankin

CLOCK GALLERY

Right: Add a splash of bright color and personality to a simple clock background with polymer clay. Designer: Irene Semanchuk Dean

Below: A lovely collection of wood trims and cutouts frame a weathered-wood background. Designer: Rolf Holmquist

FINISHING

Do you recall those delightful hours in nursery school in which you were free to slap bright colors onto chunks of wood, conjuring a house or a spaceship or, perhaps, just a glowing tribute to your own happiness? For adults, painting wood is still a lot of fun, but now you get to paint picture frames, wooden lamps, curtain rods, furniture, and more. Look for sprays, pens, antiquing, and crackling compounds. Wood work, after all, is just serious play!

MATERIALS AND TOOLS

PAINTS
Water-based paints and top coats are recommended. High in quality, easy to use and clean up, and completely nontoxic, many of these lines are economical as well. You may also want to experiment with house paints or other specialty paints designed for crafters.

PAINTBRUSHES
A wide variety of flat and round brushes will come in handy. Also look for specialty brushes, such as blending and dragging brushes made especially for craft painters.

DROP CLOTHS
They may seem like a hassle, but they're worth their weight in gold.

WOOD PUTTY
If you're working with unfinished wood, the few minutes of time spent repairing the wood can make a world of difference in the finished piece.

SANDPAPER
150-grit and 220-grit are the most commonly used.

PAINTER'S TAPE
This low tack tape is great for masking off shapes and areas you don't want painted.

TACK CLOTH
This adherent cloth removes wood shavings, dust, and lint from wood. Use it after sanding and before painting. Look for it in painting supply sections.

GLAZING MEDIUM
Water-based glazing mediums are a great way to add special effects. They can also be tinted with the color of your choice.

This clear liquid can be found in painting sections. Read the label carefully before purchasing to be sure the product will give you the desired effect.

SPRAY POLYURETHANE
This clear topcoat is great for small projects and easily disturbed finishes. Choose the amount of gloss by preference and to withstand the amount of wear an object will receive.

BASIC TECHNIQUES

PREPARING UNFINISHED WOOD

You may be itching to start painting right away, but a few extra minutes of preparation can make all the difference in the quality of your finished projects.

1 Remove hardware and ornament where necessary. If you must sand the wood, use the 150-grit sandpaper first, and then the 220-grit, to achieve a very smooth surface. Amend rough-cut patches on a piece with light-weight hole filler and a putty knife; allow to dry, and sand again. Prime the piece or use a base coat product. If you're priming with latex paint, be sure to sand lightly between coats: water-based products will raise the grain of the wood. After sanding, remove all dust and debris with tack cloth.

2 Patch any cracks or holes with filler, then sand the piece lightly with 150-grit paper to create a slightly rough surface for the new paint to "grip." Remove dust with tack cloth.

DESIGNER TIP

Test your finishing technique on an inconspicuous area first. Even if your skills are perfect, the unique combination of your particular wood, paints, and finishing technique can have varying looks. The back side or inside of a piece of furniture is a good choice; for smaller pieces, such as switch plates or candle holders, just purchase an extra one for testing purposes.

CRACKLING

Crackled finishes are a great way to add an aged finish to your favorite wood items. Read the labels carefully when purchasing crackling medium—some products create a porcelainlike crackled finish, while others create much larger crackled patterns.

1 To crackle a surface, first apply a base coat of color and allow to completely dry.

2 Next, apply the crackle medium, taking care to use smooth, even strokes. Allow to dry as directed by the manufacturer.

3 Apply a light top coat in the same color or in a contrasting one, taking care to use smooth, even strokes. The paint will start "crackling" as it dries. If you're unhappy with any areas, simply sand them down and start over.

2 Glazes are another way to add a hint of color. You can add them over bare wood, or use them over painted backgrounds to add visual depth. Clear glazes can be tinted with color, or you can purchase colored glazes.

WASHES AND GLAZES

Sometimes you may prefer to add just a little color, allowing the natural grain of the wood to show through your paint. There are several simple ways to achieve this effect.

1 Washes are an easy way to add just a hint of color. To create a wash, simply dilute your favorite acrylic paint color with water. The more water, the thinner the paint and the more the wood will show through. For best results, test your wash dilution on a piece of scrap wood, then adjust the amount of water or paint to your preference.

TINTING A GLAZE

Glazing is the finish that adds the je ne sais quoi to so many decorating projects: it brings color without bulk, it draws and holds light, and it can imperceptibly shift a surface toward antiquity. Start with about 2 teaspoons of glazing medium and a very small amount of tint. Add color in increments, rather than starting with more. Test the results on white poster board, and keep a record of shades you use, in notes and swatches, for each project.

BLOOMING CANDLE HOLDERS

Layers of paint washes create shading and dimensionality to even simple designs. Even if you've never painted anything before, you can get great results with this simple graduated wash technique.

MATERIALS AND TOOLS

Wood candle holders
Sandpaper
½-inch (13 mm) flat brush
Background acrylic paint in color of your choice (a rosy pink was used for the candle holders shown here)

Black acrylic paint
Palette or paper plate
3 small bowls
Paper towels
Scrap piece of wood

WHAT TO DO

1 To make the darker wash, add half a teaspoon of black paint to the first bowl and stir in 2 tablespoons of water. Mix well.

2 To make the medium wash, remove a teaspoon of the paint mixture from the first bowl and place it in the second bowl. Stir in 2 tablespoons of water and mix well.

3 To make the light wash, remove a teaspoon of the paint mixture front the second bowl and place it in the third bowl. Stir in 2 tablespoons of water and mix well.

4 Test your three washes on the scrap piece of wood. Since the washes are so wet, dab your brush on a paper towel to remove excess liquid so the wash won't drip off your brush. Add small amounts of extra paint or water to lighten or darken your washes if desired.

5 Sand away any rough edges with the sandpaper, then paint a single base coat of background color.

6 While the background paint is still wet, create flower petal outlines with C shapes using the darker wash, referring to the photograph as a guide.

7 Outline the petals with the medium wash, then outline them again with the lighter wash, referring to the photograph as a guide.

8 Allow the candle holders to completely dry before handling.

Designer: Susan Greenelsh

A slightly different color scheme can create a dramatically different look, so have fun experimenting.

TWO-TONED CRACKLED FINISH

Although one-color crackled finishes look great, a two-color version lets you create a more antiqued look, and the finished piece will blend in nicely with its surroundings. Choose your favorite color for the top coat since it will be dominant, while just a little of the bottom coat will show through the "cracks."

MATERIALS AND TOOLS

Wood furniture of your choosing
Sandpaper
2 pints of acrylic paint, one several
  shades darker than the other
Crackle medium
Small paint rollers and trays
Small foam brush
Clear sealant

WHAT TO DO

1 Sand and prime the wood surface if necessary.

2 Working on the back side of the furniture, apply a base coat of acrylic paint. Allow to completely dry.

3 Apply a coat of crackling medium over the base coat, taking care to apply it evenly and in the same direction as the wood's grain. Allow to completely dry.

4 Apply the top coat over the crackling layer, taking care to apply it evenly and in the same direction as the wood's grain. Allow to completely dry.

5 If you're happy with the colors and effect, repeat Steps 1–3 on the rest of the furniture, using a foam brush in difficult-to-reach areas. If you're unhappy, repaint the back and try again with different colors.

6 When the coats have completely dried, check the finished piece for any areas that did not crackle well. Lightly sand any bad areas and rework them, if desired.

7 Allow piece to finish drying— approximately six days, as directed by the manufacturer—and then apply a protective sealant coat.

CONTROLLING CRACKLE

If your base coat is much darker than your top coat, the crackles will show dark veins through the top coat. If the colors are closer in value, you will get a subtler effect.

When applying paint over the crackle medium, work in one direction. Painting over your strokes, will minimize the crackle effect. Keep in mind that long strokes create long crackles, while short strokes create short crackles.

Designer: Will Albrecht

WHIMSICAL HOUSE NUMBERS

Identify your home with style and whimsy. Ordinary craft paints thinned with water function like wood stain, giving the decorative painter a whole new array of "stains" to choose from. An inexpensive paint pen is used to add a fun touch that is all your own.

MATERIALS AND TOOLS

Wooden house letters
220-grit sandpaper
Tack cloth
Water-based acrylic craft paints
Plastic containers
Scrap piece of wood

Small paintbrushes
Metallic paint pen
Water-based, clear, spray
 polyurethane

WHAT TO DO

1 Sand the house numbers with 220-grit sandpaper. Remove dust from the surface of the wood with a tack cloth.

2 Thin paint in plastic containers by adding water to paint. Begin with a small amount of water, then continue to thin paint until desired color is achieved.

3 Test colors by painting on a scrap of wood. Add more paint or water to mixture, if necessary, to intensify or dilute color. Note: You can also layer coats of paint to intensify color.

4 Apply paint to the house numbers, as desired (see photograph), beginning at the bottom of the number and working your way to the top surface. To prevent bleeding among paint colors, allow each section to dry thoroughly before painting the next. It's helpful to leave a small, unpainted area between each section.

Designer: Susan Greenelsh

5 Once the house numbers are completely painted and thoroughly dry, use the paint pen to fill in unpainted areas and embellish with spirals, stars, lines, or any other motif of your choice.

6 Seal the finished house numbers with a clear coat of polyurethane spray.

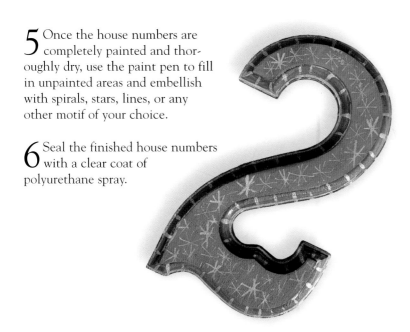

FINISHED FINIALS

Small wood items can be the perfect surface to play with different finishing effects. The finials shown here capture a light-hearted feeling of lovingly-handled, aged furnishings, and can be adapted to a country home or city apartment by selecting complementary window treatments. Crackling and staining techniques were used for these finials, but you can also try pickled, stained, and antiqued finishes.

MATERIALS AND TOOLS

Crackle Finish Finial
One wooden finial
Light blue water-based paint
White water-based paint
Medium flat paintbrush
Crackle medium
Clear acrylic spray sealer, in a satin finish

Washed Finial
Wood finials
Light blue paint
Medium flat paintbrush
Soft rag
Clear acrylic spray sealer, in satin finish

DESIGNER TIP

Brushstrokes can please the eye by creating anticipated "motion." Brush paint horizontally on flat surfaces such as a bureau top; go vertical on the sides. When painting or staining a wood floor, brush with the grain for the background color, at least.

WHAT TO DO

CRACKLE FINISH FINIAL (RIGHT)

1 Paint finial blue and allow to dry.

2 Paint crackle medium onto painted finial and allow it to dry as directed by the manufacturer.

3 Paint over crackle medium with white paint and allow to completely dry, then finish with two or three coats of clear acrylic sealant, allowing each coat to completely dry before adding the next.

WASHED FINIAL (LEFT)

1 Dilute paint with water, about half and half, then paint the finial. Immediately rub some of the paint off with a rag, allowing more color to remain in the crevices. Allow to dry.

2 Spray the stained finial with a coat clear acrylic sealant. Allow to completely dry before using.

DISTRESSED TABLE

Age a brand-new (and remarkably inexpensive) wood table in hours with a few coats of paint. Use a couple of paintbrushes and a rag to apply the paint in a random and varied fashion, and you'll have the charm of an antique table in no time.

MATERIALS AND TOOLS

Unfinished wood table
Piece of plastic or old sheet
Interior latex enamel satin paint:
   white and taupe
2-inch (5 cm) nylon/polyester
   flat paintbrush
Mixing container
Water-based translucent glaze
   (formulated for mixing with
   interior latex paint)
Wax paper
Wallpaper paste brush or other
   stiff-bristle brush
Old rag
Clear matte spray topcoat

Designer: Diana Light

WHAT TO DO

1 Position the table upside down on a piece of plastic or an old sheet to protect the work surface.

2 Use the 2-inch (5 cm) brush to apply white paint to the underside and legs of the table. Turn table right side up and finish painting. Allow table to dry. If necessary, apply a second coat and/or touch up where wood grain is still visible. Allow table to dry thoroughly.

3 Mix together four parts glaze to one part taupe paint.

4 Position the table upside down and begin to apply glaze mixture. (Note: It's a good idea to practice on the underside of the shelves and on any other areas of the table that are not visible.) Use the flat brush to lay the glaze onto a piece of wax paper, then use the wallpaper paste brush to lift the glaze off the paper. With the wallpaper paste brush, work the glaze into the corners, joints, and edges of the table—wherever the table would naturally show age and wear.

5 Continue to apply the glaze mixture to the table. Use an old rag to apply and wipe off glaze; use the flat brush to fling the glaze onto the table to create a speckled appearance; and use the wallpaper paste brush to dab the table to create random marks. Continue to apply glaze with the brushes and rag until you are pleased with the appearance. Turn table right side up and finish painting. Allow table to dry thoroughly.

6 Seal the table with a coat of clear matte topcoat. Allow table to dry thoroughly. Note: If your table will be kept outside, use a topcoat that is formulated for exterior use.

Right: Old shutters were transformed into a room divider by replacing the top panels with windows and attaching them together with door hinges. The wood finish was created with multiple layers of paint applied with wide brush strokes and sanded to allow the base coat layer to show through. Designer: Douglas Madaras

Bottom right: This interesting effect was created with an orange base coat that was then sanded and covered with a coat of red paint. After the paint dried, it was sanded with coarse sandpaper in some areas so the base coat would show through. Designer: Lindsey Morgan

Bottom left: These vibrant stacking boxes were created with gold and bright-colored paints and crackling medium. Designer: Chris Rankin

Opposite page, top: The aged look of these wood finishes was created by painting the doors in bright colors, then sanding off some of the paint in random areas. Designer: Lorin Knouse

Opposite page, far right: The opaque latex paint used on this piece mimics the look of the vintage milk paint. Crackle medium was applied in random areas to increase the antiqued look. Designer: Traci Dee Neil-Taylor

Opposite page, bottom: A colorful sponged pattern contrasts well with a wood finish. Designer: Kevin Fulford

WOOD FINISHING GALLERY

CRAFT PAINTING

Even if you can't draw—let alone paint!—a straight
line, you can master the marvelous painting techniques
in this chapter. Transform wood to marble with a
fabulous faux finish. Give an ordinary box a lux,
gilded make-over. Use stencils to create everything
from simple borders to complex murals.

GILDING

The appeal of gilding lies in the magic of transformation. By applying metallic leaf to everyday items, you can make them shimmer with a new richness. While you might think of gold when you hear the word gilding, you can also use silver, copper, and even variegated colors to create interesting effects. With an understanding of a few simple techniques and a willingness to experiment, you can gild just about anything.

MATERIALS AND TOOLS

BRUSHES
You will need an assortment of artist's brushes and bristle brushes as well as disposable brushes for gilding. A 2-inch (5 cm) bristle brush comes in handy for brushing off excess leaf.

METALLIC LEAF
There are several different types of metallic leaf. *Leaf is made by rolling metal into sheets until it is thinner than fine tissue paper. It comes in packets, known as books, with paper separating each sheet of leaf.*

Gold leaf is pure 24-karat gold. It is strong and will not tarnish. Its price fluctuates with current gold markets.

Composition gold leaf is made from brass. It comes in four shades of gold, ranging from deep red-gold to a bright yellow.

Edible gold leaf, or food-grade gold leaf, is commonly 23-karat gold. It contains gold with a very small amount of silver.

Silver leaf contains only silver, which tarnishes easily

Aluminum leaf is a great substitute for silver leaf since it is less costly.

Copper leaf's red hue is a complement to any warm palette.

Variegated leaf is composition leaf that has been heat-treated to create colorful surface patterns. It comes in multicolor as well as shades of red, green, and blue.

PAINT
Paint acts as a colored base coat for your object. It imparts a tone of color to the leaf and provides a color that will show through any cracks in the leaf.

PRIMER
A primer seals a porous surface so it can accept the size. The type of primer you use depends on your object's material. Use a paint primer for wood and metal, and gesso or spray fixative or spray lacquer for paper.

RAGS
Lint-free rags come in handy when working with paint, glue, and leaf.

SCISSORS
Any sharp, easy-to-handle scissors will serve.

SEALER
To prevent leaf from tarnishing, you will need to use a sealer on composition, silver, copper, and variegated leaf. Water- or oil-based varnishes work well and are readily available

SIZE
Size is the glue that holds the leaf to the object. You can find size under different names such as leaf adhesive, leaf size, or gold leaf size, and in both water- and oil-based preparations. Water-based is easier to clean up.

TACK CLOTHS
Because you want your surface as smooth as possible, use a tack cloth (available in most painting supply departments) to remove any loose dirt or small debris.

BASIC TECHNIQUES

PREPARING THE SURFACE

Preparing the surface is one of the most important steps to gilding. Done properly, it will make gilding easier and lead to quality results. This step varies according to the composition and the condition of the surface you'll be gilding.

If your object is made of wood, you want the surface to be as smooth as possible. For new wood, sand the surface and use wood filler to fill in any cracks or holes. After sanding, use a tack cloth to remove any debris, then apply a primer. If the object already has a finish on it that is in good condition, sanding to smooth out rough spots may be all you need before applying the primer. If the old finish is in bad shape, you may want to consider stripping it.

If you are gilding a previously painted metal object, remove the old finish with a steel brush and sandpaper. If the metal is one that rusts, use a rust-inhibiting primer. If you plan to paint a metal surface before gilding, you may need to use bonding liquid before applying the paint to make sure the paint will adhere to the surface.

Paper and fiber objects with porous surfaces need to be sealed; otherwise the size will soak into the fibers. Gesso works well on paper. You can also use a spray fixative or spray lacquer.

Glass and glazed ceramics are nonporous and are ready to accept the base coat or leaf size.

APPLYING THE PAINT

A painted base coat acts to highlight the gilding. Since this coat shows through any cracks in the leaf, select a color that will complement the leaf you are using

The paint you use will depend on your object. For large surfaces, such as furniture, you may use either alkyd- or latex-based paint from a paint store. Artist's acrylics work well for smaller objects. You can also use spray paint for the base coat. It is important to apply the paint as smoothly as possible—the leaf is so thin, brush marks will show through. You may find that using a disposable brush gives you a smoother application. When using spray paint, be careful to apply it in several light layers to avoid drips that may show through the leaf. Allow the surface to dry completely before going on to the next step. You may decide not to use paint on some objects—items that don't need much preparation or are already a color you prefer.

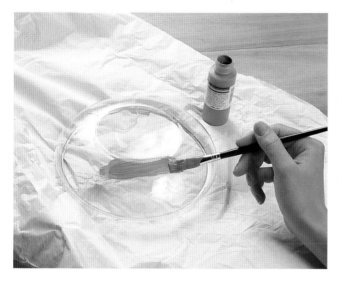

APPLYING THE SIZE

Though size is the adhesive that fixes the leaf to the surface, it behaves differently than other glues, so be sure to carefully read the manufacturer's instructions before using.

Apply your size to the surface, then wait until it dries to a tacky state before laying the leaf. The size usually becomes tacky within 15 to 20 minutes of application. If the humidity is high, the size may take longer to reach tack. You will know the size is ready when it is no longer wet and your finger hesitates as you gently rub it over the surface. The size will remain tacky for several hours before drying out and losing tack.

BE PATIENT

Water-based size is milky white in color, but as it dries it turns clear, giving a good indication that it is ready. If you apply the leaf when the size is still wet, you'll drown the leaf. While the leaf will stick to the surface, it will loose its luster and the leaf will be rough in appearance.

LAYING THE LEAF

You will need to practice working with leaf—the slightest breeze or sneeze can send it in the opposite direction.

If your book of leaf has a binding, cut it away with your scissors. If you need to cut or tear sheets into smaller pieces, do so between two pieces of the tissue paper. The easiest way to pick up leaf and lay it on a surface is to pick up the tissue and leaf and lay the leaf face down on the sized surface.

BASIC TECHNIQUES

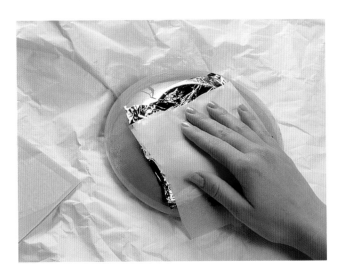

Gently rub the tissue paper to help the leaf adhere. Use a light overlap when applying more leaf. It's best to work from the inside to the outside of an object, and from the bottom to the top.

Once you've laid a section of leaf, go over it gently with a soft-bristle brush. Don't worry if you miss a spot, since the size remains tacky for several hours, you can always go back and apply more leaf. After laying the leaf, let the piece dry, which means giving the size time to dry thoroughly.

MAKE YOUR OWN BOB

A useful tool for laying leaf is a bob that pats and smoothes the leaf during application without harming the surface. You can make your own bob. Start by cutting a 4-inch (10 cm) square of lint-free cotton. Place three cotton balls in the middle of the square, then draw the corners together, securing them close to the cotton balls with a rubber band.

106

REMOVING EXCESS LEAF

The object begins to emerge from the gilding process when you brush off the excess leaf. The ragged edges of leaf are brushed away and the gilded surface is smooth and shiny.

Use a bristle brush to remove any excess leaf. Always brush in the direction of any overlaps to prevent the leaf from tearing. As you brush, small pieces of leaf, known as skewings, will fall away. Save these for filling any small cracks or separations in the leaf.

To fill in cracks, pick up some of the skewings on the tip of a soft brush and apply them to the cracks. You may need to resize areas if the sizing is no longer tacky.

SEALING THE SURFACE

You will need to seal any leaf that tarnishes, such as composition leaf, silver leaf, variegated leaf, and copper leaf. Real gold leaf and aluminum leaf do not tarnish, though the aluminum may darken with age.

The best sealer for leaf is varnish. You can get oil- or water-based preparations. Varnish comes in matte, satin, and gloss finishes (matte has no shine, satin a moderate

shine, and gloss is the shiniest). The finish you select will depend on the final look you want for your project. Water-based varnish cleans easily with water, while oil-based needs mineral spirits for clean up. Though using water-based varnish is easier, oil varnish will give you a more durable finish.

You can also use spray sealers, known as spray fixatives and lacquers. These will give very light protection to the surface, so don't use them for surfaces that will get much wear. Spray sealers are ideal for paper projects.

ALTERING THE SURFACE

You can make leaf look older, over paint it, tone down the color, or add surface decorations. If you want a more antiqued look, use artist's oil colors to shade areas of the leafed surface—use oil paints, since artist's acrylics are opaque and will not give you the washed effect. You can also use wood wiping stains. If you want to affix paper to the surface of leaf, spray fixative works well. Before using glue on the surface, make sure the size underneath the leaf has had a chance to dry thoroughly.

GILDED STORAGE BOX

This lovely box looks like an heirloom antique. It's a perfect place to store treasured letters, prized photographs, and other precious momentos.

MATERIALS AND TOOLS

Decorative wood trim
Decorative embossed carving
Unfinished wood box
Wood glue
Wood putty
Fine sandpaper
Red acrylic paint
Paintbrush

Adhesive spray
Gold color imitiation metal leaf
Gold leaf sealer
Wax paper
Soft paintbrush
Mitre saw
Ruler

RAISED OR CURVED SURFACES

Take extra care when working on raised and curved surfaces. Use smaller pieces of leaf as you move over the hills and valleys of the object.

WHAT TO DO

1 Sand unfinished wood box with fine sandpaper. Use wood glue to affix embossed carving to the face of the box.

2 Measure the top of the unfinished box. Using mitre saw, cut decorative wood trim to create a border on the top of the box. Use wood glue to affix the pieces to the top of the box. If there are any gaps at the corner joints, fill them in with wood putty. Allow to dry.

3 Apply one coat of red acrylic paint to box. Make sure to paint the feet as well as the bottom of the box lid. Allow to dry.

4 Spray the box with adhesive spray. (Adhesive spray is recommended for textured surfaces; however, you can also use liquid adhesive.)

5 Cut pieces of wax paper a bit larger than the leaf. Lay the wax paper over the leaf and rub gently with your hand until the leaf sticks to the paper.

6 Lay the leaf on the adhesived surface. Rub lightly with soft paintbrush to be sure leaf is well adhered. Continue until the entire box is covered with leaf. (You may need to go over areas a second time

Designer: Megan Kirby

to obtain adequate coverage.) Use the soft paintbrush to adhere gold leaf "dust" to small areas. It's okay if the red base coat shows through in some areas.

7 When you are done applying the leaf, seal it with varnish. The designer of this project chose an antique varnish for a mellower, aged look.

TAKE A HOLIDAY

Small cracks that expose the paint underneath often occur during the leafing process. You can leave these faults—also known as "holidays"—if you like the look, or you can fill them in later with small bits of leaf.

PICKLED GLASS BOWL

Whether you fill it with flowers or use it as a centerpiece for your table, this bowl brings a new richness to any room. Since the surface of the glass doesn't need preparation before gilding, this project is quick and easy to make.

MATERIALS AND TOOLS

Clear glass bowl
Leaf adhesive
Gold leaf or composition leaf
Red spray glass paint
   (stained glass paint)

½-inch (12 mm) flat brush
Soft, natural-bristle artist's brush
5/16-inch (8 mm) brush with
   medium-stiff bristles
Wax paper

Homemade Bob (see page 106 for
   instructions)
Old newspapers or newsprint for
   covering your work surface

WHAT TO DO

1 Clean and dry the glass bowl.

2 Using the ½-inch brush, apply the leaf adhesive to the back side of the bowl. Allow the adhesive to become tacky before applying the leaf

3 Holding the leaf in one hand and the soft-bristle artist's brush in the other, tear the leaf into small pieces. Allow the pieces of leaf to fall on the bowl and use the brush to tamp and smooth the leaf as you work. Use as much leaf as you want to get the coverage you desire.

4 Using the same soft-bristle brush, go over the leaf, making sure the edges of the leaf are smooth and that the leaf is adhering to the bowl.

5 Smooth the leaf further by gently placing a piece of wax paper over the bowl. Smooth with your hands, then gently remove the wax paper. (The wax prevents the paper from sticking to the size and pulling up the leaf.) Allow the leaf adhesive to dry thoroughly.

6 Using the 5/16-inch brush, gently remove any excess leaf. Use the bob to smooth over any rough spots and to remove any small pieces of leaf that may be sticking up. Save any leaf scraps in a plastic container for future projects.

7 Allowing for adequate ventilation, follow the instructions on the can of spray paint to paint the entire back of the bowl. You will be painting over the leaf, but the gold will show through the glass on the front side.

8 Allow the paint to dry thoroughly before handling.

Note: Gently hand wash your bowl and wipe clean after every use. Never allow the painted side to come in contact with food.

BLUE-AND-SILVER PHOTO FRAME

This crisp combination of dark blue with shimmery silver leaf will handsomely frame any photo that finds its way into this frame. The random pattern allows you to add as much or as little to the design as you want.

MATERIALS AND TOOLS

Wood frame
Primer or gesso
Dark blue acrylic paint
Leaf adhesive
Silver leaf
Clear matte spray lacquer

Fine-grain sandpaper
1-inch (2.5 cm) flat brush
½-inch (1.3 cm) flat brush
Scissors
5/16-inch (8 mm) brush with
  medium-stiff bristles

Soft, natural-bristle artist's brush
Wax paper
Craft knife
Old newspapers or newsprint for
  covering your work surface

WHAT TO DO

1 Line your work surface with newspapers, then sand the frame to remove rough spots.

2 Using the 1-inch (2.5 cm) brush, apply the primer or gesso to the frame and allow to dry.

3 Using the 1-inch brush, apply the acrylic paint and allow to dry.

4 Using the ½-inch brush, apply the leaf adhesive only on the front of the frame. Allow the adhesive to become tacky before applying the leaf.

5 Keeping the silver leaf between two pieces of tissue paper from the book of leaf, use the scissors to cut long narrow strips of leaf approximately ⅛ to ¼ inches (3 to 6 mm) wide. Remove the tissue paper.

6 With the frame face up, hold a strip of leaf slightly above the frame. Using the scissors, cut sections of the strips into rectangular pieces approximately ⅜ inch (9 cm) long, and allow them to fall on the frame. Keep moving your hands around the frame to randomly but evenly cover the surface.

7 Use the 5/16-inch (8 mm) brush to carefully tamp the silver pieces on to the frame.

8 Repeat step 5, this time cutting the strips approximately twice as wide. As you hold the strips over the frame, cut them into square shapes and allow them to fall on the frame.

9 Cut the leaf into approximately ½-inch squares, allowing the squares to fall on your work surface. Using the soft-bristle artist's brush, pick up a square and place it on the frame. To easily pick up the square, lightly brush the brush over a square a few times to allow a buildup of static electricity to make the square cling to the brush hairs. Lay the square on the frame, tamping it in place with the brush. Repeat, placing the squares randomly on the frame until you are satisfied with the design.

10 To smooth the leaf, lay a piece of wax paper over the frame and press gently before removing the wax paper. (The wax prevents the paper from sticking to the frame and pulling up the leaf.) Use a craft knife to carefully cut away any leaf that may be sticking up or hanging over the inside or outside edges of the frames. Allow the leaf to dry thoroughly.

11 Spray the front of the frame with clear lacquer and allow to completely dry before handling.

Designer: Diana Light

SHIMMERY PAINTED CANDLES

Why should the wick get to have all the fun? Use this simple technique to give the rest of the candle some glow and glamour, too.

MATERIALS AND TOOLS

Candles
Paper towel and rubbing alcohol
Candle painting medium
Powdered mica pigment

Paper plate
Sea sponge
Water

WHAT TO DO

1 Wipe the surface of the candles clean with a paper towel moistened with rubbing alcohol.

2 Following the manufacturer's instructions, mix the candle painting medium and the mica powder together on the paper plate.

3 Dampen the sea sponge slightly with a little water, then dip it into the paint mixture. Tap any excess paint onto the plate.

4 Lightly sponge the mixture onto the candles. If you'd like denser coverage, allow the first coat of mica pigment to dry, then sponge on a second and, if desired, a third coat.

QUICK-CHANGE CANDLEHOLDERS

Within an hour, you can give new life to an old set of wooden candleholders that will reflect the shimmer of your painted candles. First, paint the candleholders a rich deep color. Allow the paint to dry, then use a sea sponge to dab on a sheer layer of dappled gold or silver metallic paint. If you don't want a dappled effect, mix mica pigments into your paint for a subtle sheen. The combination is up to you. The technique is so easy, you can change the color at will to coordinate with any table setting or holiday.

Designer: Lynn Krucke

GILDING GALLERY

Above: All four of these candle holders were made by simply painting and gilding plain wood candle holders. The slight color variation in two of the candle holders was created by rubbing a mixture of burnt umber oil paint and linseed oil over the gilding, then buffing off the excess. Designer: Kathleen Burke

Above right: Plain wooden eggs were transformed with costume jewelry, composition leaf, and antiquing glaze. Designer: Terry Taylor

Right: A copper gilded triptych makes a glowing frame for a special photograph. Designer: Fred Gaylor

Above: These stunning shades were created by taping a stencil in place and then applying composition leaf to the exposed areas. Designer: Gay Grimsley

Top left: Composition gold leaf highlights and an antique finish create the sophisticated allure of this chair. Designer: Sharon Thompkins

Top right: Easy-to-make black polymer clay beads shimmer when gilded with gold composition leaf. Designer: Susan Kinney

STENCILING

In Colonial New England, the birthplace of "modern" stenciling, only the wealthiest homeowners could afford a stenciled decor. They would hire itinerant artists to paint elaborate murals and delicate designs throughout their homes. With the advent of mass-produced stencils and easy-to-use paints made especially for the craft, anyone can enjoy stenciling today! From borders to boxes, stenciling is the perfect way to tie a room together, giving everything in your home a little decorative polish.

MATERIALS AND TOOLS

STENCILS
So many shapes and styles! See page 120 for a comprehensive survey of what's available.

STENCIL BRUSHES
Designed specifically for the craft, stencil brushes have round, flat heads and densely packed bristles that distribute paint evenly while preventing it from seeping under your stencils. They come in a variety of sizes, with bristles that range from very stiff to very soft.

STENCIL ROLLERS
Stencil rollers look and work like smaller versions of regular paint rollers. They offer quick coverage of large areas, yet produce delicate, even shading. The larger amount of paint a stencil roller holds and applies increases the risk that some will seep under your stencil; prevent

this from happening by using spray stencil adhesive to firmly affix your stencils in place.

SPONGES
Sponges offer interesting, variegated applications of paint. The resulting textures are particularly effective when used to paint stencils that depict objects that might naturally have grains similar to those which can be achieved with sponges: motifs of fluffy clouds, for instance, or rough river rock.

SKETCH PAPER, BLACK GRAPHITE PAPER, PENCIL, AND RULER
These materials are used to mark stencil positions on your project's surface.

MASKING AND INVISIBLE TAPE
If you accidentally sever a bridge (see page 120) in your stencil, use a bit of tape to fix it.

STENCIL ADHESIVE
Available in spray and roll-on forms, these adhesives will hold your stencil in place while you paint, and release easily when you're done.

STENCIL TAPE OR LOW-TACK MASKING TAPE
Made especially to hold and mask stencils (see page 122), this tape

removes easily without stripping paint or leaving residue.

PAINTS

See Choosing Paint on page 121 for tips on selecting the best paint for your project.

PAINT-APPROPRIATE MEDIUM OR SOLVENT

Paint for stenciling should have the consistency of heavy cream.

Maintain that consistency with an appropriate additive, per the paint manufacturer's instructions.

CLEANUP MATERIALS

You can clean some paints up with a little soap and water. Others require special solvents. Follow the paint manufacturer's instructions.

BASIC TECHNIQUES

ABOUT STENCILS

Just about anything that will mask (or block) paint from one area while allowing it through to another can act as a stencil—even your hand!

All stencils work in basically the same way: Paint is applied through a pattern, or window, cut in an impermeable material such as acetate or waxed cardboard. The bits between windows—the spaces between the petals in a flower, for instance—are called bridges. Single overlay stencils, the most basic kind, consist of very simple patterns, such as hearts or circles, and may not even have bridges. The entire pattern can be painted with just one stencil, which is why they're referred to as "single overlay." If you're new to stenciling, master the process by working with these stencils first before moving on to more complex multioverlay and theorem stencils.

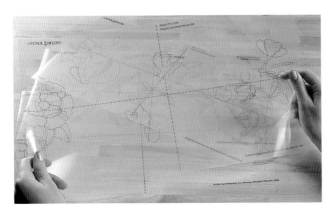

Multioverlay stencils are stencils that require multiple sheets, or overlays, to produce the complete stenciled image. Each overlay may show the entire scene, but windows are cut for only those components that are to be painted the same color. It's less complicated than it sounds. Imagine a stencil of a flowering vine: The first overlay may have the vine and leaves cut from it. Paint the vine and leaves green, let the paint dry; then align the second overlay, with the flowers cut from it, on top of the painted vine and leaves. (Many precut multioverlay stencils are made with registration marks that will take the guesswork out of aligning successive overlays.) Paint the flowers the appropriate color(s). Each component in the design will be crisp and exact, and your finished pattern will look as if it was painted with a single, bridged stencil.

Theorem stencils work on the same principle as multioverlay stencils: The complete design is created by painting through successive overlays. Unlike multioverlay stencils, however, theorem stencils must be used in a particular order, indicated on the overlays themselves. Because each successive overlay builds on the previous one, often without bridges, the finished project can look as if it was painted by hand rather than by stencil. The most complex stencils—detailed murals and trompe l'oeil (literally, "deceive the eye," in reference to this type of painting's realistic and often three-dimensional appearance)—require theorem stencils. Heeding registration marks is particularly important when using these elaborate templates.

There are two common types of registration marks. The first consists of horizontal, vertical, and sometimes diagonal lines that intersect in the exact center of a stencil, helping you place the stencil straight. They'll also help you keep track of the distance between the centerline of one repeat (complete design) and the next. The second kind of registration mark is a small hole cut in each corner of a stencil. To use these registration marks, place a self-adhesive note under each corner of the first sheet of the stencil and mark the holes' positions on the notes with a pencil. Then align each successive stencil using these marks. Remove the self-adhesive notes when you're done.

CHOOSING PAINTS

You can use just about any paint you'd like for stenciling, but some kinds are better than others for particular jobs. The more popular choices follow.

Stencil crémes and stencil gels, as their names suggest, are designed expressly for stenciling. The crémes are thick, creamy, oil-based paints that won't drip or run. Because they stay moist for some time, they're easy to blend and shade, but smear readily. Stencil crémes are self-sealing, forming a thin film when not in use; to remove the film, wipe it away with a paper towel or a clean cloth. Like crémes, stencil gels are thick, blend well, and won't drip or run. Unlike stencil crémes, these semitranslucent paints are waterbased, so they're nontoxic, quickdrying, and relatively smudge-resistant. Stencil crémes are available in a large range of colors; gel color choices are more limited. Both can be applied to wood, metal, fabric, paper, and walls, although you should check the manufacturer's instructions for recommended uses.

Acrylic paints offer the same advantages in stenciling as they do in most other crafts: They're inexpensive, available in a huge range of colors, and they're easy to work with and clean up. Best of all for stenciling, they dry quickly. Acrylic paints don't blend well, though, so they're not the best choice for projects that require delicate or subtle shading and application. They're also fairly liquid and will drip if applied with a heavy hand. Choose acrylics for simple, bold patterns such as checkerboards, and take extra care loading and blotting your applicator (see pages 122 and 123) before you begin painting. Acrylic paints will work well on wood, metal, and—when blended with textile medium—fabrics.

If you want to cover a lot of area quickly, you're going to like spray paints. You can apply them to most surfaces, but the rather restricted palette in which they're available may limit your use of them. Applied in a fine mist, they produce a delicate, almost hazy coverage, which can be built up for denser coloration. When using spray paints, protect the areas around your stencil by masking them with newspapers or drop cloths, and protect yourself from potentially harmful fumes by wearing goggles and a face mask. Spray paints can be drippy—not a desirable quality for stenciling. Avoid "run-unders" by firmly and completely adhering stencils to your project surface with spray stencil adhesive, and use a light touch as you apply the paint.

Most paints refuse to stay put on nonporous surfaces such as glass and ceramic. Overcome this obstacle in your stencil projects by using air-dry enamel paint, which not only sticks to glass and ceramic, but becomes dishwasher safe after it's been baked. (Follow the manufacturer's instructions.) These paints dry quickly, which helps prevent smudging, but prohibits thorough blending. Beginning stencilers may find the sticky consistency of air-dry enamel paints difficult to work with and quick to build up on stencils. Plus, they're very runny, so take extra care loading and blotting your applicator (see pages 122 and 123), and avoid seepage by using spray stencil adhesive to affix stencils firmly to your project surface.

Glazes are thick and easy to apply to most surfaces. Their solid coverage works especially well on walls and fabric, particularly for creating bold patterns that require dense coloring. Thanks to their thick consistency, glazes won't seep under stencils and they dry slowly enough to allow thorough blending. These paints aren't available in a huge number of colors, but you can expand your range of choices by mixing the glaze colors that you do find with acrylic paints, which come in just about every hue imaginable. After applying a glaze to a fabric, be sure to heat-set it according to the manufacturer's instructions.

Outdoor paints, fabric paints, and ink stamp pads are some other possible choices for stenciling. Their names suggest their intended functions and the manufacturer's instructions will guide you in their use. If you want to stencil a project that will spend a lot of time outdoors in the weather, outdoor paint is a good choice; just be sure to allow it adequate time—usually three to four hours—to cure between coats. You can stencil teeshirts and pillow cases with a variety of other paints, but fabric paint is specially formulated to adhere to cloth surfaces. Ink stamp pads, created for use with stamps offer good colors in a relatively dry and easy-to-apply form.

BASIC TECHNIQUES

POSITIONING STENCILS

You can just smack a stencil on the wall and start painting—but you'll probably like the results better if you position your stencil properly first.

Before you get down to the fun business of painting and creating, take a few minutes to chart where your stencils will go. Many stencilers make paper proofs of exactly what they plan to paint. Simply paint the motif on a length of paper; then tape the paper in place on the project. This is especially useful for stenciling borders and other running patterns along walls, because the paper proofs will allow you to see how the design will actually look before you commit any paint to your precious walls. When you're satisfied with your positioning, mark the exact position of each stencil placement using a piece of chalk and the stencils themselves.

ADHERING STENCILS

1 If you're using masking tape to hold your stencil in place, simply place a small piece at each corner. If a window is very close to an edge, you may want to apply tape along the edge of the stencil to avoid getting paint on the project. If you're using a roll-on or spray stencil adhesive, apply it to the back of the stencil. The roll-on needs to be applied only in a few spots, but should be allowed to dry for at least five minutes before the stencil is placed. When using a spray adhesive, wear goggles and a face mask. Apply the spray in a light, even coat and allow it to dry for a few minutes and become tacky before positioning the stencil against the project. Spray adhesive, unlike tape or roll-on adhesive, forms a bond with the project, effectively preventing paint from running under stencils.

LOADING THE APPLICATOR

Putting paint on a brush may seem like a simple enough procedure—and it is! There's just a specific way to do it for stenciling. Learn the technique, and your success is practically guaranteed. In stenciling, you'll always use a dry-brush technique. The method varies slightly by applicator, but the rule remains the same: Less (paint) is more!

1 Start by placing about a teaspoon of paint on your palette. If you're working with stencil crème, load your brush directly from the container of paint, removing the self-sealing film first. If you're using a sponge as an applicator, it should be just the slightest bit moist—not even damp, just no longer stiff. Holding your applicator perpendicular, lightly place it in the paint. Still holding it perpendicular (to load the paint into the center of the applicator, rather than onto the sides), gently rotate the brush as if you were driving a screw.

2 Now that you've loaded your applicator with paint, you need to remove almost all of it before you can begin stenciling. Tape a piece of paper towel or a bit of clean cloth to your work surface to hold it firmly in place; then blot your applicator on it, using gentle circular strokes. When the paint your brush is discharging appears to be dry, stroke an X onto your blotting surface to remove any paint that might be on the applicator's sides or edges. Finally, before you begin painting, take a test stroke on an uncut portion of the stencil. If the paint seems at all wet, blot your applicator on the paper towel again. Your applicator should be almost completely dry as you begin painting.

3 If you're working with a stencil roller, start by rolling out lengths of brown paper and paper towel; you'll use both to blot the loaded roller. Place 2 to 3 tablespoons of paint on your palette and work the paint into the roller. Now, remove as much paint as possible by blotting the roller first on the brown paper, then on the paper towel. As with other applicators, the roller should be almost dry before you start stenciling with it. Test it on an uncut portion of the stencil. If the paint still appears wet, blot the roller on the paper towel again.

APPLYING PAINT

For most projects, you'll use one of three strokes: a circular stroke, a pouncing stroke, or a sweeping stroke.

The goal in stenciling is to apply only a hint of color at a time, layering paint gradually. By working this way, you'll be able to create depth, nuance, and shading in your coloration—and, even more important, you'll prevent paint from seeping under your stencils. You'll be able to create a variety of effects using the strokes described in the following steps, but for the best results, choose just one stroke per stencil and stick with it for each repeat. If at all possible, dedicate a separate brush or applicator for each color you plan to apply. Otherwise, clean your applicator thoroughly between colors (see page 125).

For a smooth, even application of paint, use the circular stroke. Keeping your applicator perpendicular to the surface you're painting, move it in a gentle swirling motion. Paint around the edges of the window first and apply more pressure as the brush becomes drier. Move into the center of the window gradually, blending paint from the edges toward the middle. This stroke is most effective when used with stencil crémes and stencil brushes. Due to the risk of seepage, it should probably be avoided if you're working with any kind of sponge applicator or runnier paints such as air-dry enamels and acrylics.

Applying paint with a pouncing stroke will produce a faintly dappled, textured effect. To apply paint this way, simply "pounce" your applicator in an up-and-

123

BASIC TECHNIQUES

down motion, keeping it perpendicular to your stencil surface. Start at the center of the window and work toward the stencil's edges. For heavier coverage, use a firmer pounce. For more delicate coverage, use a lighter pounce. You can use this stroke with any kind of paint or applicator, but it works particularly well with sponge applicators—sea sponges, makeup sponges, sponge pouncers, etc. Pouncing is a good technique for beginners because it's less likely to result in seepage and other mistakes than a circular or sweeping stroke.

If you want to incite controversy in a roomful of stencilers (and who wouldn't?), ask if you should ever use a sweeping stroke when painting stencils. For some, this stroke is anathema. For others it's an important technique, particularly valuable for filling in large areas. Paint applied with a sweeping stroke will have a discernible direction to its texture. Working from the edge of the window toward the center, stroke the paint on by sweeping the applicator back and forth. The best applicators to use when working with a sweeping stroke are makeup sponges and sponge pouncers. Using a stencil brush will create a very obvious texture in the paint.

There's no better way to paint a large stencil than with a stencil roller. If loaded properly with paint, a roller will produce delicate, even coverage—quickly! Using firm but even pressure, roll from one end of the stencil to the other. Repeat from the opposite direction, applying more pressure as the paint begins to adhere to the surface. After you've painted the entire area, you can add highlights using a brush or another applicator. Keep your roller fresh between applications by rolling it over a moistened paper towel, then wrapping it in plastic wrap or aluminum foil.

MASKING MOTIFS

You've finally found a stencil with the perfect bumblebee motif. Unfortunately, the bumblebee is flying through daisies—which you don't want on your project. No problem. Simply cover the daisies with several strips of masking tape, leaving only the bee.

TROUBLE-SHOOTING

Paint drips, bristles slip, cats walk by and run their tails through fresh designs—accidents happen to even the most experienced stencilers. Fortunately, where there's a problem, there's usually a solution.

The most common problem in stenciling is smudging under the edge of a stencil. If the smudge is light, allow the paint to set; then remove it with a kneaded artist's eraser. You can also remove light smudges with a cotton swab dipped in a solvent appropriate for the paint. If a smudge is dark or very obvious, either shift the stencil slightly to incorporate the mistake into the painted area or paint a different, small motif over it. If all else fails, paint over the offending smudge with the base color. Allow it to dry completely; then paint the stencil again.

CLEANING AND CARING FOR YOUR STENCILS AND APPLICATORS

After you've finished stenciling, clean your applicators thoroughly with soap and warm water. Give special attention to your stencil brushes, working the soap into them carefully to remove all residual paint. Rinse the applicators under running water—don't soak them; then blot them on paper towels or a clean cloth to remove excess water. Preserve the shape of a stencil brush's bristles by looping a rubber band around them, rolling it up near the bristle tips. Store the brushes on their sides in a dry box and don't use them again until they're completely dry. Clean your stencils with baby oil: Place each stencil on a flat surface, on top of a paper towel; then rub away all the paint on each one with a paper towel moistened with baby oil. Blot the stencils dry and store them flat.

CLEANING AS YOU GO

Sounds fun, right? It may not be the most exciting part of stenciling, but keeping your applicators, stencils, and paints in good order while you work will save time and improve your results.

After you've used every bit of paint you loaded into your applicator, you'll need to start over again. But before you reload, take a moment to "rejuvenate" your applicator. Moisten a folded square of paper towel with a little paint solvent. (Rubbing alcohol is fine for water-based paints and mineral spirits will work for oil-based paints.) Pull the head of the applicator through the paper towel; this not only prevents buildup on your brush, but keeps the bristles flexible, too. While the applicator is still slightly damp from the solvent (work quickly—the solvent evaporates rapidly!), swab it around the uncut portions of your stencil to clean off any paint buildup. Be careful to avoid the windows—the solvent will smear the paint you just worked so diligently to apply.

If your applicator picked up a lot of paint as you cleaned it, you may want to pull it through the solvent-moistened paper towel again. Now, before you dip your brush back into it, check your paint. Liquid paints may thicken and become gummy and crème paints will develop a self-sealing film when not in use. To rejuvenate liquid paint, mist it or add just a drop of solvent to it and blend well. Ideally, you should be able to restore the paint to its original consistency. To remove film from a crème paint, simply wipe it off with a clean cloth or a paper towel. Reload your applicator as before and start again.

BOLD FLOWER-BORDER FRAME

Once you find a design you like, you can tie an entire room together by stenciling the motif on various accessories, even adding a border along the wall. We've included instructions for the handsome frame; refer to the Basic Techniques section for general tips on stencilling.

MATERIALS AND TOOLS

Square wood frame
Ivory acrylic paint
2-inch (5 cm) paintbrush
Sandpaper
Floral stencil
Stencil adhesive
Stencil brushes
Shader stencil brush
Stencil cremes (or other paints) in olive green, hunter green, golden yellow, red, purple, and soft blue
Spray clear matte sealer

WHAT TO DO

1 Prime and sand the wood frame, if necessary.

2 Apply two coats of ivory acrylic paint to the frame, allowing the paint to dry and sanding lightly after each coat.

3 Spray the back of the stencil with stencil adhesive and position the stencil on the frame. Using the stencil brush, stencil three flowers in one corner and a single flower in the opposite corner, using red, yellow, and blue for the flowers and olive green for the leaves and stems.

4 Using the shading stencil brush, shade the stenciled areas as indicated in the photo, darkening the outer edges of the yellow petals with additional yellow paint, then shading the red petals with the red paint. Shade the leaves and stems with hunter green, and shade the blue flower with the purple.

5 After all paint has dried thoroughly, spray on a clear matte sealer.

Designer: Bill Palasty

CELTIC GARDEN STONE

Looking for a quick way to brighten your garden and jump into the craft of stenciling? Look no further. A custom-painted stepping stone makes a lovely addition to any outdoor pathway, and it's easy enough for even a beginning stenciler to complete in just an afternoon. Choose a stencil and a "stone" (ours is actually made of molded fiberglass) that complement your garden and your personality.

MATERIALS AND TOOLS

Square garden stone (available at garden centers)
Paper towels
Rubbing alcohol
Ruler
Stencil
Stencil tape
Stencil gels (or other paint) in the colors of your choice (We used green, blue, and sandstone)
Palette
Stencil brushes, one for each color
Cotton swabs or eraser
Clear matte lacquer spray

WHAT TO DO

1 Clean your garden stone with a paper towel moistened with rubbing alcohol, if needed.

2 Using the ruler and pencil, find and mark the center of your stone. Next, very lightly mark two, straight intersecting diagonal lines, one connecting each pair of opposite corners. The point where the lines intersect is the stone's center.

3 If your stencil has horizontal, vertical, and/or diagonal registration marks, use these and the lines you just marked to center your stencil on the stepping-stone. If your stencil does not have this type of registration mark, use the technique described in Step 2 to find and mark the center of each overlay. Align the first overlay of your stencil and fasten it in place with stencil tape.

4 Choose a stencil brush in a size appropriate for the overlay you're about to paint: If it has small windows and slim bridges, work with a small brush; if it has larger windows and bridges, use a larger brush. Referring to the instructions on pages 122 and 123, load the brush with your first color of paint.

5 Using a soft, circular stroke, paint each window in the overlay. When you're done, remove the overlay and allow the paint to dry.

6 Repeat Steps 4 and 5 to paint the remaining overlays, remembering to align each one properly using the registration marks.

7 When all the paint has dried, use an eraser or a cotton swab moistened with rubbing alcohol to carefully remove any pencil marks remaining from Step 2.

8 If desired, paint any highlights you'd like to add, working freehand. For instance, in the project shown, the crevices along the stone's border have been highlighted with the same shade of green used to paint one of the stencil overlays.

9 Allow the paint to dry; then, following the manufacturer's instructions, apply clear matte lacquer spray to protect and weatherproof your stenciling.

Designer: Heidi Kronen

FLEUR-DE-LIS LAMP SHADE

Add charm to that plain lamp in the corner and turn it into the perfect accent piece for your room. The trick is to keep a steady hand and use that measuring tool. This is a great project for advanced stencilers, as well as for beginners who don't mind a challenge.

MATERIALS AND TOOLS

Black lamp shade with gold interior
Gold paint
Stencils of fleur-de-lis in two sizes
Stencils of diamonds (for borders)
  in two sizes

Stencil tape or spray adhesive
Cloth tape measure
Light erasable marker

Palette
Stenciling brushes in assorted sizes
Paper towels

WHAT TO DO

1 Select your lamp shade before you buy your stencils and paint. The type of material your shade is made from will determine the best kind of paint to use, and you'll want to choose your fleur-de-lis and diamond stencils in sizes that are in proportion with it. The lamp shade shown in the project photo is made from black cardboard with gold paper backing, and the designer used stencil crème to paint the stencils.

2 Working with large stencils on a curved and relatively small lamp shade can be difficult. To make placement and painting easier, cut a fleur-de-lis in each size from the main body of the stencil and work with these cutouts instead.

3 Determine how you'd like to arrange the fleur-de-lis on the shade. The project shown features a row of the larger fleur-de-lis centered along the lamp shade's height, bordered by a row of smaller fleur-de-lis both top and bottom.

4 To ensure even placement of your pattern, use the cloth tape measure to determine the circumference of the shade along each meridian that you plan to stencil. Then measure each stencil cutout from one edge of the pattern to the other. Using these measurements,

determine how many repeats of the pattern will fit on your shade and how much space you'll need to leave between each one. Lightly mark the position of each repeat using the erasable marker.

5 Using stencil tape or stencil spray adhesive, adhere the first stencil in place. Using a stencil brush that's appropriate for the size of the stencil, load your brush with paint. Slowly brush color into the stencil window using a soft, circular stroke. When you're done, remove the stencil, adhere it at the next marked position, and repeat.

6 Repeat the process with each component of your design, taking care not to smudge the fresh paint.

7 Finish by stenciling the borders around the top and bottom of the shade. In the project shown, the larger diamonds are used along the bottom and the smaller diamonds are used along the top.

8 Allow the paint to dry completely before placing the shade on your lamp.

Designer: Heidi Kronen

STENCILED ROOM DIVIDER

With an elegantly stenciled room divider, you can instantly turn one room into two, seal off an intimate corner, or simply (and attractively) hide a heap of untidy laundry from surprise visitors. Stenciling something as large as what amounts to a faux wall, however, takes some practice and patience. If you're new to stenciling, don't take this on as your first project!

MATERIALS AND TOOLS

Room divider with wooden panels
Sandpaper
Clean cloth
Acrylic paint for the base coat on the wooden panels
Acrylic paint in a contrasting color for the divider's frame
2 paintbrushes
Ruler or cloth tape measure
Butcher paper
Pencil or erasable marker
Stencil
Stencil tape
Stencil brushes, one for each color
Stencil crèmes (or other paints) in the colors of your choice
Paper towels
Clear matte lacquer spray

WHAT TO DO

1 Sand smooth all the surfaces on the divider that you plan to paint; then dust the divider with a clean cloth. Paint the frame and the panels contrasting colors, if desired, using acrylic paint. (We used flat light blue on the panels and flat black on the frame.)

2 While the acrylic base coat is drying, make paper mock-ups of the panels. Measure and mark the placement of your stencils on the mock-ups, working from the center of each "panel" out.

3 Tape the mock-ups to a wall, stand back, and see how the design you created looks. Does any element need to be adjusted? If so, adjust it now at this stage, rather than risking your expensive room divider!

4 Adjust the mock-ups as necessary until you're happy with the design. Then paint them with the stencil exactly as you plan to paint the room divider. Once again, tape the mock-ups to the wall and take a good look. You may even want to

tape them in place on the room divider (make sure the acrylic base paint is dry first, though).

5 When you are completely happy with your design, go to work on the room divider itself. Transfer your final design to the panels, using a pencil or an erasable marker.

6 Tape the first overlay of the stencil in place, working from the center of the panel outward. Referring to the instructions on page 123, load your stencil brush with the first color of paint and, using a soft circular stroke, apply color through the windows.

7 Repeat the process with each overlay and paint color until you've completed your design.

8 After you've stenciled the entire room divider, seal the paint with a coat of clear matte lacquer spray, following the manufacturer's instructions.

Designer: Heidi Kronen

Above: An inexpensive cardboard box can become a cherished room accent the doubles as storage with the addition of stenciled flowers. Designer: Chris Rank

Left: Simple seashell stencils can be used as a wall border pattern or in unique combinations on furniture. Designer: Tammie Wilson

STENCILING GALLERY

Left: A blooming border stencil can be used on multiple surfaces as shown here on a wall, box, vase, and pillow. Designer: Bill Palasty

Below: Add a designer touch to your porch with a simple stenciled pattern. Designer: Derick Tickle

Opposite page, top left: Add a decorator touch to anywhere in your home with a classic ivy pattern. Designer: Cheryl Ball

Opposite page, top right: Use a simple fruit stencil to create a faux mosaic effect. Designer: Bill Palasty

FAUX FINISHING

Pssssst . . . don't tell: Faux finishing may well be the most forgiving, and the most fun, of all the craft techniques in this book. By its nature, you simply can't make a mistake, and each project you make will be wonderfully unique. Start with small projects, such as picture frames and boxes, then work your way up to furniture, walls, and maybe even your neighbor's car!

MATERIALS AND TOOLS

BRUSHES
The more sizes and shapes of brushes, the better. Look for specialty brushes, such as splattering brushes, in the craft painting section of your favorite craft store.

SPONGES
Sponges are a great way to add texture to faux finishing projects. Buy as many sizes and shapes as you can find.

PAINTS
Many faux finishing projects can be created with acrylic paints. They can easily be diluted with water or blended in multiple color combinations to create special effects.

SURFACE PRIMERS
Depending on the surface you've chosen to finish, you may need to use a primer. For wood surfaces that are very porous (and not receptive to paint), prepare them with a quick sanding and a coat of primer.

SEALANTS
Your faux finished project may look perfect, but it won't last that way without a protective sealant (also known as a top coat). Look for sealants such as varnish and polyurethane in craft painting sections.

WORK SURFACE PROTECTANT
Your paint may look oh so innocent and predictable sitting in a pallete, but don't be fooled. Splatters are inevitable, so protect your work surface with a drop cloth or newspapers.

136

BASIC TECHNIQUES

PRACTICE BLOTTERS

Most faux finishing techniques aren't difficult, but they do require using just the right amount of paint to get the right look. The tips below will guide you to success.

When working with sponges, you ideally want the texture of the sponge to show in the finished piece, not to fill in with thick globs of paint. To achieve the right effect, keep a practice blotter near your work space. When you're happy with the look on the blotter, then start working on your craft project. Ideally, your practice blotter should be made of the same material as your project: a wood blotter for wood projects, fabric for fabric projects, and ceramic for ceramic projects. The blotter needn't be anything expensive—just a scrap works fine.

Blotters are also extremely helpful when working with washes. The overly wet nature of paint/wash mixtures means that dripping brushes can distort or destroy your painted projects. To use the blotter, dip your brush in the wash mixture and dab it gently in a folded-up paper towel, then paint strokes on the blotter until you're happy with the effect.

ADDING HIGHLIGHT

The easiest way to add highlight is to lightly echo the patterns or design of a base color with a slightly lighter or contrasting color.

Start by adding the base color. Then, while the paint is still wet, lightly add highlights in a contrasting or lighter color. The highlights should lightly cover part of the base coat color, not all of it. If you accidentally add too much highlight color, just go over the area again with the base coat and start again.

You can create even more dramatic effects by using three or four highlight colors. Just be sure to apply them without a rigid pattern (in multiple directions, for instance) and to blend them well with a damp terry cloth.

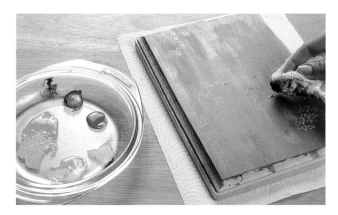

CREATING DEPTH

"Depth" is the key to many well-done faux finishing projects. It creates a dramatic effect that tricks the eye into believing the faux finish is real.

1 Often the trick to adding depth is to use multiple colors in closely related tones. To apply the base coat, add the colors by dabbing your brush in one color, adding to your project with a downward, mashing motion. When you add the next color, don't rinse your brush. Don't wait for one color to dry before

adding the next—the wet paint will help with the blending effect.

2 Create depth by adding a contrasting color of paint with the same downward, mashing motion. Try to work in a random pattern—you don't want the pattern to become predictable to the eye.

3 Create even more depth by adding speckles of paint in the same contrasting color or in a second contrasting color. To make the splatters, dip a ½-inch (13 mm) brush into paint that has been slightly diluted with water. Hold the brush against your painted surface and pull the bristles back toward you. When you release the bristles, small paint dots will be splattered across the surface. This effect can also be easily created with a splattering brush.

SPONGE PAINTED VASE

You can find an assortment of solid-color ceramic vases in the floral department of your craft supply store. Maybe you bought one years ago to go with the color scheme of a room that you have since redecorated. Don't get rid of the vase—transform it! Sponge painting will add texture and depth to give an old vase a new look. (Or a new vase a dramatic uplift!) By selecting colors for sponging that match or coordinate with your fabric, paint, or wallpaper, you can easily harmonize a room.

MATERIALS AND TOOLS

Solid-color ceramic vase
2 colors of acrylic paint, used here blue-green and blue
Paper plate and paper towels
Small sea sponge
Spray varnish (optional)

DESIGNER TIP

Obviously, the shape of your sponge will affect the finished look. Buy extra sponges in lots of sizes and shapes (they're cheap!), and experiment with them on your practice blotter. If you're not happy with the look, cut the sponges into any size or shape you like with ordinary household scissors.

WHAT TO DO

1 You may want to do a test to see if you want to sponge from the lighter color to the darkest or the darkest to the lightest. Keep in mind that the color of the vase acts as a third color. Since you are using acrylic paint, you can do your test on a small section of the vase, then, if you don't like the effect , you can wipe the paint off before it dries and try again.

2 Pour a small amount of the first color you will be using on a paper plate. Dip the sea sponge in the paint and apply it to the vase using a dabbing motion. Be careful not to drag the sponge over the surface since this will smear the paint. Continue dabbing until you have an allover design. Allow the paint to dry.

3 Using the second color, repeat Step 2. If desired, you may want to apply more than two colors—just make sure you allow each coat to dry before applying the next one.

4 You may want to apply a coat of clear spray varnish to protect the paint . If you do, avoid drips by applying two light coats rather than one heavy one.

Designer: Megan Kirby

HANS PFAALL

Designer: Susan Greenelsh

FAUX LEATHER FRAME

The easy faux finish technique used to create a leather look on this frame can be used on just about any wood surface with great results. Try it on shelving, tabletops, bookcases, chairs, and more.

MATERIALS AND TOOLS

Unfinished wood frame
Sandpaper
Acrylic paints in black, bright red, olive green, antique gold, and yellow
Palette or paper plate

New sponge cut into 1¼-inch (3 cm) squares
½ inch (13 mm) flat brush
Small glass bowl
Clear sealant

WHAT TO DO

1 Decide how much of the frame's surface area you want to be covered with the faux leather finish and mark off with painter's tape.

2 Paint the marked off area with two coats of red paint, allowing the first coat to completely dry before adding the second. Remove the painter's tape.

3 While the second coat of red paint is still wet, dip a dry brush in black paint. Gently add subtle brush strokes around the red surface, taking care to work in different directions. Allow the frame to dry for 20 minutes before proceeding with Step 4.

4 Dilute a small amount of red paint with 3 tablespoons of water. Dip your brush in the wash, then dab off any excess liquid so the brush is not dripping. Brush on a coat of this wash over your red and black paint. The wash will blend the colors and add dimension. Allow the frame to completely dry before proceeding to Step 5.

5 Paint the remaining bare surface area with two coats of black, allowing the first coat to completely dry before adding the next. Note: The line where your black paint butts against the red will probably not be exactly straight, which increases the faux look.

6 Make sure your sponge is the correct size by dabbing it all the way around the frame, leaving a ¼-inch (6 mm) gap between dabs. If you end up with too much room left over or not enough room, solve the problem by either increasing the size of the gaps between sponge prints or trimming the sponge to a smaller width.

7 Squeeze out some olive green paint and gently dip the sponge in it. Press the sponge against a scrap piece of paper several times until you're happy with the effect. The goal is to add the sponge's texture in paint so that some of the black still shows through. Work your way around the top and side surfaces, leaving a gap of solid black between applications to serve as a faux border.

8 While the paint from Step 7 is still wet, mix together equal amounts of antique gold and bright yellow. Dip a clean sponge in the paint, test it as you did in Step 7, and then lightly sponge on top of the antique olive sponged areas. Again, the goal is to sponge lightly enough to allow the colors below to show through. Any areas you are unhappy with can be responged.

9 Apply a coat of clear sealant after the paint has completely dried. Enjoy!

MARBLED CORNER SHELVES

Since faux marbled effects are created by blending multiple colors, you can easily make custom pieces that tie together the colors in your home.

MATERIALS AND TOOLS

Wood shelf
Sandpaper
3 tones of the same color acrylic paint (The project shown here

used a light, a medium, and a dark pink)
Black and white acrylic paint

½-inch (13 mm) flat brush
Fine artist's brush
Palette or paper plate

WHAT TO DO

1 Sand the wood shelf well, then squeeze out small amounts of your pink paints (or other color, if desired) on the palette.

2 Dab your ½-inch brush in one of the colors and press it against the wood in a twisting motion. Return to your paint and get another color and repeat. (There's no need to rinse your brush between colors since you're trying to create a blended effect.) Continue working in this way, using all three colors, until you have covered the entire surface. Remember that with this technique, you're emulating real marble, which has an incredible range of variation in it. Thus, there is no formal order or pattern to adding the paint colors. Just have fun!

3 While the paints in Step 2 are still wet, squeeze out a little white paint and twist it into the pink paints in a random pattern.

4 Squeeze out a little black paint. Then, while the paints from Steps 2 and 3 are still wet, dip the tip of the fine artist's brush in the black paint. Create small marbling "veins" randomly around the shelf.

5 To finish the look, add small white splatters around the shelf. To make the splatters, dip the ½-inch brush into white paint. Hold it near the shelf and pull the bristles back toward you. When you release the bristles, small white paint dots will be splattered around the marbling.

Designer: Susan Greenelsh

FAUX COPPER SWITCH PLATES

Painted highlights are fun to create, and the range of effects you can create with them is quite amazing. Here, a faux copper look was made with simple paint and texture combinations. Vary the amount of copper and highlight colors to create a custom look that's just right for your home.

MATERIALS AND TOOLS

Wood switch plates
Sandpaper
Copper acrylic paint
2 shades of green acrylic paint, one
   light and one medium
Brown acrylic paint
½-inch (13 mm) flat brush
Small face cloth cut in quarters

DESIGNER TIP

When copper is exposed to air or seawater for long periods of time, a greenish crust forms on its surface. This layer of copper sulfate is known as verdigris and is a beautiful natural finish prized by interior designers. You'll find that bringing this antiqued look into your house will add a welcoming warmth.

When you create a faux verdigris finish, as you do for the light switches in this project, you, not mother nature, are in control. Any amount of weathering and aging your object goes through is in your hands. Layering the paint, as detailed here, is one way to create a verdigris finish. There are also commercial paint products available that will help you create this effect.

WHAT TO DO

1 Sand the switch plates to remove any rough edges, then paint them with a background coat of copper. Do not worry about nice, neat paint strokes; occasional odd marks will increase the coppery look.

2 While the copper paint is still wet, add intermittent strokes of the medium green paint with a dry brush. Make sure some of the strokes come up and over the sides of the switch plate. Wad up one of the face cloth squares and use it to streak the paint brush marks. (See page 139.)

3 While the copper and green paints are still wet, add intermittent strokes of the light green paint with a dry brush, going over the medium green paint in some areas. Use a second face cloth square to streak the paintbrush marks.

4 Repeat Step 3 with the brown paint, taking care to work in different directions.

FAUX SUEDE DRAWERS

There's an amazing variety of faux spray paints that allow you to create special effects in minutes. Look for paints that let you spray faux crackling, suede, and even faux granite.

MATERIALS AND TOOLS

Unfinished chest of drawers
Sandpaper
Faux suede spray paint in 3 contrasting colors

WHAT TO DO

1 Remove the drawer pulls and set them aside, then remove the drawers. Sand and prime the wood surface if necessary.

2 Working outdoors, spray the back side of the furniture with a light coat of your chosen main color, working in a back and forth motion. When the paint has completely dried, add a second light coat of spray paint. If you're happy with the color and the effect, proceed to Step 3; if not, resand the surface and try again.

3 Spray the front side of the furniture with a light coat of your main color. Allow to completely dry, then add a second light coat.

4 Spray the top and bottom drawer, plus one of the drawer pulls, with a light coat of secondary color. Allow to completely dry, then add a second light coat.

5 Repeat Step 4 with the middle drawer and the two remaining drawer pulls.

6 When the paint has completely dried, replace the drawer pulls in the drawers, choosing contrasting colors.

A TOUCH OF TEXTURE

Spray on textures can create a tactile as well as visual sensation. For a child's room use ABC stencils to spray faux suede letters onto a colorful chest of drawers. Little hands can trace the letters while learning their alphabet. Or, use a teddy bear stencil and spray faux suede to provide a friendly companion.

Designer: Will Albrecht

FAUX FINISHING GALLERY

Opposite page, top left: Faux marbling looks great on both wood and fabric. Here, a dark-colored fabric lamp shade was embellished with brushed-on paint, metallic paint pens, and puff fabric paint. Designer: Mary Jane Miller

Opposite page, top right: Two coats of yellow base paint were covered with a terra-cotta glaze to create this color-washed wall. To create a textured look, the glaze was dabbed with cheesecloth while it was still wet. Designer: Sheila Ennis

Opposite page, bottom left: A diamond-shaped pattern creates this wood finish known as faux bois. Designer: Sheila Ennis

Opposite page, bottom right: A metallic color wash over a base coat of gray makes a great wall finish for formal living rooms. Designer: Sheila Ennis

Above: A four-paneled wood screen makes a fabulous surface for showcasing your favorite faux finishes. The techniques include sponging, stenciling, rag rolling, and washing. Designer: Lyna Farkas

Left: A craft comb was pulled across wet paint in two directions to create the latticelike effect on these garden pots. Designer: Elena Lange

151

HOME DECORATING CRAFTS

Turn your house into a home with beautiful, practical projects. Start with candles: Make them from traditional materials or from super-versatile candle gels. Learn inventive techniques for decorating purchased candles, and master the art of candlescaping. Move on to soap making—it's easier than you think! Finally, transform the ordinary to extraordinary with mosaic.

DECORATING CANDLES

Whether it's a romantic dinner for two, an elegant evening soiree, or a solitary soak in a bubble-filled tub, when we long for ambiance, we switch off the electric bulbs and light the candles. Give these special moments an even more personal touch by adorning your candles for the occasion. Available in an abundance of styles and colors, candles offer an endless choice of palettes. The techniques and projects in this chapter represent merely a few creative possibilities. You will no doubt discover many of your own in no time.

MATERIALS AND TOOLS

CANDLES
If you plan to decorate'em, you better have some around. See page 156 for information about types of candles.

PAPER, RULER, AND TAPE
Unless you have a cloth measuring tape, you'll need these materials to determine your candle's circumference.

COOKIE CUTTERS
Cut appliqués from sheets of wax using cookie cutters in various shapes.

HAIR-DRYER OR EMBOSSING TOOL
Use a hair dryer or embossing tool to gently heat the surface of candles before pressing materials into them.

RUBBING ALCOHOL
Swab your candles with paper towels moistened with rubbing alcohol to prep their surface for paint or glue.

PANTYHOSE SCRAPS
Run in your hose? Don't throw them away. Instead, use old pantyhose to polish scratches and accidental melts from your candles.

WHITE CRAFT GLUE
No need to break out the hot-glue gun for paper or fabric. White craft glue works just fine.

HOT-GLUE GUN
A hot-glue gun is the perfect tool when you're adhering three-dimensional objects to a candle.

CANDLE-PAINTING MEDIUM
Available at craft stores, this material helps acrylic paint adhere to wax.

ACRYLIC PAINTS
Acrylic paints are the best choices for painting on wax.

STRAIGHT PIN
Use a straight pin, rather than a marker or pencil, to mark the position of an appliqué or other material on your candle.

TACKS, SEQUIN PINS, AND DECORATIVE STUDS
All can be used to jazz up candles on their own or to pin other materials to candles.

BASIC TECHNIQUES

MATCHING CANDLES TO DECORATIVE TECHNIQUES

From slender tapers to massive pillars, there are candles in every shape and size imaginable. Some make better palettes for particular decorating techniques than others, though. Let the following steps guide your selection.

◆ Tapers are the candles that come to mind when you hear the word "candlestick." Tall and slim, they're generally wider at the bottom and taper to a narrower point at the top. They range in size from the tiny tapers that top birthday cakes to the elegant wands that fill candelabras. When decorating these candles, stick to simple techniques suitable for their limited surface area; painting and wrapping are good choices. Because tapers are very slender, their wicks (and thus their flames) will be quite close to any decoration applied to their surface. Avoid using paper and other highly flammable material to adorn anything but the base of a taper, and even then, you'll want to keep a very close eye on a taper that's decorated this way while it's lit.

◆ Freestanding and offering a breadth of artistically inviting surface area, pillar candles are perfect candidates for just about any decorative idea you can dream up—stenciling, stamping, wrapping, tacking, and painting are just a few to try. Although the name suggests a simple columnar form, pillar candles are also available in shapes ranging from pyramids and spheres to ovals and rectangles. Because they're quite thick, their wicks burn at a safe distance from their sides, making them a good choice for decorative techniques that involve flammable materials. If you're dying to wrap a candle in swaths of tulle, for instance, a pillar should be your first pick. (Nevertheless, you should exercise caution when burning any candle adorned with combustible materials.)

◆ From hearts and roses to Christmas trees and cowboy boots, there's a novelty candle for every taste and occasion. The shape and size of your candle will determine, in large part, which decorative techniques will work well on it. A snowman candle might look jaunty "dressed" in a bright, painted-on Hawaiian shirt. Use caution when inserting tacks or pins in a candle that has protrusions or fine details; you may end up snapping off a rose petal when all you were trying to do was pin a sparkling bead dewdrop to it.

◆ Container candles are made from low-melting-point paraffin wax that's poured into any type of container that might make a pretty candle. Gel and soy candles are other types of container candles. When decorating a container candle, you'll probably be embellishing the container rather than the candle itself. Thus, the container will dictate the appropriate method of decoration. A strand of beaded wire can add glitz and sparkle to a candle in a plain glass tumbler. A stenciled row of daisies or ladybugs might brighten a terra-cotta garden pot that houses your shoo-fly citronella candles. Use your imagination—and your commonsense! Even container candles need supervision if they're adorned with flammable materials.

◆ Votive candles are typically 2 inches (5 cm) tall and about 1½ inches (4 cm) thick. They're designed to fit and burn inside small containers, often glass, which contain the melting wax. Because they're usually hidden inside these containers and are fairly small, votives (and their smaller cousins, tea lights) may not be your first choice for decorating projects. They are, however, inexpensive, which makes them ideal "test candles" for experimenting with new techniques and ideas. Many votive containers can be decorated the same way you would a container candle.

MEASURING CANDLES

Whether you're trying to determine what length of ribbon to cut or designing a template for stenciling, you'll need to know the circumference of your candle.

Ideally, there's a simple cloth tape measure buried in your sewing kit or craft box, in which case all you'll need to do is wrap the tape measure around your candle. If not, just use a piece of yarn or other flexible material. Mark the overlap, then add ¼ to ½ inch (6 to 12 mm) to the length, just to be sure. You can always trim away some excess, but it's a little harder to add back a shortfall.

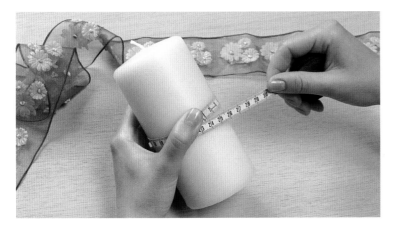

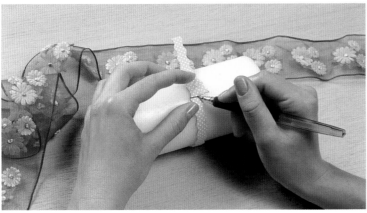

DESIGNER TIP

You wouldn't be decorating candles if you didn't really care about how they'll look once they're on display! While there are plenty of candles that can be safely burned without the support of a candleholder—pillars, for instance—there are just as many that do require some form of external propping. Here are some tips for choosing a candleholder:

* If possible, bring your candle or candles with you when you go shopping for a candleholder—you'll want to test for a perfect fit!

* Make sure the candleholder will hold the candle upright and securely in or on a nonflammable surface.

* The candleholder should protect the surface on which the candle is to be displayed from dripping wax.

* The candle or candles should never overpower the holder (or vice-versa).

* Don't rely on retailers alone to supply your candleholders! Look around your home and you'll find all kinds of candleholders secretly masquerading as other objects: seldom-used mugs, a piece of driftwood, a bowl full of pebbles.

* Although pillars don't necessarily require candleholders, you may still want to protect the surface on which they're placed (the dyes in some candles may stain certain surfaces). Simply place a pretty mat or plate under the pillar.

BASIC TECHNIQUES

TRANSFERRING PATTERNS

If you think of a candle as a three-dimensional canvas, you begin to realize that just about any type of pattern can be used to decorate candles.

1 For elaborate patterns with curved edges, graphite paper is the best way to transfer a design. Simply reduce or enlarge the pattern on a photocopier until the size suits your candle. Position the pattern on your candle, then slide a piece of graphite paper under the pattern, tape the two in place, and lightly trace over the design with a ballpoint pen.

2 For straight line designs, hold a ruler against your candle and mark the lines by gently pressing the blade of a craft knife into the wax. Patterns can also be marked with masking tape, which is easy to remove after painting, beading, etc.

PAINTING CANDLES

Painting is one of the most versatile techniques you can use to customize your candles. Whether you're stenciling a few pretty roses or composing a freehand masterpiece, the following tips will improve your end results.

1 To paint a candle, first prepare the surface by wiping the candle with rubbing alcohol. If you don't want to work freehand, transfer a pattern as described at left.

2 Dilute acrylic paint colors with candle painting medium as directed by the manufacturer's instructions.

3 Paint the candle as you would paint any other surface, then allow to dry completely before using.

158

ATTACHING EMBELLISHMENTS

Fasteners such as sequin pins, tacks, and decorative studs do triple duty in candle decoration. They can be used as "invisible markers," taking backstage to the material they're holding, or stand alone as embellishments in and of themselves. Warm wax is another option, as is hot glue and white craft glue.

Sequins and studs are a great way to dress up plain candles. Arrange them randomly or follow a pattern you've transferred. Whether you're pinning a line of sequins in place or studding a candle with decorative tacks, take a moment to warm the candle's surface before embedding anything in it. If your hands are nice and warm, simply hold the candle between them for a few minutes. Otherwise, use a hair dryer or embossing tool to gently heat the candle's surface for a few seconds. Then, using steady pressure and twisting as if you were inserting a screw, embed the pin or tack in the candle. Don't be tempted to use a hammer to pound tacks in—you'll almost certainly shatter your candle.

Lightweight materials such as dried leaves, paper, and flimsier fabrics will adhere just fine when pressed into the warmed surface of a candle. Use an embossing tool or a hair dryer to carefully heat a small area of your candle. You'll be able to see the wax begin to liquefy, but don't apply too much heat too quickly, or you may over-melt the wax, causing unsightly drips. (If you do accidentally over-melt any portion of your candle, shave drips off with a craft knife and polish the surface smooth with a scrap of pantyhose.) Holding a piece of wax paper over it, gently press the decorative material into place and allow the cooling wax to "grip" the material. For

added holding power and an intriguing visual effect, you may want to over-dip the decorated candle in uncolored paraffin wax.

Inexpensive ribbon can be quickly attached to a candle with hot glue. Special ribbon can be attached with sequin or map pins by just pressing the pin through the ribbon and into the candle on the back side and as needed in other areas. Then, when you're through with the candle and want the ribbon back, all you have to do is unpin it. To finish the back side, fold the top edge over for a clean seam, then cover with pins, tacks, beads, or buttons.

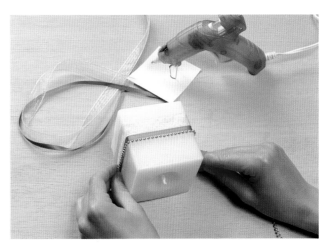

An incredible variety of stickers can be found in memory card and scrapbooking sections of larger crafts stores. Just peel, arrange, and stick!

Pretty-in-Plaid Pillar Candles

Tidy grids of green-and-blue plaid give this pair of pillars a certain air of preppy refinement.

Designer: Diana Light

160

MATERIALS AND TOOLS

2 pillar candles
Paper
Pencil
Masking tape
Ruler
Craft knife
Scissors
Paper towels
Rubbing alcohol
Acrylic craft paint in two shades of
    blue and two shades of green
Candle and soap painting medium
Palette
Paint brushes (You may want to use a
    different width of brush for each
    color.)
Plastic wrap
Rinse cup and water
Cotton swabs

WHAT TO DO

1 Referring to the instructions on page 157, measure the circumference of your candles with a piece of paper. Then use the ruler to measure the candles' height. Subtract 2¼ inches (6 cm) from the height measurement to leave room for borders.

2 Using a ruler and pencil, draw a rectangle on a sheet of paper with the dimensions you measured in Step 2. The rectangle will be as wide as the candle's circumference and as tall as the candle's height, less 2¼ inches.

3 Determine how you'd like to space the stripes that will create the grid for your plaid. In the project shown, the wide, light blue vertical stripes are ⅜ inches (9 mm) wide and spaced 2 inches (5 cm) apart. The thin, dark blue vertical stripes are ⅛ inch (3 mm) wide, spaced 1½ inches (4 cm) apart, and start ¼ inch (6 mm) from the nearest wide, light blue verti-

cal stripe. The outside edge of the uppermost wide, light green horizontal stripes is 1 inch from the top of the candle. The outside edge of the lowermost wide, light green horizontal stripe is 1¼ inch from the bottom of the candle. Each wide, light green stripe is ¼ inch wide and the stripes in both the upper and lower pair of stripes are spaced ½ inch apart. A ¼-inch-wide, horizontal dark green stripe runs directly between each pair of light green stripes, spaced exactly ¼ inch from each one. Use these measurements or your own to mark a grid in the rectangle you drew in Step 3.

4 Measure 1 inch (2.5 cm) down from the top of your candle; use a craft knife to lightly score this 1-inch mark at four equidistant points around the top of your candle. Measure 1¼ inch up from the bottom of the candle and mark four equidistant points the same way.

5 Wrap a length of masking tape around the top of the candle, with the tape's upper edge right at the 1-inch points you just scored. Wrap another length of tape around the bottom of the candle, with the tape's lower edge right at the 1¼-inch points.

6 Use the craft knife to lightly score a line all the way around the top and bottom of the candle, using the outer edges of the strips of masking tape as guides. These marks will define the upper and lower borders of your plaid pattern.

7 Cut your grid from the paper and secure it in place on your candle, between the lines you scored in Step 7. Use a craft knife to mark the position of each horizontal line, making several marks along each line. Remove the paper grid and place a strip of masking tape along each set of marks on the candle, just as you did in Step 7.

Score the lines with a craft knife, using the edges of the masking tape as a guide. Remove the tape.

8 Tape the grid back in place on the candle and mark the vertical lines just as you marked the horizontal lines. Remove the grid, place masking tape along the vertical lines, and score them with a craft knife. When you're finished, you will have transferred the entire grid to the candle.

9 Wipe away any tiny shavings and clean your candle with a paper towel moistened with rubbing alcohol.

10 Mix the lightest color first on your palette, following the paint and candle and soap painting medium's manufacturers' instructions. Paint the appropriate stripes, leaving the small rectangles where lines cross blank—you'll fill these areas in later with a mix of the two stripe colors.

11 Mix the second lightest color on your palette with medium, and paint the next set of lines, once again remembering not to paint those areas where lines cross. Mix and paint the remaining colors. You may want to cover each color on your palette with a little plastic wrap to prevent it from drying out.

12 After you've painted all the lines, paint the areas where lines intersect. To do this, start by mixing together the two colors of paints from the intersecting lines. You'll end up with four new colors. Carefully fill in the small squares where the lines intersect with the appropriate color blends.

13 Use a cotton swab moistened with rubbing alcohol to clean up any mistakes you may have made. Then allow the paint to dry thoroughly before handling the candle.

CARVED CANDLE

Beeswax candles were once too expensive for the common man. Tallow candles, made from a mixture of rendered fat from sheep and cattle, lit the rooms of humbler homes. Today candles are most often made of paraffin wax, a byproduct of the petroleum industry. Because wax is both firm and soft, it is the perfect medium for aspiring carvers.

MATERIALS AND TOOLS

White or ivory pillar candle
Cloth tape measure; or a sheet of
 paper, tape, and a ruler
Template
Scissors
Tape
Graphite paper
Ball-tipped stylus or a pencil with a
 dull point
Paper towel and rubbing alcohol
Candle painting medium
Acrylic paint in burnt umber
Disposable gloves (optional)
Foam brush
Cotton rag
Newspaper to protect work area
Paper plate

WHAT TO DO

1 Measure the circumference (see page 157) and height of your candle. Then use a photocopier to enlarge or reduce the template on page 515 to a size that will fit your candle. Make several photocopies of the template and cut them out. Tape the cutouts around the candle, spacing them evenly.

2 When you're satisfied with the spacing and placement of the cutouts, slip a sheet of graphite paper under them and tape in place. Trace around each one with your stylus or pencil. Use light pressure—you won't have to press hard to leave an impression on the candle.

3 After you've traced around all the cutouts, remove them from the candle. Then, using firm but even pressure, go over each line on the candle again with your stylus or pencil. Press harder this time, brushing away excess wax as you work.

4 Prep your candle by cleaning its surface with paper towel moistened with rubbing alcohol.

5 Using the paper plate as a palatte and following the manufacturer's instructions, mix the candle painting medium with the paint.

6 Protect your work surface with a layer of newspaper and your hands with a pair of gloves. Then apply the paint mixture over entire candle with the foam brush. Use the cotton rag to wipe most of the paint from the surface of the candle, leaving paint in the carved areas. Allow the paint to dry.

Designer: Lynn Krucke

Designer: Lynn Krucke

CLIMBING IVY CANDLES

Bring the elegance of an English garden indoors by "training" ivy to climb a set of white candles. Purchase dried ivy leaves at your local craft store, or press your own leaves between sheets of heavy paper or between the pages of a thick book.

MATERIALS AND TOOLS

Assorted white candles
Pressed ivy leaves
Straight pin
Wax paper
Embossing tool or hair dryer
Craft knife
Scrap of pantyhose

WHAT TO DO

1 Select the leaves to use and experiment with possible placements on the candles. Use a straight pin to lightly mark where you plan to place each leaf.

2 With the embossing tool or hair dryer, carefully warm the surface of the candle and apply one of the leaves. Place a piece of wax paper over the leaf and continue to heat, pressing the leaf into the warmed wax to secure it.

3 Repeat for the remaining leaves. Work carefully to avoid overmelting the wax. If drips or smears do occur, shave them off with the craft knife; then polish the area with the scrap of pantyhose.

Safety Note: Dried leaves are highly flammable. If you plan to burn candles decorated using the technique described in this project, choose wide pillars with wicks that are a sizable distance from the candles' sides. If you simply must adorn your dining room tapers this way, apply the leaves only to the bottom third of the candles and extinguish them before the flame burns to the level of the leaves.

DECORATING CANDLES AND SAFETY

Decorating candles is a great way to craft unique treasures, and it's a lot of fun. Never forget, though, that they can be a fire hazard if not used properly. Be sure to keep the following safety tips in mind:

*Never position flammable materials anywhere near the flame.

*Burn decorated candles for short periods of time, and never when you're not right there to watch them.

*When the candle burns down more than an inch (2.5 cm), it's time to discard the candle and decorate a new one.

*Never give a decorated candle as a gift to someone whithout explaining safety precautions. If you don't think they will follow them, find another gift.

ALL-BUTTONED-UP CANDLES

Everyone who sews has a box full of ribbon scraps and notions and jars of spare buttons. Here's a novel way to put some of those extras to good use.

MATERIALS AND TOOLS

Pillar candles (Because this project uses flammable materials, be sure to choose wide candles whose wicks will burn at a safe distance from the decorated sides.)
Paper
Tape
Ruler
Wire-edged ribbon, 2 inches wide
Cloth ribbon, 1 inch wide
Paper towel
Rubbing alcohol
Hot-glue gun and glue stick
Thread in color that matches candles
Needle
Large wooden button

WHAT TO DO

1 Referring to Step 1 on page 157, determine the circumference of your candle using the paper, tape, and ruler.

2 Fold the wire-edged ribbon into 1-inch (2.5 cm) pleats. It can be hard to tell how long a piece of ribbon you'll need to encircle the entire candle until you've actually made the pleats, so wait until you've pleated enough ribbon to cover the candle's circumference—plus 1 inch—before you cut your ribbon from the spool.

3 Cut a length of cloth ribbon about ½ inch (13 mm) longer than the circumference of your candle.

4 Wipe the surface of your candle clean with a paper towel moistened with rubbing alcohol.

5 Determine the position of the ribbon on the candle; then apply a small amount of hot glue to one end of the pleated, wire-edged ribbon. Allow the glue to cool slightly before adhering the ribbon to the candle.

6 Wrap the ribbon around the candle just tightly enough so it will stay in place. Trim any excess ribbon. Apply a small amount of hot glue to the ribbon's loose end and press it against the other end of the ribbon (not the candle), tucking it under a pleat. (By using glue in just one small spot on the candle, you'll be able to easily detach the ribbon and slide it down as the candle burns.)

7 Apply a thin line of hot glue along the back of the cloth ribbon and press it into place on the candle, centering it along the wire-edged ribbon's width.

8 Thread the needle and take a few passes through the button, as if you were sewing it onto a piece of fabric. Knot the thread at the back of the button.

9 Apply a bit of hot glue to the back of the button and press it into place on the candle, right where the two ends of the cloth ribbon meet.

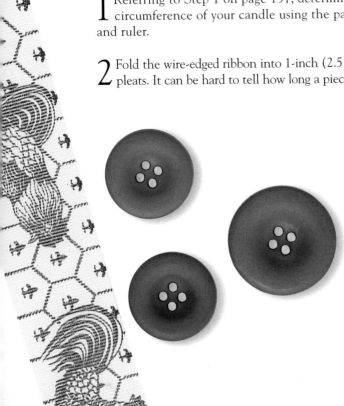

DECORATING CANDLES GALLERY

Opposite page, near right: Lace-like skeleton leaves can be found in your favorite craft store and make a dramatic addition to candles. Designer: Lynn Krucke

Opposite page, far right: Create a faux mosaic surface with eggshells painted in your favorite colors. Designer: Jean Tomaso Moore

Opposite page, below: Personalize your candles (or your gifts) with sealing wax medallions and ribbon. Designer: Terry Burgin

Below: Temporary tatoos are a great way to jazz up simple candles. They come in a wide variety of colors and styles and take just minutes to apply. Designer: Megan Kirby

Right: Photocopy your favorite images, then transfer them onto pillar candles with transfer solvent. Designer: Nicole Tuggle

GEL CANDLES

Candle gel is, well, remarkable. It can be colored, fragranced, and decorated. It can be remelted, recolored, recyled, and replenished. It emits a soft, lovely glow, burns a long time, and can be poured and repoured into a variety of containers—without causing the container any harm. This is about as easy and rewarding as crafting gets.

MATERIALS AND TOOLS

GEL

Candle gel is sold at craft stores in solid form. To determine how much gel to melt, measure the amount of water required to fill the chosen container. This is the amount of gel you will need. (Since candle gel is reusable, it makes sense to overestimate rather than underestimate.)

DYES

Though there are dyes made specifically for gel candles (sold in both liquid and solid form), you can also use dyes made for paraffin wax, though bear in mind that paraffin dyes create a more opaque color. Never use ordinary food coloring to color candle gel.

FRAGRANCES

It is important to use only gel-compatible fragrances (check the label), as other fragrances may cloud the finished candle, or cause the candle to be unsafe by lowering the flashpoint.

WICKS

Zinc-cored wicks are ideal for gel candles, since they are stiff and stay straight in gel. Wicks are available with or without anchors (or tabs). All wicks (including those with a wax coating) will need to be pretreated to avoid bubbling (see page 174). Sticky dots are available to attach anchors to the bottom of the containers, though these are not essential. Do not use paper wicking in gel candles.

COOKING VESSEL

An electric slow cooker with a temperature adjustment gauge is the ideal container for heating gel, but any ordinary cooking pan (used with a clip-on thermometer, see below) will work.

A pot with a pouring spout and a heat-resistant handle is the best choice for stovetop melting. Clean any vessel you use with grease-dissolving detergent after each use.

THERMOMETER

Clip-on thermometers are inexpensive and found wherever candy-making supplies are sold. Since melted gel looks the same at any temperature, a thermometer is essential, unless you are using a cooker with its own temperature gauge.

HEAT GUN

Though certainly not a necessity in making gel candles, a heat gun works wonders to smooth the tops of candles and to eliminate air bubbles (simply warm the container from the outside to remove bubbles). Make sure you follow the manufacturer's guidelines for safe and proper use.

METAL UTENSILS

Always use metal utensils (not wood or plastic) when working with candle gel. Metal ladles, spoons, knives, scissors, tweezers, and skewers are all useful in making gel candles. Note: Wood utensils will create bubbles, and are a good choice when you want a bubbled candle.

BUBBLE STICK
Found where canning supplies are sold, plastic bubble sticks are for stirring gel immediately following pouring to remove bubbles from candles before the gel cools.

EMBEDS
Though, in theory, any nonflammable object can be embedded in a gel candle, some items make better embeds than others. To avoid bubbling, embeds should be pretreated (see page 174). Try items made from glass, ceramic, polymer clay, and metal. Beads, marbles, and silk flowers are good choices. Avoid organic items (paper, fabric, dried flowers, and foliage), plastic, and rubber, as these items are flammable.

CONTAINERS
Oh, the possibilities! Though you should avoid thin glass and containers that are narrower at the top than at the base, any glass container will work. Sometimes, in fact, an interesting container requires only clear gel and a wick to become spectacular.

171

BASIC TECHNIQUES

HEATING & DYEING GEL

It's crucial that you follow the manufacturer's instructions exactly when working with candle gel, particularly regarding heating temperatures. Here are some general guidelines for preparing gel for pouring. See page 174 for important safety information.

1 To remove gel from its container, use a knife to cut small chunks, then scoop out the pieces with your bare hands. Place chunks into a pan or cooker. Attach thermometer to the pan, if applicable.

2 Clean the candle container thoroughly, then preheat it in a warm oven (175° F or 80° C) for about 10 minutes to decrease bubbling; if you want bubbles, preheating is not necessary.

3 While the container is warming, heat gel slowly to the proper temperature, as recommended by the manufacturer, until it becomes liquid (usually 180° F to 220° F or 82° C to 104° C). Note: if you don't want bubbles, heat the gel to the highest temperature recommended by the manufacturer.

4 Carefully stir in dye with a metal spoon in small amounts until the desired color is achieved. Note that the color will appear somewhat darker in pan. If you add too much color, add clear gel to the pan in small amounts to make adjustments in color. Add gel-compatible fragrance to the gel, if desired, just prior to pouring, so the scent will not evaporate.

POURING GEL

Though you may be anxious to see the finished candle, this is the point at which you need to take your time and be careful with the melted gel. It's a good idea to keep children and pets out of the way as well.

1 If you are using an anchored wick, dip the anchor into hot gel and press it to the bottom of the container with a metal skewer; or you can attach the anchor with a sticky dot specifically designed for this purpose. Loop the excess wick around a skewer and lay skewer across the top of the container. Note: To avoid bubbling, make sure the wick is pretreated.

2 Place warmed candle container on a level surface, and position embeds, if desired (see page 175). Double-check the temperature, then carefully pour the gel into the container. Tilt the container at an angle when pouring to reduce bubbles, if desired.

3 If you are not using an anchored wick, position wick at this point (see wick manufacturer's guidelines for length and size). Either loop the excess wick around a skewer and place skewer across the top of the container, or insert a wick once the gel has cooled enough to hold it snugly. Trim wick to ¼ inch (6 mm). Note: Do not place wick near flammable embeds.

4 Place newly poured candles in a secure place for several hours to cool. To prevent bubbles, you can slow down the cooling process by wrapping the candle in towels or by putting the candle in a warm oven (no more than 175° F or 80° C) for several hours.

173

BASIC TECHNIQUES

PRETREATING EMBEDS & WICKS

Anything that will be placed inside a gel candle, including the wick, should be pretreated to avoid bubbles. Of course, bubbles are important to some designs; in those cases, skip this process.

1 To pretreat an embed or a wick, place the item in a pan with a small amount of melted gel (this gel should not be reused).

2 If bubbles do not appear in the gel, use tweezers to remove the embed or the wick from the gel. Hold embed over the pan until the gel hardens. Once you lift the wick from the gel and it has cooled to the touch, remove excess gel by running fingers along wick.

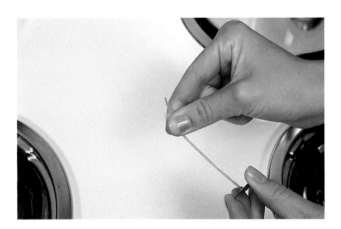

3 If bubbles do appear, stir the gel occasionally with a metal utensil until bubbling stops. If the bubbling continues after a few minutes, do not use the item in your gel candle.

SAFETY

Candle gel is flammable. Read all instructions and guidelines provided by gel and wick manufacturers, particularly with regard to pouring temperatures. Take your time and work carefully. Because gel heats up very quickly (and thus reaches its flash point very quickly), do not leave gel heating on the stovetop unattended and do not exceed the temperature recommended by the manufacturer. If your gel does ignite, do not put water on the fire. If the fire is small, cover and remove from heat or smother the fire with baking soda; for larger fires, use a fire extinguisher. Avoid hot gel coming in contact with skin; always use potholders and kitchen mitts. Apply ice to any skin burns immediately.

POSITIONING EMBEDS

Whether your design is whimsical, elegant, or somewhere in between, embeds are a great way to add a personal touch to gel candles—and creative positioning is part of the fun.

1 If you want your embeds to rest on the bottom of the container, position those items first. Use tweezers or cooking skewers, if necessary, to arrange them inside container.

3 Once gel is poured, use a metal skewer to rearrange embeds in the container, as needed. As the gel cools, gently remove thread.

2 To create floating embeds, suspend the items from sewing thread and tape the ends of thread to the outside of the container, or suspend the embeds from a skewer that has been positioned across the top of the container. Take care to postion all embeds away from where the wick will be. To prevent any chance that embeds will come in contact with the wick, you may choose to use a very short wick (1 to 2 inches, 2.5 to 5 cm).

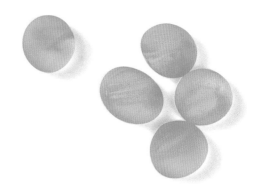

JEL DESSERT CANDLES

Enjoy the fun of summertime gelatin desserts year 'round with these festive look-alike candles. They're simple to make, and the addition of a little gel candle glitter creates a brilliant, sparkling effect.

MATERIALS AND TOOLS

Clip-on pan thermometer
Pan
Sundae dessert bowls
Clear candle gel
Gel candle dyes
Gel candle glitter
Large metal spoon
Square or rectangular baking pan
Wick
Sharp, nonserrated kitchen knife

DESIGNER TIP

Use glitter made specifically for gel candles (not regular craft glitter, which may be flammable) to add a unique sparkle to your designs. Glitter should be stirred into melted gel just before pouring.

WHAT TO DO

1 Melt the gel over low heat in the pan until it reaches the temperature recommended by the manufacturer.

2 Tint the gel to the desired color by adding dye one drop at a time, stirring well. Double-check the color by removing a small amount of gel on a spoon and placing it on a sheet of heavy white paper. Add additional gel to the pan if the color is too dark, or additional dye if the color is too light.

3 Carefully add the desired amount of gel glitter, stirring well.

4 Dip the bottom of the wick anchor in the melted gel, then position it in the center bottom of the dessert dish.

5 Pour the gel into the square or rectangular pan until it's ¾ to 1 inch (18 to 25 mm) thick. Allow the gel to cool undisturbed for several hours.

6 Cut the gel into squares with a knife, then remove them from the pan and arrange them around the wick.

7 Repeat Steps 1 through 6 in another fruity color if desired.

Designer: Dawn Cusick

ETCHED GLASS GEL CANDLES

Etched glass containers are available in an incredible range of styles and shapes, often for meager sums. Choose a floral design on a small votive shape or a geometric pattern on a taller bud vase. These candles make an ideal first gel candle project: Just melt, tint, and pour the gel.

MATERIALS AND TOOLS

Clip-on pan thermometer
Pan
Etched glass containers
Clear candle gel
Gel candle dyes
Large metal spoon
Wick

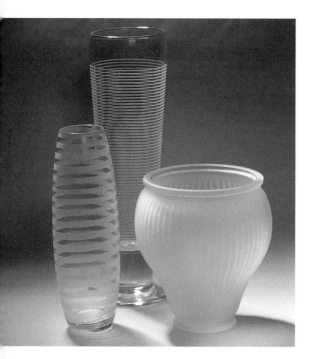

A variety of etched containers

WHAT TO DO

1 Melt the gel over low heat in the pan until it reaches the temperature recommended by the manufacturer.

2 Tint the gel to the desired color by adding dye one drop at a time, stirring well.

3 Double-check the color by removing a small amount of gel on a spoon and placing it on a sheet of heavy white paper. Add additional gel to the pan if the color is too dark or additional dye if the color is too light.

4 Dip the bottom of the wick anchor in the melted gel, then position it in the center bottom of the container.

5 Pour the tinted gel into the container, then allow to cool several hours undisturbed.

6 Repeat Steps 1 through 5 with another color if desired.

Designer: Dawn Cusick

DESIGNER TIP

If gel spills on a nonporous surface, the best course of action is to wait until the gel has cooled, then peel it off. To remove gel from a porous surface, such as fabric, hand-launder the item with a grease-dissolving detergent, then air-dry. Since candle gel is oil-based, there's no guarantee the gel will come out, so take care, work slowly, and try to avoid spills altogether.

AMBER GEL CANDLES

The beauty of gel candles is that you can easily create custom colors to match your favorite flower vase, your curtains, or even your couch! Here, clear gel was tinted to match a collection of vintage dishware.

MATERIALS AND TOOLS

Clip-on pan thermometer
Pan
Glass bowls
Candle gel
Gel candle dyes
Large metal spoon
Wick

DESIGNER TIP

Imperfect gel candles—perhaps an out-of-place wick or too many bubbles?—can be reheated at a low heat in the oven. Place the candle on a foil-lined cookie sheet to avoid spills. Do not reheat candles if you used embeds that can melt, floating embeds, or if it's a layered candle.

WHAT TO DO

1 Melt the gel over low heat in the pan until it reaches the temperature recommended by the manufacturer.

2 Tint the gel to the desired color by adding dye one drop at a time, stirring well.

3 Double-check the color by removing a small amount of gel on a spoon and placing it on a sheet of heavy white paper.

4 Adjust the color of the gel if desired by adding additional clear gel to the pan if the color is too dark or additional dye if the color is too light.

5 Pour the tinted gel into the container. Position a short wick in the center of the candle, then allow the gel to cool undisturbed for several hours.

BUBBLY CHAMPAGNE CANDLES

What better way to toast a special occasion than by the romantic flicker of these elegant gel candles? Just as a champagne flute is the perfect vessel for bubbly liquid, so is it an ideal gel-candle holder, because it accentuates the air bubbles that naturally form in the gel. Embellish the glasses for any occasion (a wedding, perhaps?) with ribbon, flowers, or beads.

MATERIALS AND TOOLS

Clip-on pan thermometer
Clear candle gel
Gel candle dye
Large metal spoon
Champagne glasses
Wick
Wood skewer
Pan

WHAT TO DO

1 Melt the gel over low heat in the pan until it just begins to melt, stirring as little as possible.

2 Add just enough yellow dye to lightly tint the gel a pale champagne color. Double-check the color by removing a small amount of gel on a spoon and placing it on a sheet of heavy white paper. Add additional gel to the pan if the color is too dark or additional dye if the color is too light.

3 Pour the tinted gel into the glasses and arrange a short wick. Create extra bubbles by gently moving the wood skewer across the top surface.

4 Allow the gel to cool undisturbed for several hours.

Designer: Dawn Cusick

LAVENDER LIGHTS

An inexpensive melt-and-pour soap-making mold was used to create colorful gel highlights to add color to these candles. Drop the lavender gel into a cooling clear gel candle to create subtle swirls of color and extra bubbles.

MATERIALS AND TOOLS

Clip-on pan thermometer
Pan
Large decorative glass
Clear candle gel
Gel candle dyes
Large metal spoon
Wick
Candy or soap mold

WHAT TO DO

1 Melt a small amount of gel over low heat in the pan until it reaches the temperature recommended by the manufacturer. Add dye by the drop and stir until you're happy with the color.

2 Allow the tinted gel to cool for a few minutes, stirring occasionally to keep it from solidifying, then pour the gel into the molds.

3 After the gel has solidified, remove it from the molds and place the shapes on a paper towel. A pointed object, such as a toothpick, can be helpful in removing gel from molds.

4 Remove any remaining tinted gel from the pan, then melt enough clear gel to fill the glass.

5 Pour the melted clear gel into the glass and allow to cool for several minutes.

6 Drop several tinted gel shapes into the glass. Allow the gel to cool for another few minutes, then add several more tinted gel shapes. Repeat until you are happy with the effect.

7 Position a short wick and allow the candle to cool undisturbed for several hours.

DESIGNER TIP

The smart and money-wise candlemaker always saves bits of unused gel. Simply remove scraps of gel from the container or pan and store in a sealed plastic bag or glass container. These pieces can be reheated to make another candle or used to add color to clear gel (just drop them in the pan during the melting process).

Designer: Dawn Cusick

Right: Celebrate in style with the ultimate gel candle. The bottom layer was made from pink gel; a "frosting" layer was created by adding grated white crayon to melted gel; and the opaque, third layer was created by folding tinted gel over a butter knife as it cooled until the color changed. Desinger: Megan Kirby

Below: Design your own zen rock candle by layering river stones on the bottom of a nicely shaped glass container, then pouring gel over the stones. Multiple wicks add to the appeal. Desinger: Terry Taylor

Opposite page, left: Ceramic miniatures positioned on a layer of green sand make a great gel candle for your favorite gardener. Designer: Theresa Gwynn

Opposite page, right: Ceramic sharks, beach sand, and aqua-tinted gel create the perfect underwater scene. Designer: Megan Kirby

Opposite page, below: Candlescaping with gel candles is as easy as pouring tinted gel into small juice jars decorated with colorful sequins. Designer: Terry Taylor

GEL GALLERY

CANDLESCAPING

Nothing creates ambience and evokes romance quite like candles. A single candle in a simple candlestick has its own charm, to be sure, but why not use a variety of items in combination with candles to embellish a spot in your home? And though you may think of displaying candles only at holidays or special events, candlescaping is an easy way to decorate indoors and out, every day of the year.

MATERIALS AND TOOLS

CANDLES

Candles are widely available in craft, home décor, and home improvement stores, as well as in discount stores and supermarkets. You can find plain ones, fancy ones, scented, or unscented; indeed, candles seem to come in just about every color, shape, size, and price range (the dripless, slow-burning varieties are the most expensive). Paraffin and beeswax are the most common types of wax used, though candles made from wax blends—soy wax and gel wax, for example—are also available. Candles should be stored in a cool, dry place.

CONTAINER CANDLES

As the name implies, these are candles made by pouring low-melting-point paraffin wax into a container. This is a particularly fun and easy type of candle to make at home (see page 208).

TAPERS

Tapers are tall, thin candles that require a candlestick or another snug holder. Store tapers flat in a cool location to prevent warping.

PILLAR OR BLOCK CANDLES

These are sturdy, freestanding candles that can be placed on any flat, nonflammable surface. Very large pillars with multiple wicks are available, as are a wide variety of pillars with decorative surfaces.

VOTIVES

Also known as vigil candles, these are small candles (usually several inches or 5 cm tall) designed to be held in a simple (often glass) container.

TEA CANDLES

These are among the smallest candles available. Tea candles are generally round and fitted into disposable metal cups.

CANDLE HOLDERS

Glass, metal, ceramic, and wood are traditional materials used to make candle holders, though almost anything can be used. Just make sure

that any holder made of a flammable material keeps the flame at a safe distance from the holder. (This is not an issue, of course, if you are not planning to light the candle.) Very large block or pillar candles can be placed directly on any flat surface, which allows for a great deal of creativity when choosing a holder.

CANDLE ADHESIVE
This puttylike material is useful when placed on the base of the candle to prevent the candle from tipping. Usually only a small portion is required. Be mindful not to use so large an amount as to cause the candle to become unstable.

STABILIZERS
The possibilities are endless: sand, marbles, seashells, nuts, pebbles, Easter eggs, holiday ornaments, even Mardi Gras beads or faux pearls. Although these elements can be important in stabilizing candles, they can also be used for purely decorative purposes.

BASIC TECHNIQUES

CHOOSING CANDLE HOLDERS

When choosing a holder for your candle, think outside the box (or brass candlestick, if you will). Sure, there are vast assortments of candle holders available in the market- place, but why not save time and money and devise some- thing unique? Mismatched china or ceramic dishes or teacups, smooth stones, slabs of wood, discarded toys or wagons—all can become interesting candle holders, not to mention conversation pieces!

1 Choose holders that complement your candles in color, shape, and texture. Candles illuminate and accentuate the texture and shape of many containers. Try a container that allows light to show through, such as a lantern, an orchid pot, or even an aluminum can in which you have punched holes. If necessary, line the bottom of the holder with foil to protect it from drips.

2 Make sure the holder will keep the candle upright and prevent wax from dripping. If necessary, press a small ball of candle adhesive to the base of the candle

for a snug fit. If the base of the candle is too wide, use a paring knife to shave around the edges of the candle. If you are using a wood candle holder, sometimes a well- placed finish nail can serve to keep the candle upright.

3 Position the candle in the holder. If you have lined the holder with foil (see Step 1), you may want to disguise the foil with moss, potpourri, or another similar material.

CANDLESCAPING TIP

So many colors to choose! When it comes to grouping candles, why take the easy way by only using candles of the same color? You can add more drama to your arrangements by combining different shades of the same color—say a green grouping from deep jade to pale sage. Or, combine opposite colors in complementary tones, such as periwinkle and yellow, or teal and deep rose.

CHOOSING & PREPARING CANDLES

If you have already chosen your candle holders, then the type of candles you need may already be decided. On the other hand, if you happen upon some fantastic candles first, the design process can begin there. Whether you are going for sleek and understated or bold and whimsical, the candles you choose are an important element in designing an effective candlescape.

1 Consider the candle holder. A candle should never overpower its holder, and vice versa. For stability and safety, use pillar or block candles when it is important that wax not spill.

DESIGNER TIP

Be considerate when using scented candles, as many people are very sensitive (or even allergic) to scents. Also, do not burn scented candles while dining, as the scent interferes and competes with the aroma of the food.

2 Determine the color. Candles do not need to "match" the décor, though you should try to choose colors that complement or contrast with your existing color palette in a pleasing way. Consider whether you want a monochromatic design or a mixture of colors. A colored glass container may work best with a simple white votive, for example.

3 Candle wicks should be trimmed to ¼ inch (6 mm). This not only allows the candle to burn more evenly, it helps keep the candle from sputtering and wax from overflowing. Light and extinguish candles once before burning them (just before guests arrive works well); this makes them burn more evenly.

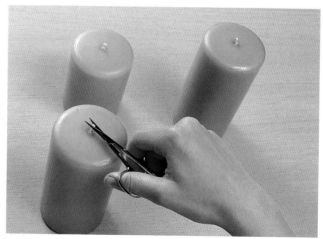

BASIC TECHNIQUES

Choosing a Location
& Planning the Design

Have a blah corner or an unoccupied tabletop? Candlescaping is a terrific way to lend color and atmosphere to any uninteresting area of your home. Take a walk through your living space, and consider where candlescaping will have the biggest impact.

1 Consider the candles and candle holders you want to use or the ones you would like to make or buy, and the overall look you would like to achieve, then select a location. For fragile or complicated candlescapes, pick a low-traffic spot. Simple designs can be positioned anywhere. Avoid elaborate candlescapes on the dining table, as they inhibit conversation and form a visual barrier between dinner companions. Though mantels and dining tables and windowsills are obvious choices, a little extra thought can yield some unusual possibilities.

Designer Tip

Sometimes candle wicks burn too low and become embedded in the candle, which makes the candle very difficult to light and causes it to burn ineffectively. This problem can be alleviated. Use a sharp knife to carefully remove wax from around the base of the wick so that at least ¼ inch (6 mm) of fresh wick is exposed.

2 Plan the design and determine the materials you will use. Sketch the candlescape, if desired; this is especially helpful when working with complicated designs. Try either varying the height of the materials and positioning candles so that flames are on different planes, or lining up similarly shaped items on the same plane. Repetition is a simple, and very effective, way to create striking designs. To create a more interesting and dynamic design when working with materials that have similar heights, vary heights by creating ledges (boxes, flat stones, and overturned bowls work well).

3 Arrange the candle holders first, then position candles. Make sure candles fit snugly in their holders and are not close to any flammable item or surface.

4 If any materials will be arranged around the base of the candle holders or on the surface below—such as flowers, potpourri, mementos, or collectibles—position these items last. Stand back from the design, and make any necessary adjustments.

DESIGNER TIP

Tired of your old standard candlesticks? Use fruits and vegetables! Try squashes, apples, pears, oranges, peppers, onions, to name only a few. Simply remove any stem then make a hole in the food with an apple corer or a small paring knife, then insert candle. (It's best to begin with a smaller hole, then enlarge as needed.)

DESIGNER TIP

For a quick, unique candle presentation, nestle a candle or candles in a stabilizer of your choice in a bowl, basket (line with foil), or other container. Even the most humble materials take on a magical feel when accentuated by a candle's lovely glow. If you are using a taper, secure candle to the base of the container with a small amount of candle adhesive.

TOWER OF LIGHT

You found that old plant stand at a flea market one weekend, and immediately imagined using it to transform a corner of your bedroom into a lush, tropical fern garden. That was before you discovered that your cats harbor an unholy fascination with all things feathery and green. Not a single fern survived. No matter. With those ferns out of the way, the stand's true calling becomes apparent: What that dim corner really needs is light, glorious, flickering, romantic candlelight—tier upon tier of it.

MATERIALS AND TOOLS

Metal plant stand with several tiers
  (see Step 1)
Dish detergent, optional
Wire brush or steel wool, optional
Cloth, optional
Vinegar, optional

Metal primer, optional
Enamel in the color of your choice,
  optional
Assortment of container candles
Dim corner in need of candlelit pizzazz

WHAT TO DO

1 Before paying top dollar for a brand new plant stand (available at most garden supply stores and discount retailers), hit a few yard sales and flea markets. Chances are you'll find a fabulous—and inexpensive!—vintage stand that you can refurbish and make your own. If you're working with a new stand, proceed to Step 4. Otherwise, read on.

2 To bring an old metal plant stand back to life, start by cleaning it with warm water and a mild dish detergent to remove any dirt or rust. Then remove any peeling or loose paint with a wire brush or steel wool. Wipe the entire stand clean with a cloth and vinegar.

3 Allow the stand to dry completely; then coat it with metal primer. After the primer has dried, apply a coat or two

of enamel in the color of your choice. (Classic black is always a good choice.) Make sure the enamel is completely dry before proceeding.

4 Position your stand as desired, making sure to leave plenty of free space above and around it. Then arrange the candles on the tiers. For a more pulled-together, formal look, use candles that are all the same style, as shown in the project photo. For a more eclectic look, vary the candles, perhaps using a different style on each tier.

5 To light the candles, be sure to start at the top tier and work your way down—remember that heat rises!

Designer: Megan Kirby

DESIGNER TIP

Don't let cleanup keep you from burning your candles. It's actually quite easy to remove wax from candle holders. One technique is to soak the candle holder in warm, soapy water, then use a sponge or a cloth to remove wax. For more tenacious wax, try putting the candle holder in the freezer for at least half an hour, then use a blunt tool, such as a toothpick, to remove the wax.

GARDEN CHANDELIERS

Set your next garden party a-sparkle with a scattering of crystal, candlelit chandeliers. So what if the wind snuffs a candle or two? These fabulous hanging holders will look just as gorgeous lit by starshine. Besides, beauty and romance always trump practicality, particularly when it comes to entertaining out-of-doors!

MATERIALS AND TOOLS

Assortment of candle holders made from wire and glass beads (see Step 1)
Fine-gauge chain
Wire cutters
Needle-nose pliers
Large jump rings, one for each candle holder
Wire hooks, one for each candle holder
Small candles that fit the candle holders

WHAT TO DO

1 Specialty candle suppliers stock a huge variety of fabulous candle holders. If you can't find any you like, though, try making your own—a quick review of pages 496–499 should get you up to snuff on working with beads and wire.

2 To turn a regular candle holder into a hanging candle holder, start by cutting three lengths of chain, all the same size, using your wire cutters. Attach the pieces equidistantly around the top of the candle holder: To do this, pinch the cut link of each chain piece around the wire of the candle holder, using your needle-nose pliers.

3 Attach the tops of the wire to a single jump ring, again using your needle-nose pliers to squeeze a cut link around the wire of the ring.

4 Slip a hook onto the jump ring and a candle into the holder. Find a branch that can bear the weight of your miniature, outdoor chandelier and hang it in place. Let the party begin!

196

Designer: Megan Kirby

LUMINOUS HARVEST

Put some real shine on those apples! This unusual project is easy to make and can be adapted to reflect the season's bounty—summer peaches, autumn apples, winter squash, spring mangoes. Just be sure to choose fruits or vegetables that are firm enough to hold a candle.

MATERIALS AND TOOLS

Assortment of apples or other
  firm-fleshed fruits or vegetables
Paring knife or apple corer

Tea lights
Candle adhesive
Basket

WHAT TO DO

1 Wash and dry all the apples. Then select several that you think will make good candle holders. Set the others aside.

2 Working at the stem end, use the paring knife or corer to carve out a shallow hole in each of the apples you selected in Step 1. You may want to hold a tea light against the area to be cut and lightly trace around it with the paring knife; then cut the hole slightly smaller to ensure a snug fit.

3 Test the depth of each hole by placing a tea light in it. The candle's top edge should sit flush with the apple's surface.

4 If a candle fits a little loosely, remove it and apply a bit of candle adhesive to its base before fitting it back into the apple.

5 Arrange the apples in the basket, interspersing the ones with the candle holders in among the others. Make sure that the candle-holding apples are very stable, and—if your basket has a handle—that they don't sit directly under it.

198

Designer: Megan Kirby

Designer:
Megan Kirby

A CELEBRATION OF THE SUBTLETY OF HUE

We're all the same. And we're all different, too—just like the glass-sheathed votives that form this lovely, luminous row. The subtle change in hue from one candle to the next is a perfect reminder of the beautiful harmony that can arise when we make constructive use of our similarities and our diversities.

MATERIALS AND TOOLS

Assortment of votives
 (see Steps 1 and 2)
Glass candle holders to hold
 the votives
Empty windowsill

WHAT TO DO

1 Choose votives that are all the same size and in the same basic color family. Odd numbers make more pleasing arrangements than even, so choose three, five, seven, or nine candles, rather than four, six, or eight.

2 You can experiment not only with pleasing arrangements of hues, but scents as well. For instance, you could combine vanilla-, apple-, and cinnamon-scented candles in your arrangement for an apple-pie effect.

3 Place the votives in the glass candle holders and arrange them along an empty windowsill in ascending order, from lightest to darkest—or in whatever order seems best to you!

200

THE MIDAS TOUCH

Nothing adds the feeling of richness to a room like gold. Don't go overboard like old Midas, though! Practice some restraint by confining your golden bounty to a single, simple, stunning arrangement. For a cooler look, try this project using silver candles in a silver-toned serving dish.

MATERIALS AND TOOLS

Assortment of gold candles
(see Step 1)
Ornate, gold-toned planter or
serving dish
Clean water

WHAT TO DO

1 Visit your favorite candle supplier for an array of gold-colored candles. To keep the look unified, we selected candles in varying sizes of the same shape. Choose an assortment of pillars, or a combination of pillars and floating candles.

2 Arrange the candles in the dish, interspersing the smaller candles among the larger ones. Add water until it's almost flush with the tops of the pillar candles.

Designer: Megan Kirby

FIERY, FLOWERING WATER GARDEN

Pretty and elegant, this combination of fire, flowers, and water makes a dramatic centerpiece. It's the perfect way to stretch a bouquet, too—when the larger flowers in your Mother's Day arrangement begin to turn, simply pick out the blooms that remain fresh and use them to make this entirely new display.

MATERIALS AND TOOLS

Assortment of clear, glass vases
Glass pebbles
Short, wide clear glass bowl
Taper candles
Candle adhesive

Floating candles (flower shapes are nice for this project)
Fresh flowers
Ivy vines or other greenery

WHAT TO DO

1 Start by matching candles to vases. For instance, in the project shown, each tall vase accommodates a tall, slim taper.

2 Place an inch or two of glass pebbles in the bottom of each vase that will be supporting a taper candle. Add a handful of pebbles to the bottom of the glass bowl, too.

3 If you're not working in the area where you plan to display the arrangement, move your supplies to that area now. (Transporting the finished arrangement would be a little tricky.)

4 Apply a bit of candle adhesive to the bottom of each taper candle; then nestle each one into the pebbles in the base of its vase. Don't worry if the candles seem a little wobbly—the water you'll add in the next step will help anchor the tapers.

5 Pour clean water into the vases and the bowl. Add the floating candles to the glass bowl, along with several flowers. Arrange the remaining flowers and the greenery around the vases and the bowl to create a unified feel.

202

Designer: Michelle Keenan

CANDLESCAPING GALLERY

Opposite page, top left: Line your driveway or garden path with paper bag luminaries. The bags can be decorated as you choose (rubber stamp designs were used here). Designer: Nicole Tuggle

Opposite page, bottom left: This romantic candlescaping arrangement is perfect for a bridal shower or special birthday. Designer: Anne McCloskey

Above: A blending of pillar and tea candles creates a striking display in a large bowl. Designer: Terry Taylor

Above left: Small terra-cotta pots can be painted in any number of styles, making them a versatile candlescaping design tool. Here, they were painted in the spirit of the Southwest, then arranged on a platter with desert sand and cactus. Designer: Shelley Lowell

Below left: Celebrate your favorite festive occasion with a colorful display of candle holders and simple tapers. Designer: Max Keller

CANDLEMAKING

Candlemaking is an ancient craft that hasn't lost its appeal. Indeed, creating handmade candles is surprisingly easy to do at home and there's no end to the variations and decorative possibilities. And who among us can resist the allure of a flickering flame?

MATERIALS AND TOOLS

WAX
Here's where you shouldn't skimp. Buy high-quality wax with the appropriate melting point for your candle projects. Paraffin wax is probably the most commonly used wax in candlemaking, since it is easy to work with and releases well from molds. Beeswax is also available in both block and sheets; it burns more slowly than paraffin and does not require topping off, though it is sticky and, thus, more difficult to release from molds.

WICKS
The size of the wick you use is directly proportional to the diameter of the candle—consult wick manufacturer instructions when choosing wicks. There are also a variety of wick types. Square-braided wicks are used for block candles, flat-braided wicks are most commonly used for tapers, and wire-core wicks are used in container candles and votives. Wick anchors (also called wick tabs) are used to secure wicks to the bottom of containers.

FRAGRANCE
Fragrance oils (synthetic) and essential oils (natural) can both be added to wax to create scented candles.

Add fragrance in small amounts at a time—it's easy to add scent, but not to take it away!

ADDITIVES
This category includes substances that are added to wax to impart a variety of characteristics. Stearic acid is one of the most popular additives. It makes the wax color opaque, makes the wax easier to remove from molds, and makes finished candles burn longer. Additives have a variety of designations, so read all packaging and instructions carefully before using.

DYES
Candle dye comes in both block and powder form. Follow instructions on the dye package, and add color gradually to melted wax after any additives have been added and just before any fragrance.

MOLDS
As candlemaking becomes more popular, the array of molds available continues to expand. You will find different molds useful for different types of candles. Metal molds, for example, are often used for block candles or candles with very crisp lines, though molds with a lot of detail are often made of plastic or rubber.

MOLD SEALER
Mold sealer is a puttylike substance that is used to seal wick holes in molds to prevent wax seepage.

MOLD WEIGHTS
These are flexible lengths of lead that are used to stabilize molds to prevent wax from spilling out of open-top molds. Two or three mold weights should be enough for most molds.

WAX MELTER
The best choice is a durable, seamless wax melting pot with a sturdy handle and a flat bottom. An old-fashioned, stove-top coffeepot works well as a wax melter.

DOUBLE-BOILER BOTTOM
Occasionally you will need a pot or other vessel filled with water to hold cans of dye or wax or to serve as the base for the dipping vat. Since the double-boiler bottom is sure to get damaged (at the very least, coated with wax), an old pan or a thrift-store find is a good choice.

DIPPING VAT
A vessel for dipping is a must when making tapers. Although galvanized vats are widely available—and indeed are quite effective—you can also improvise with household containers. Make sure the vat is 3 inches

(7.5 cm) longer than the desired length of the tapers.

DIPPING FRAME
Dipping frames are sold where candlemaking supplies are found. It's used for dipping tapers and keeps wicks taut and in place while they are being submerged in and lifted from the dipping vat. Dipping frames are a great investment if you want to make multiple tapers at once.

THERMOMETER
Either a clip-on candy thermometer (available at supermarkets) or a wax thermometer will serve you well in candlemaking. Make sure your thermometer reads from 150°F to 300°F (66° to 149°C).

WICK RODS
You can purchase rods (often they come with molds) that are designed specifically for holding wicks in place while wax hardens. A skewer, a length of coat-hanger wire, or a pencil works just as well.

KITCHEN FIRE EXTIINGUISHER
Just in case!

BASIC TECHNIQUES

Any nonflammable container with a fairly wide (2 inches or 5 cm) opening is suitable for a candle container. It's a great way to lend function and beauty to unused vessels around the house. Try mismatched teacups, old bottles or bowls, and terra-cotta pots.

1 For container candles, use paraffin wax (or a combination of waxes) with a melting point of 128°F (53°C). The addition of a microcrystalline wax (specifically, micro opalescent wax creates more of a glowing effect) is also a good idea for containers—consult manufacturer guidelines. Soy wax is another good choice. Place waxes in a wax melter with a thermometer and turn to medium heat. Stir waxes together while you bring temperature of wax to the pouring temperature, between 160° and 180°F (71° to 82°C).

SAFETY TIP

Remember that candle wax is flammable. Before you begin any candlemaking project, organize your tools and materials on a flat surface in a well-ventilated area and cover your work surface with wax paper. Never leave wax unattended on the stovetop. Extinguish any wax fires with baking soda or a fire extinguisher.

2 Shave your dye into small pieces and add them to your melting wax. Add fragrance at this point, if desired. Stir until completely blended.

3 Prime the wick (see page 209). Secure a wick end to an anchor (also called a tab), then use a small amount of melted wax and a metal skewer to attach anchor to the bottom of the container. Wrap the other end of the wick around a wick rod or the metal skewer, and position across the top of the container.

4 Place the container on a foil-covered cookie pan. When the correct pouring temperature has been reached (see Step 1), pour the melted wax into the container. Adjust the wick, if necessary.

5 A well will form in the candle when it hardens. Once the well has formed, pierce the wax around the entire length of the wick with a length of coat-hanger wire or the metal skewer. Bring the wax back to the pouring temperature (see Step 1) and fill the well. Allow the wax to harden, then trim wick to ½ to ¾ inch (12 to 18 mm).

WICKING A MOLD

You should follow all manufacturer's instructions for wicking molds, though these general guidelines should help get you started.

1 Any mold you buy or make will need a hole in the center bottom for the wick to pass through. Many molds, such as metal molds, already have such a hole; if yours does not, you will need to create one with an awl or another sharp piercing tool. If you are using a metal mold that has a screw in the wick hole, remove the screw.

2 Draw the wick through the hole (use a sharp tool, if needed), leaving about an inch (2.5 cm) of wick on the underside, then seal the hole with mold sealer on the underside of the mold.

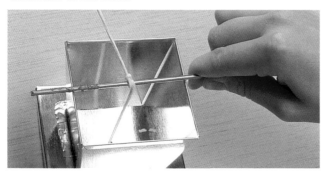

3 Cut the wick several inches longer than needed at the top of the mold, tie the excess wick around a wick rod or metal skewer, then position skewer across the top of the mold so that the wick is taut. If applicable, replace screw in metal molds.

PRIMING A WICK

It's prudent to take the time (only a few minutes!) to prime your wick before you begin a candle project, since primed wicks light more easily and burn better. To prime a wick, melt a small amount of wax in a wax melter, then dip wick into wax until wick is coated completely with wax. Allow the wax to harden, then dip wick again. Once hardened, the wick is primed and ready to use.

MAKING MOLDED CANDLES

There are a wide variety of candle molds available, including those made from metal, rubber, and plastic. You can also experiment with a variety of molds fashioned from household items; just make sure you choose items that are not flammable and will hold up to hot wax. Again, read all instructions carefully before you begin.

1 For molded candles, a variety of waxes and additives can be used. To begin, try 100% paraffin wax with a melting point of 140° to 145°F (60° to 65°C); as you get more proficient at molded candles, you can also use beeswax, as well as a number of additives. Place wax in a wax melter with a thermometer and melt together on medium heat. Stir waxes until they are combined thoroughly.

BASIC TECHNIQUES

2 Once the wax has melted, add 3 heaping table-spoons of stearic acid per pound of wax. Note: Additives can have subtle affects on candles; over time, you may find you have a personal preference for more or less stearic acid (or other additive).

3 Prime the wick(s) you will need for your chosen mold (see page 209) and wick the mold (see page 209). If you are using a peel-back or pop-out mold, secure the mold by placing a rubber band around its mid-section to keep mold lined up and the melted wax in.

4 Bring the wax to the pouring temperature recom-mended by the mold manufacturer, then add any dyes or fragrance. Stir together thoroughly.

5 If you are using a metal mold, run warm water on the outside immediately prior to pouring, taking care not to get any moisture into the mold. Optional step to speed hardening: Set up a cool-water bath in a container that is deep enough to accommodate the mold. Do not use a cool-water bath with beeswax candles.

6 Tip the mold slightly, then slowly pour the melted wax into the mold. Adjust wick as necessary. Once the candle has settled for several minutes, use a wood-en spoon to tap the sides of the mold; this will help remove any air pockets that have formed on the inside of the mold.

7 Place the candle into a cool-water bath, if desired. Use mold weights to stabilize mold. If not using a cool-water bath, skip to Step 8.

8 When well forms, top off as described in Step 5 of Making Container Candles (see page 208). Once candle has hardened, untie wick and trim to ½ to ¾ inch (12 to 20 mm). Remove mold sealer and/or screw, and trim wick on underside of candle as closely as possi-ble. Gently tap the mold and slowly remove candle.

DESIGNER TIP

To estimate the amount of wax you will need in a contain-er or a mold, fill the vessel with water, then pour out the water and measure. For every 9 ounces (252 g) of water, you will need 8 ounces or ½ pound (227 g) of solid wax.

OVERDIPPING TAPERS

The rhythmic dipping of tapers in wax can be very satisfying. If you like the process of dipping tapers, a dipping frame is a wonderful investment.

1 To overdip candles, you'll need a large pot and a dipping container for each color of wax you're making. Clean, empty tin cans make excellent dipping containers. You'll also need paraffin wax with a melting point of 140°F (78°C), a sharp paring knife, a candy or wax thermometer, wax dye in the colors of your choice, a wooden spoon for each color, and an oven mitt. Make sure your dipping containers are big enough to accommodate the candle you'll be dipping into them by filling each one halfway with water. Hold the candle by its wick and immerse it in the water. If water spills over the edge of the can, you need a larger container.

2 To help the wax melt more quickly, cut it into shavings with a sharp paring knife. Make enough shavings to fill each of your dipping containers about halfway. Make shavings of the dye or crayons, too, but don't add them to the wax yet. Fill the large pot halfway with water and place the dipping containers in it. Bring the water to a boil; then reduce the heat to keep it at a simmer. Stir the wax in the dipping containers to help it melt. Bring the wax to between 140° and 160°F (81° and 89°C), using the wax or candy thermometer to check the temperature. When the wax has melted completely and reached the correct temperature, start adding the dye a few shavings at a time. Stir with a wooden spoon and keep adding dye until the wax is the desired color.

3 Holding your candle by its wick, immerse it in the melted, colored wax for a few seconds. Raise the candle straight out of the wax and hold it over the dipping container to let the excess wax drip off. You may have to dip the candle several times to obtain the intensity of color you want. After the candle is appropriately colored, allow it to dry. Add additional layers by dipping it into another color of wax. You can add as many layers as you'd like. Using the oven mitt to protect your hand, remove the dipping container from the pot of water and place it somewhere out of the way to cool. If you choose to dip two candles at the same time, take care not to let them touch while you work. Don't throw away the wax; you can remelt it and use it again.

DESIGNER TIP

To smooth lumpy tapers, allow candles to harden slightly, then roll them on a sheet of wax paper. To remove seams created by candle molds, use a paring knife to evenly trim off excess wax.

SOY CANDLES

This project is the ultimate in simplicity—just melt and pour. A cleaner-burning alternative to paraffin, soy wax is clear when poured, but turns to a milky, opaque color as it cools. This quality makes for very lovely pastel candles.

MATERIALS AND TOOLS

Heat-proof glass containers
Wick (in size appropriate for chosen container)
Pencil
Soy wax chips
Microwave-safe container or double boiler
Candy thermometer
Candle dye

WHAT TO DO

1 Wash and dry the glass containers and position on a towel or newpaper. Prime the wick (see page 209). Wrap the wick around a pencil or any other wick support and position wick over container (see page 208 for more information on wicking container candles).

2 Slowly melt the wax in a microwave or over a double boiler with a thermometer until it reaches the pouring temperature recommended by the soy wax manufacturer.

3 Melt candle dye (see page 208), add to wax, and stir well. Soy candles lighten considerably as they cool, so you may need to add more color than you would when making paraffin or gel candles.

4 Warm the container (see page 210), carefully pour wax into the container, top off the wax, then allow candle to cool, undisturbed, for at least an hour (longer if using a large container). Trim the wick, light, and enjoy!

Designer: Dawn Cusick

Layered Candles

These candles looks sophisticated, but they are oh-so-easy!
The trick is making sure you allow the wax to cool somewhat
between layers. By varying the dye colors, the thickness and
angle of the layers, and the shape of the mold, you can make a
totally unique layered candle every time.

Materials and Tools

Paraffin wax
2 slow cookers
Candy thermometer
Stearic acid
Candle dye block(s)

Candle mold of your choice
Wick (appropriate size for mold)
Clean tin cans
Pencil

What To Do

1 Place the paraffin wax on high heat in a slow cooker with a thermometer. When the temperature reaches 160°F (71°C), turn heat to low. When the temperature is between 160°and 180°F (71° and 82°C), add the stearic acid (2–5 tablespoons per pound [454 g] of paraffin wax) and stir until completely dissolved.

2 Separate the wax into batches, according to how many layers you want the candle to have, and add candle dye to each. Shave small amounts of dye until desired level of color is achieved. Repeat this step with as many colors as desired.

3 Prime and wick the mold, as described on page 209, and secure wick to a pencil, a wire, or any other wick support. Place the mold in a mold holder or in another container that will keep the mold upright.

4 Pour a small amount of wax into the mold to make the first layer. Allow the wax to cool enough so that there is a thick film on top. (If the film is not thick enough, the layers will blend.)

5 Repeat Step 4 to create as many layers as desired. Once the mold is completely filled, top off wax and allow candle to harden. See Steps 4 through 7 in Making Molded Candles (page 210) for additional information on pouring and topping off molded candles, as well as on using a cool-water bath.

6 Once candle has hardened, untie wick and trim to ½ to ¾ inch (12 to 18 mm), and remove candle from mold (see Step 8, page 210). If difficult to remove, place candle in refrigerator for several hours and try again.

Designer Tip

To make an angled layered candle, carefully tip the mold and secure in
the tilted position until wax hardens, making sure the wick is centered.

214

Designer: Pamela Brown

Designer: Megan Kirby

BEESWAX CANDLES

There's something wonderful about beeswax candles—perhaps it's the lovely pattern or the distinctive aroma. And candlemaking doesn't get any easier than this! Choose from the variety of colors available to coordinate these lovely candles with your decor.

MATERIALS AND TOOLS

Beeswax sheets, one each white and pink
Hair dryer
Small kitchen knife
Metal ruler
Wick #500 (burns longer) or #360 (burns brighter)
Cutting board

DESIGNER TIP

If you plan to make a lot of tapers, invest in an end former. This inexpensive gadget is used by professional and amateur candlemakers alike to create crimped ends on tapers so they will fit more snugly into a candle holder. It's as simple as pressing the end of the taper into the end former when the taper is still soft.

WHAT TO DO

1 Gently warm the beeswax sheets with a hair dryer until they become pliable, but not brittle.

2 Working on a flat surface, use a knife and a metal ruler to cut an 8- x 8-inch (20 x 20 cm) rectangle from each of the beeswax sheets.

3 Again using the ruler and knife, cut each section in half to create two 4- x 8-inch (10 x 20 cm) sheets in each color. Cut the resulting sections in half again to create four 2- x 8-inch (5 x 20 cm) sheets in each color.

4 Place four of the sheets (two of each color) on a flat surface with the edges aligned, alternating colors. Gently warm the sheets with a hair dryer. Overlap the edges of the sheets slightly and press the edges together.

5 Cut the wick about 1 inch (2.5 cm) longer than the length of the candle. Lay the wick on the stacked sheets, ¼ inch (6 mm) from the edge. Gently fold the wax over the wick, then press to secure the wick in place.

6 Roll the candle as tightly as possible, taking care not to damage the honeycomb. You may need to squeeze the bottom of the candle to fit the chosen candle holder.

7 Repeat Steps 1 through 6 to make another candle.

Beeswax comes in so many colors and the best thing is they are so easy to make no dye, no melting. Keep a few sheets around the house to make quick gifts for friends.

PYRAMID CHUNK CANDLES

*Chunk candles are a great way to make use of leftover bits of wax.
A fun variation is to cut wax shapes with cookie cutters (while the
wax is still soft, of course) and position the shapes along the sides of
the mold so that they will be visible once the candle has been poured.*

MATERIALS AND TOOLS

Paraffin wax, 1½ pounds (681 g)
Stearic acid, 2–5 tablespoons
  (30 to 74 ml)
2 wax melters

Candy thermometer
Candle dye(s) of your choice
Pie plate(s) or other shallow pan(s)
Knife

Pyramid mold
Wick (appropriate size for mold)
Pencil
Propane torch (optional)

WHAT TO DO

1 Place 1 pound (454 g) of the
paraffin wax in a wax melter
with a thermometer on medium
heat. When the temperature reaches
between 160° and 180°F (71° to
82°C), add the stearic acid and stir
until completely dissolved.

2 Melt candle dye (see page 208)
and add to wax. If you would
like the chunks to be different
colors, divide wax and mix batches
separately.

3 Melt the remainder (½ pound
or 227 g) of the paraffin wax in
a separate wax melter. (Do not add
any stearic acid to this batch of
paraffin.) Either add a small amount
of candle dye to make the wax a
pale color, or leave wax white.

4 Bring the (colored) batch of
wax to the pouring temperature
recommended by the mold manufacturer. Pour the wax into the pie
plate(s) or other shallow pan(s).

Allow wax to cool until firm, but
not hard, then cut wax into small
chunks. Repeat this step with as
many colors of wax as desired.

5 Prime and wick the mold, as
described on page 209, and
secure wick to a pencil (or any
other wick support). Place the
mold in a mold holder or in
another container that will keep
the mold upright.

6 Fill mold with colored chunks
of wax. You can either create
colored layers or arrange the chunks
randomly.

7 Bring the remainder of the wax
(the lighter color) to the pouring temperature recommended by the
mold manufacturer, and carefully
pour the wax into the mold, filling to
the top.

8 As the wax cools, make holes in
the wax with a pencil, wire, or

other similar object then fill with
additional wax. Let cool for several
hours or use a cool-water bath. See
Steps 4 through 7 in Making
Molded Candles (page 210) for
additional information on pouring
and topping off molded candles as
well as on using a cool-water bath.

9 Once candle has hardened,
untie wick and trim to ½ to ¾
inch (12 to 18 mm), and remove
candle from mold (see Step 8, page
210). If difficult to remove, place
candle in refrigerator for several
hours and try again.

DESIGNER TIP

*Light a propane torch on low
flame and wave flame lightly
over the sides of the candle to
melt off some of the wax; this
allows chunks to become
more visible.*

Designer: Pamela Brown

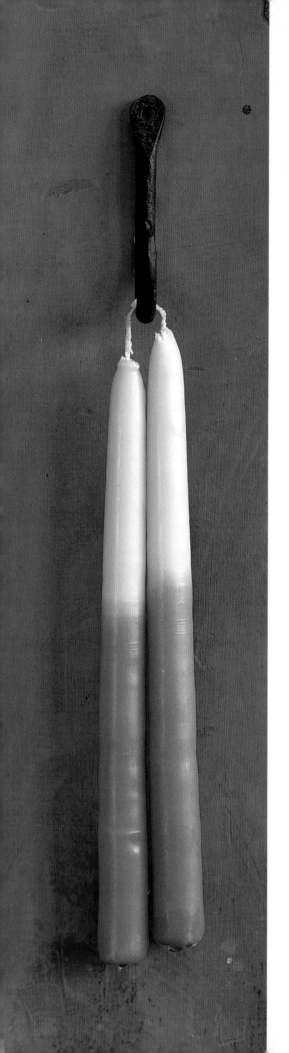

MULTICOLORED DIPPED TAPERS

Overdipping light-colored tapers with colored wax is an effective way to create all sorts of decorative results. A fun alternative is to use a cutting tool to carve designs in the overdipped candle to reveal the color underneath.

MATERIALS AND TOOLS

Paraffin wax
Metal dipping vat
Candy thermometer
Large saucepan

Stearic acid
Wick for standard tapers
Dipping frame (optional)
Candle dye, in colors of your choice

WHAT TO DO

1 Cut wax into chunks, place chunks in a dipping vat (see page 211), attach a thermometer, and place vat in a saucepan that is about half full of water. Heat the water on the stove top until the wax melts. When the temperature of the wax is between 160°and 180°F (71° and 82°C), add the stearic acid (2–5 tablespoons per pound [454 g] of paraffin wax) and stir until completely dissolved.

2 To make two 10-inch (25 cm) tapers, you will need a 22-inch (55 cm) wick. Prime the wick (see page 209). Drape the wick across a piece of wood, your fingers, or a similar object or position wick on a dipping frame. Make sure the two wick halves are separated by at least 1 inch (2.5 cm).

3 Dip the wicks into the wax for about four seconds, remove wicks from wax, then allow to cool for one to three seconds. Continue this process of dipping and cooling until the tapers are almost to the desired thickness.

4 Add more wax to the dipping vat and add stearic acid as above (see Step 1). Allow temperature to reach 145°F (63°C). Melt candle dye, add to wax, and stir together.

5 Carefully dip the candles into colored wax by hand until one-half of the candle is completely submerged. Hold in wax for four to five seconds. Remove from wax and allow to cool.

6 Repeat Step 5 to dip the other halves of the tapers. Another option is to add more dye to darken the wax color, then dip the other halves of the tapers into the darker color. Hang tapers and allow to harden.

Designer: Pamela Brown

CANDLEMAKING GALLERY

Above: Relief patterns in candles can hold a surprising amount of detail. For best results, be sure your mold is cleaned well before each use. Designer: Bright Lights

Right: Faux bamboo candles add a decorator touch and a bright, rosy glow to your home. Designer: Susan Schadt Designs

Above: Sheets of different colored beeswax cut in triangles were bonded together with the heat from a hair dryer, then rolled into a patchwork-style candle. Designer: Let There be Light

Above right: Candle molds come in an incredible variety of sizes and shapes. These colorful candles feature grooves and ridges. Designer: Pamela Brown

Right: Layered candles are a fun way to use up leftover scraps of colored wax, and can be custom designed to match any home decor accent. Designer: Pamela Brown

SOAP MAKING

MELT AND POUR SOAP BASE
To make melt and pour soaps, you'll start with a commercially available base. See page 226 for more details.

SHARP KNIFE AND WASHABLE CUTTING BOARD
You'll need a sharp knife and a washable cutting board to cut the soap base into smaller pieces and to slice finished loaves of soap into bars.

ESSENTIAL OILS AND FRAGRANCE OILS
Use essential oils and fragrance oils to imbue your homemade soaps with delicious, personalized scent. See page 233 for details.

COLORANTS
Soap-appropriate colorants range from mineral pigments to liquid soap dyes. See page 247 for details.

MOLDS
Choose molds designed specifically for soap making or enlist other flexible, lye-resistant (for cold-process soaps) containers for the job.

MEASURING SPOONS AND MEASURING CUPS
To be on the safe side, choose measuring implements that are lye resistant.

MICROWAVE-SAFE BOWLS OR A DOUBLE BOILER
Melt melt-and-pour soap bases in the microwave or in a double boiler.

LONG-HANDLED WOODEN OR STAINLESS STEEL SPOONS
Set aside two or three spoons specifically for soap making. Be aware that cold-process soap making will eventually eat away wooden spoons.

GLASS EYEDROPPERS
Add liquid scents and colorants by the drop. Use glass because dyes may stain plastic and some essential oils will corrode it.

KITCHEN LADLE
Ladling soap into molds can be easier and more precise than pouring. Make sure it's lye-resistant (plastic or stainless steel) if you're working with cold-process soaps.

COSMETIC-GRADE SPRAYER FILLED WITH RUBBING ALCOHOL
When small bubbles form on the surface of melt and pour soaps, a spritz of alcohol will remove them.

SAFETY GLASSES AND RUBBER OR LATEX GLOVES
You'll need these items to protect your eyes and hands from caustic lye when making cold-process soaps.

WHITE VINEGAR
Vinegar neutralizes lye. Keep a jug nearby when you're making cold-process soaps.

DIGITAL SCALE
To ensure you're using the exact amount of lye and fat specified, use a digital scale that weighs in tenths of ounces.

LYE
Lye (sodium hydroxide) is available at grocery and hardware stores. Make sure to purchase pure sodium hydroxide that does not contain additional ingredients.

2 LYE-RESISTANT PITCHERS OR POURING JARS
Use a smaller plastic pitcher with a lid to mix and pour the lye-and-water solution. Use a larger pitcher to pour the freshly made soap into molds.

LYE-RESISTANT SAUCEPAN

Use a glass, enamel, or stainless steel saucepan that's large enough to hold all the ingredients to melt fats and heat oils and to mix the soap.

2 STAINLESS STEEL MEAT THERMOMETERS

Choose thermometers that measure temperatures between 70°F and 200°F and that return accurate readings within seconds, rather than minutes.

FATS AND OILS

You try to avoid over-indulging in this food group, but you'll need plenty of fat for making cold-process soap. Individual projects will specify types and amounts.

2 CONTAINERS FOR WATER BATHS

Adjust the temperatures of the lye-and-water solution and the melted fat in water baths. A double sink or several large plastic tubs are fine.

RUBBER SPATULA

Use a rubber spatula to scrape every drizzle of soap from the pouring pitcher into the soap molds.

OLD BLANKETS OR TOWELS

Use these to insulate the molds for the first 48 hours that cold-process soap is curing.

DRYING RACK

Flat wooden or metal racks work fine, as do plastic needlepoint screens and even white butcher paper.

HOME DECORATING CRAFTS

BASIC TECHNIQUES

PREPARING MOLDS FOR SOAP MAKING

Don't wait until you're pouring hot soap to discover that your molds aren't large enough or that they're a bit grimy. Save yourself some trouble by taking these precautionary steps beforehand.

1. Making cold-process soap is—let's face it—something of an ordeal, and you will be loath to waste even a single drop of your precious soap after you've gone to the trouble of creating it. But waste it you will if you don't have enough room in your molds to accommodate all the soap you've made. And although melting more melt and pour soap than you have space for in your molds isn't a disaster, it is a nuisance. To make sure your molds have sufficient capacity before you get started, simply place an empty dish on your scale and reset the scale to zero. Fill the molds with water; then pour the water into the dish to weigh it. Your molds will hold an equal amount of soap.

2. The best "mold" for making a single, large loaf of cold-process soap is a plastic or stainless steel pan (2½ x 9 x 11 inches [7 x 23 x 28 cm] is a good size), equipped with a tight-fitting lid. To prepare this mold for soap, grease it, line it with freezer paper, then grease the freezer paper, too: Place the pan, rim side down, on the freezer paper and trace around it with a fine-tipped marker. Cut the freezer paper

From crystal-clear glycerin to creamy, opaque coconut oil soaps, new melt and pour bases come on the market seemingly every month. Let your project—and your creative spirit—guide your choices!

1 In the beginning of the melt and pour craze, there was glycerin—and only glycerin. Skin-soothing and cleansing, this colorless, translucent base is a byproduct of the soap-making process. Plain, unadorned glycerin soap base is still available and still quite popular. Think of it as a blank palette for soap making, just waiting for your inspired additions of color, scent, herbs—even toys! Just about anything you add to plain glycerin will remain in view in your finished project—imagine a red, heart-shaped soap embedded inside a clear bar of glycerin soap, for instance. If you'd rather start with a colored palette, glycerin bases are now available in a wide variety of pre-dyed translucent colors and even in opaque white for more "traditional-looking" soaps.

2 Manufacturers have responded to melt and pour soap making's popularity by offering a slew of bases beyond basic and not-so-basic gylcerins. Peruse your craft store, and you'll find blocks of bases in creamy, opaque pastels; pre-scored slabs of scented specialty soaps; bases labeled "suspension formula" that will hold additives in an even distribution throughout your soap as it sets; and all manner of other melt and pour base options. Before you get carried away with this bounty, keep two things in mind: First, most skin types will be happiest when cleansed with soaps created from bases made from pure vegetable and nut oils. Second, if you don't want to wash up with wax and alcohol, don't buy a base that contains these additives. If you're in doubt on either count, simply look for bases labeled "hypoallergenic," and you should be safe.

MELTING AND POURING

Yes, making melt and pour soaps really is as easy as it sounds: Simply melt the base soap, add fun stuff as desired, and pour into pretty molds.

1 Assemble all your materials in your workspace, including any additives such as herbs, dyes, and scents. Read and follow the manufacturer's instructions for melting the soap base. In general, you'll need to cut the soap base into small cubes. Place these cubes in a microwave-safe bowl or cup and heat in the microwave as directed, taking care not to boil or overheat the soap. You may also melt soap base in a double boiler: Heat water to a boil in the larger pot; set the smaller pot, containing the soap cubes, in the boiling water. Cover the smaller pot to keep moisture in. Reduce the heat so the water remains at a simmer. Remove the pot from the heat when the soap has melted, leaving the lid on the pot until you're ready to add ingredients or pour the soap.

2 If you're using a microwave, it may take a few tries to melt the soap completely. Be patient: Heat the soap at short, two-minute intervals rather than blasting it for ten minutes at a stretch. You may gently mix or nudge any unmelted chunks in between heating intervals with a wooden spoon, but don't stir with too much vigor—otherwise, you risk creating bubbles in your soap base. Soap melted over a double boiler should melt relatively smoothly, without any additional aid from you. When the soap has melted completely, let it cool for just a moment before adding anything to it.

about 2 inches (5 cm) beyond the lines you just traced. Grease the sides and bottom of the pan with solid vegetable shortening; then fit the piece of freezer paper into it. To make the paper fit smoothly, cut a small wedge out of each corner. Press the paper flat, sticking it to the bottom and sides of the pan, then trim it flush to the rim. Finally, grease the paper, too.

3. For melt and pour soaps, a quick swipe with a clean, damp cloth should be sufficient to remove any dust or residue from your molds. Warm water and—what else?—soap will take care of more persistent stuff. Wipe away any remaining moisture with a dry cloth or allow the molds to air-dry before filling them with soap. That's all you'll need to do if you're using molds designed specifically for melt and pour soap making—your finished soaps should pop right out of them. Other molds—molds that didn't start life as molds, per se—might not release your projects as nicely. If that's the case, coat the insides of your non-mold molds with a very light layer of vegetable oil cooking spray or petroleum jelly. (Be forewarned, however, that this technique may leave a greasy residue on your finished soaps.)

BASIC TECHNIQUES

3 Add scent first, releasing just a drop or two into the base at a time and mixing very gently to disperse it evenly. Keep adding scent this way until you've obtained the desired potency. For most scents, one to four drops to each ounce of soap base is a good ratio. Add color next, again adding just a little at a time to avoid over-coloring the soap. Liquid soap dyes are an especially good choice for melt and pour soaps. Finally, add any other ingredients you may be using, such as herbs, pearlescent powders, emollients, or exfoliants. Work quickly but carefully: If you don't work fast enough, your soap may begin to harden before you've finished adding ingredients, but if you're not careful, you may stir bubbles into your soap.

4 Pour the soap into molds. You may find it easier to transfer the soap to a pouring pitcher before filling

your molds, particularly if your molds are very small. Otherwise, ladle the soap into the molds, filling them completely, but not so full that soap drips over the sides. If bubbles have formed on the surface of your poured soap, mist it lightly with rubbing alcohol, then simply allow the soap to cool and harden. It's ready to unmold when it's cool and very firm to the touch. This can take one to two hours. Some soap makers like to speed the process by placing the soap in the fridge or freezer after it's cooled at room temperature for 30 minutes. The manufacturer's instructions should tell you whether it's okay to cool your soap this way.

5 When the soap is cool and firm to the touch, pop it out of the mold. You can suds up with it right away! If you have trouble releasing your soap, try running hot water over the back of the mold; this may re-melt the surface of the soap that's right next to the mold, causing it to separate from the sides and pop out. You can also try placing the mold in the freezer for ten or fifteen minutes. When you remove it, the contrasting temperature may help release the soap. (Don't use this method if the soap manufacturer's instructions advise against freezing.)

MAKING COLD-PROCESS SOAP

Making soap from scratch by combining lye and fat isn't hard; but it does require patience, attention to detail, and caution. Read the following steps all the way through before starting.

1 Set aside at least three hours when you know you won't be interrupted. Line your work surface and floors with newspaper. Dress in comfortable long pants and a long-sleeved shirt that you won't mind possibly damaging. Assemble your materials, making sure you have all the necessary ingredients and equipment and room to work with them comfortably. Choose and prepare your molds, as described on page 226. Then, wearing safety glasses and protective gloves, measure the lye. Do this by placing one of the lye-resistant measuring cups on the scale. Reset the scale to zero; then add the amount of lye called for by the recipe you're following. Set the lye aside and, using a clean measuring cup, measure the necessary amount of tepid water the same way you measured the lye.

2 Still wearing protective gloves and goggles, use a wooden spoon or plastic spatula to stir the lye into the water, being careful to avoid splashing or breathing the mixture's fumes directly. The chemical reaction between lye and water creates intense heat; this mixture will be very hot—hot enough to burn you severely. If you get lye on yourself, wash it off with plain, white vinegar—not water, which will only increase the heat. Stir until the lye is completely dissolved. Carefully place one of the thermometers in the pitcher to monitor the solution's temperature. Leaving the thermometer in place, cover the pitcher, but leave the pouring lid open to allow gases to escape. Set the lye mixture aside to cool while you melt the fat.

3 Measure any solid fats required by your recipe first. Place the lye-resistant pot on the scale, then reset the scale to zero. Add the necessary amount of fat. Measure any liquid oils required by your recipe, but don't add them to the pot yet. Melt the fat over medium-low heat, being careful not to overheat it and stirring to break up any large or floating lumps. When the fat is completely melted, remove the pot from the heat and stir in the liquid oils, blending thoroughly. Place the other thermometer into its contents, being careful not to let the thermometer touch the bottom.

BASIC TECHNIQUES

4 For saponification (the chemical reaction that results in soap) to take place, the lye solution and the fats must be the same (or very close to the same) temperature when they are blended together. Both mixtures should be between 95°F and 100°F and as close in temperature as possible. Adjust the temperatures by placing the containers in water baths and stirring. Use a cold water bath to reduce temperature, and a hot water bath to increase temperature. This step can be tricky and will take some practice. Don't get frustrated—just keep placing the containers in hot or cold water baths as necessary until the temperatures of the lye solution and the fat match and are within the recommended temperature range.

5 Double check to make sure the lye solution and the melted fat are both between 95°F and 100°F. Wearing safety glasses and protective gloves, secure the pitcher containing the lye solution. Slowly pour the solution in a thin, steady stream into the pot with the fat, using one hand to pour and the other hand to stir the mixture continuously. If substantial amounts of lye solution collect on top of the fat, stop pouring and stir to blend the lye completely. Resume pouring until all the lye solution has been added. Keep in mind that the lye is still caustic—and will remain that way until the soap has cured—so continue to exercise caution and wear safety glasses and gloves for the remaining steps.

6 Continue to stir the mixture gently until it thickens, or "traces." You may stir the soap by hand or use the beater portion of a milk shake mixer. To do the later, plug the mixer in, place it in the soap until it hits the bottom of the pan, and mix using the lowest speed.

7 Stir or mix until the soap thickens enough for a drizzle to hold its shape on the soap's surface for a few seconds, a sign that your soap has traced. Stirred by hand, soap may take more than an hour to trace. Using a mixer, it should trace within 15 minutes. If, after an hour of hand-stirring, your soap isn't showing signs of tracing, proceed as if it has; the signs are probably there, but you may not be experienced enough to see them.

8 You may add scents (see page 233), colors (see page 247), and other additives (see page 234) after your soap traces and just before you're ready to pour it into molds. Because the lye in your soap is still caustic at this point, it may effect the scents and colors of your additives. Don't be disappointed or discouraged if your finished bars don't turn out smelling or looking quite as you had anticipated. Making soap from scratch takes some practice, but eventually you'll get a feel for the process and your soaps will come out just right.

9 Pour the soap from the pot into the large pitcher; this will make pouring the soap into molds much easier and more precise. You may also spoon the soap into the molds with a kitchen ladle. Carefully fill the molds with soap. Use a spatula to scrap the sides of the pitcher, getting every last bit of soap. If you're using a plastic or stainless steel pan as a mold, place its lid on tightly. For molds that don't have their own lids, cover with a sheet of freezer paper and top with something flat and heavy, such as a cutting board. Then, to keep the soap from cooling too fast and separating, wrap each covered mold in a double-layer or blanket or towel. Allow the soap to rest, covered and undisturbed, for 48 hours.

FATS AND OILS FOR COLD-PROCESS SOAPS

All of the soap recipes in this book specify particular fats and oils. Should you decide to strike out on your own, though, here's a quick primer.

Tallow: *Rendered beef or pig fat. Makes mild, long-lasting soaps with small, creamy bubbles.*

Lard: *Rendered pig fat. Makes mild, long-lasting soaps that don't lather well.*

Palm oil: *Expressed from the fruits of various types of palm trees. Makes very mild, soft soap with a rich lather.*

Coconut oil: *Solid at room temperature. Makes a somewhat hard, drying soap with a creamy lather.*

Cocoa butter: *From the seeds of the cacao tree. Forms a hard, creamy, skin-softening soap.*

Vegetable shortening: *May be used in place of animal fats such as tallow and lard.*

Olive oil: *Makes a hard, brittle soap that's mild on skin and long-lasting in the shower.*

10 After 48 hours, unwrap the molds and remove the lids. Be careful, because the soap is still caustic at this point. Wearing a protective glove, test the soap's surface; it should be warm to the touch and firm, but still soft enough that your finger will leave an impression. If the soap is too soft, leave the lid off and let it air-dry for a day or two. When the soap has become firm enough to hold the impression of your gloved finger, it's time to remove it from the molds. Working over a sink or some other lye-resistant surface, pull the sides of the molds back from the soap. Then turn the mold over and press the bottom to release the soap. If the soap doesn't come out easily, allow it to dry for a while longer.

11 If you made one large loaf of soap, now is the time to cut it into manageable bars. Still wearing protective gloves, peel away and discard the freezer paper. Place the released soap on a clean, dry cutting board. Don't use a cutting board that's stained, though, because those stains might leech into your soap. Using a very sharp kitchen knife, cut the loaf into slices. Homemade cold-process soap must cure for several weeks before it can be used. Place your soap on a drying rack and store it in a warm, dry place with good ventilation. The recipe you're following should specify the exact amount of time the soap should cure.

SIMPLE GUEST SOAPS

These sweet little no-fuss soaps are a fine example of what folks mean when they refer to life's simple pleasures. This straightforward project allows even the busiest crafter the opportunity to enjoy the satisfaction of offering guests genuine homemade soaps.

MATERIALS AND TOOLS

Melt and pour soap base (See Step 1)
Vegetable-oil cooking spray or petroleum jelly (optional)
Small soap molds in basic designs

Sharp knife
Cutting board
Microwave and microwave-safe bowl, or a stovetop and double boiler

WHAT TO DO

1 Save yourself a few minutes by choosing a natural-colored melt and pour soap base or a base that's already colored to suit your taste; this way, you'll be able to skip additional dying or coloration.

2 Prepare your soap molds with a light coating of vegetable-oil cooking spray or petroleum jelly. Cut your soap base into small cubes and place them in the microwave safe bowl.

3 Melt the cubes according to the manufacturer's instructions. (See Steps 1 and 2 on page 227.) Allow the soap to cool slightly. If desired, you may add a few drops of scent at this time (refer to page 233). However, if you do in fact plan to offer these soaps to guests, it may be best to leave them scent-free to avoid possible allergic reactions.

4 Pour or ladle the soap into the molds. No matter how carefully you've measured, you may have melted more soap base than will fit into your molds. Don't throw away the leftovers, though! Skip to Step 8 for tips on using scraps and leftovers.

5 Referring to Step 5 on page 228, allow the soap to harden. When it's cool and firm to the touch, pop it out of the molds. Your soap is ready to use.

6 If you find yourself with dribs and drabs of leftover soap base, don't despair. Invest in a couple of very small molds in simple designs and save your leftover soap until you have 2 or 3 ounces. Then re-melt the scraps (taking extra care not to overheat the soap—which is easier to do with a little soap than with a lot), and pour as usual.

Designer: Dawn Cusick

SOAP SCENTS

Imagine lathering up every day with your very favorite smells—warm cinnamon, zesty lemon, soothing lavender. Let the following steps guide your way to soapy, scentsational abandon.

1. You'll add scents just before pouring your soap into molds, as noted in the general instructions for making cold-process soaps (pages 229–231) and melt and pour soaps (pages 226–228), as well as in specific projects. Keep a few cautions in mind. First, remember that you can always add more scent to your soap, but you can't remove excess—so add just a drop or two at a time. In general, one to four drops of fragrance will scent about one ounce of soap. Be aware that excessive amounts of fragrance can cause skin irritations. If you have a history of allergies, test your scented soaps on a small area—the inside of your upper arm, for instance—before slathering your whole body with it. Finally, no matter how yummy they may smell, don't ingest essential or fragrance oils. (See step 2.)

2. Essential oils offer the best means of imbuing your soap with scent. Extracted from individual plant sources, these natural oils are highly potent and long-lasting. Drop for drop, essential oils will generally scent more soap than their synthetic cousins, fragrance oils—which is one way of justifying their rather steep price tags. Some common essential oils include cinnamon, vanilla, lavender, orange, rose, clove, peppermint, almond, patchouli, and lilac. Almost as potent as essential oils and somewhat less expensive, fragrance oils are available in just about any "flavor" you can imagine. While essential oils come in single-note scents only, fragrance oils come in a huge array of scent "alloys:" ocean, Christmas, rain forest, apple blossom, summer, and so on. Both essential oils and fragrance oils are available through online retailers or at natural food stores and some craft stores.

RELIEF ACCENT SOAPS

Looking for a simple, pretty way to dress up melt and pour soaps? Choose a mold with a recessed design, then highlight the recessed area with a second soap color or with seed beads.

ADVANTAGEOUS ADDITIVES

From oil-absorbing clays to skin sloughing exfolliants, there dozens of materials you can add to personalize your soaps. Following are just a few you might consider and their purported benefits.

FACIAL CLAY
Draws out and absorbs oil from the skin

COFFEE GROUNDS
Absorbs odors

GROUND, DRIED GINGER
Warms the skin

HONEY
Softens and smooths

CUCUMBER
Acts as a mild astringent and cleanser

COCOA BUTTER
A rich emollient

OATMEAL
Soothes irritated skin

VITAMIN E OIL
Softens skin and prevents wrinkles

MATERIALS AND TOOLS

Vegetable-oil cooking spray or petroleum jelly (optional)
Recessed soap molds
Small seed beads in the color(s) of your choice
Melt and pour soap base in the color(s) of your choice
Sharp knife
Cutting board
Microwave and microwave-safe bowl, or a stovetop and double boiler

WHAT TO DO

1 Prepare the molds, referring to Steps 1 and 3 on page 226. Sprinkle the bottom of each with seed beads, if desired.

2 Melt the soap base according to the manufacturer's instructions. (See Steps 1 and 2 on page 227.) If you're making two-toned soaps, melt the accent color first.

3 Allow the soap to cool slightly. Add any scents or colors at this point, if desired. Then pour or ladle the soap into the mold. If you're using an accent color, pour it in first and allow it to harden and cool before melting and pouring the second color.

4 If you're using a second color, melt it and add color and scent as desired, then pour it on top of the accent color, filling the mold.

5 Referring to Step 5 on page 228, allow the soap to harden. When it's cool and firm to the touch, pop it out of the molds. Your soap is ready to use!

Designer: Dawn Cusick

BLOOMING ROSE SOAP

Like a perfect rose garden, this gorgeous double-layered soap brings together the old and the new, combining the tradition of cold process soap making with the ease of melt and pour technology. Be sure to re-read the steps for both techniques all the way through before getting started. See pages 226–231.

MATERIALS AND TOOLS

5 to 6 ounces clear glycerine base soap
Microwave-safe bowl
Long-handled wooden or stainless steel spoons
Pink liquid soap dye
Variety of round soap molds
White freezer paper
Fine-tipped marker
Scissors
Rubber gloves and goggles
Lye-resistant measuring cup,
   with a capacity of at least 4 cups
2 stainless steel meat thermometers
2 large lye-resistant pitchers or pouring jars
Digital scale
16 ounces distilled water
6 ounces lye
Lye-resistant saucepan,
   with a capacity of at least 8 quarts
12 ounces solid vegetable shortening
11 ounces coconut oil
11 ounces palm oil
9 ounces olive oil
½ ounce rose essential oil
Pink mineral pigment
Oiled butcher paper or waxed paper
One large or several small cutting boards
   or other heavy, flat object
Old hand towels, one for each mold

WHAT TO DO

1 Referring to Steps 1 and 2 on page 227, melt the glycerin soap base. When it's completely melted, add the pink liquid soap dye, a little at a time, until the desired color is obtained. Add a few drops of rose essential oil, too, if desired.

2 Pour ¼ to ½ inch (6 to 12 mm) of glycerin soap into each mold. Set the molds aside while you make the cold process soap.

3 Don your gloves and goggles. Working in a well-ventilated area and referring to Step 1 on page 229, measure the water and lye. Pour the measured water into one of the lye-resistant pitchers or pouring jars.

4 Referring to Step 2 on page 229, carefully mix the measured lye into the water in the lye-resistant pitcher. Be very cautious with this mixture! It's extremely hot and its fumes are toxic. When the lye and water are thoroughly blended, place one of the thermometers in the pitcher; then put the lid on, leaving the pour spout open to allow gases to escape. Set the pitcher aside, well out of your way.

5 Referring to Step 3 on page 229, measure the solid vegetable shortening, coconut oil, palm oil, and olive oil. Add all but the olive oil to the lye-resistant saucepan and melt them over medium-low heat. When the solid fats have melted completely, remove the saucepan from heat and stir in the olive oil. Place the second thermometer into the hot oil mixture.

6 Referring to Step 4 on page 230, use water baths to bring the temperatures of the lye mixture and the oil mixture to 100°F.

7 Wearing gloves and goggles and referring to Step 5 on page 230, slowly add the lye mixture to the oil mixture.

8 Referring to Step 6 on page 230, stir the soap to trace. When the soap begins to trace, add the rose essential oil and mix well.

9 Still wearing gloves and goggles, scoop out 1 cup of the uncolored soap and set it aside. Add the pink mineral pigment to the remaining soap, a little at a

Designer: Lee Partin

time, until you've obtained the desired color, then gently swirl the uncolored soap into the colored soap to create a pretty variegation.

10 Carefully pour the cold process soap on top of the glycerine soap, filling each mold completely. Cover each mold with a piece of oiled butcher paper or waxed paper. Place one large cutting board over all the

molds or top each individual mold with a flat, heavy object. Wrap the covered molds, individually or separately, in towels or blankets.

11 Allow the molds to rest undisturbed for 48 hours. Then, wearing gloves, remove the soaps from the molds. Allow the cold-process portion of this soap to cure for at least 4 weeks.

Summer Splash Soap

Who says you can't go back in time? Recapture the feel of long lazy days with this fruit-scented soap. The citrus undertones of mango combine with the subtleties of peach to create a soap that is sweet, sensual, and summery.

Materials and Tools

White freezer paper
Fine-tipped marker
Scissors
Solid vegetable shortening (for greasing pans)
Plastic or stainless steel pan with a tight-fitting lid,
  2-½ x 9 x 11 inches
Rubber gloves and goggles
Lye-resistant measuring cup, with a capacity of
  at least 4 cups
2 stainless steel meat thermometers
2 large lye-resistant pitchers or pouring jars
Digital scale
16 ounces distilled water
6 ounces lye
Long-handled wooden or stainless steel spoons
Lye-resistant saucepan, with a capacity of
  at least 8 quarts
12 ounces solid vegetable shortening
11 ounces coconut oil
11 ounces palm oil
9 ounces olive oil
⅓ ounce of Mango fragrance oil
⅓ ounce Peach fragrance oil
2 old towels or blankets
Sharp kitchen knife and cutting surface

What To Do

1 Grease and line the pan with freezer paper, as described in Step 2 on page 226.

2 Don your gloves and goggles. Working in a well-ventilated area and referring to Step 1 on page 229, measure the water and lye. Pour the measured water into one of the lye-resistant pitchers or pouring jars.

3 Referring to Step 2 on page 229, carefully mix the measured lye into the water in the lye-resistant pitcher. Be very cautious with this mixture! It's extremely hot and its fumes are toxic. When the lye and water are thoroughly blended, place one of the thermometers in the pitcher; then put the lid on, leaving the pour spout open to allow gases to escape. Set the pitcher aside, well out of your way.

4 Referring to Step 3 on page 229, measure the solid vegetable shortening, coconut oil, palm oil, and olive oil. Add all but the olive oil to the lye-resistant saucepan and melt them over medium-low heat. When the solid fats have melted completely, remove the saucepan from heat and stir in the olive oil. Place the second thermometer into the hot oil mixture.

5 Referring to Step 4 on page 230, use water baths to bring the temperatures of the lye mixture and the oil mixture to 100°F.

6 Wearing gloves and goggles and referring to Step 5 on page 230, slowly add the lye mixture to the oil mixture.

7 Referring to Step 6 on page 230, stir the soap to trace. When the soap begins to trace, add the fragrance oils and mix well.

8 Still wearing your gloves and goggles, pour the soap into the greased and paper-lined pan. Place the lid on the pan tightly. Wrap the pan well in a blanket or towel and let it rest undisturbed for 48 hours.

9 Referring to Steps 10 and 11 on page 231, remove the soap from the mold(s) and cut it into bars. Allow the soap to cure for at least 4 weeks before using.

10 Wrap each bar in a beautiful paper and tie with raffia.

Designer: Lee Partin

CINNAMON BALSAM FIR SOAP

Warm and woodsy, this is a soap men will enjoy using and women will love smelling. Be sure to re-read the steps for making cold-process soaps on pages 229–231 all the way through before getting started.

MATERIALS AND TOOLS

White freezer paper
Fine-tipped marker
Scissors
Solid vegetable shortening
   (for greasing pans)
Plastic or stainless steel pan with a
   tight-fitting lid,
   2½ x 9 x 11 inches
Rubber gloves and goggles
Lye-resistant measuring cup, with a
   capacity of at least 4 cups
2 stainless steel meat thermometers
2 large lye-resistant pitchers or
   pouring jars
Digital scale
16 ounces distilled water
6 ounces lye
Long-handled wooden or stainless
   steel spoons
Lye-resistant saucepan, with a
   capacity of at least 8 quarts
12 ounces solid vegetable shortening
11 ounces coconut oil
11 ounces palm oil
9 ounces olive oil
1 ounce cinnamon essential oil
1 ounce balsam fir or
   pine fragrance oil
Green mineral colorant
Rubber spatula
2 old towels or blankets
Sharp kitchen knife and
   cutting surface

WHAT TO DO

1 Grease and line the pan with freezer paper, as described in Step 2 on page 226.

2 Don your gloves and goggles. Working in a well-ventilated area and referring to Step 1 on page 229, measure the water and lye. Pour the measured water into one of the lye-resistant pitchers or pouring jars.

3 Referring to Step 2 on page 229, carefully mix the measured lye into the water in the lye-resistant pitcher. Be very cautious with this mixture! It's extremely hot and its fumes are toxic. When the lye and water are thoroughly blended, place one of the thermometers in the pitcher; then put the lid on, leaving the pour spout open to allow gases to escape. Set the pitcher aside, well out of your way.

4 Referring to Step 3 on page 229, measure the solid vegetable shortening, coconut oil, palm oil, and olive oil. Add all but the olive oil to the lye-resistant saucepan and melt them over medium-low heat. When the solid fats have melted completely, remove the saucepan from heat and stir in the olive oil. Place the second thermometer into the hot oil mixture.

5 Referring to Step 4 on page 230, use water baths to bring the temperatures of the lye mixture and the oil mixture to 100°F.

6 Wearing gloves and goggles and referring to Step 5 on page 230, slowly add the lye mixture to the oil mixture.

7 Referring to Step 6 on page 230, stir the soap to trace. When the soap begins to trace, add the essential oils and mix well.

8 Still wearing your gloves and goggles, pour all but 1 cup of the soap into the greased and paper-lined pan. Add the green mineral colorant to the remaining cup of soap, stirring to blend thoroughly. Gently pour the cup of green soap on top of soap in the pan. Using the rubber spatula, carefully fold the colored soap into the upper layer, creating this soap's swirled appearance.

9 Referring to Steps 10 and 11 on page 231, remove the soap from the molds and cut it into bars. Allow the soap to cure for at least 4 weeks before using.

CITRUS CINNAMON SOAP

With its refreshing citrus scent and warm hints of cinnamon, this soap will turn your morning shower into a heavenly awakening! Be sure to re-read the steps for making cold-process soaps on pages 229–231 all the way through before getting started.

MATERIALS AND TOOLS

White freezer paper
Fine-tipped marker
Scissors
Solid vegetable shortening
   (for greasing pans)
Plastic or stainless steel pan
   with a tight-fitting lid,
   2½ x 9 x 11 inches
Rubber gloves and goggles
Lye-resistant measuring cup, with a
   capacity of at least 4 cups
2 stainless steel meat thermometers
2 large lye-resistant pitchers or
   pouring jars
Digital scale
16 ounces distilled water
6 ounces lye
Long-handled wooden or stainless
   steel spoons
Lye-resistant saucepan, with a
   capacity of at least 8 quarts
12 ounces solid vegetable
   shortening
11 ounces coconut oil
11 ounces palm oil
9 ounces olive oil
1 ounce orange essential oil or citrus fragrance oil
3 to 4 tablespoons ground
   cinnamon
Rubber spatula
2 old towels or blankets
Sharp kitchen knife and
   cutting surface

WHAT TO DO

1 Grease and line the pan with freezer paper, as described in Step 2 on page 226.

2 Don your gloves and goggles. Working in a well-ventilated area and referring to Step 1 on page 229, measure the water and lye. Pour the measured water into one of the lye-resistant pitchers or pouring jars.

3 Referring to Step 2 on page 229, carefully mix the measured lye into the water in the lye-resistant pitcher. Be very cautious with this mixture! It's extremely hot and its fumes are toxic. When the lye and water are thoroughly blended, place one of the thermometers in the pitcher; then put the lid on, leaving the pour spout open to allow gases to escape. Set the pitcher aside, well out of your way.

4 Referring to Step 3 on page 229, measure the solid vegetable shortening, coconut oil, palm oil, and olive oil. Add all but the olive oil to the lye-resistant saucepan and melt them over medium-low heat. When the solid fats have melted completely, remove the saucepan from heat and stir in the olive oil. Place the second thermometer into the hot oil mixture.

5 Referring to Step 4 on page 230, use water baths to bring the temperatures of the lye mixture and the oil mixture to 100°F.

6 Wearing gloves and goggles and referring to Step 5 on page 230, slowly add the lye mixture to the oil mixture.

7 Referring to Step 6 on page 230, stir the soap to trace. When the soap begins to trace, add the orange essential oil or citrus fragrance oil to the soap and mix well. Pour all but 1 cup of the soap into the greased and paper-lined pan. Add the ground cinnamon into the remaining cup of soap, stirring to blend thoroughly.

8 Gently pour the cup of cinnamon soap on top of soap in the pan. Using the rubber spatula, carefully fold the cinnamon soap into the upper layer, creating this soap's distinctive brown swirls.

9 Referring to Steps 10 and 11 on page 231, remove the soap from the molds and cut it into bars. Allow the soap to cure for at least 4 weeks before using.

Designer: Lee Partin

Designer: Bonnie Wilber

PEPPERMINT POLKA DOT SOAP

Bathing with these whimsical bars is a little like sudsing up with big, pepper-minty dominoes. Be sure to re-read the steps for making cold-process soaps on pages 229–231 all the way through before getting started.

MATERIALS AND TOOLS

Solid vegetable shortening
Plastic wrap
2 stainless steel meat thermometers
2 large lye-resistant pitchers or pouring jars
Digital scale
Lye-resistant measuring spoons
Rubber spatula
Old towels
PH strips (available at pool-supply stores)
Large, lye-resistant spoon
Large, lye-resistant airtight container

For 1 pound of polka dots:
Small, stainless steel loaf pan

2 ounces (3 level tablespoons) lye
5½ ounces distilled water
Stainless steel saucepan, 1-quart capacity
4 ounces vegetable oil
6 ounces palm kernel oil
6 ounces palm oil
2 large plates
Black, cosmetic-grade pigment

For 2 pounds of base soap:
Sturdy cardboard box, measuring 3½ x 3¼ x 10 inches
Sturdy cardboard box, measuring 3½ x 3¾ x 10½ inches
Duct tape

Scissors
Contact paper
Masking tape
4 ounces (six level tablespoons) lye, divided evenly
11 ounces distilled water, divided evenly
Stainless steel saucepan, 2-quart capacity
12 ounces palm kernel oil
12 ounces palm oil
8 ounces vegetable cooking oil
Glass measuring cup, 4-cup capacity
½ ounce peppermint essential oil
Paper towels
Black, cosmetic-grade pigment

WHAT TO DO

1 Grease the small, stainless steel loaf pan with solid vegetable shortening, line it with plastic wrap, and grease the wrap.

2 Make the polka dots first: Don your gloves and goggles. Working in a well-ventilated area and referring to Step 1 on page 229, measure the water and lye. Pour the measured water into one of the lye-resistant pitchers or pouring jars.

3 Referring to Step 2 on page 229, carefully mix the measured lye into the water in the lye-resistant pitcher. Be very cautious with this mixture! It's extremely hot and its fumes are toxic. When the lye and water are thoroughly blended, place one of the thermometers in the pitcher; then put the lid on, leaving the pour spout open to allow gases to escape. Set the pitcher aside, well out of your way.

4 Measure the solid oils and melt them in the 1-quart saucepan over medium-low heat until they're completely melted. Then add the vegetable oil. Stir to blend well. Place one of the thermometers into the oil, being careful not to let it touch the bottom of the pan. Keep heating until the oil reaches 200°F. Heating the oil to this high temperature will ensure that the soap neutralizes quickly, allowing you to handle it in 24–48 hours.

5 Remove the oil from heat. Wearing gloves and goggles and referring to Step 5 on page 230, slowly add the lye mixture to the oil mixture.

6 Referring to Step 6 on page 230, stir the soap to trace. After the soap has reached trace, pour it into the small, stainless steel loaf pan. Cover the pan with either a lid or plastic wrap; then wrap it in an old towel or blanket and let it rest for 24 hours.

7 After 24 hours, test the soap for neutrality, using PH strips. It should have the consistency of moist clay and it should not sting your bare hands. If it does sting your skin, rinse your hands with white vinegar and, wearing rubber gloves, place the soap in an airtight container. After 24 hours, test the soap again. Keep testing it until it's neutral.

8 When the soap has neutralized, scoop half of it out of the loaf pan. Pinch off a little of this soap at a time. Roll each pinch between your hands to create round marbles, using the entire half of the soap you scooped out. Set the marbles aside on one of the large plates. These will be the white polka dots.

9 Add ¼ teaspoon of black cosmetic-grade pigment to the remaining half of the soap. Using your hands, mix the pigment into the soap thoroughly. If the soap appears gray rather than black, add a little more dye and mix again. Then roll the black soap into marbles and place them on the other plate. These will be the black polka dots.

10 Heat your oven to 180°F and place the polka dots in it while you make the soap for the black and white layers. (The polka dots must be hot when you add them to the soap layers; otherwise,

they'll bring down the temperature of the other soap too quickly.)

11 Make a mold for the soap from the two cardboard boxes: The smaller box will hold the soap and will sit inside the larger box, which will act as an insulator and stabilizer. Make a cut from the rim to the bottom at each corner of the smaller box so that you can spread the box flat, then cover it front and back with contact paper and grease the inside with solid vegetable shortening. Spread plastic sheeting over the entire inside surface, smoothing it flat; then bring the box's corners together, pulling any excess plastic sheeting to the outside. Secure the corners by running masking tape around the entire box several times. Line the inside of the larger box with plastic sheeting, securing it with masking tape; then tape its outside corners with duct tape to make sure it won't fall apart.

12 Wearing goggles and gloves and referring to Step 2 on page 229, carefully mix 2 ounces of lye into 5½ ounces of distilled water in each of the two lye-resistant pitchers or pouring jars. Set the pitchers aside while you heat the oils.

13 Measure the solid oils for the base soap and melt them in the 2-quart saucepan over medium-low heat until they're completely melted. Then add the vegetable oil. Stir to blend well. Place one of the thermometers into the oil, being careful not to let it touch the bottom of the pan. Keep heating until the oil reaches 160°F. Remove the oil from heat.

14 Very carefully pour half of the melted oil into the 4-cup glass measuring cup. There should be exactly 2 cups of oil in the cup;

check it at eye-level to make sure you've poured the correct amount.

15 Add the lye mixture from one of the pitchers to the melted oil in the measuring cup. Referring to Step 6 on page 230, stir the soap to trace. After the soap has reached trace, add ¼ of an ounce (about 1 teaspoon) of peppermint essential oil and mix well.

16 Pour the scented soap into the smaller cardboard box. Remove the black polka dots from the oven and gently stir them into the soap or, if you prefer, place them in even rows throughout the soap. (Just be sure to wear rubber gloves; the fresh soap is still caustic and can burn you.) Cover the mold with plastic wrap, wrap it in an old blanket or towel, and set it aside.

17 Quickly make the black layer of soap: If necessary, re-heat the remaining oil to 160°F. While the oil is heating, wipe the glass measuring cup clean with paper towels (be sure to wear rubber gloves and place the used paper towels in a plastic bag before throwing them away.)

18 Pour the heated oil into the measuring cup, making sure you have exactly 2 cups. If there's too much oil, pour a little out. If there's not enough, add vegetable oil to make up the difference. Add the remaining lye mixture to the oil in the measuring cup and stir to trace.

19 When the soap has reached trace, blend in the remaining peppermint essential oil and about ½ teaspoon of black cosmetic-grade pigment. If the soap seems gray rather than black, add a little more pigment.

20 Unwrap the mold with the white soap and black polka dots. Using a large spoon and wearing rubber gloves, carefully ladle a 1½-inch layer of black soap over the white layer. Try not to mix the two layers together. Remove the white polka dots from the oven. You may either blend them into the black soap in the measuring cup, or place them in even rows in the soap that you just spooned in. In either case, add the remaining black soap to the mold, using the rubber spatula to scrape the inside of the measuring cup clean.

21 Tightly cover the mold with plastic wrap; then wrap it in several layers of towels or blankets. Set the mold in a very warm place for at least 12 hours. When the soap is cool to the touch, release it from the mold by removing the masking tape from the smaller box and pushing the cut corners flat.

22 Store the soap in an airtight container. After one week, use PH strips to test the soap's neutrality. If it isn't neutral, return it to the airtight container and test it again after several more days. When the soap is neutral, cut it into bars. It should be ready to use!

CREATIVE COLORING

Naturally hued soaps are undeniably beautiful. But if you want bars that match your bathroom or that clue you in to their scent by sight alone, by all means—add some color!

1. You'll add color, if you choose to do so, right after you've added fragrance. (The general instructions for making melt and pour and cold-process soaps, as well as the specific project instructions, will clue you in.) As with adding scents, use a light hand when adding color—add just a little at a time, let it disperse, then add more if necessary. Your soap's suds should always be white; if it lathers some version of its dyed color, it will likely transfer that color to towels, tubs, and—yikes!—your skin: Discard any soaps with suds that are any color other than white. Finally, be aware of potential allergic reactions; test dyed soaps on an inconspicuous part of your body before using them all over.

2. Today's soap makers have many options for coloring homemade soaps, including dyes that are custom-made for the craft. Liquid soap dyes, available online and at craft stores, are one of the best choices for melt and pour soaps. Their intense colors disperse evenly, without detracting from the clarity of glycerin bases. Soap dyes are also available in solid forms, including shavings and blocks; these melt right into your soap. Some soap makers cross craft boundaries and use candle and fabric dyes in liquid and solid forms; if you choose one of these options, be particularly wary of possible allergic reactions. Pigment powders—which are ground, colored, minerals—give soap a subtle, grainy hue. Ground spices and herbs, such as cinnamon and turmeric, offer a similar effect. Food dyes are the least appropriate option—use them only as a last resort.

Top left: Soap balls? Yes, soap balls! To make them, simply add warm water to a bowl of soap scraps and shavings. Allow the soap to moisten for 10 minutes, then mold the soap into balls with your hands. Designer: Norma Coney

Above: These checkerboard soaps add a splash of fun and color to your bathroom. To make them, cut tinted glycerin soap into strips, then arrange the strips in a soap mold with space between them and pour opaque soap into the spaces. Designers: Allison Smith and Terry Taylor

Left: Marbled swirls of color were created in a peppermint soap base for a soap that's beautiful and fragrant. Designer: Bonnie Wilber

SOAP MAKING GALLERY

Right: These simple soaps were created by embedding a skeletonized leaf in a layer of clear soap that was topped with a layer of opaque soap. Designers: Terry Taylor and Allison Smith

Bottom right: The top layer of these soaps features a pink pearlescent powder, while the bottom layer was made from a mixture of opaque soap base and dried rose petals. Designers: Terry Taylor and Allison Smith

Below: Pearlescent powder and clear soap base create sparkling soaps in celestial shapes. Designers: Allison Smith and Terry Taylor

MOSAICS

It must be something innate in the human psyche, this desire to create wholeness, order, and beauty from bits, pieces, and shattered fragments. After all, humans have been decorating surfaces with mosaic for thousands of years. With a handful of glass tiles or pottery shards, a little glue and grout, and a few hours, you can turn just about any surface in your home or garden into an object d'art worthy of the Byzantines or the ancient Romans.

MATERIALS AND TOOLS

PRECAUTIONARY STUFF
Your toolbox of mosaic supplies should include goggles, gloves, and a dust mask for you; and kraft paper or plastic sheeting for your work surface.

TRACING SUPPLIES
Use tracing paper, a pencil, black graphite paper, masking tape, and a permanent marker to transfer a design from template to project.

TESSERAE
These are the small(ish), hard pieces that form the mosaic's design. Descriptions of some common of types of tesserae follow.

VITREOUS GLASS TILE
Precut, nonporous (that's what vitreous means) glass tiles are available in ¾- and ⅜-inch (18 and 9 mm) squares.

STAINED GLASS, TEXTURED GLASS, AND MIRROR
Cutting your own tiles from stained glass, textured glass, or mirror is relatively simple. (See pages 252 and 253.)

CERAMIC TILE
Choose tiles that are specifically made for mosaics; these are usually frost proof and suitable for indoor and outdoor projects.

CHINA
Chipped teacup? Hardly—it's art in the making. Break it up (carefully, following the instructions on pages 252 and 253) for perfect tesserae.

BEADS, PEBBLES, STONES, SEASHELLS, RHINESTONES...
The list goes on. If you can glue and grout it in place, it's tesserae.

GLASS CUTTER AND RUNNING PLIERS
You'll score the glass with the first tool and make a clean break in it with the second.

GLASS MOSAIC CUTTERS
A cross between pliers and glass-cutting scissors, this tool is good for shaping pieces of glass.

CERAMIC TILE NIPPERS
Trim ceramic tiles and china into tesserae and shape vitreous glass with this hand-held tool.

HAMMER
Need to break a lot of china and relieve stress at the same time? A hammer's the perfect tool.

BASE OBJECT
This is the surface to which you'll apply your mosaic. The choices are endless, ranging from wooden boards to garden walls.

ADHESIVES
Make sure your design stays put by choosing the right adhesive. See the instructions on page 255 for types and techniques.

CRAFT STICKS
They're not just for model-making and popsicle-holding anymore! Have plenty on hand for spreading adhesives and "buttering" tesserae.

GROUT
Use this cement-based material to fill the spaces between tesserae and to reinforce your adhesive's holding power.

SPONGE AND POLISHING CLOTH
Swipe excess grout from your project with a moist sponge and polish it clean with a soft cloth.

CLEANING TOOLS
Scrape hardened grout from projects with single-edge razor blades or dental picks (check flea markets and dentists' offices).

CONTAINERS
Finally—a use for all those plastic tubs you've been meaning to recycle: Mix grout, store tesserae, and clean sponges in them.

BASIC TECHNIQUES

CUTTING TILES FROM GLASS AND MIRROR

With the right tools and a little practice, cutting glass isn't difficult. And after you've mastered the technique, you can create tiles in any of the colors available in a stained glass shop—a practically endless array!

1 Set the sheet of glass or mirror you'll be cutting on a flat, unyielding surface. Determine the width of the tiles you plan to cut; then measure and lightly mark the sheet accordingly. Place a ruler along the sheet's length at the first width mark. Working with the wheeled end of your glass cutter and using the ruler as a straightedge, score a line along the sheet's length: Push the glass cutter forward with just enough downward pressure to score the glass or mirror's surface. Repeat to score parallel lines at the remaining width marks.

2 If you're not using the entire sheet of glass, snap off the scored portion with your running pliers. Grasp one edge of the sheet with the running pliers, aligning the mark on the pliers' upper jaw directly over the score line where you want the glass to snap. Gently squeeze the pliers; the pressure will press the glass down against the raised ridge inside the pliers' lower jaw, and the glass should snap right along the score line.

WORKING WITH TILE NIPPERS

Although smashing old plates and teacups with a hammer (see page 253) can be satisfying, using tile nippers to snip china into neat pieces offers more control over the end result.

1 Snipping china with a hand-held tool may seem as if it would require a lot of hand strength, but tile nippers are designed to provide maximum leverage, allowing you to exert minimum effort. Start by donning safety goggles. If you're cutting a plate, remove its rim from its flat bottom first: Grip the plate with your tile nippers, overlapping the edge by about ⅛ inch (3 mm) and lining up the jaws so that they point in the direction you want to cut. Squeeze the handles firmly, but gently. A large chunk of the rim should break off. Work around the plate to remove the entire rim. Depending on your design, you may want to snip the rim pieces into smaller chunks, but leave their smooth edges intact; use these rim pieces to finish borders, giving your mosaic a more polished look.

2 Snip the plate's flat bottom into pieces. To give your mosaic a more orderly appearance, cut pieces of approximately the same size and shape. For a mosaic with more motion, cut the pieces in a variety of sizes and shapes. If the plate's face has a pattern, you may want to preserve it in your finished mosaic; in that case, arrange the pieces in the pattern's original order. (Be sure to do this on an out-of-the-way portion of your work surface to minimize the chances of sweeping the pattern into disarray with a careless brush of your elbow.) Otherwise, simply sort the flat bottom pieces into one container and the rim pieces into another.

3 The protruding handle of a teacup or mug can add an interesting three-dimensional effect to your mosaic. The trick is removing the handle intact. To do this, start by breaking the teacup or mug in half: Grip the edge of the cup's rim with your tile nippers, selecting a spot that's neither directly opposite the handle nor directly above it. Gently squeeze the handles together until the cup breaks. Working on the half with the handle, carefully nip away small bits until all that remains is the small rectangular or oblong shard to which the handle is attached.

Breaking Ceramic with a Hammer

Quicker (and, let's face it, often more satisfying) than using tile nippers, smashing plates and tiles with a hammer is the best way to create a lot of tesserae in a hurry.

Fold a thick cloth or towel into a double thickness and place it on a flat, unyielding work surface. Set the tile or plate to be broken on top of the towel, face down. Put on your safety goggles. Grip your hammer firmly and strike the center of the tile or plate. It should break into three or four large pieces. You can break these into smaller pieces with the hammer, or you can snip them into pieces and shapes with your tile nippers.

BASIC TECHNIQUES

SHAPING GLASS AND CERAMIC TESSERAE

Creating triangles and even curves and half-moon shapes in glass and ceramic tesserae is easier than it sounds. All you need are ceramic tile nippers or mosaic glass cutters and a little practice.

1 You can use ceramic tile nippers to shape either ceramic or glass, although mosaic glass cutters are a better choice for shaping the latter. To make triangles, start with roughly square-shaped tiles. You can use pre-cut tiles or tiles you've made yourself. To make triangle shapes, simply cut a tile in half diagonally. Snip each resulting half in two to make smaller triangles. To make a half-moon shape, snip off the outside corner of a triangle; then nibble out the middle. To make a roughly circular shape, nibble off the corners of a square tile; then take small nips around the resulting shape until the piece is round.

PUTTING TOGETHER THE PUZZLE

Creating a mosaic design really is a little like piecing together a puzzle – except that there's a literally infinite number of solutions!

1 Before you butter the back of your first tile, play with your tesserae and a full-size line drawing of your design. Begin by sorting your tesserae by shape, size, and

color. Then place the drawing on a flat surface and start experimenting—what fits where? Do those colors really go together? In general, try building the most important elements of a design first: If a big, red rose is the focal point of your mosaic, start by piecing it together; then create its leaves and stem. Fill in the background last. As you're experimenting, you may want to trim pieces to the approximate size you'll need. Wait until you're ready to start adhering the pieces to your project before you snip them to the exact shape you want.

TRANSFERRING PATTERNS

You can, of course, sketch your design right onto a base object or even work free-form. Sometimes, however, you'll want to transfer a pattern from paper onto an object of soon-to-be art.

1 If the template of your pattern is smaller than the size indicated in the project instructions, start by enlarging it using a copy machine. Tape the pattern to the back of a piece of black graphite paper. (Note that black graphite paper, a special wax-free paper designed specifically for transferring patterns and sold by most art and craft suppliers, is not the same thing as carbon paper, which is used for typing.)

2 If you're working on a flat surface, simply tape the joined pieces of paper to the base object, graphiteside down, aligning the design carefully. If you're transferring

a design to a three-dimensional object, skip to Step 3. Use a pencil to go over all the lines on the pattern, pressing firmly enough to transfer the design through the graphite paper and onto the base object. When you're done, remove the pieces of paper. To prevent smudging or accidental erasure, trace over the graphite lines with a fine-tipped permanent marker.

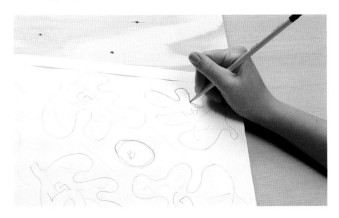

3 Transferring a design to a three-dimensional object such as a vase requires a little more care. Basically, you'll have to work on the pattern one section at a time, making sure all the while that each section you're tracing aligns properly with the other sections. Start by taping the top of the joined pieces of paper to the base object, leaving the sides and bottom loose. Smooth the pattern around the object to make sure the pattern will be aligned properly. Then use a pencil to trace over the portion of the design in front of you. When you're done with one portion, turn the object and move the tape to hold the paper over the next section you'll be tracing. Continue until you've transferred the entire pattern. Remove the paper and trace over the graphite lines with a permanent marker.

CHOOSING ADHESIVES

The key to making your mosaic stick is choosing the right adhesive. Cement-based tile adhesive (Step 1) and silicone and multipurpose waterproof glues (Step 2) are the most common choices.

1 If you're applying a mosaic—particularly one created from ceramic tesserae—to a cement-based surface (a cement birdbath or stepping stone, for instance), the best "glue" for the job is cement-based tile adhesive, also known as thin-set mortar. Available at hardware stores and craft suppliers, this adhesive consists of a blend of Portland cement and sand to which you'll add water. Read and follow the manufacturer's instructions for mixing and applying cement-based tile adhesive, paying particular attention to temperature requirements.

2 Silicone glues, sometimes called silicone sealant, can adhere just about any kind of material to any other kind of material. If you're gluing glass tesserae to a cement base, silicone glue is an even better choice for the job than cement-based tile adhesive. Buy these glues in tubes, which are easier to handle than the caulking-gun cartridges in which they are also available. For outdoor projects, be sure to purchase glue that's rated for exterior use. When you're working with very small base objects and tesserae, however, silicone glues can be difficult to apply and spread. For these situations, choose a multipurpose waterproof glue, which—with the exception of cement-based stuff—will stick most things together. Don't confuse this type of glue with common hobby PVA (polyvinyl acetate) "white glue," which isn't waterproof.

3 Premixed ceramic tile mastic is also a good adhesive for projects that will remain indoors. You can spread the mastic just as you would thin-set mortar, or butter the back of tessarae individually. It's simply a matter of choice of which type of adhesive—silicone, multipurpose waterproof glue, or tile mastic—you wish to use and feel comfortable working with. Experience will guide your choices.

BASIC TECHNIQUES

Although adhesives are meant to remain behind the scenes, how they're applied will affect your project's appearance. Follow Steps 1 and 2 if you're working with glue, and Step 4 if you're using thin-set mortar.

1 Unless you're working with very large tesserae, applying glue to the back of each individual piece (a technique known as "buttering") is messy and impractical. Instead, apply the glue directly to the surface of your base object and gently press the tesserae into it. When gluing small areas, use the applicator tip of the glue's tube to spread the adhesive evenly. For larger areas, smooth the glue with a flat knife or a craft stick. Spread the glue to an even thickness—about $1/16$ inch (1.5 mm) for glass or mirror tesserae and about $1/8$ inch (3 mm) for other materials—and only over the amount of area you can tile before the adhesive dries. Keep in mind that silicone glue dries in 5 to 10 minutes.

2 If your glue dries before you're able to set tesserae in it, you'll have to scrape it off and start over. (Applying fresh glue on top of old glue will create a lumpy, uneven surface, which will result in a lumpy, uneven mosaic.) You can use a flat knife or a single-edge razor blade for this job. No matter how careful you are to apply glue evenly, some of it will squeeze up between tesserae. Use a dental pick or some other pointed tool to remove glue that squeezes up between tesserae before it dries.

3 Start by mixing your thin-set mortar according to the manufacturer's instructions. Use a flat bed trowel with a smooth surface to spread the mortar over only as large an area of your base object as you'll be able to tile before the mortar sets. Spread the mortar evenly to a thickness of about $1/8$ inch. You may want to use a small pointing trowel to apply mortar in tight spots. Then, using a flat knife or a craft stick, "butter" the back of your tesserae with a $1/8$-inch thickness of mortar, being careful to coat the entire surface. Gently press the tesserae onto the base object. Scrape away any excess mortar that squeezes out with a craft stick or your knife.

4 Regardless of the type of adhesive you're using or how carefully you've applied it, you'll need to do a final and thorough cleaning before you move on to grouting your project. Working with a single-edge razor blade, scrape away dried adhesive from the top surfaces of the tesserae. Use a dental pick or other sharp, pointed object to pick out excess adhesive from between the cracks. Any adhesive residue that remains on your project's surface or in the cracks between tesserae will mar your mosaic's final appearance, so don't be tempted to skip or skimp on this step!

Gluing tesserae directly to a base object is known as the "direct method," which is appropriate for most projects.

1 Whether you're using glue or thin-set mortar, there are a couple of things to keep in mind as you begin adhering tesserae to your base surface. If you're working on a vertical surface, work from the bottom up, applying the adhesive, then the tesserae, upward. This way, the lower pieces will keep the higher pieces from slipping down before their adhesive dries. Space tesserae consistently: $1/16$ inch to $1/8$ inch apart for glass tesserae, and $1/8$ to $3/16$ inch for ceramic tile. When tiling curved areas, use tesserae that are small enough to lie flat against the surface. When tiling along an edge, place the tesserae flush to the edge, creating a stronger border and a more polished appearance.

2 To tile an edge itself, start by measuring its thickness; then cut several strips of material (glass, mirror, ceramic, etc.) to that exact width. Snip the strips into tiles, lining up the tiles on your work surface in the same order in which you cut them. Apply adhesive to the edge and press the tiles into place along the edge, in the order in which you cut them. If the edge curves, you may have to cut some of the tiles into smaller tesserae so they'll lie flat against the project's surface. Make sure that each tile is flush to both sides of the edge; otherwise, they'll be prone to popping off and they'll lack a polished, finished appearance.

CHOOSING, MIXING, AND APPLYING GROUT

Not only will grout fill the spaces in between tesserae, adding to your project's appeal, it will also strengthen the overall design, ensuring that tiles stay put.

1 Grout is available in sanded and unsanded versions. Most mosaic artists use unsanded grout for projects in which the tesserae are spaced less than ⅛ inch apart and sanded grout for projects with wider spacing. (Unsanded grout tends to crack when used in wide spaces.) Some artists, however, use sanded grout for all their projects, citing the material's greater sculptural quality. You may want to add acrylic grout fortifier to increase the grout's strength and durability. Grout comes in white, as well as a variety of colors. You can also custom color grout by adding colorant(s) to white or colored grout; liquid pure pigment (available at art supply stores) is the best choice, but acrylic art paints and powdered pigments work, too.

2 You'll mix your grout right before you're ready to apply it. Keep in mind that once you've started grouting, you can't stop until you've finished the entire project. Most mosaic artists like to mix their grout by hand—literally. Wearing latex gloves, scoop and blend the grout manually. Mix grout according to the manufacturer's instructions, starting by adding colorants first. Then pour in water and grout fortifier, adding a little at a time until the grout has reached the consistency of thick oatmeal. Grout that's too dry can be difficult to work and may crack after it's dried. Grout that's too wet is sloppy and hard to apply to edges and vertical surfaces. Naturally, it's easier to add more moisture to dry grout than to remove it from overly wet grout.

3 When the grout is mixed, it's time to apply it to your mosaic. Work on one small section at a time, grouting it thoroughly before moving to the next section. Still wearing latex gloves, scoop out a small handful and work it onto the surface of your mosaic. Gently but firmly press the grout into the spaces between the tesserae, smoothing and rubbing until you've filled all the gaps and have covered the entire surface of the section you're working on. Finish the primary surfaces first, then move on to the edges, working grout into all the spaces and over all the surfaces. You may want to elevate your project on an old book so you can reach the bottom edges better.

4 As soon as you've grouted the whole project, dip a clean sponge into water and wring it out well. Use the damp sponge to wipe the grout off the surface of the mosaic, being careful not to remove too much grout from between the tesserae. Clean your sponge often by dipping it into water and wringing it out well. After you've wiped the entire project clean with the sponge, wait several minutes for the surface to dry. A haze will form from the grout residue. Use a soft cloth to polish off the residue, then use a dental pick or a craft knife to scrape away any excess grout that remains on the surface. Behold your finished project!

DELFTWARE MOSAIC PLANTER

You can save chipped pieces of blue Delftware to make this pretty planter, use dishes from an old matched set, or work out a color scheme with non-matching but compatible pieces rescued from flea markets and thrift stores. If you can't find a planter exactly the same size and shape, don't worry—just adapt the instructions to fit your project.

MATERIALS AND TOOLS

Ceramic planter, with top opening
  12 inches (30.5 cm) across
Assortment of broken china
Plastic bag
Hammer
Leather gloves
Ceramic tile nippers
Safety goggles
Plastic for covering work surface

Paper plates for holding tiles
Polymer-fortified thin-set
  tile adhesive
Craft sticks
Latex gloves
Sponge or damp cloth
Plastic for wrapping object
Cleaning tools (abrasive cleaning
  pad, razor blade, etc.)

Lazy Susan (optional)
Containers for mixing grout
Container for water
4 pounds (1.8 kg) of white
  sanded grout
Acrylic grout fortifier
Polishing cloth
Razor blades

WHAT TO DO

1 Using a hammer and wearing leather gloves, roughly break up plates by putting them in a plastic bag and hitting it with a hammer. Use tile nippers to cut the broken tiles into irregular pieces small enough to lie flat on the planter's curving surface. Set aside the smallest pieces to use for the rim of the planter. Make sure you wear safety goggles to protect your eyes.

2 Mix the thin-set tile adhesive according to the manufacturer's instructions. Starting with the rim of the planter, use a craft stick to butter the smallest pieces with adhesive; then press them into position on the rim of the planter. Use the remaining pieces and the same technique to finish covering the

pot. Use a craft stick to clean away any adhesive that comes up into the spaces between pieces, and wipe off the tiles with a sponge or damp cloth as you work. It's a good idea to wear latex gloves while you do this to avoid getting the adhesive on your hands.

3 Cut, nip, and glue irregular pieces of tile to the planter until you've completely filled in the background. Remember to keep the spacing between tiles as uniform as possible.

4 Wrap the planter in plastic and let the adhesive dry overnight.

5 Put the planter on a lazy Susan if you have one. Use cleaning tools to remove any dried adhesive from the surface.

6 Mix the grout and acrylic fortifier. Start grouting the planter on the inside rim, then work grout into the edge pieces along the top. Use a finger to smooth the joints on both sides of the edge.

7 Now work your way down and around the planter, pressing grout firmly into all the spaces.

8 Wipe the grouted planter with a damp sponge. Allow time for the surface to haze over, then polish it with a soft cloth. Remove any stubborn dried grout with a razor blade.

9 Wrap the planter in plastic or kraft paper and let it cure for three days.

Designer: Megan Kirby

259

Designer: Terry Taylor

GARDEN MOSAIC BALL

Mosaic balls make delightful accents among your garden blooms. Be sure to protect your mosaic from freeze/thaw cycles by bringing it indoors in the winter.

MATERIALS AND TOOLS

Polystyrene foam ball or hard plastic ball

Variety of ceramic plates and saucers: you'll need more than you think, so buy 10 or 15 plates at thrift stores and yard sales.

Tile nippers

Safety goggles or glasses

Premixed tile mastic

White sanded grout

Acrylic paint (optional)

Grout spreader and polyethylene foam wrap (white packing material)

Mixing container for grout

Palette knife

Sponge and lint-free rags

WHAT TO DO

1 Prepare a supply of mosaic shards by breaking plates in half with tile nippers. Remove the rims from the plates. Trim the rims into small, rectangular pieces. Break the flat portions of the plate into small pieces, then sort your pieces by color on paper plates or in another type of container.

2 Use the tile mastic to adhere the shards of pottery to the ball. Place them close together, but not touching. Work on half of the ball, then let the ball sit overnight to dry.

3 Turn the ball over and finish attaching shards to it. Allow the mosaic to dry overnight before grouting.

4 Mix the white sanded grout according to the manufacturer's instructions. If desired, add a small amount of acrylic paint to the mixture to color the grout.

5 Use a grout spreader or the polyethylene foam wrap to spread the grout over the surface of the mosaic. Use pressure to force the grout into all the spaces between the shards. Allow the grout to set for about 15 minutes, then begin removing the excess grout with polyethylene foam wrap or clean, lint-free rags. Follow the manufacturer's recommendations on the grout for removing any grout haze that develops.

WHERE TO FIND BROKEN CHINA

Ok, we've all dropped a plate or two. But if it's been awhile, finding china for your mosaic project may be as enjoyable as making the project itself. Be on the lookout for interesting patterns and colors as you browse flea markets and thrift stores. Chipped and cracked plates give you bargaining leverage. Or, go to the source. China shops pottery outlets, even antique stores are bound to have broken goods slated for the dumpster.

Mosaic Mélange Stepping Stone

Every crafter has drawers and baskets full of odd little things: a handful of gorgeous glass marbles, a collection of beads salvaged from mismatched earrings, several summers' worth of seashells. Creating a lovely mosaic stepping stone is the perfect way to put at least some of your personal mélange of crafting goodies to excellent use.

Materials and Tools

Concrete paving stone (available at garden supply stores)
Mélange of tesserae: beads, glass pebbles, shells, pottery shards, etc.
Pencil
Cement-based tile adhesive or silicone glue
Craft sticks

Tile nippers (if working with pottery shards)
Sanded grout
Latex gloves
Sponge with small pores
Toothbrush or single-edged razor blade
Tile sealant

What To Do

1 Take a few minutes to sort your tesserae and get a feel for what you have to work with. Experiment with various arrangements and patterns on your paving stone. When you're happy with a design, lightly mark it on the stone in pencil so you'll have a pattern to follow as you glue the pieces in place.

2 If you're working with large tesserae (larger than 1 inch, 2.5 cm), you may want to butter (apply adhesive to the back of) each piece using a craft stick. Otherwise, spread a ⅛-inch (3 mm) layer of the adhesive over a small area of the stone. Press the tesserae into place, following the pattern you marked in Step 1. If necessary, use your tile nippers to trim pottery shards to fit properly.

3 Continue either buttering tesserae individually or spreading tile adhesive over small sections of the stone and placing the tesserae until you've tiled the entire stone.

4 Use a craft stick to scrape away any excess adhesive from between the tesserae. If any adhesive has gotten on the upper surface of the pieces, carefully wipe it away with a damp cloth. (Be careful not to shift the pattern as you do this; the adhesive probably hasn't set long enough at this point to hold the tesserae firmly in place.)

5 Allow the adhesive to dry for at least 24 hours. Then, referring to choosing, mixing, and applying grout on page 257 and following the grout manufacturer's instructions, mix the grout.

6 Wearing latex gloves to protect your hands, use a damp (not wet) sponge to spread the grout over the tesserae, packing it into the spaces between the pieces.

7 After you've grouted the entire stone, clean the sponge well and use it to wipe the surface of the tesserae clean, rinsing and wringing the sponge frequently. Don't worry if a thin layer of grout remains after this initial cleaning. Wait 15 to 30 minutes, then sponge the tesserae again. Repeat until only a hazy film remains.

8 Allow the grout to set for 2 to 3 hours. Then use a clean cloth to remove any remaining film from the surface of the tesserae. Use a toothbrush or a single-edged razor blade to scrape away any particularly stubborn spots.

9 Allow the grout to set for seven days. Then, following the manufacturer's instructions, apply a tile sealant to weatherproof your stone. Place in your garden and enjoy!

Designer: Melanie Gidley

263

MOSAIC SERVING TRAY

Funky old trays and chipped china abound at flea markets and thrift stores. With a little artful mosaic, these elements can transcend the realm of castoffs to become a chic means of delivering (or receiving) your next breakfast in bed.

MATERIALS AND TOOLS

Serving tray
Sandpaper
Clean cloth
Acrylic paint in the color of your choice
Paintbrush
Assortment of china in various patterns
Ceramic tile nippers or a hammer, towel, and safety glasses
Pencil
Cement-based tile adhesive
Craft sticks
Sanded grout
Latex gloves
Sponge with small pores
Toothbrush or single-edged razor blade
Epoxy resin finish

WHAT TO DO

1 If you acquired your serving tray from a flea market or thrift store, it may need a little freshening: Sand it smooth, wipe away any dust, and give it a fresh coat of paint.

2 While you wait for the paint to dry, break the china into pieces. (Refer to working with tile nippers on page 252 and breaking ceramic with a hammer on page 253.) For the project shown, the designer arranged the tesserae in designs that maintained the china's original patterns. If you'd like to create a similar look, keep your china pieces in order as you break them.

3 Take a few minutes to experiment with various arrangements of your tesserae on your tray. When you're happy with a design, lightly mark it on the tray in pencil so you'll have a pattern to follow as you glue the tesserae in place.

4 If you're working with large pieces of china (larger than 1 inch, 2.5 cm), you may want to butter (apply tile adhesive to the back of) each piece using a craft stick. Otherwise, spread a ⅛-inch (3 mm) layer of the adhesive over a small area of the tray. Press the tesserae into place, following the pattern you marked in Step 3. If necessary, use your tile nippers to trim pieces to fit properly.

5 Continue either buttering tesserae individually or spreading tile adhesive over small sections of the tray and placing the tesserae until you've tiled the entire tray.

6 Use a craft stick to scrape away any excess tile adhesive from between the tesserae. If any adhesive has gotten on the upper surface of the tiles, carefully wipe it away with a damp cloth. (Be careful not to shift the pattern as you do this; the adhesive probably hasn't set long enough at this point to hold the tesserae firmly in place.)

7 Allow the tile adhesive to dry for at least 24 hours. Then, referring to choosing, mixing, and applying grout on page 257 and following the grout manufacturer's instructions, mix the grout.

8 Wearing latex gloves to protect your hands, use a damp (not wet) sponge to spread the grout over the tile, packing it into the spaces between the tesserae.

9 After you've grouted the entire tray, clean the sponge well and use it to wipe the surface of the tesserae clean, rinsing and wringing the sponge frequently. Don't worry if a thin layer of grout remains after this initial cleaning.

Wait 15 to 30 minutes, then sponge the tesserae again. Repeat until only a hazy film remains.

10 Allow the grout to set for 2 to 3 hours. Then use a clean cloth to remove any remaining film from the surface of the tesserae. Use a toothbrush or a single-edged razor blade to scrape away any particularly stubborn spots.

11 Allow the grout to set for seven days. Then, following the manufacturer's instructions, mix and apply the epoxy resin finish, paying close attention to any safety considerations and suggested curing time.

Designer: Melanie Gidley

265

MOON AND STARS MIRROR MONTAGE

A broken mirror may foretell bad luck in other realms, but in mosaic, bits of shimmering reflective glass portend years of decorative beauty. Set this stunning stepping stone in a garden pathway to reflect the ever-changing skies above; or place it in a sunny window to invite a little sun-, moon-, and starshine inside.

MATERIALS AND TOOLS

Round concrete paving stone
    (available at garden-supply stores)
Pencil
1 sheet of blue stained glass
1 sheet mirror
Glass cutter
Running pliers
Containers for sorting glass pieces
Glass mosaic cutters
Silicone glue or cement-based tile
    adhesive
Craft sticks
Latex gloves
Grout
Sponge
Soft cloth
Toothbrush
Flat razor blade or dental pick

◆ Commonsense precaution: Glass and mirror pieces are sharp! Use extreme care when working with them!

WHAT TO DO

1 Draw the pattern directly onto your paving stone with a pencil, or transfer the pattern following the instructions on pages 254 and 255.

2 Referring to the instructions for cutting tiles from glass and mirror on page 252, use the glass cutter and running pliers to cut the blue stained glass and the mirror into roughly 1-inch-square (2.5 cm) tiles. Sort the blue tiles and the mirrored tiles into separate containers, being very careful of their sharp edges.

3 Referring to the instructions for shaping glass and ceramic tesserae on page 254, cut the square tiles you created in Step 2 into triangle shapes. Don't worry if some of your triangles don't look exactly like triangles; these irregular pieces will come in handy, too.

4 Take a few minutes to play with your tesserae to get a feel for how they'll fit together to form your pattern and to make sure you have enough pieces to complete your project.

5 When you're ready to start gluing pieces in place, start with the primary elements of the design—the stars and moon, in this project. Referring to applying adhesives on page 255 and placing and spacing tesserae, use a craft stick to smooth a thin layer (about 1/16 inch, 1.5 mm, thick) over one of the penciled stars. Working quickly but carefully, gently press mirrored tesserae in place to form the star. You may have to trim the triangles to smaller sizes or different shapes for a good fit.

6 Repeat Step 5 to tile the remaining stars and the moon, remembering to spread the glue evenly each time.

7 Fill in the background with the blue stained glass tesserrae, continuing to apply the glue in an even, thin layer. After you've tiled the entire paving stone, use a craft stick to remove any excess adhesive, then allow the glue to dry for at least 24 hours.

8 Don your latex gloves. Referring to choosing, mixing, and applying grout on page 257 and following the manufacturer's instructions for your specific grout, mix your grout by hand.

9 Working on one small section of the paving stone at a time, smooth a handful of grout into the spaces between the tesserae. Gently press it into all the gaps and completely cover surface of the section you're working on. Again, be very careful of the glass and mirror tesseraes' sharp edges! Repeat until you've applied grout to the entire tiled surface of the paving stone and all around its edges.

10 As soon as you've finished applying the grout, wipe the paving stone with a damp (not wet) sponge to begin removing the grout from its surface. Be careful not to remove too much grout from between the glass tiles! Clean your sponge often, dipping it into water and wringing it out well.

11 After you've sponged the grout from the paving stone, a haze will form on its surface. Use a clean cloth to polish away this hazy residue and a toothbrush to scrub off any stubborn areas. You may need to use a flat razor blade or a dental pick to remove really tough grout.

12 Allow the grout to set for 24 hours before moving the paving stone to its intended destination.

267

MOSAIC GALLERY

Right: Ceramic saucers and plates were used to make mosaic chips for this lovely pastel table. Designer: Terry Taylor

Bottom left: Tumbled stones make an interesting mosaic material, especially when placed around a mirror. Designer: Catherine Delgado

Bottom right: A plain wooden box (available in larger craft supply stores) transforms into a unique jewelry box when decorated with a stained glass mosaic. Designer: Catherine Delgado

Opposite page, top left: Functional and gorgeous, mosaic house numbers are a great way to announce your artistic nature to the world. Designer: Jill MacKay

Opposite page, top right: Tea cups, sugar bowls, and a creamer on the sides and top of this planter creates extra planting areas and a novel look. Designer: Jill MacKay

Opposite page, bottom left: Mosaics can be made from more than just ceramic chips, as this welcome sign illustrates. The letters were formed with painted nail heads (inserted into a pine board base), and the gaps were filled with finishing tacks. Designer: Jean Tomaso Moore

Opposite page, bottom right: Transform an ordinary table top into a mosaic showpiece with your favorite colors and patterns. Designer: Jill MacKay

FLORAL CRAFTS

Enjoy the beauty and fragrance of flowers year 'round. Dried blossoms offer all the appeal of fresh, without the wilting. Silk blooms are even more enduring and just as lovely. For pure scent appeal, we've included fragrant crafts, too—scented sachets and aromatic potpourris, just for starters.

SACHETS & POTPOURRIS

Just as your garden provides beauty, color, and fragrance to your home in the warmer months, potpourri can offer these qualities year 'round. Indeed, your summer garden can live on in gorgeous bowls of potpourri, in sachets, and in a variety of other fragrance-based crafts. What better gift than a lovely, fragrant sachet?

MATERIALS AND TOOLS

PURCHASED POTPOURRIS
Commericially made potpourris are available in dozens of colors and fragrances.

FLOWERS AND HERBS
Dried plants of all kinds, with or without natural color or fragrance, can make terrific materials for potpourri. Whether you grow your own plant materials or purchase them, experiment with a variety of flowers, herbs, and spices to find the ones that best suit your tastes.

FILLER MATERIAL
Wood shavings are popular filler material for homemade potpourris since they are inexpensive, readily absorb fragrance, and provide a nice texture to potpourris. Clean straw and moss are also good choices. Depending on the potpourri you choose, a filler material may not be necessary.

FRAGRANCE
Fragrance oils, also called essential oils, are becoming less expensive and more widely available, and make it practical to use nonfragrant plant material just for the sake of color or texture. Add these oils in small amounts until the desired fragrance level is achieved, then as needed to refresh potpourris. (Be careful: these oils can leave stains on wood, fabric, and walls.) There are many ways to impart fragrance, so be creative; for example, scented wax or even shavings from a scented bar of soap can lend fragrance.

FABRIC
Because most sachets are quite small, and thus require very little fabric, you can treat yourself to high-quality fabrics. Though any fabric will work as a sachet, natural fibers (such as cotton, silk, or linen) are more effective at releasing scent. Wedding netting, tulle, and lace are also good choices.

EMBELLISHMENTS
Think of your sachet as a blank

canvas just waiting for your own creative touch. Buttons, ribbons, lace, dried or silk flowers, beads, stamps, and fabric paint can turn a simple sachet into a special item— and you will need only a few embell- ishments to make a big impact.

HOT-GLUE GUN
This is a great tool for securing ribbons, buttons, and other embell- ishments to sachets, as well as for attaching pieces of floral material. If you don't have a sewing machine or the time to hand stitch, hot glue can be used to make simple sachets.

FABRIC GLUE
If you don't have a sewing machine or the inclination to sew, fabric glue can be used to make a variety of simple sachets. Look for it in sewing departments.

273

BASIC TECHNIQUES

MAKING POTPOURRI

Though potpourri is widely available, crafters have long understood the benefits of making one's own special potpourri blend. Remember that everyone (yes, everyone) has fragrance preferences. Before you begin a potpourri project, take a moment to consider your preferences or those of the recipient.

1. Create a fragrant base by combining an assortment of scented, fully dried plant materials in a large, non-metal bowl. At this point, you should focus on scent, so continue to add ingredients until you are pleased with the fragrance.

2. Now, make your potpourri look pretty by adding dried blooms, leaves, seed pods, berries, or other plant material. Add any filler material at this time, as well. Choose materials with complementary colors and textures. Mix everything together loosely with your hands or a wooden spoon. Note: If your potpourri will be used for a sachet, this step may be unnecessary.

SEWING A SACHET

These simple sachets require only small pieces of fabric and simple sewing skills. Go ahead, splurge on fancy cottons and rich silks!

1 Cut a piece of fabric 12 inches wide x 10 inches high (30 x 25 cm). Turn down a narrow hem across one long edge. Press and stitch.

2 Press down a second, larger hem (about an inch, 2.5 cm), then fold the fabric in half with right sides facing. Pin the side and bottom seams, then stitch.

3 Turn right sides out and press. Fill with potpourri and tie with a pretty ribbon.

◆ Note: Interesting variations can be made when using cotton eyelet fabrics. Just arrange the embroidered openings at the top and thread the ribbon through them to tie.

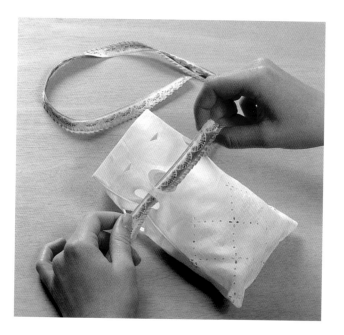

3. *Add the fixative of your choice. For every cup of potpourri, add 1 tablespoon of fixative. (Fixatives are natural materials such as orrisroot, gum benzoin resin, tonka beans, sandalwood bark, and patchouli leaves.)*

4. *To intensify the fragrance, add a few drops of essential oil, if desired. (Choose a fragrance that is the same as or complementary to the scented materials you've used in Step 1.) Use a wooden spoon to carefully combine all the ingredients.*

5. *Place potpourri in a paper bag, and roll the top of the bag several times to close tightly. Store bag in a dark location and shake it once a day for a week to distribute and blend the scents. For the following five weeks, shake the bag once a week. In six weeks, your potpourri is ready to display and enjoy.*

BASIC TECHNIQUES

TWO-MINUTE SACHETS

Need a quick gift? Give a handkerchief sachet as a gift by itself or tie one into a bow on a wrapped package.

1 Place the handkerchief face down on a flat surface, then add several large spoonfuls of potpourri to the center.

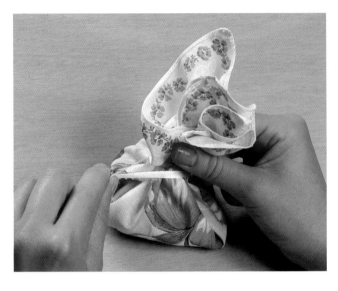

QUICK NO-SEW SACHETS

A few simple supplies — fabric glue, pinking shears, and a small piece of pretty fabric — are all you need to create great sachets.

1 Cut out two 5-inch (12.5 cm) squares of fabric. Pink the edges to prevent the fabric from unraveling.

DESIGNER TIP

Have the perfect container but not enough potpourri to fill it? Just fill the bottom with a piece of floral foam or some newspaper or tissue paper. Just make sure the potpourri covers the filler material below completely.

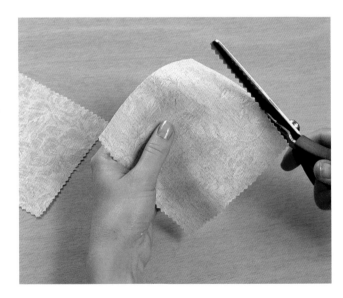

2 Place one square face down on a flat surface, then place a large spoonful of potpourri in the center of it.

3 Outline the fabric square about ¼ inch (6 mm) in from each edge with fabric glue.

The ancient Greeks placed a muslin sachet beside each guest at banquets; surely you can find many uses for sachets in your home as well. Though a sachet can also be secured with a hot-glue gun, a sewn sachet will be more secure and long lasting. The sachet described at left is finished on all sides, but you can also leave one side open, finish the open end with a simple stitch, then tie with a ribbon.

4 Place the second square on top of the first, right side facing up, and press it gently into the glue. Allow it to completely dry before handling.

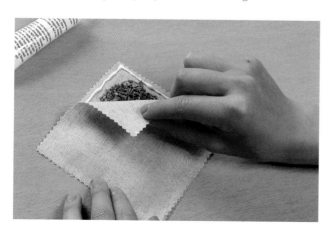

PERFECTLY SIMPLE POTPOURRIS

Simple potpourris radiate both beauty and fragrance. You can purchase special bowls to display your potpourris, or simply use something pretty from your china cabinet.

MATERIALS AND TOOLS

Potpourri of your choice (store bought or homemade)
Display bowls
Fragrant oils

WHAT TO DO

1 Place your potpourri in a bowl and add a drop or two of fragrant oil if needed.

2 Choose a display location away from direct sunlight and high moisture. (Sunlight quickly fades the bright colors of potpourri, while moist areas cause the dried blooms to reabsorb moisture.)

DESIGNER TIP

Making your own potpourri is a fun alternative to store-bought varieties. Here are some fragrant plant materials that work well in potpourri: roses, lemon verbena, scented geraniums, honeysuckle, eucalyptus, lemon balm, lemon thyme, lemon basil, lemon grass, lavender, mint, sassafras, dried citrus peel, rosemary, allspice, nutmeg, cloves, bay, sage, star anise, or cinnamon sticks.

Designer: Megan Kirby

No-Sew Hankie Sachets

Perhaps you're lucky enough to have a box filled with your grandmother's cherished handkerchiefs. If not, check out flea markets and vintage shops for old-fashioned handkerchiefs made of fine linen and embellished with hand embroidery or tatting. Here's a great way to make great use of them without causing the hankie itself any harm.

MATERIALS AND TOOLS

Assorted handkerchiefs
Potpourri of your choice
Ribbon
Beads (optional)

WHAT TO DO

RIBBON-TIED HANKIE SACHET

1 Launder and press the handkerchief and position the fabric, with the decorative side facing down, on a clean, flat surface.

2 Place a small amount of potpourri in the center of the handkerchief. (Several small spoonfuls should be plenty.) Optional: If you want to use less potpourri, then add a few drops of essential oil to a couple cotton balls, and put those on the hankie with the potpourri.

3 Draw up all four sides of the handkerchief, then tie ribbon to secure. Thread beads on the ends of the ribbons, if desired.

FOLDED HANKIE SACHET

◆ Sew or glue the decorative edges together to form an envelope, leaving one side open to insert potpourri. Fill sachet, then glue remaining edge closed.

DESIGNER TIP

Look in unexpected places for materials to make sachets. An old pair of lace or crocheted gloves—perhaps you own a pair or can find one at a thrift store—makes a terrific sachet when stuffed with potpourri and tied with a pretty ribbon. Antique linens that are too damaged or stained to use as a tablecloth or bed sheet surely have a corner or section that can be salvaged to make a darling sachet for your lingerie drawer. A loose-tea strainer is a marvelous container for fragrant potpourris.

Designer: Catherine Ham

Designer: Catherine Ham

DREAM PILLOWS

These dream pillows are the ultimate pamper-yourself gift and are charming when presented as sets tied with ribbons and adorned with beads— try a stack of different-colored sachets all in the same size, a set of pillows in graduated sizes, as we've done here, or perhaps an array of interesting shapes (hearts, circles, and diamonds, for example). In no time you can make dozens of these scented treasures and have a handy stash of inexpensive, one-of-a-kind gifts.

MATERIALS AND TOOLS

Fabric of your choice
Needle and thread or
  sewing machine

Potpourri (or other fragrant filling
  of your choice)

WHAT TO DO

1 Determine what sizes you would like for your pillows to be. These are 4 x 6 inches (10 x 15 cm), 5 x 7 inches (12.5 x 17.5 cm), and 6 x 8 inches (15 x 20 cm).

2 Cut two pieces of fabric to the chosen dimensions. Position the fabric with right sides together and sew them together, leaving an opening for turning. Trim seams and turn right sides out.

3 Fill the pillow. It works well to fill small pillows with potpourri. For larger pillows, it may be overwhelmingly fragrant or too expensive to fill them with potpourri alone; you may want to use a combination of potpourri and cotton balls, adding a few drops of fragrance oil, if desired. Slip stitch the opening closed.

DESIGNER TIP

Another easy sachet: Purchase a muslin tea bag at any health food store, fill with your favorite potpourri blend, then pull string tight to secure. These little bags are inexpensive and easy to embellish and are great for tucking all around the house.

RELAXING BATH BARS

Have fun coordinating fragrance and color when making these bars: green dye with peppermint scent, red with sandalwood, yellow with lemon, and so forth. A batch of these bars makes a terrific gift; they are also lovely when displayed on a decorative dish in the bathroom.

MATERIALS AND TOOLS

Epsom salts
Baking soda
Mixing bowl
Glycerin
Spa or soap dye
Rose-scented fragrance oil
Small dessert molds
Butter knife

WHAT TO DO

1 Combine ⅔ cup Epsom salts and ⅓ cup baking soda in a mixing bowl. Add five drops glycerin and just enough water to moisten the mixture. Stir well.

2 Add dye gradually, stirring the mixture well between drops, until you are happy with the color. Stir in three drops of fragrance oil and mix well. (For additional fragrance, continue to add oil, one drop at a time.)

3 Fill each mold with the mixture. Press the mixture into the mold firmly, then use a butter knife to smooth the top of the mold (as you would frosting on a cake). Remove excess mixture from the sides of the mold.

4 Invert the molds on a paper towel and tap lightly to remove the bath bar. Allow to dry undisturbed overnight. If your bath bar doesn't invert perfectly, simply place the mixture back in the bowl and repeat Step 3. To use, dissolve bars under hot, running water.

DESIGNER TIP

Vast amounts of information about the meaning and lore of various plants are available, and can be of great benefit and amusement to the potpourri-maker. Check out a book at the library or invest in one of your own, then make potpourris that convey a particular sentiment. Make sure you write this information on the gift card before you present the potpourri to the lucky recipient.

SCENTED BOX DECORATIONS

Don't hesitate to use fragrance oils to add scent to nonscented floral decorations. These boxes can be used purely as ornamental elements in the home or as snazzy gift boxes. Any flower variety can be used, though try to choose a fragrance oil that complements the chosen silk materials.

MATERIALS AND TOOLS

Cardboard
Scissors
Satin wired ribbon
Floral wire
Hot-glue gun
Silk hydrangea blossom
Silk irises (optional)
Fragrance oil
Decorative boxes

WHAT TO DO

1 Cut a piece of cardboard to the size and shape you would like your decoration to be. Tie several ribbon bows by creating multiple loops of ribbon and securing the center with floral wire. (We used two bows for the smaller decoration, and three for the larger one.) Leave long ribbon ends.

2 Hot-glue the bows to the center of the cardboard. Use your fingers to separate and spread out the loops of the bows, and position and hot-glue the ribbon ends so that they trail off the cardboard in a pleasing manner. Trim ends, if necessary.

3 Cut off individual flowers and unopened buds from the hydrangea blossom, and hot-glue these elements to the cardboard, nestling them in and around the ribbon. (This design looks best when flowers in varying stages of development are used.) In the larger decoration, silk irises were also used. Continue to add floral pieces until the cardboard is completely covered. You can also hot-glue flowers to the ends of the ribbon for a little added whimsy.

4 Once the design is complete, add the fragrance of your choice. Begin with a few drops in the centers of several of the flowers, then continue to add oil until the desired level of fragrance is achieved. Lastly, hot-glue the decoration to the top of the box.

Designer: Cynthia Gillooly

Right: Lavender basket: Welcome overnight guests with a scented bath basket decorated with lavender sprigs and filled with lavender soap and lavender sachet bags. Designers: Corinne Kurzmann and Terry Taylor

Below left: Need a great gift? Mix up a lavender/oatmeal bath with 1 cup oatmeal, ½ cup sea salt, ¼ cup powdered milk, and ¼ cup dried lavender or other dried herbs. Designers: Heidi Tyline King and Nancy Worrell

Below right: Lace netting makes a lovely sachet material. Look for vintage scraps in antique stores. Designer: Joyce E. Cusick

Opposite page, left: Showcase your favorite potpourri blend in a colorful sachet decorated with dried flowers and ribbon. Designer: Joan Morris

Opposite page, top: Scented hot pad: Fill a hot pad with a spicy potpourri—its fragrance will be released when you place hot pots on it. Designer: Tracy Munn

Opposite page, bottom: Fill the centers of colorful fabric squares with fragrant potpourri (or scented cotton balls), then tuck them in drawers, under your car seat, in your purse, etc. Designer: Catherine Ham

SCENTED
GALLERY

DRIED FLOWERS

The natural beauty of fresh flowers is retained in many types of dried flowers and greenery. Dried flowers are a remarkably versatile crafting material. You can create large, expansive arrangements, small nosegays, garlands, and much more. They can be used in traditional ways—as a centerpiece on a dining room table, for example—or in much more novel ways— as curtain tiebacks, for example.

MATERIALS AND TOOLS

DRIED FLOWERS
Dried flowers offer a wonderfully complex array of textures and colors, and can serve as focal or accent flowers as well as background or filler material. Because of their versatility, dried flowers work well when combined with silks and fresh flowers, and can be used in all sorts of craft projects.

FLORAL FOAM
Used as a stabilizer for floral arrangements, floral foam comes in a variety of shapes and sizes. Delicate dried flowers will need to be attached to floral picks or floral wire to add extra support; more sturdy dried material can be inserted directly into the floral foam.

FLORAL WIRE
This wire comes in a variety of thicknesses, or gauges, and is used to attach dried flowers as well as other materials to a base. Try to position wire where it will not show in the finished design.

FLORAL TAPE
Floral tape, also called stem wrap, comes in an array of widths and colors. It's handy for securing floral foam to containers, binding together several stems or pieces of foam, and lending extra support to delicate materials. For best results, pull the tape taut as you wrap; this makes the tape sticky, and thus allows for a secure hold.

FLORAL PINS
These U-shaped pins (also called U pins or moss pins) are curved pieces of wire used to secure moss and ribbon to the base material as well as to attach plant materials to straw or foam bases.

FLORAL PICKS
These are wooden picks with an attached wire that are used to give extra support to delicate stems, to bundle several stems together, or to serve as a stem lengthener.

BASES
Straw, grapevine, foam, polystyrene, and wire forms make creating wreaths, topiaries, and swags easy. Visit your local craft store and you'll be amazed by the assortment. Although each type of base has its own benefits and drawbacks, when working with delicate, wispy dried flowers, a wire base is ideal.

HOT-GLUE GUN
Crafters swear by this trusty tool, and dried-flower designers in particular can find many uses for a glue gun. A dab of hot glue is the perfect (and invisible) way to attach delicate dried flowers to a base without damaging the flower.

290

BASIC TECHNIQUES

USING FLORAL PICKS

Floral picks prevent damage to delicate stems and can save you a significant amount of time.

1 To attach materials to a floral pick, arrange several stems of dried flowers together in a mini bouquet. Place the stems next to the pick about midpoint down the pick with the pick's pointed side facing down.

2 With the blooms and pick held together in your left hand, use your right hand to wrap the wire around the stems several times in the same place, then spiral the remaining wire down the stems.

3 To use a picked mini bouquet, simply insert it by the tip into floral foam (for a low-based arrangement) or into a wreath base. When inserting bouquets into wreath bases, be sure to insert them at an angle. You may need to add a small amount of hot glue at the tip of the pick to help it stay in place.

USING FLORAL TAPE

Floral tape comes in hues of green and brown. You will need to use floral tape only when there's a chance that your picked mini bouquet will show in your finished project, so be sure to choose the color that will be the least conspicuous in your finished project.

1 To use floral tape, hold it against your picked bouquet. Stretch it slightly, then spiral it down the picked stems.

2 To use a taped floral bouquet, insert or glue it into a base material.

◄ WORKING WITH SINGLE BLOOMS ►

Single blooms are easy to work with and can create a wide array of projects. If you have a lot of blooms, you can cover an entire surface area, such as a topiary ball or a wreath base, with blooms. Otherwise, simply follow the instructions below.

1 Cover the surface you plan to decorate with moss using floral pins or hot glue.

2 Remove the stems from the blooms and add a dab of hot glue to their backs, then press them into the moss.

3 For maximum effect, vary the size and color of the blooms you use.

◆ Note: See the Silk Flowers section (pages 308 and 309) for information on creating arrangements.

DRIED ROSE TOPIARY

Simply elegant or sweetly simple? You choose. By using florals—rosebuds or rose petals—or herbals—lavender or potpourri, you can make this topiary a delight to look at or an aromatic centerpiece. Mix and match the florals with the herbals for a bedroom delight, or use only rosebuds to create captivating table adornments for a bridal shower. Your choice of ribbon will dress it up or down—grosgrain, satin, or raffia. While the hint of Spanish moss adds a texture that takes you to remembrances of gentle and gracious summer evenings.

MATERIALS AND TOOLS

4-inch-diameter (10 cm)
  polystyrene ball
Loose rosebuds, lavender, rose
  petals, or potpourri
Floral foam
6-inch-diameter (15 cm) terra
  cotta pot
½-inch-diameter (1.5 cm) twig,
  15 inches (38 cm) long
Spanish moss
Ribbon (optional)
Hot-glue gun and glue sticks

WHAT TO DO

1 Cover a small portion of the polystyrene ball with hot glue, then stick rosebuds onto ball one at a time until the entire ball is covered.

2 Cut a piece of floral foam to fit snugly inside the terra-cotta pot and wedge into place.

3 Stick the end of the twig into the bottom of the ball and the other end into the florae foam.

4 Cover the top of the floral foam with Spanish moss.

5 If desired, tie a bow around the center of the twig or around the top of the pot.

DESIGNER TIP

Pressing has been a popular method of drying and preserving flowers for centuries, and it is still a lot of fun. And though flower presses are widely available, a simple press is easy and inexpensive to improvise at home. Just remove the blooms and leaves from their stems, then arrange the plant material on a sheet of porous paper. Make sure you allow an adequate amount of space between plants. Cover the plants with another sheet of paper then position the pages inside a heavy book. Open the book every few weeks to check the drying process.

Designers: Heidi Tyline King &
Nancy Worrell

Designer: Cynthia Gillooly

CURTAIN TIEBACKS

You don't need a fancy floral arrangement to make a big impact with dried flowers in your home. These darling little bouquets can be tucked anywhere (even displayed in a small vase). Here, they are coupled with decorative cording to serve as unique curtain tiebacks. Of course, substitute dried flowers as you wish to make bouquets that coordinate with your decor.

MATERIALS AND TOOLS

Dried flowers
Scissors
Floral tape
Cording

WHAT TO DO

1 The best way to form these bouquets is to begin with the central flower, the gardenia. Holding the gardenia in one hand, position dried miniature red roses in an uneven number around the gardenia. Because it will be viewed only from one side, don't worry about how the bouquet looks from the back; of course, do consider the back side if you have different plans for your bouquet.

2 Finish the bouquet by adding blue statice, then artemisia until you are satisfied with the design.

3 Cut the ends of the stems to the desired length, then wrap the stems with floral tape. Tie curtain back and tuck bouquet behind knotted cording.

PRETTY-IN-PINK BOUQUET

Dried flowers may not be the traditional choice for wedding parties, but they certainly can be lovely, and—unlike their hothouse counterparts—they'll make a lasting keepsake. Tucked into a simple glass vase, this stunning bouquet will serve as an endearing reminder of a special day, as well as a graceful means of beautifying any coffee table or mantel.

MATERIALS AND TOOLS

Large flower to serve as the bouquet's center, 1 per bouquet
Assorted dried flowers in varying shades of two colors (We used pinks and creams.)
Scissors
Floral tape
Hot-glue gun and glue sticks
2½-inch-wide (8 cm) wire-edged ribbon in color that matches flowers, approximately 2 yards (1.8 m) per bouquet
Wide glass vase

The view from above

WHAT TO DO

1 Trim all the flower stalks to about 9 inches (23 cm) long. Then separate the flowers into piles by color and type.

2 Start with the large flower that will be at the center of the bouquet. Place a ring of flowers in a contrasting color around the center flower. Secure the flowers by wrapping a bit of floral tape around their stems, near the top.

3 Place a row of flowers in the first color (the color of the center flower) around the row you just taped in place, positioning their blooms just below the blooms in the first row. Tape their stems as before.

4 Continue adding rows of flowers in alternating colors, placing each successive row just slightly below the one before it, until you're happy with the size of your bouquet. Wrap the entire bunch of stems, from top to bottom, with several turns of floral tape.

5 Trim the bottom of the stems so that the bouquet will fit in vase.

6 To make the loops of ribbon that surround the bouquet, fold the ribbon into a half bow under the flowers, holding the ribbon in place with one hand while continuing to make half-bow loops all the way around the stems. Secure the looped ribbon in place with floral tape and cut the end of the ribbon.

7 Wrap the remaining ribbon around the stem starting at the top and securing it with a dab of hot glue. Wrap the ribbon all the way down the stem, and glue the bottom in place. If desired, you can go back to the bouquet and attach additional buds with a little hot glue.

8 Allow the glue to dry completely; then place the bouquet in the glass vase, or head down the aisle with it!

Designer: Joan K. Morris

Raffia Garland

Bunches of raffia are knotted together to create an appealing swag that can be as thick or as long as you want it to be. This garland measures 10 feet (9 m)— a great length for draping around doors or large windows.

Materials and Tools

Package of raffia
4 yards (3.6 m) sheer organza ribbon, 2 inches (5 cm) wide
Bunch of dried German statice

Bunch of dried purple annual statice
16 dried roses
1½ yard (1.4 m) wired satin ribbon, 1 inch (2.5 cm) wide

Hot-glue gun
Floral tape

What To Do

1 Measure the length of the area where you would like to hang the swag. Separate the raffia and gather strands together into the desired thickness, then tie the lengths together in knots until the desired length is achieved.

2 Thread organza ribbon through the raffia; tie to the raffia at intervals to secure.

3 You will need to make a bouquet for every raffia knot in your swag. Here, we've alternated large and small bouquets. Make the large bouquets by arranging the dried flowers into three bouquets of seven to nine stems and securing the stems with floral tape. Secure the large bouquets at the raffia knots by inserting the stem into the knots, then tying at the base of bouquet with loose strands of raffia. Finish off by tying each large bouquet with a knotted bow made with ½ yard (.45 m) of the 1-inch (2.5 cm) ribbon.

4 Make the small bouquets by hot-gluing five to seven stems of flowers in a pleasing arrangement directly to every other knot.

Designer Tip

Stored and used properly, dried flowers will last a long time. That being said, a little extra effort can prolong them even longer. To preserve and protect your dried flower treasures, spray them lightly either with a coat of clear plastic spray (available at craft or paint stores) or with regular hairspray.

Designer: Cynthia Gillooly

ELEGANT NATURAL WREATH

Sometimes inspiration can come when you least expect it. This designer found some lovely braided silk cording with tassels and used the rich color palette as a springboard for this charming dried-flower wreath.

MATERIALS AND TOOLS

Grapevine wreath base
2 lengths of braided cording with tassels
Hot-glue gun
4 dried pinecone gardenias
9 dried red roses
1 small bunch of dried protea
1 small bunch of dried German statice
1 small bunch of dried annual statice
Spanish and green moss

DESIGNER TIP

Here are some flower varieties that dry well: blue and red salvia, cockscomb, strawflower, lavender, globe amaranth, pansy, statice, rose, hydrangea, larkspur, marigold, zinnia, artemisia, pearly everlasting, and Queen Anne's lace. Although these are great beginnings, experiment to see what surprises different flowers can reveal when dried.

WHAT TO DO

1 Tie the braided cording onto the wreath base; tie one length on the top left and the other on the bottom right, using the photograph as a guide.

2 First, create a focal point at the top left. Hot-glue gardenias, roses, and protea around the cording in a pleasing arrangement, then fill in with small sprigs of German statice and annual statice.

3 Repeat Step 2 around the cording at the bottom right of the wreath. Once the focal points have been established, fill in the wreath by hot-gluing small sprigs of Spanish and green moss, taking care to leave some of the natural base visible.

Designer: Cynthia Gillooly

DRIED FLOWER GALLERY

Right: Single blooms of pressed flowers can be purchased inexpensively and used to decorate a variety of items, from greeting cards to candles. Designers: Allison Smith and Terry Taylor

Below right: Pussy willow branches form a lovely base for spring blooms. As the flowers fade, replace them with summer blooms. Designer: Josena Aiello-Bader

Below left: A straw hat makes a creative base for dried flower blooms. Wear it in the garden or hang it on a bedroom wall. Designer: Vicki Baker

Opposite page, top left: Foam balls in different sizes were covered with strawflowers using a glue gun. Designer: Terry Taylor

Opposite page, top right: Add a special touch to your correspondence with pressed flowers. A drop of fragrant oil can be added for a subtle scent. Designer: Nicole Tuggle

Opposite page, below: Tie stems of dried flowers, greenery, or pressed blooms into a sheer bow and you have a magical gift box. Designer: Molly Sieburg (box design by Patrice Tappe)

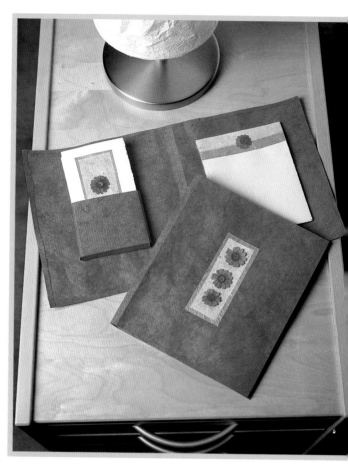

SILK FLOWERS

Colorful and natural-looking artificial flowers, fruits, vegetables, grasses, and foliage are readily available, often in abundant supply, at craft- and art-supply stores. Though rarely made of real silk, all artificial plants are referred to as "silks." Silks are a joy to work with, because silk arrangements are long-lasting, can be re-created at the designer's whim, and the finished arrangements require very little care.

MATERIALS AND TOOLS

FLORAL FOAM/POLYSTYRENE
Use porous, green floral foam (soaked in water) as a stabilizing base when combining silks with fresh flowers. Use only dry, gray or green floral foam when working exclusively with silks. Polystyrene is a less-expensive option and works very well with materials attached to floral picks; it is not a good choice for dried or delicate stems.

FLORAL PICKS
Floral picks are used to give support to delicate stems, to lengthen stems, and to connect several stems. That said, picks may not be necessary for all silks, since many silk flowers are sold already wired.

FLORAL PINS
These U-shaped pins (also called U pins or moss pins) are indispensable in securing moss and ribbon to the base material as well as in attaching silks to straw or foam bases.

FLORAL TAPE
Floral tape, also called stem wrap, is handy for securing floral foam to containers, binding together several pieces of foam, and, when used with floral wire (see below), extending stems. The key to working with floral tape is pulling the tape taut as you wrap it; this makes the tape sticky, and thus allows for a secure hold.

FLORAL WIRE
Floral wire comes in a variety of gauges and colors, and is used chiefly to extend and strengthen stems, though it is also useful in attaching flowers and foliage to wreaths, swags, and topiaries.

FLOWER FROGS/STABILIZERS
Flower frogs, which come in a variety of shapes and sizes, stabilize flowers at the bottom of an arrangement when floral foam is not being used. Use adhesive clay to secure the frog at the base. For a translucent container or vase, consider using marbles, pieces of glass, stones, or another filler that will both stabilize stems and add character to the design. To create the illusion of water, acrylic water is available in craft and floral supply stores and also serves as a stabilizer.

HOT-GLUE GUN
This crafter's mainstay is essential to the silk-flower designer. Use hot glue to affix flowers to bases and to make repairs to individual silks. A slow-drying gun works well for silk-flower design, since it allows the designer time to reposition flowers as needed.

WIRE CUTTERS

Because most silk flowers have a wire running the length of the stem (for stability and to aid in manipulating the blooms), you will need a sturdy pair of wire cutters to make necessary adjustments. (Scissors can be used to cut very thin or unwired stems.)

BASES

Commercially prepared bases or forms are useful when creating topiaries, swags, and wreaths, and are usually made of straw, grapevine, floral foam, or polystyrene. Of course you can make your own, though most designers find purchased bases are worth the minimal expense.

CONTAINERS

Just about any container can be used for silk-flower arrangements, from ceramic vases to terra-cotta pots to baskets. Choose a container that best suits the style of the particular arrangement. Use your imagination—since a silk-flower arrangement doesn't need to hold water, the possibilities are limitless.

BASIC TECHNIQUES

Sometimes the best designs begin with an interesting container; on the other hand, a selection of gorgeous silks is also a grand start. Whatever your inspiration, a little preparation will help a great deal.

1 Use a serrated knife to cut floral foam or polystyrene to fit inside the container. For vertical arrangements, the foam should fall just below the rim of the container. For arrangements with cascading elements, the foam should extend several inches above the container. Floral foam can often be wedged securely in place, though floral tape or hot glue may also be used, if necessary.

2 If the foam and/or floral tape will be visible in the finished piece, secure moss to the foam with floral pins or hot glue. (These components can be disguised later with well-positioned flowers.) Spray the moss slightly with water and press down with fingers, if desired, to achieve a snug fit.

3 Choose the flowers and other elements for the design and position materials on the work surface. For a more pleasing arrangement, use materials with a variety of textures, colors, and shapes. Experimenting with combinations of silk materials is the fun part!

4 Make sure the stems will fit securely into the floral foam or polystyrene. Delicate flowers, as well as large, top-heavy flowers, most likely will require additional support. For double-wired stems, separate the wires with scissors to form a fork. If necessary, affix wire with floral tape or use floral picks to create additional support for single-wired stems.

CONTAINER ARRANGEMENTS

Having an infinite number of container possibilities is one of the biggest advantages to working with silks. This may also save you time and money, since you probably already have the perfect vessel in your house or garden!

1 Establish the approximate dimensions of the arrangement—the height, width, and shape—by inserting several larger stems to form a framework. In general, flowers should be about 1½ times as tall as the container, though this is certainly not written in stone. Dip stems in craft glue before inserting them into base. If you are using very thick branches or stems, use an awl or other sharp tool to make a hole in the foam, then insert the stem.

2 Beginning with the central elements and focal flowers, and ending with filler materials, gradually fill in the arrangement with the remaining flowers and foliage. Turn the base as you work to make sure the piece looks good from every side. Position plants on different planes and manipulate the flower heads so that they face a variety of angles.

3 Stand back from the arrangement and see where adjustments or additions need to be made. Turn any visible wire spines away from the front side, or wrap stems with floral tape for a more authentic look. (Nothing gives away an artificial flower like an exposed wire.) If necessary, hot-glue individual flowers to the arrangement to conceal empty spaces.

DESIGNER TIP

Naturalize silk arrangements by combining silk flowers with dried or real flowers and foliage. Including scented fresh flowers, in particular, lends authenticity to silk designs. When the fresh plants have withered, just replace them, or substitute another variety, dried blooms, or more silks to create a completely different design.

DESIGNER TIP

To create a bouquet-style arrangement that looks like it was just gathered from the garden, position the flowers with the largest, most prominent flowers or greenery. Holding these stems in one hand, insert other flowers, foliage, and filler material, adjusting and bending the stems as you work to create a natural appearance. Connect all the stems with a rubber band or floral tape, then place entire bouquet in a vase.

309

Spring Arrangement

Have a touch of spring fever in January? Here's a cure for even the most severe case: bright blooms in a darling spring arrangement. Instant gratification!

Materials and Tools

Basket
Floral foam
Hot-glue gun
Floral tape

Moss
Floral pins
Assorted spring silks
Craft glue

What To Do

1 Use a serrated knife to cut floral foam to fit inside and extend 2 inches (5 cm) above the top of the basket. Use hot glue or floral tape to secure the foam. Disguise the top of the foam with moss and secure with floral pins.

2 Plan the design and gather silk materials. Here we've used irises, lilies, daffodils, narcissus blooms, roses, and a variety of smaller blooms and filler materials. Look for spring flowers with a variety of shapes, colors, and textures. Attach floral picks to flowers, if necessary. Wrap wire stems with floral tape for a more authentic look.

3 Begin the design. Remembering that the arrangement should be about 1½ times the height of your basket, establish the dimensions of the design by inserting the central and focal flowers. Use floral picks, floral pins, or hot glue (whichever method is most suitable for each piece) to secure flowers to the foam. Position the flowers on a variety of planes. Dip floral picks in craft glue before inserting into floral foam.

4 Turning the basket as you work and beginning with the largest elements, fill in with the rest of the flowers. Position some flowers and leaves so that they spill over the edge of the basket. Continue to position silk materials until you are pleased with the arrangement from every side.

Designer: Cynthia Gillooly

Designer: Susan McBride

GARDEN-FRESH ARRANGEMENTS

Each of these baskets is made with a lovely combination of purple and yellow flowers, and each looks as if its contents have been just gathered from the garden. The flowers are different in each basket, demonstrating the flexibility of silk materials, as well as the subtle effects created by using different types of flowers and foliage. More random—and less symmetrical—arrangements of this sort make for pleasantly casual designs.

MATERIALS AND TOOLS

White painted baskets with handles
Floral foam
Hot-glue gun
Floral tape
Assorted silk flowers and foliage
Craft glue

DESIGNER TIP

Although high-quality silks can be expensive, they last a long time, and there is very little waste. Stems that have been cut too short can be "regenerated" by attaching a floral pick or a length of floral wire to the stem and wrapping with floral tape. Keep any unused blooms, leaves, stems, and plant pieces to use in a later design. Sometimes pieces can be hot-glued to empty spaces in an arrangement (on a wreath, for example) to cleverly fill a troublesome void.

WHAT TO DO

1 Use a serrated knife to cut floral foam to fit inside each basket. Use hot glue or floral tape to secure the foam.

2 Plan the design and gather silk materials. Here we've used an assortment of purple flowers (hydrangeas, larkspur, snapdragons, delphinium, heather, lilacs) and yellow flowers (yarrow), filling in with a wonderful variety of greenery, including ruffled bells of Ireland, spikes of ornamental grasses, and other foliage.

3 Attach floral picks to flowers, and wrap wire stems with floral tape, if necessary, for a more authentic look.

4 Begin the design. Remembering that the arrangement should be about 1½ times the height of your baskets, establish the dimensions of the design by inserting the central and focal flowers.

5 Use floral picks, floral pins, or hot glue (whichever method is most suitable for each piece) to

secure flowers to the foam. Position the flowers on a variety of planes. Dip floral picks in craft glue before inserting into floral foam.

6 Beginning with the largest elements, fill in with the rest of the flowers and filler material, turning the baskets as you work. Position some flowers and leaves so that they spill over the edge of the basket and conceal any exposed foam. Continue to position silk materials until you are pleased with the arrangement from every side.

SILK-FLOWER GIFT DECORATIONS

Use leftover silk flowers and individual leaves to fashion super-easy, super-impressive gift decorations. Even the simplest designs have amazing impact when they feature a strong floral element. Covering the entire top surface of the package with smaller blooms can also make for a lovely presentation.

MATERIALS AND TOOLS

Paper or gift wrap
Raffia, ribbon, or twine
Assorted silks
Scissors
Hot-glue gun

WHAT TO DO

1 Wrap the gift. Here we've used white paper to provide a nice contrast to the silk flowers. Craft paper or any gift wrap will work, though do try to choose a color or design that coordinates with your silks.

2 Tie raffia, twine, or ribbon around the present. Center the raffia (or other material) across the top of the package, wind around to the back side and twist, then bring around to the front again and knot. For the sunflower package here, we tied an additional length of raffia around the knot and fluffed the material for a more dramatic effect.

3 Remove the stem of the silk flower and hot-glue the flower to the center of the package.

4 If desired, position and hot-glue leaves to the design as well. If you are using ivy or any other trailing silk material, wrap stem around the tied material, hot-gluing in spots to secure, and allow ends to spill over edge of package.

314

Designer: Megan Kirby

Designer: Susan McBride

ROSE PILLOW

Here's a terrific way to give a tired old throw pillow a lively update. You can cover the entire front surface of the pillow with the same type of silk bloom (as we've done here), choose an assortment of flowers, or use individual flowers to embellish a favorite pillow (which works especially well with garden-themed fabrics).

MATERIALS AND TOOLS

23 silk roses, approximately 3½ inches (9 cm) in diameter (or enough for your chosen design)
Scissors or wire cutters
12- x 12-inch (30.5 x 30.5cm) pillow
Hot-glue gun or needle and transparent thread

WHAT TO DO

1 Remove the roses from their stems with scissors or wire cutters. Trim the backs of the flowers and remove any plastic backing so that flowers will sit flat against the pillow.

2 Determine how the flowers will be positioned on the pillow. If you are covering the entire surface, make sure you have plenty of flowers. Laying the blooms out on your work surface (just as you would on the pillow) is a good way to plan the design and to see if you have enough materials.

3 To hot-glue the blooms to the pillow, simple apply glue to the underside of the flower (either in the center of the flower or on the petals), position flower on the pillow, and press firmly in place until glue sets. If you are sewing the flowers, skip to Step 4.

4 If desired, hand-sew the flowers to the pillow with transparent thread. Note: It's a good idea to use a thimble when hand-sewing.

DESIGNER TIP

Silk-flower arrangements require very little maintenance, though you should try to keep them out of direct sunlight, which will eventually fade the colors. Dust will eventually collect on silks, so dust them regularly, either by hand or with a blow dryer on a low setting. Silks that have become wrinkled or misshapen can be usually be manipulated back into shape by hand, although steam-ironing on a low setting also works well. Commercial sprays designed for cleaning silks are also available and are quite effective.

VEGETABLE BASKET

There's no need to settle for a vegetable harvest that doesn't last. Many silk and artificial vegetables look remarkably authentic, and a handsome basket filled with a varied selection makes for a charming centerpiece.

MATERIALS AND TOOLS

Basket
Floral foam
Hot-glue gun
Floral tape
Straw

Floral pins
Assorted silk vegetables
Twine
Craft glue

WHAT TO DO

1 Use a serrated knife to cut floral foam to fit inside and extend 2 inches (5 cm) above the top of the basket. Use hot glue, floral tape, or florist's frogs to secure the foam. Cover the top of the foam with straw and attach the straw with hot glue and/or floral pins.

2 Plan the design and gather the silk materials. Here we've chosen vegetables in a variety of colors, shapes, and textures: eggplant, potatoes, carrots, radishes, scallions, asparagus, green beans, peas, tomatoes, onions, squashes. Tie twine around vegetables (asparagus and scallions were used here) to create groupings, if desired.

3 Determine how the vegetables will be attached to the foam. Some will have picks already attached; for those that do not,

either affix floral picks or use a hot-glue gun to secure items to the foam. Wrap wire stems with floral tape.

4 Begin the design. Remembering that the arrangement should be about 1½ times the height of your basket, establish the dimensions of the design by inserting the larger vegetables. Position the focal vegetables on a variety of planes. Dip floral picks and stems in craft glue before inserting into floral foam to secure.

5 Beginning with the largest elements, fill in with the rest of the vegetables, turning the basket as you work. If any of the silk vegetables have attached foliage, position these so that the leaves spill over the edge of the basket. Continue to position vegetables until you are pleased with the arrangement from every side.

Designer: Cynthia Gillooly

SILK FLOWER GALLERY

Right: Transform an ordinary cake into an extraordinary celebration with a few stems of silk blooms arranged in a bouquet. Designer: Cathy Barnhardt

Below: Welcome spring with a whimsical wreath of silk blooms. Designer: Susan Partain

Opposite page, top left: Welcome visitors with a simple bouquet of silk hydrangea blooms arranged in a stiffened doily container. Designer: Susan McBride

Opposite page, top right: These leaf-wrapped posies make a quick, thoughtful gift. Designer: Susan McBride

Opposite page, bottom: Grace your bed frame with an everlasting rose garland for the sweetest dreams ever. Designer: Joann Handley

PAPER CRAFTS

It started in kindergarten, with a tiny pair of scissors and a stack of colored paper. Somewhere along the way, though, you became too "grown up" for paper crafts. Or so you thought. As you'll see in this chapter, decoupage, memory cards, scrapbooking, and stamping have raised paper crafts to new levels of sophistication.

DECOUPAGE

You learned the skills you need for decoupage in kindergarten: cutting and pasting. Though the techniques are basic, you can create amazingly sophisticated and long-lasting decorative items and works of art with a few simple tools and your imagination.

MATERIALS AND TOOLS

CUTOUTS
Once you start looking for paper scraps and printed images to use in decoupage, you will quickly have a large supply. Keep a box or storage container handy and deposit any potential scraps. Use a photocopy machine or a scanner to enlarge or reduce images or to make color images black and white. The lighter-weight the paper, the better the results usually are.

ADHESIVES
A number of adhesives can be used in decoupage, including PVA (white) glue, wallpaper paste, wood glue, and spray adhesive. Which type you use depends on the cutout being applied and the surface you're applying it to. Often, PVA glue is a good choice.

PAINT
Consider the object that will be painted when choosing paint for your project. Decorative painting and decoupage often go hand in hand, and the painting techniques you choose can be as complicated or as simple as you wish.

PAINTBRUSHES
Available in a variety of sizes and widths, paintbrushes are very useful in applying glue, paint, and varnish. Use clean, high-quality brushes to minimize stray hairs or bristles getting caught in paint or varnish.

VARNISHES
Polyurethane varnishes work well on wood surfaces; in addition, varnishes are sold that create a colored, tinted, or crackled surface. Use the varnish that best suits the material that is being coated, and always read the manufacturer's instructions before using. Water-based varnishes will not affect the color of the piece, while oil-based varnishes impart a yellowish color. PVA glue acts as a varnish as well.

PAPER SEALER
Print fixative spray, shellac, and white French polish (sometimes called button polish) are a few of the paper sealers that prevent paper cutouts from discoloring. This step, while not always essential, also helps give structure and durability to flimsy or poor-quality papers.

SCISSORS/CRAFT KNIFE
Sometimes scissors work best to cut out decoupage scraps, while a craft knife is useful for cutting very straight lines or detail work. Make sure your craft knife has a very sharp blade and that you use a mat or piece of cardboard to protect the work surface. Small manicure or embroidery scissors (again, with a very sharp blade) are good tools for cutting out small pieces.

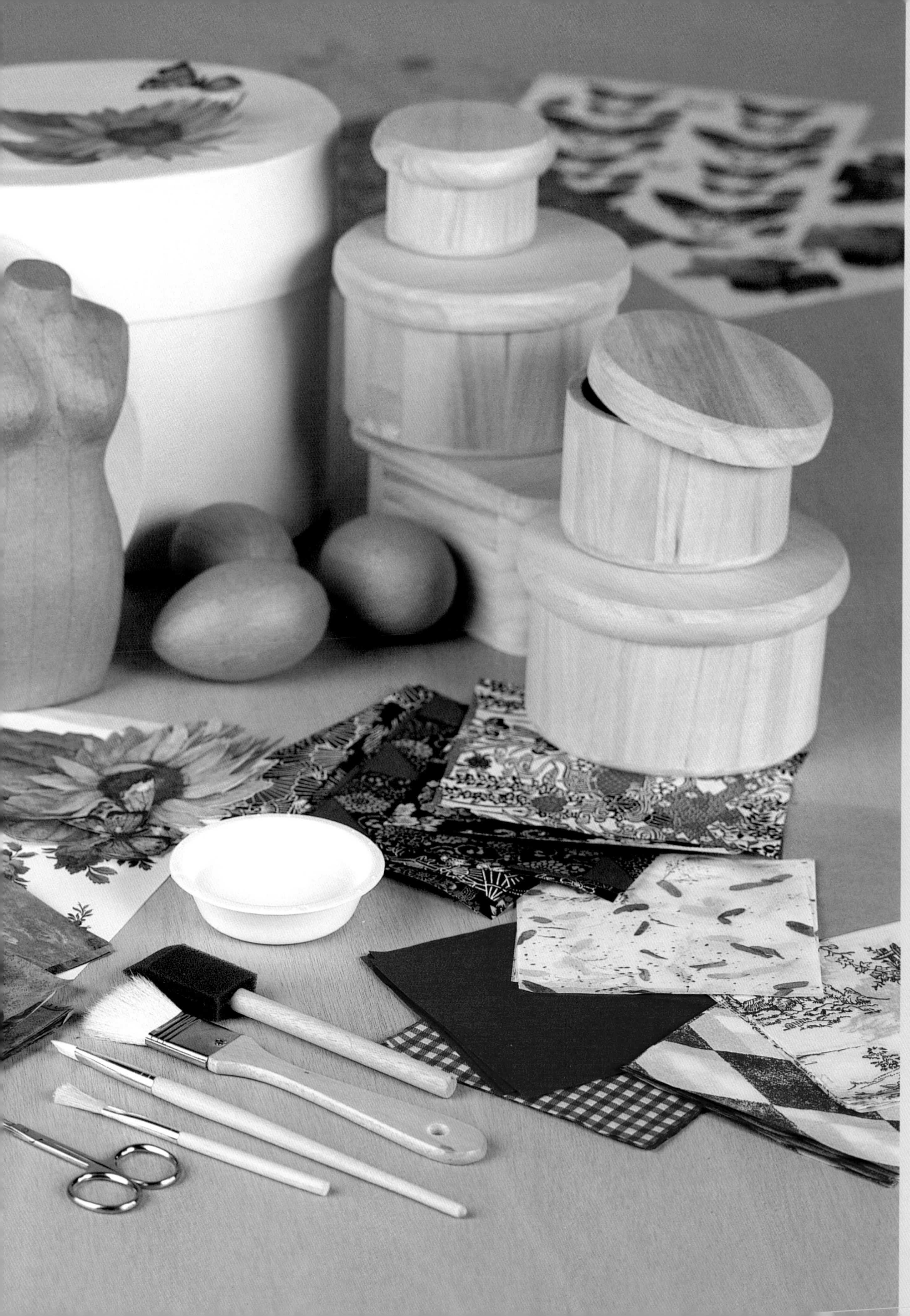

BASIC TECHNIQUES

A hard surface made of just about anything—metal, wood, ceramic, or paper, to name only a few—is suitable for decoupage. As you become more experienced with this craft, you will find the process of applying cutouts to found objects (rescuing them, if you will) very pleasing.

1 Thoroughly clean the surface of the object to be decoupaged with a mild detergent and warm water, and allow to dry. If using a metal object, remove rust with steel wool, then wash surface with a solution of half vinegar and half water. Clean and sand wood surfaces and fill any holes with wood putty.

2 Prime or seal the object. Any porous object will need to be sealed with a sealant or varnish. Wood surfaces will need to be primed (for painting) or sealed (for projects in which you want the wood to show). Metal surfaces will need a primer coat; a coat of rust-proofing sealant is an optional step. Apply gesso, if desired.

3 Paint the object, if desired. Usually, several coats of paint are necessary. Sand lightly between coats. Lightly sand the surface of the object one last time with fine sandpaper so that cutouts will adhere more easily.

Your decoupage project is only as interesting as the cutouts you choose. Wrapping paper, photocopies from books, magazine images, and even stickers and fabric scraps can result in terrific, one-of-a-kind decoupage designs.

1 Use scissors to cut the paper into manageable sizes, then use smaller scissors or a craft knife to cut out the shapes. To avoid white edges that may show in the final piece, cut at a slight angle.

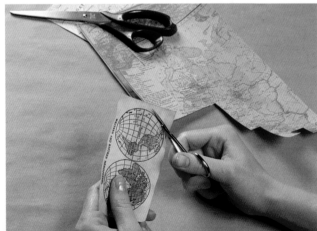

326

2 Determine how the cutouts will be positioned on the surface of the object and arrange on the work surface. This is easy when using a flat surface, and more challenging with curved surfaces.

APPLYING THE CUTOUTS & FINISHING

Sometimes you will find that randomly applying cutouts is the most fun, although it always makes sense to put a little thought into the design before you begin to glue. An adhesive with a longer drying time will make it easier to rearrange cutouts as you work.

1 Apply adhesive. Spread glue with a paintbrush onto the base surface (not to the underside of the cutout). Spray adhesive should be sprayed directly on the cutout, using a piece of scrap paper underneath to protect the work surface.

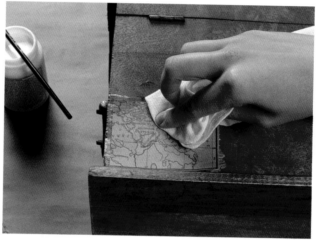

2 Press the cutout down on the surface and rub firmly from the center to the outside with a clean, soft cloth. Try to remove any air bubbles as you apply pressure. Allow adhesive to dry, then wipe off any excess glue with a warm, wet cloth. (Note: Follow manufacturer's guidelines for glue drying times, as some glue dries very quickly and some very slowly.)

3 Apply varnish in thin, even strokes, according to manufacturer's instructions. Allow to dry thoroughly, then apply additional layers of varnish, if desired. Once varnish has dried, you can consider your decoupage project to be complete. Apply any additional finishes, such as antique wax or crackle finish, last.

GARDEN DECOUPAGE DINNER PLATE

Look at that stack of lovely paper napkins leftover from your garden tea party. Don't you wish you had a set of dishes in that pattern? Wish no more.

MATERIALS AND TOOLS

Clear glass plate
Floral-printed paper dinner napkins
Scissors
Glass cleaner

Paper towels or lint-free cloth
Light-colored scrap paper
Decoupage medium, matte finish
Flat paintbrush, 1 inch (2.5 cm) wide

Flat paintbrush, 2 inches (5 cm) wide
White or cream-colored glass paint
Clear aerosol varnish

WHAT TO DO

1 Cut the flowers and other attractive images or text from the napkins. Experiment with their arrangement on the plate as you go to refine the layout you'll use and to determine how many cutout images you'll need.

2 Place the light-colored scrap paper on your work surface (you'll need a light background to work on so you can see how your design will look.) Wipe your plate clean—front and back—with glass cleaner and a paper towel or lint-free cloth. Then place the plate on the scrap paper, face down.

3 Your napkin images may be several layers thick, but for maximum transparency, you'll just need the upper printed layer. Peel away the other layers just before you're ready to begin gluing the images in place.

4 Select an area on the back of the plate to begin decoupaging.

Keep in mind that you're essentially working in reverse—the images at the forefront of the design should be applied first. (For the plate shown, for instance, the cluster of flowers at the center was applied first; then the text image was added "on top" of it.)

5 Using the 1-inch-wide paintbrush, apply a thin, even layer of decoupage medium over an area of the plate just slightly larger than the image you're about to place. Carefully position the napkin image with the image side facing the glue. Use your fingers to lightly press the napkin to the surface, creating a secure bond and smoothing out any wrinkles or bubbles. Apply another layer of decoupage medium over the back of the napkin, sealing it in place.

6 Repeat Step 5 until your design is complete, allowing the decoupage medium to dry between each paper application. If you find

it difficult to work in reverse, lift the plate by its edges and turn it toward you to check the image placement.

7 After you've completed the collage, use the 2-inch-wide brush to apply a thin but even layer of white or cream-colored glass paint to entire back of the plate. Allow the paint to dry. Then, working in a well-ventilated area and following the manufacturer's instructions, spray the back of the plate with varnish. If you choose to apply additional coats of varnish, be sure to allow the previous coats to dry first.

- Milk
- Cat food
- Bakery
- Tea

Jeff's dent.
appt.
2:15 Thur

Rebecca's recit
7:30 Friday

MAGNETIC DECOUPAGE

Finally, refrigerator magnets that are just as wonderful as the prized drawings and photographs they hold. Because they're made from clear glass and decoupage paper, you can create a set of magnets to fit a theme, match a room, or complement a personality. Go ahead—express yourself!

MATERIALS AND TOOLS

Clear glass half-marbles
Decoupage papers
Decoupage medium, matte and gloss finish
Epoxy glue
Flat paintbrush, 1 inch (2.5 cm) wide

Fine-tip artist's paintbrush
Glass cleaner
Paper towels or a lint-free cloth
Fixed-blade craft knife
Sponge brush, 1 inch (2.5 cm) wide
¼-inch (6 mm) circular magnets

WHAT TO DO

1 Cut the selected images out of the decoupage paper with scissors, allowing a generous border on all sides. A square of decoupage paper that's 2 x 2 inches (5 cm) accommodates both large and small half-marbles. Make sure the picture or pattern you want to show through the half-marble is in the center of the square.

2 The quality of the half-marbles varies greatly, even within the same package, so discard those that are cracked, scratched, or have large bubbles in the glass. Clean the flat surface of one half-marble with glass cleaner and a paper towel or lint-free cloth.

3 Dip the flat brush into the matte decoupage medium and apply a thin, even coat to the flat surface of the half-marble. Place the marble on the center of one paper square. Lift the marble and paper off your work surface and squeeze them together to distribute the decoupage medium. Check the position of the image and make any small adjustments in the paper's placement, taking care not to cause wrinkles or tears. Let the glue dry completely. Repeat this process for all the marbles, letting them completely dry before proceeding to Step 4.

4 Use scissors or the craft knife to trim away the excess paper from the marble. Because they have a curved surface, it's easy to make a close cut that's slightly underneath the outer edge of the glass. With the fine-tip paint-brush, re-glue any paper edges as needed. Allow this glue to dry.

5 With the sponge brush paint a thin topcoat of gloss-finish decoupage medium over the back of the paper. The glue acts as a varnish and gives the back of the magnets a nice finish. Allow the glue to completely dry.

6 Glue the magnets to the paper-backed glass with a few drops of epoxy, then hold them firmly together until the epoxy forms a tight bond.

Designer: Marthe Le Van

DECOUPAGE EGGS

Even the humble paper napkin can be used in decoupage to create something out of the ordinary: in this case, an assortment of papier-mâché eggs. Though we've used egg shapes in a variety of sizes, this technique can be used on items with just about any surface, in any size or shape.

MATERIALS AND TOOLS

Papier-mâché eggs (wood or foam
  eggs can be substituted)
Acrylic paint
Paintbrush
Floral paper napkins
Scissors
Gloss decoupage glue
1-inch (2.5 cm) foam brush
Clear spray varnish, gloss or satin
  finish (optional)

WHAT TO DO

1 Paint all of the eggs a background color of your choice. White or other pale colors work well. Allow paint to completely dry.

2 Most paper napkins consist of several layers: a top layer with the design, and one or two white layers underneath. Carefully remove all of the bottom (unpatterned) napkin layers. Determine which of the napkin's flower designs you would like to use on the eggs, and tear or cut out those designs. If you want the eggs to be completely covered, tear the napkin into strips.

3 Use a foam brush to apply decoupage glue to the egg in the area you would like to put a flower or a strip of napkin, then carefully position the piece of paper on the glued area. (If you are using strips, apply the strips to the egg parallel to each other and at an angle.) Use your fingertips or a clean cloth to smooth out any wrinkles, taking care not to tear the paper. Apply another layer of glue on top of the paper. Repeat this process over the entire surface of each egg, pausing occasionally to allow the glue to dry.

4 To give the eggs a protective finish, apply two or three coats of glue, or spray on a layer of clear varnish.

Designer: Joan K. Morris

Designer: Marthe Le Van

GIFT WRAP CHEST

Don't just throw your gift-wrapping gear in the back of the closet—store it in style. Simple wood chests can be had for very little money, although you may well have a suitable piece in your attic or basement. Choose themed papers—wedding, birthday, Christmas, and so forth—to help create a visual organization system.

MATERIALS AND TOOLS

Wooden chest with drawers
Wood putty and putty knife (optional)
Sandpaper
Clean cloth
Gloss latex paint
Paintbrush
Gift wrap
Scissors
Foam brush
Decoupage medium, matte or gloss finish
Cutting board
Craft knife
Acrylic craft paint (optional)

WHAT TO DO

1 Remove any drawer pulls on the chest. Following the putty manufacturer's instructions, fill any holes, splits, or knots with wood putty. Let the putty dry, then sand. (You will not need to fill the drawer pull holes, as they will be hidden.)

2 Sand the chest and the drawers, as needed, to smooth any rough surfaces, uneven edges, or seams. Wipe the surface of chest and drawers with a clean cloth.

3 Use a paintbrush to apply gloss latex paint in the color of your choice to the chest and the sides of the drawers. Paint as many coats as necessary to achieve the desired color saturation and gloss level, allowing paint to dry thoroughly between coats.

4 Determine which areas of the gift wrap you would like to use for the drawer front. Measure the dimensions of the drawer, then cut a section from the gift wrap to a size that is slightly larger than the size of the drawer. Repeat this step until you have a piece of gift wrap for each drawer.

5 Lightly dip the foam brush into the decoupage medium, then spread a very thin and even coat of medium over the entire surface of a drawer front.

6 Carefully position a piece of gift wrap so that it completely covers the drawer front. Use your fingers to carefully smooth the paper to remove any air bubbles. Set aside drawer to dry. Repeat Steps 5 and 6 until all the drawer fronts are covered.

7 Turn the drawers upside down on top of a cutting board and carefully trim the excess gift wrap with a very sharp craft knife.

8 Place the covered drawers back into the chest in a pleasing arrangement. If desired, use acrylic craft paints to cover any unfinished drawer edges.

DESIGNER TIP

One of the best sources for paper scraps is your mailbox. Postcards, catalogs, greeting cards, and all manner of junk mail are gold mines for colorful and interesting images. So before you discard the day's mail, consider its decoupage potential!

MAP CHEST

Decoupage a simple chest with an interesting shape and pretty hardware and watch it transform before your eyes. This project looks best when a large variety of maps are used. Maps are easy to find on the Internet and look great when reproduced on a color printer; old books and atlases from secondhand bookstores are also great sources.

MATERIALS AND TOOLS

Wood chest
Sandpaper or palm sander
Clean cloth
Assorted maps
Scissors
Foam brush
Decoupage medium, matte
   or gloss finish
Acrylic craft paint (optional)

DESIGNER TIP

Before applying cutouts to an object, try altering them for a more unique look. Tint black-and-white images with watercolor paint or colored pencils, or soak images in brewed tea to create a vintage, aged look.

WHAT TO DO

1 Remove any ornamentation on the chest that may interfere with the decoupage. (On this chest, the designer removed decorative metal strips and finish nails with pliers and wire cutters.)

2 Use sandpaper or a palm sander to smooth uneven edges or wood seams on the chest. Wipe the chest with a clean cloth.

3 Look at the maps you have collected and identify areas of visual interest. Cut the maps into squares or rectangles of various sizes. You can begin with a few pieces, then cut additional pieces as you work.

4 Work on one surface of the chest at a time, and begin with a piece that fits on one corner of the surface. Lightly dip the foam brush into the decoupage medium, spread a very thin and even coat of medium, then position the map piece. Use your fingers to smooth any wrinkles or air bubbles.

5 Select another map piece and attach it adjacent to the first, as described in Step 4. Continue to glue pieces to the chest in this manner, cutting additional pieces as needed,

until the first surface of the chest has been completely covered. Use small map pieces to cover any exposed wood. Continue to cover the rest of the chest, one surface at a time.

6 Paint any exposed wood edges with acrylic craft paint in a coordinating color, if desired.

Designer: Marthe Le Van

DECOUPAGE GALLERY

Above: Say "Happy Birthday!" in style with a gift box decoupaged with gift wrap papers. Designer: Maggie D. Jones

Right: Decoupaging with wallpaper? You bet! The techniques are the same and the results are fabulous. Designer: Lyna Farkas

Opposite page, top left: Light up an ordinary lamp shade with out-of-the-ordinary decoupage paper. (Sewing patterns were used here.) Designer: Ellen Zahorec

Opposite page, top right: This paper napkin decoupaged photo frame was finished with crackling medium to create a porcelain effect. Designer: Terry Taylor

Opposite page, bottom: Transform an old suitcase into a one-of-a kind travel companion with your favorite trip mementos. Designer: Ellen Zahorec

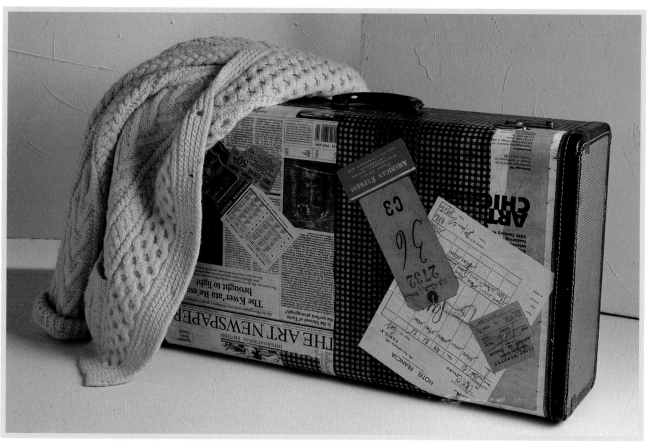

CARD MAKING

If you're a crafter looking for a new creative canvas, memory cards offer a fun way to explore the simple joy of the handcrafted gesture. With a multitude of possible materials and a few easy steps, you can honor cherished memories and create new ones with cards that will be treasured for years to come.

MATERIALS AND TOOLS

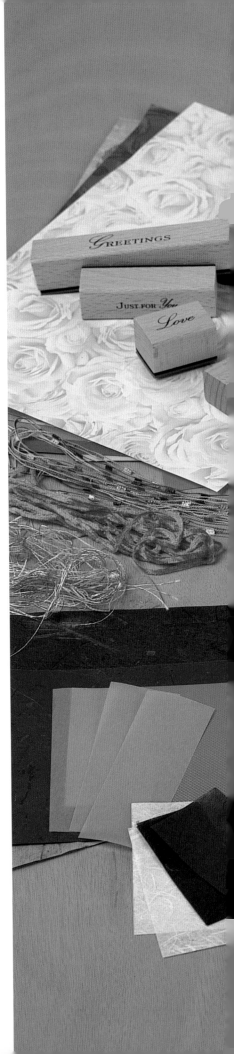

PAPER
The most essential material for card making, paper now comes in an astonishingly wide range of weights, colors, patterns, and textures.

GLUE
PVA (polyvinyl acetate) is the common white craft glue that dries clear and works well for almost any gluing job. Other options include glue sticks, spray adhesive, double-sided tape, and hot glue.

CRAFT KNIFE
Keep one of these at hand and replace the blades often to make a variety of precise, sharp cuts.

CUTTING MAT
Protect your work surface with a purchased self-healing cutting mat. When in a bind, an ordinary kitchen cutting board will suffice.

METAL RULER
A metal ruler provides necessary measuring guidelines while also serving as a straightedge for scoring and cutting.

SCISSORS
Besides the ordinary household scissors, there are also many paper edgers that can create interesting decorative effects—from a deckled edge to zigzags—on cards and collage materials.

HOLE & SHAPED PUNCHES
Use a common hole punch or shaped craft punches to create paper shapes for collage or negative space in a larger piece of paper.

BONE FOLDER
This inexpensive tool is invaluable in creating crisp folds and a flat, even finish to glued papers.

DECORATIVE ELEMENTS
Anything goes: junk jewelry, pressed flowers, hardware store finds, craft wire, fabric, eyelets, beads, buttons, photocopies, natural materials, ribbon, and so much more!

BASIC TECHNIQUES

Whether your glue of choice comes in a spray can, a stick, or a bottle, there is one method you should follow to glue materials to cards.

1 Lay the piece of paper on a scrap piece of paper, with the side that will be adhered facing up.

2 Brush, cover, or spray your adhesive on the entire paper surface, extending past the edges.

3 To seal the bond between the glued and dry surfaces (called burnishing), place a piece of scrap paper over the surface you have just glued, and press firmly along the entire area with a bone folder. The bone folder can alter the appearance of the paper it is burnishing, so the scrap paper provides a protective layer to keep you from damaging your card surface.

◆ Note: Be sure to use a fresh sheet of paper each time you are gluing to prevent sticky residue from transferring onto your new paper.

EMBELLISHING

The joy is in the details, especially when making cards. From decorative papers to photographs, fibers to three-dimensional objects, there is an infinite variety of eme-bellishment materials waiting to be transformed into a mailable piece of artwork. Leftover scraps from other craft projects and even ordinary household items can find new life in the small canvas of a card. The only limit is your own imagination.

MAKING A BLANK CARD

While blank cards are widely available, you may wish to create your own blank card to suit your own particular needs.

1 Decide what size card you would like to create, and cut a piece of card stock that measures twice that size. For example, if you wish to create a 4- x 5-inch (10 x 12.5 cm) card, cut a piece of card stock measuring 8 x 5 inches (20 x 12.5 cm) If you are making a card to fit in a premade envelope, it will need to be approximately ⅛ to ⅜ inch (3 to 9 mm) smaller than the envelope.

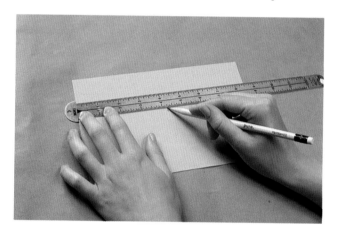

2 Lightly mark the midpoint on the inside of the card paper. Line up a ruler along this midpoint. Using a bone folder, score along this line from one end to the other. This breaks the top layer of paper fibers, making it easier to create a good fold.

3 Fold the card in half along the scored midpoint. Run the edge of the bone folder across the fold, pressing firmly.

◆ NOTE: You can add an interesting border to your card by cutting the front edge with a pair of decorative scissors or tear it along a deckle-edged ruler.

HANDLE WITH CARE: POSTAL TIPS

Now that you've spent your valuable time and creativity crafting a card, make sure that your card arrives at its destination safe and sound and in a timely manner. Handmade cards often use bulky, weighted materials and unconventional envelope sizes. Take the extra effort to protect your card. An extra layer of paper wrapped around the card before placing in an envelope can make all the difference. If you can, take your cards to the post office so that each item can be properly weighed and stamped as "fragile."

SETTING EYELETS

Eyelets make beautiful additions to hand-crafted cards. See page 369 in the Scrapbooking section for step-by-step instructions on setting eyelets.

BASIC TECHNIQUES

AGING MATERIALS WITH TEA AND COFFEE DYES

Create an antiqued look by dyeing fabric or paper using a very strong brew of tea or coffee. Add a teaspoon of vinegar to the dye solution to keep your dyed items from fading.

Chamomile tea results in a yellow color, while many fruit teas can create shades of orange and red. Black teas such as oolong or pekoe vary from brown to beige. Coffee creates a rich amber to dark brown effect.

Dip the paper or fabric in the dye, and let it sit for 20 to 60 minutes, depending on the darkness you want to achieve. If the color is not dark enough, return it to the solution. You can also paint on the dye solution for a more controlled effect. If the dye runs into an area where you don't want it, use a cottonball or tissue to soak up excess.

NOTE: The tannic acid in tea is not archival and eventually (after 30 years or so) it will degrade your work, as all acids will do. Coffee dyes should not degrade work for 75 to 100 years.

CUTTING WINDOWS

Windowed cards are easy to make and let you create all sorts of interesting special effects.

1 To make a window, first measure and mark the area you'd like open on the front side of your card.

2 Open the card up (so there's no chance you'll cut through the back side), and cut out the window with a craft knife. If you are having trouble getting smooth, clean cuts, switch to a new blade.

MAKING MULTILAYERED CARDS

Multilayered cards are a great way to showcase specialty papers such as vellums. When layering, be sure to choose papers that are distinctly different in color and/or texture for maximum effect.

1 To make a mulitlayered card, first make multiple blank cards with the same dimensions. Pierce holes about an inch (2.5 cm) from the edges of the fold line at top and bottom.

2 Align the cards so their right sides face up, then thread an embroidery needle with 12 inches (30 cm) of ribbon (or yarn, colored wire, embroidery floss, etc.). Insert the threaded needle through hole at the top edge of the card on the inside and bring it up on the outside of the card. Unthread the needle, then go back to the inside of the card and rethread the needle. Bring it up through the hole closest to the bottom edge and out on the front side.

3 Turn the card over and tie the ribbon ends in a bow.

COLORFUL CRAYON CARD

Die-cut paper shapes are available in most craft stores, and offer an easy, inexpensive foundation for card-making creativity. This card can be made with any long, symmetrical die-cut shape. Simply write your message on the reverse side to surprise any young recipient.

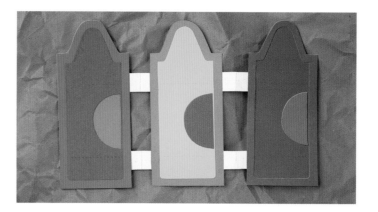

MATERIALS AND TOOLS

3 large crayon-shaped paper die cuts, approximately 5 inches (12.5 cm) long
3 pages of primary colored card stock
2 pieces of white card stock, measuring 1 x 7 inches (2.5 x 17 cm)
Ruler
Bone folder
Scissors
Craft brush
Clear-drying craft glue

WHAT TO DO

1 Cut three half circles approximately 2 inches (5 cm) in diameter in three different colors. Glue one half circle at the right middle side of each crayon shape. Set aside to dry.

2 Brush a thin layer of glue along the entire back side of one of the crayon shapes. Press down onto a sheet of card stock in a different color. Burnish the surface to remove any wrinkles or air bubbles. With a pencil, lightly draw a line approximately ¼ inch (6 mm) around the entire crayon shape, following the contours. Cut along the pencil line. Repeat with other two crayon shapes.

3 Glue down the center of one of the white strips of card stock along the back of one of the crayon shapes, ½ inch (12 mm) from bottom. Glue the center of the other white strip ½ inch from the top.

4 Glue the two left strap ends to the back side of a second crayon shape, leaving ¾ inch (19 mm) of white paper between the two

shapes. Glue the right two straps to the back side of the third crayon shape. Set aside to dry.

5 Using a bone folder, score the center point of each strap between each crayon shape. Fold along each score line. Fold again in the opposite direction so the card will fold upon itself with ease.

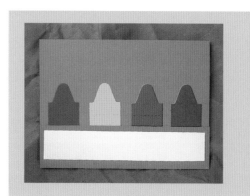

VARIATION

Glue smaller crayon-shaped die cuts onto a rectangular card to create a playful crayon-box effect.

To: Linnea and Gavin

Designer: Nicole Tuggle

HERITAGE CARDS

With a quick trip to a copy shop, old treasured photos can become rich raw materials for new keepsake cards. Whether they're snapshots of a family member from years ago or mysterious thrift store find, black-and-white photos honor the beauty and significance of our own past.

MATERIALS AND TOOLS

Purchased blank card
Color copy of vintage photo
Decorative paper scraps
Cotton muslin or vintage fabric
Wood veneer scrap
Found object
Clear-drying craft glue
Craft brush
Epoxy glue

KEEPSAKE ITEM CARD

Salvage a forgotten object (a key, locket, or watch face) and transform it into this card's centerpiece.

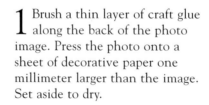

WHAT TO DO

1 Brush a thin layer of craft glue along the back of the photo image. Press the photo onto a sheet of decorative paper one millimeter larger than the image. Set aside to dry.

2 Apply a thin layer of glue to the back of a piece of cotton muslin or fabric remnant. Press down to the bottom right side of the card front.

3 Brush glue along a scrap of wood veneer or a long paper scrap and press down onto the left side of the card.

4 Add glue to the back of the framed photo image, then place onto the center point of the card. You may need to press the card under some heavy books to ensure that it adheres well and dries flat.

5 Glue the found object to a piece of thick paper, taking care not to let the glue seep out the sides. Set aside to dry.

6 Glue the thick piece of paper, object intact, onto another piece of paper 1 mm larger than the first to create a frame effect. Glue down to the left side of the photo.

◆ Note: Due to the extra weight of this card, you will need extra postage if mailing. You may also want to write "hand cancel" on your envelope to prevent the card from getting jammed in the postal machines.

348

memory (mem'o-ri), n. 1. Faculty of the mind by which it retains the knowledge of previous thoughts or events. 2. Thing remembered. [See MEMOIR.] [reminiscence; tradition. Syn. Recollection; remembrance;

Designer: Nicole Tuggle

OVAL CAMEO CARD

Recreate the timeless beauty of a treasured cameo with the simple addition of decorative beads and vintage buttons.

MATERIALS AND TOOLS

Purchased blank card
Color copy of oval-shaped vintage
  photo
Decorative paper
Pencil
Needle
Beading thread
Amber colored beads, 12
Waxed linen thread
Vintage buttons
Clear-drying glue
Craft brush

WHAT TO DO

1 Cut the photo image small enough to fit on the card, leaving enough room around the image for embellishment. Glue the image onto a sheet of slightly larger dark paper to create an attractive frame and strengthen the image for the embellishment process.

2 Carefully mark along the sides of the oval with a pencil where you would like the beads to go. Poke through each pencil mark with the needle so you can see where to thread the needle when you are working from the back of the image.

3 Thread the needle, leaving a substantial knot at the end. If needed, place a dot of glue onto the knot to hold. Move through the back side of the image, starting with the first hole. Once through the front, thread a single bead onto the thread, and then work the needle back through the same hole. Repeat until all the beads have been added. Knot the thread's end so it's secure. If needed, place a dot of glue onto the knot to hold.

4 Sew the vintage buttons to the top and bottom center points of the image, using waxed linen thread for an added decorative touch.

5 Apply a generous layer of glue to the back of the image and glue down onto a lighter piece of paper slightly larger than the first. This will help you hide the sewn side and knots. Glue the entire framed image onto the center point of the card.

◆ Note: Due to the delicate nature of these cards, you may want to write "hand cancel" on the envelope if mailing, so it will not be damaged in postal machinery.

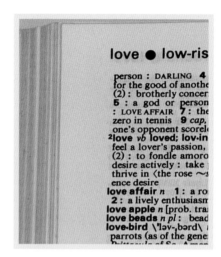

DICTIONARY DEFINITION CARD

Sometimes a single word can capture just the emotion you want to communicate. Cut up a thrift-store dictionary, or simply photocopy a dictionary page.

MATERIALS AND TOOLS

Purchased blank card
Color copy of vintage photo
Decorative paper scraps
Parchment or vellum
Dictionary definition
Mica or metal foil
Color copy of handwritten letter
Clear-drying glue
Craft brush

1 Glue the photo onto a piece of light-colored paper one millimeter larger than the image. Glue this paper onto another sheet of dark-colored paper one millimeter larger. Repeat on a sheet of parchment or vellum paper. Set aside to dry.

2 Cut a piece from the handwritten letter slightly smaller than the card face. Coat the back with a thin layer of glue and press down onto the front of the card.

3 Apply a thin layer of glue along the entire back edge of your multiframed image. Press down onto the center point of the handwritten sheet.

4 Glue the dictionary definition onto a small frame of mica or metal foil. Glue down at the very top of the photo image.

SILHOUETTE TAG CARD

This card captures a sense of playfulness and whimsy, making it a lovely gesture to mark special birthdays.

MATERIALS AND TOOLS

Purchased blank card
Color copies of vintage photos, 2 each measuring 1½ by 2¼ inches (4 x 6 cm) or smaller
Decorative paper scraps, 3 each measuring 1½ by 6¼ inches (4 x 16 cm)
Blank tags, 2
Deckle-edged ruler or scissors
Clear-drying glue
Craft brush
Craft knife
Cutting mat

WHAT TO DO

1 Cut the edge off one long side of each piece of paper using a deckle-edged ruler or scissors. Glue the paper horizontally to the front of the card, making sure there are deckled edges facing the outside.

2 On a cutting mat, cut along the outside edges of the photo image. Glue the image down to the front of a blank tag. Cut off any excess from the bottom edge. Repeat with second image and tag.

3 Glue the tags down onto the card in a playful angle.

EYELET CARDS

Eyelets are one of the hottest trends in crafting. Available in a rainbow of colors and an ever-increasing variety of shapes and sizes, they serve as practical connective tools, add visual flair, and open a world of creative possibilities to the inventive card maker.

THANK-YOU CARD

Take the time to show your gratitude with this simply elegant card. The use of the French word "Merci" adds a touch of worldly class.

MATERIALS AND TOOLS

Light blue folded paper card,
   measuring 5½ x 4 inches (14 x 10 cm)
2 pieces of dark gray paper,
   measuring 1¾ x 2½ inches (4.5 x 6 cm)
2 pieces of light gray paper,
   measuring 1¾ x 2½ inches
5 ⅛-inch round blue eyelets
Circular metal-framed tag
Metal eyelet letters
Eyelet punch
Eyelet setting tool
Hammer
Clear-drying glue
Craft brush
Bone folder
Pencil

WHAT TO DO

1 Brush a thin layer of glue along the back side of one of the pieces of dark gray paper. Press down onto the top right corner of the card front, leaving approximately ⅛ inch (3 mm) of blank space along all sides. Glue one of the light gray pieces of paper onto the bottom right corner of the card. Repeat this step on the left side of the card with the other pieces of paper so that the dark piece is on the bottom left and the light on the top left. Be sure to leave ⅛ inch (3 mm) of blank space along all sides. Place a piece of scrap paper over the card surface, and burnish. Set aside to dry.

2 Select the letters needed for your chosen word. Place them on the dry card and play with layout options. Once you have decided how the letters will sit on the card, set all the letters aside.

3 Place the metal-framed tag on the exact spot on the card where it will appear. Mark the spot through the hole at the top with a pencil. Open the card so the back is safely out of the way of your punching surface, and place on a suitable surface. (If you do not have a punching mat, a small stack of magazines will do.) Punch a hole in the card directly over the pencil mark. Insert the eyelet into the hole of the first letter, through the hole of the circular tag, then through the paper surface of the card. Carefully turn the project over, keeping the eyelet in place. To set the eyelet, position the setting tool into the back of the eyelet, then strike the setting tool with a hammer to flatten out the eyelet and secure it in place.

4 Repeat Step 3 for the remaining letters. Always be sure to open the card flat, leaving the back of the card out of the punching area.

352

Designer: Nicole Tuggle

CIRCULAR FRAME CARD

Eyelets are a great way to hold photos or other images in place. Here a photocopy of an old engraving takes center stage in this stunning study in blue.

MATERIALS AND TOOLS

Bright blue folded paper card, measuring 5 x 7 inches
  (12.5 x 18 cm)
Text paper (Try an old letter or page from an old book),
  measuring 3 x 4½ inches (7.5 x 11.5 cm)
Blue vellum, measuring 3¼ x 4¾ inches (8 x 12 cm)
4 ⅛ inch round blue eyelets
1 ⅛ inch round aluminum eyelet
Circular metal-framed tag
Photocopied image
Metal screen
Eyelet punch
Eyelet setting tool
Hammer
Clear-drying glue
Hot glue
Craft brush
Bone folder
Pencil

WHAT TO DO

1 Brush a thin layer of glue onto the back of the text page, and glue to the center of the card front. Burnish. Place the vellum over the text, add mark with a pencil approximately ¼ inch (6 mm) in at each corner.

2 Open the card so the back is safely out of the way and place it on a suitable surface. (If you do not have a punching mat, a small stack of magazines will do.) Holding the vellum in place over the text, punch a hole in the card directly over each pencil mark. Insert a blue eyelet into one of the holes, through the hole on the surface of the card. Carefully turn the project over, keeping the eyelet in place. To set the eyelet, position the setting tool into the back of the eyelet. Strike the setting tool with a hammer to flatten out the eyelet and secure it in place.

3 Repeat the above step with the remaining three corner eyelets. Always be sure to open the card flat, leaving the back of the card out of the punching area.

4 Place a dime-sized amount of hot glue on the center of the card. Press the metal screen down into the glue, taking care not to burn your fingers.

5 If you have a tag with a vellum face, brush a thin layer of glue onto the front surface of the photocopied image. Press the tag onto the surface of the image, cutting off any remaining paper from the metal frame with scissors. If you have a tag with a plain white face, brush glue along the back side of the photocopied image. Press the image onto the tag, and cut off any excess paper with scissors.

6 Pierce through the top hole of the tag, then drop in the aluminum eyelet. Carefully turn over the tag onto a safe punching surface, position the setting tool into the back of the eyelet, and strike the tool with a hammer.

7 To finish, add a dime-sized amount of hot glue to the back of the tag, then press down lightly onto the metal screen.

CRAFT PUNCH CARD WITH RIBBON CLOSURE

Craft punches—available in a wide variety of fun shapes—serve as the centerpiece for this card. The clever ribbon closure demonstrates one of many practical functions for eyelets.

MATERIALS AND TOOLS

Light blue folded paper card, measuring 5½ x 4 inches
  (22 x 10 cm)
1 piece of dark gray paper, measuring 2½ x 4 inches
  (7.5 x 10 cm)
2 pieces of light blue paper, 1 inch (2.5 cm) square
Scrap of bright blue paper
Shaped craft punch
3 ⅛ inch round aluminum eyelets
2 ³⁄₁₆ inch square aluminum eyelets
Thin ribbon, measuring 12 inches (30 cm) long
Eyelet punch
Eyelet setting tool
Hammer
Clear-drying glue
Craft brush
Bone folder
Pencil

WHAT TO DO

1 Brush a thin layer of glue along the back side of the dark gray paper. Press down onto the center of the card front. Glue one of the light blue pieces of paper onto the top center point of the gray paper, leaving approximately ¼ inch (6 mm) of gray paper above the blue. Repeat this step with the second piece of blue paper, placing it at the bottom center point. Place a piece of scrap paper over the card surface and burnish, then set aside to dry.

2 Take the bright blue scrap paper and slip it inside the craft punch. Press down to punch out the paper shape. Repeat two more times. Glue one shape onto the center point of each light blue square, and glue the third shape at the exact center point of the card. Set aside to dry.

3 Open the card so that the card back is safely out of the way of your punching surface. Place on a suitable surface. If you do not have a punching mat, a small stack of magazines will do. Using the eyelet punch, make three holes directly over the center point of each punched paper shape. Insert a round eyelet into one of the holes, through the hole on the surface of the card. Carefully turn the project over, keeping the eyelet in place. To set the eyelet, position the setting tool into the back of the eyelet. Strike the setting tool with a hammer to flatten out the eyelet and secure it in place. Repeat with the other two holes.

4 Lightly mark the center point of the opening flap of the card with a pencil. Make sure this mark is at least ¼ inch (6 mm) in from the edge. Repeat Step 3, this time adding the slightly larger square eyelet. Repeat this entire step for the eyelet that will appear at the center point on the back flap of the card.

5 Thread the ribbon through each of the holes, and lightly tie in a bow. As the lucky recipient unties the card's bow to read your message, they will feel like they've received a gift!

ACCORDION FOLD CARDS

Here's a great card idea that takes advantage of today's growing array of colorful, patterned scrapbooking paper. There's so much room on this card that you could write an entire letter!

HARD COVERED ACCORDION FOLD CARD

The hard cover provides a sturdy canvas for added embellishment.

MATERIALS AND TOOLS

1 piece of solid colored scrapbooking paper, measuring 12 inches (30 cm) square
1 piece of patterned scrapbooking paper, measuring 12 inches square
2 pieces of binder's board or illustration board, measuring 3¼ x 4¼ inches (8 x 11.5 cm)
Ruler
Pencil
Bone folder
Craft brush
Clear-drying craft glue

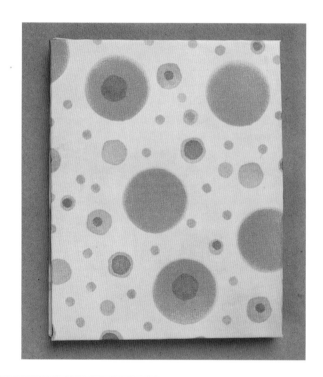

WHAT TO DO

1 Divide the sheet of colored paper into thirds and mark them lightly with a pencil. Cut the paper into the three pieces, each measuring 4 x 12 inches (10 x 30 cm). NOTE: You will use only one of these pieces for the card. Set aside the other two to make additional cards later or as scrap paper to make a collage embellishment for the cover.

2 Fold the colored piece of paper in half lengthwise. Take the flap and fold in half again toward the first fold. Turn the paper over and fold the other flap in half toward the first fold. You should now have an accordion fold measuring 3 x 4 inches (7.5 x 10 cm).

3 Place the patterned paper right side down on your work surface. Mark lightly with a pencil two rec-

tangles measuring 4¼ x 5¼ inches (11.5 x 22 cm). Cut out each rectangle. Set the other paper scraps aside.

4 Take one of the board pieces and cover the entire surface with a thin layer of glue. Place face down on the back side of the patterned paper, leaving an even amount of blank paper along each edge of the board. Turn the board

Designer: Nicole Tuggle

over and burnish the surface of the paper with a bone folder, eliminating any wrinkles or air bubbles.

5 Brush glue onto the side flaps and fold them over the board, smoothing the paper with fingers or bone folder. Dab a small amount of glue to the flaps at the top corners. Fold over each corner at a 45-degree angle. Be sure to angle the fold so the paper will not hang over the edges of the board. Repeat on the bottom corners.

6 Brush glue on the top and bottom flaps and fold them down onto the board. Take care to keep the angled corners tucked on the inside of the boards to prevent them from showing on the outside of the card.

7 Repeat Steps 4 through 6 for the other cover.

8 Brush a thin layer of glue onto the front flap of the accordion fold paper, taking care not to get glue on the other flaps. Press the glued flap down onto the center

point of the uncovered side of one cover. Burnish with a bone folder.

9 Brush a thin layer of glue onto the back flap of the accordion fold paper. Press this last flap onto the center point of the uncovered side of the other cover. Burnish.

10 Press finished card between a couple heavy books to get a nice, flat finish.

ACCORDION FOLD JOURNAL

Use a much longer piece of paper to create a fun, snakelike accordion card that can double as a small gift journal.

MATERIALS AND TOOLS

1 piece of white paper, measuring 5½ x 34 inches (14 x 86 cm)
2 pieces of patterned scrapbooking paper, 12 inches (30 cm) square
2 pieces of binder's board or illustration board, measuring 4¾ x 6 inches (12 x 15 cm)
2 pieces of binder's board, one measuring 1 by 3 inches (2.5 x 7.5 cm), the other 2 x 4¼ (5 x 11 cm)
Decorative paper scraps
Ruler
Pencil
Bone folder
Craft brush
Clear-Drying Craft Glue
Hot glue
Decorative fiber

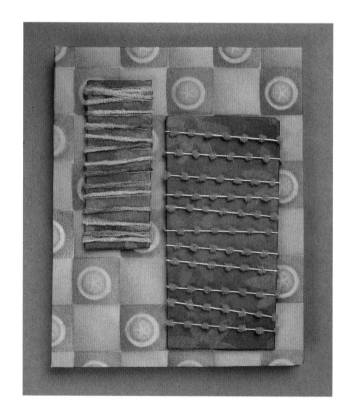

WHAT TO DO

1 Fold the white piece of paper in half lengthwise, then fold the flap in half again toward the first fold. Turn the paper over, and fold the other flap, in half toward the first fold. Repeat once more, until you have an accordion fold measuring 4½ x 5½ inches (12 x 14 cm).

2 Place one sheet of patterned paper right side down on your work surface. Mark lightly with a pencil a rectangle measuring 5¾ x 7 inches (14 x 18 cm). Cut out the rectangle. Repeat with second sheet of patterned paper. Set the other paper scraps aside.

3 Take one of the board pieces and cover the entire surface with a thin layer of glue. Place face down on the back side of the patterned paper, leaving an even amount of blank paper along each edge of the board. Turn the board over and burnish the surface of the paper with a bone folder, eliminating any wrinkles or air bubbles.

4 Brush glue onto the side flaps, and fold them over the board, smoothing the paper with fingers or bone folder. Dab a small amount of glue to the flaps at the top corners. Fold over each corner at a 45-degree angle. Be sure to angle the fold so the paper will not hang over the edges of the board. Repeat on the bottom corners.

5 Brush glue on the top and bottom flaps and fold them down onto the board. Take care to keep the angled corners tucked on the inside of the boards to prevent them from showing on the outside of the card.

6 Repeat Steps 3 through 5 for the other cover.

7 Brush a thin layer of glue onto the front flap of the accordion fold paper, taking care not to get glue on the other flaps. Press the glued flap down onto the center point of the uncovered side of one cover, then burnish with a bone folder.

8 Brush a thin layer of glue onto the back flap of the accordion fold paper. Press this last flap onto the center point of the uncovered side of the other cover. Burnish.

9 Press finished card between a couple heavy books to get a nice, flat finish.

10 Brush one side of the two smaller pieces of binder's board with glue and cover with decorative paper (a great use for scraps). Once dry, wrap a single strand of decorative fiber around the board, adhering the ends to the back side with a dab of hot glue. Glue the small pieces of decorated board onto the cover of the card wherever you want.

FIBER EMBELLISHMENTS

Many fabulous fibers—from threads and yarns to ribbons and cords—can add an eye-catching effect to your cards. Simply weave, twist, tie, or wrap fibers through the card surface or around other embellishments that can be added to the card surface. It couldn't be easier!

ROMANTIC LAYERED CARD

Offer this beautiful card as a touching gesture to a loved one. Keep your message on the innermost layer as a surprise, or add a touch of anticipation by writing a line on every page.

MATERIALS AND TOOLS

Sheet of burgundy card stock,
  5½ x 8½ inches (14 x 22 cm)
Sheet of gray card stock,
  5½ x 8½ inches
Sheet of botanical printed paper,
  5½ x 8½ inches
24-inch length of thin organza
  ribbon,
Pencil
Awl
Ruler
Bone folder
Cutting mat

DESIGNER TIP

Miniature envelopes are the perfect way to conceal a secret message to a sweetheart, tuck away a surprise gift or keepsake memento, or simply add an extra element of discovery to your cards. Paper, metallic, and see-through vellum varieties are readily available in craft and stationery stores.

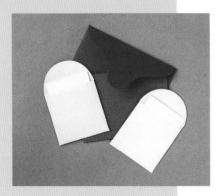

WHAT TO DO

1 Fold each piece of paper in half to form a folded sheet measuring 4¼ x 5½ inches. Hold the edges together with one hand and press down along the crease with a bone folder, taking care to match the corners exactly.

2 Stack the folded sheets together, one inside the next with the botanical paper on the outside, followed by the gray paper, and then the burgundy paper.

3 Open the stack of paper, folded edge facing down. Measure 1 inch (2.5 cm) down from the top and bottom edge on the fold line and mark lightly with a pencil.

4 Holding all the layers together, carefully poke through each pencil mark with an awl. Be sure to go through all three sheets of paper.

5 Thread the ribbon through the holes, starting from the inside of the card. If you are using wide ribbon, you may need to poke the ribbon through the hole with the aid of the awl. Don't worry about fraying the edges of the ribbon, as the ends can be cut.

6 Tie the ribbon in a bow along the spine of the card.

PEEKABOO WINDOW VARIATION

Place the gray paper on the outside, botanical paper next, and burgundy paper on the inside. Follow the remaining steps above. Take the finished card, measure 1 inch in from each side, and mark an internal line with a pencil. Place the cover over a cutting mat, making sure the rest of the card is safely placed to the left. Using a craft knife and ruler, cut along the marked lines. Remove the cut rectangle to reveal a charming window through which the botanical paper can be seen.

Designer: Nicole Tuggle

CARD MAKING GALLERY

Above: Celebrate nature with a handmade card that uses seed pods as embellishment. Designer: Susan L'Hommedieu

Above right: Stamp your way into a lovely collection of handmade greeting cards. Designer: Deborah Randolph Wildman

Below right: Paper mosaics are a wonderful way to use up leftover paper scraps, and you can create virtually any simple motif. Designer: Margaret Desmond Dahm

Above: Appeal to your favorite child (or child at heart) with a whimsical handmade card. Designer: Barbara Bussolari

Above right: Envelope cards are a great way to include special tidbits for the lucky recipients of your cards. The tea bag slides right out of this card. Designer: Kimiko Cards

Right: Computer collage decorates the front of this card, while a colorful fish cutout punctuates the interior. Designer: Tracy Page Stilwell

SCRAPBOOKING

Scrapbooking offers a world of creativity to anyone with memories and a wish to share them. Specialty papers, embellishments, stickers, die cuts, and cropping tools to suit every taste are widely available. Crafters once daunted by the tedious nature of photograph storage and display now try a new technique with every page.

MATERIALS AND TOOLS

ALBUMS AND PAGES
Choose a large-format album to hold school memorabilia, or a petite one to present to a friend in honor of a special occasion. Sturdy, removable pages are especially helpful, as you may need to add to or move them from time to time.

SPECIALTY PAPERS
Discover embossed, sueded, metallic, marbled, textured, and watercolor papers, just to list a few.

VELLUM
Vellum adds dimension and texture to your scrapbooking pages. It comes in a rich array of patterns and colors, and can be used to create terrific impressions of snow, ice, clouds, glass and windows, water, smoke, rays of sunshine, rain, fire, and bubbles. You can also write on vellum in ink, chalk, or paint.

MINIATURES
Nearly anything you want to express is available in miniature these days, from beach sandals to wedding gowns, lettering, baby themes, state symbols. If anything, you will want to edit your choices so as not to overcrowd your pages.

HOLE PUNCHES AND DIE CUTS
Use hole punches with heart, boat, or butterfly shapes to decorate paper edges and build a theme. Laser kits provide precision-cut images such as butterflies, barnyard animals, stars and moons, baby things, delicate flowers and grasses, musical instruments, and more.

POCKETS
Memorabilia pockets can be used to attach locks of hair, pressed flowers, or a button from a favorite shirt.

WIRE
Available fine or thick, colored or metallic, and easily manipulated with simple tools, wire is a dynamic element among photographs and as a connector for unusual elements.

ORNAMENTS

Embellish pages with metal charms, foreign or special postage stamps, beads, chains, fabric blossoms and leaves, pearls, eyelets and brads, glitter, and even tinsel. Let your imagination roam over your most cherished belongings, and preserve or represent them in your scrapbook.

ADHESIVES

A variety of adhesives is available for scrapbookers. Look for brands specifically labeled as "acid free."

BASIC TECHNIQUES

CREATING BORDERS

Borders add style, color, and visual interest to your scrapbooking pages. Create them with purchased border templates, or create your own with your imagination.

1 To use a border template, place the template over a piece of background paper and trace the shape.

2 Cut out the shape with a craft knife. If you have difficulty getting a clean edge, change to a new blade. Gently remove the cut paper, then position it over your photo.

3 To create a custom border, choose a paper item such as a doily that has an interesting shape. Use a craft knife to cut out a picture "window."

4 Gently remove the cutout paper, then position your photo within the opening.

5 Fancify your borders with punches or decorative-edged scissors.

LAYERING PAPERS

The days of a single background paper are over, leading to virtually endless fun for the passionate scrapbooker.

◈ To choose papers, take your photos to the craft store and play with color, pattern, and thickness. Handmade papers might be perfect. Or polka dots. Or a transparent vellum.

COLLECTING MEMORIES

* *Gather into a convenient place information about yourself, your family and its history, vacations (dates, place names, people and places visited), school records and events, and other important data. Ask family members if they have memories or, even better, photos or mementos to share. When you can, tape-record the stories of special people to be able to quote them in their own words. Determine ages of children depicted, if possible.*

* *Capture the feeling of a holiday meal together, or a great ski trip—even a summer spent at the pool—by picking up postcards, matchbooks, membership cards, and small souvenirs during the year. Group them in envelopes or shoe boxes, and store them with careful notations of date, place, and the people you want to remember.*

* *Don't you wish you knew what your ancestors thought and felt about significant events of their time? Keep a journal especially for recording reactions to what happens in the world. Where are you and who are you with when it happens? How does it affect you, physically, emotionally, spiritually? How did life change as a result? Keep clippings, emails, and notes on conversations you have about major events. Save quotations, contemporary lyrics, and headlines that say it best. You'll be grateful to have such a trove when you decide to make a statement about your experiences in your scrapbook.*

* *Once you are in the habit of collecting special objects and "memory triggers," you can relax and enjoy the fun of creating pages in your mind, before you attempt to record things permanently. Allow yourself the freedom to dream, and then practice on the page by moving things around until you achieve the look you want.*

BASIC TECHNIQUES

CROPPING PHOTOS

Let's be honest: Even our favorite photos often have unnecessary clutter in their backgrounds, and you definitely don't want clutter in your favorite scrapbooking pages.

1 To crop a photo, first measure and cut a ¼- to ½-inch (6 to 13 mm) border on the inside of a piece of paper. Now cut your narrow rectangle into two L shapes.

2 To determine precisely where to crop your photo, arrange your two L shapes in different places around the photo. When you're happy with the effect, lightly mark the new corners with a pencil.

TYPOGRAPHY

Typography possibilities are virtually endless. Look for peel-'n'-stick or press type letters, or create your own on a computer or with magazine cutouts.

❖ Remember when your first-grade teacher lectured you about keeping all of your letters on the same base line? Well, forget that rule. Position your letters however they look nice on a page—scattered about, up and down, tipped at angles—whatever you like.

TAGS

A proliferation of tag materials now lends dimension and storage capacity to a geometric shape on which to write, stamp, or otherwise decorate. Use tags for titles, quotations, photo frames, sticker blocks; tuck a blossom, ribbon, message, or 3-D trinket into a tiny envelope.

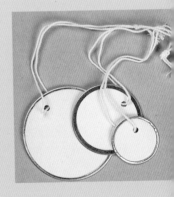

368

ADDING CHARMS

Ceramic and metal charms add a special feel to scrap-booking pages, and they're easy to attach.

◆ To attach a charm, first make two small holes in the paper with a hole piercer. Thread thin-gauge wire through the charm, then thread one end of the wire through each hole. Twist the wires on the back side of the paper until they hold the charm in place. Trim excess wire with wire cutters.

SETTING EYELETS

Eyelets are one of the most exciting newcomers on the crafting scene. They make great decorative additions to scrapbooking pages and handmade cards, and they're also a pretty way to attach letters, paper cutouts, and charms.

1 Begin by lining your work surface with a layer of cardboard or an old magazine, then use the punch portion of the eyelet setting tool to make a hole where you want the eyelet to appear by hitting the back of the tool with a small hammer.

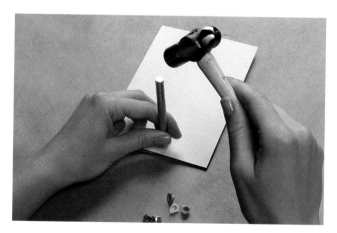

2 Push the eyelet through the hole so its front side is on the front side of your paper. If you plan to use the eyelet to attach something, place it through the hole first, then position the eyelet over it.

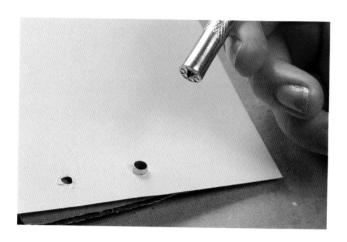

3 Turn the paper over so the front side faces downward. Match the eyelet setting tip to the size of your eyelet, then position it over the eyelet. Anchor the back of the eyelet in place by hitting the back end of the setting tool with a small hammer.

LA FRANCE

While you're on holiday, save souvenirs such as hotel tabs, tickets to museums or shows, transit tokens, currency, maps, and so forth. Capture the flavor of the place by noting common colors and textures; pay attention to foliage, architecture, and other indications of regional character. Photocopy documents, or sections of them that you wish to include, and cut the copies apart.

MATERIALS AND TOOLS

Background paper in slate, or French, blue
Photocopied snapshots, or originals as available
Coins, tokens
Coin purse
Double-coat rubber cement
Typed or printed list of sites and towns visited (these are printed in red and black on adhesive-backed, clear plastic sheets), and phrases you like
Bill from hotel or other stopover establishment
Small stack of white paper, perforated across the top
Very fine wire, about 2 inches (5 cm) long
Red, blue, and white paper for French flag, or one made with colored markers or paint
White acrylic paint
Clipped images of memorable figures (vintage wrapping paper was the source here)
Small souvenirs

WHAT TO DO

1 Clip section of hotel bill with French headings and prices. Paste onto background paper.

2 Arrange photographs and adhere to background. Paint graceful swathes of white paint to back printed names, sites, and phrases. Let dry.

3 Clip words from adhesive-backed sheets. Stick over painted white areas.

4 Run fine wire through perforated holes in stack of white paper, in tiny coils. Make a quick pencil drawing on the top sheet to turn it into a miniature sketch pad. Rubber-cement the coin purse to the background, and then glue a few francs in place emerging from the opening.

5 Paste clipped images, flag, and souvenirs around the photographs as appropriate.

Designer: Dana Irwin

THE WEDDING COUPLE

Although black and lavender aren't common wedding-theme colors, their contrasting combination creates a striking page that would look great with virtually any theme.

Designer: Tracia Williams

MATERIALS AND TOOLS

12-inch (30 cm) square sheet of black cardstock
12-inch square sheet of lavender paper
Sheet of black paper with silver or gray design
Scrap of vellum
Scraps of red, pink, and gray paper
Decorative border paper punch
Template for cutting decorative rectangles, circles, and ovals

2 decorative ceramic preprinted charms
Lettering markers
Ribbon
Heart punch
Stamp and black ink
Double-faced foam tape
Double-faced tape
Silver gel pen
White craft glue

WHAT TO DO

1 Cut two 2-inch (5 cm) strips of black paper, punch with border punch, and attach them to the lavender page with double-faced tape.

2 Ink the stamp and stamp it several times on scrap paper until you're happy with the effect. Stamp the lavender page, referring to the photograph for placement.

3 Cut out three rectangles from black patterned paper and one from the vellum with the template. Next, cut out two photos 1 inch (2.5 cm) smaller than the rectangles. Cut out a solid black oval and then a smaller-sized pink oval. Finally, cut out a black circle and smaller-sized gray circle. Mount these shapes to the lavender paper using foam tape on pieces that are attached to the lavender paper and double-faced tape on other layers.

4 Color hearts with lettering markers, tie with ribbon, attach to circle and oval with double-faced tape.

5 Punch red hearts from the scrap red paper and glue them to the oval.

6 Using gel pens, add tiny designs to any plain blank cardstock on page.

FLOWER GIRL

Although this page features a flower girl, the same design can be used to feature prom or party photos. The colored vellum creates a beautiful spectrum of colors.

MATERIALS AND TOOLS

12-inch (30 cm) square sheet of
  lavender paper
1 sheet each of pink, purple, and
  blue vellum paper
Sheet of beige decorative paper
Decorative scissors
Decorative corner punches
Ceramic princess rectangle
Ceramic princess-themed hearts
Lettering markers
Double-faced tape
Craft glue
Craft wire in your choice of color
Black marker
Paper cutter

Designer: Tracia Williams

WHAT TO DO

1 Cut two 7- x 5-inch (18 x 12.5 cm) rectangles from each color of vellum Cut six 1½-inch (4 cm) squares from each color of vellum and from the beige decorative paper. Trim edges on all of them with decorative scissors.

2 Color the ceramic shapes with lettering markers and add fun wire swirls to each.

3 Using corner scissors, cut corners on photos, and cut some odd corners from scraps of vellum. Using double-faced tape, glue rectangles to lavender paper as well as photos and odd corner pieces, referring to the photo for placement.

4 Spell out a name or verse on cardstock squares. Then, using double-faced tape, add vellum squares to page and letters. Attach the ceramic shapes with craft glue.

SCRAPBOOKING GALLERY

Above and right: This carefully planned memory page opens from the center; it is shown closed at right and opened above. The page commemorates the separation and reunion of two young people—Dot and Bud—who courted and married during World War II. The designer constructed the page to emphasize the couple's interconnection. While the thoughts of each person are recorded in a different script, each side of the page opens to reveal photos of the other person, and the two background papers reverse on the inside—his becomes hers, and hers, his. Designer: Jeanne Jacobowski

Left: The early years of the Collette family are celebrated by this handsome memory page. At left, the designer constructed a functioning memory book—the rigid cover opens to reveal 10 beautifully decorated pages of photos and mementos. At right, a photo covered in rigid acrylic (to simulate a frame) hangs from gold-colored wire strung with beads. Designer: Jeanne Jacobowski

Right A new baby is the moon and stars to his mother, and this page proclaims that two-month-old Louis is exactly that. A gold-mesh moon and stars of gold and silver paper decorate a background of blue tissue and surround mother and child. Designer: Jeanne Jacobowski

Left: This graphic page combines papers in bold colors and a quotation from a beloved author to celebrate a bold and beloved little girl. Designer: Jeanne Jacobowski

Below: This birthday page combines corrugated paper, colored wire, and three bright feathers to celebrate two buddies turning 10 years old. Designer: Jeanne Jacobowski

Opposite page: "Best friends" are well worth celebrating, and this page records a friendship that lasted through childhood and into adulthood. Designed to mimic a bulletin board, the page's background consists of paper squares with a cork board pattern. Then charms, photos, trinkets, and an excellent report card are attached as randomly and playfully as they would be on a real bulletin board. Designer: Jeanne Jacobowski

A baby is born with a need to
be loved and never outgrows it.

Frank A. Clark

Tyler Scott Philips
January 27, 2001
6:30 a.m.

Opposite page: This outstanding page uses
pockets constructed of romantic floral paper to
hold "grandmother's treasured memories"—
beloved family photos and two love notes from
her husband. The two outside pockets fold in
for a three-dimension effect. Tags identifying
the mementos are attached with striped ribbon in subtle shades. Designer: Anna Griffin

Above: As happy as the baby it celebrates,
this page uses woven strips of paper to
marvelous effect. Satin ribbon finishes
the corners of the weaving and provides a
graceful bow to top off the photo.
Designer: Anna Griffin

Right: Decorative papers enliven this
treasured heritage photo. The designer
used long strips of pink-flowered paper
for a border of flattened bows around the
edge of the page. She fringed the same
paper to frame the photo and cut floral
motifs from it as added decorations.
Designer: Anna Griffin

Joseph Conrad Carver Jr.
BORN AUGUST 1895

Above left and right: Travel memories come to life when depicted in scrapbooking pages. Here, specialty paper borders and tags showcase photographs, while pockets hold souvenirs. Designer: Megan Kirby

Right: Three generations of wedding photos grace this scrapbook page, arranged around an antique doily and dried flowers. Designer: Dana Irwin

Opposite page, top left: A treasured photo is given the attention in deserves on this stunning page, framed by two layers of pleated paper. Designer: Anna Griffin

Opposite page, top right: This stunning memory book is also an altered book. The designer used multiple techniques to decorate pages that include copies of old family photos, including stamping, decoupage, and added fringe and beads. Designer: Billie Worrell

Opposite page, bottom left: A special Christmas is remembered with ornaments, packages, and an unforgettable visit to Santa. The large medallion with the photo moves aside to reveal "believe" written in wire. Designer: Jeanne Jacobowski

Opposite page, bottom right: Life's best "firsts" deserve scrapbook pages all their own. This page combines brightly colored paper, playful lettering, and color-copied photos of the proud bubble blower. Designer: Jeanne Jacobowski

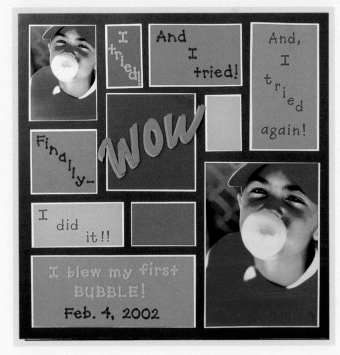

STAMPING

Watch out! Stamping is not only fun, it's addictive! Simple enough to beguile beginners, yet sophisticated enough to attract accomplished artists, this craft has seen an explosion in both popularity and new techniques. Learn the basics of stamping, and you'll soon be making your own unique impressions on paper, fabric, wood, polymer clay, ceramics—just about every surface in sight.

MATERIALS AND TOOLS

MANUFACTURED STAMPS
There are literally thousands of stamp images available. Stamps are usually made of rubber or foam mounted on a wood or plastic handle. You can also find stamps mounted onto rollers; these are good for adding borders to all sorts of surfaces, including walls.

STAMP INKS
Available wherever stamps are sold; see Stamp Inks, page 384, for an explanation of the five principal types of ink.

BRAYER
This tool is similar to a small paint roller, but is made of rubber. Use it to ink large stamps or to create colored backgrounds for stamping. Ink your brayer by rolling it on a large ink pad or by pouring paint or ink onto a sheet of glass and then rolling the brayer until it's coated.

STAMPING SURFACES
You can stamp just about any object with a smooth surface: paper, wood, fabric, polymer clay, glass, ceramic, terra-cotta, leather, and even the walls of your home. Just be sure to choose the best ink for each project

STAMP CLEANER
Many cleaners are widely available, but you can also use diluted window cleaner or non-alcohol baby wipes.

EMBOSSING POWDER
This powder is made of tiny plastic pellets that melt when heated to merge with the stamped ink and create a raised image. The powder can be clear, translucent, opaque, or glittery. Use colored powder with clear embossing ink and clear or translucent powder with colored pigment ink.

EMBOSSING OR HEAT GUN
This easy-to-use tool blows extremely hot air out of its nozzle to melt embossing powder. You can use an alternative form of heat, such as an iron, electric element, hot plate,

or toaster. Hair dryers do not blow hot enough to melt embossing powders.

MATERIALS TO ENHANCE STAMPING PROJECTS

Add color to your stamped images with colored pencils, markers, watercolor paints and watercolor pencils.

BASIC TECHNIQUES

STAMP INKS

The five principal types of ink used for stamping are described below. The type of ink that's best for your project will depend primarily on how porous that project's surface is.

DYE-BASED INKS

Translucent, water-based inks. These quick-drying inks are suitable for stamping on all papers, although the colors may bleed slightly on absorbent, uncoated papers. Dye-based inks are not fade-resistant and usually cannot be embossed.

PIGMENT INKS

Thick, opaque inks. These slow-drying inks are suitable for stamping on uncoated paper, coated paper if used with embossing powder, wood, polymer clay, and fabric.

EMBOSSING INKS

Clear or slightly tinted inks that dry slowly so embossing powders will melt and fuse with their stamped image when heat is applied.

FABRIC INKS

Water- or solvent-based inks that remain on fabric after laundering. Some must be set with heat.

PERMANENT INKS

Water- or solvent-based inks that can be used on paper, wood, glass, and fabric. Once it has dried, permanent ink won't run, so it's useful for stamping images you want to enhance with watercolor pencils or water-based markers or paints, or for projects that require a protective finish.

BASIC STAMPING

The basic technique of stamping isn't difficult once you get the hang of it. The hard part will be keeping yourself from compulsively stamping every surface in sight!

1 To start, make sure the material you're stamping is flat. Iron any wrinkles if you're working with fabric or wrinkled paper. If possible, use masking tape to hold the object you're stamping in place.

2 Lightly tap the stamp on the ink pad's top. Do not press the stamp into the pad or rub it across the pad's surface.

3 Test the stamp on scrap material (paper if you are using paper, wood if you'll be stamping wood, etc.) for too much or too little ink. Re-ink if the image is faint or spotty; blot the stamp on a paper towel if it's over-inked.

4 Hold the stamp firmly and press down on the paper or other material being stamped. Do not rock or move the stamp or the image will be blurred. You may need to stand to create more pressure when using an extra large stamp. Press each corner carefully to make sure the entire image is left behind.

5 Lift the stamp straight up, again being careful not to rock or move the stamp.

6 Clean the stamp as directed by the manufacturer after each stamping session.

MAKING A STAMP

You can make your own stamp from erasers, linoleum, wood, rubber, foam, or even fruits and vegetables. The basic steps are the same, whatever your material.

1 Draw or trace your design onto tracing paper. (Keep in mind that the image will be reversed when you stamp it, so numbers and letters must be reversed.) Transfer the design to your stamp surface by sandwiching a piece of carbon or graphite paper (treated side down) between the tracing paper and the surface, then retrace the lines. If you're using a cut fruit or vegetable, press a cookie cutter into its exposed surface instead of trying to draw on it to create a carving.

2 Insert the small V-shaped tip into the linoleum-carving knife and use it to carve a rough border around the image's lines. Remember, whatever part of the material you carve away will be unprinted white space when you use the stamp. The raised (uncut) portions will be what prints. For smooth edges, make shallow cuts, not deep gouges. You should be able to see the upper edges of your blade above the material you are carving. Use a larger, U-shaped tip to carve away large areas of the design.

3 Use a craft knife to cut around the perimeter of the stamp's design. Ink the stamp and make a test print on paper to see if any rough edges need to be trimmed.

4 When you are happy with the image the stamp prints, you can use it as is or add a handle by glueing it to a piece of wood or doweling.

TIP

To get reversed numbers or letters for your handmade stamp, first write them normally on tracing paper. Retrace them with a dark marker. Set the tracing paper image-side down on your stamp surface and sandwich a piece of carbon or graphite paper (treated side down) between the tracing paper and the surface. Now use a pencil or pen to redraw the lines showing through to the back of the tracing paper and a reverse image will transfer to the stamp surface.

RUBBER STAMPED GIFT WRAP

Create this gift wrap to show special love on Mother's Day—or on any occasion when you want to give a gift "with love." Look for compatible large floral and foliage stamps. The complementary use of metallic paint with a highlight of gold paper as a border, makes for a rich and inviting presentation.

MATERIALS AND TOOLS

Ivory wrapping paper
Acrylic paint in dusty purple and metallic gold
Paper plates and paper towels
Wedge sponges
Rubber stamps, one larger floral stamp, preferably with an engraved look; a smaller "engraved" foliage stamp; cursive script to spell "With Love"
Scissors
Cellophane tape
Glue
Paper in deep rose and metallic gold
Gold gift tag
Ribbon

WHAT TO DO

1 Lay the ivory gift wrap on a hard, flat surface.

2 Pour small amounts of the dusty purple and gold paint onto a paper plate.

3 Using one of the wedge sponges, pick up some purple paint and apply it to the large floral stamp using a patting motion. Stamp onto the wrapping paper and repeat to create an allover pattern. You may have to reapply the paint several times as you work. Allow the paint to dry and clean the stamp well.

4 Repeat the stamping process on the piece of deep rose paper using the metallic paint and the smaller foliage stamp.

5 Wrap the gift with the stamped ivory wrapping paper using cellophane tape and glue.

6 Tear a strip of the stamped deep rose paper to fit around the gift. Tear a strip from the gold paper that is slightly wider than the deep rose strip. Warp both around the gift, placing the wider strip of gold paper under the deep rose strip. Using glue, adhere the edges.

7 Using the dusty purple paint, stamp "With Love" onto the gold gift tag.

8 Tie the ribbon and gold tag around the wrapped gift.

CLEANING AND CARING FOR YOUR STAMPS

Clean your stamp after each use (and between colors). To do so, simply press your stamp onto a paper towel moistened with water and commercial stamp cleaner or diluted window cleaner until all the ink is removed. Nonalchohol baby wipes can be used instead, and the moisturizers in them will help condition the rubber. Some inks will stain your stamps. Don't worry: this stain won't affect the color of future stampings, as long as you clean your stamps well. Stamps will last for years if cared for properly. Never submerge mounted stamps in water, and always store stamps image-side down in a cool location where they'll be protected from sunlight.

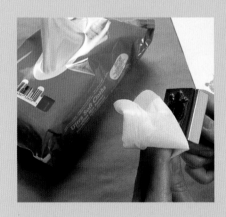

With Love

Designer: Chris Rankin

STAMPED KEEPSAKE BOX

Use your favorite stamps to create a collection of coordinated projects—from tags to greeting cards to gorgeous gift bags. If you need to impose a little organization on your creative chaos, store your gift-giving ensemble in a matching keepsake box—it's the project you get to make just for yourself!

MATERIALS AND TOOLS

Shoebox
White contact paper
Scissors
Cream-colored cardstock
White craft glue
White paper
Large background stamp
Border stamp
Focal stamps (we used a bow
   and a wreath)
Gold ink pad
Gold satin ribbon
Craft knife
Double-sided poster tape

WHAT TO DO

1 Cover the shoebox and its top in white contact paper. Fold edges over on the inside and trim excess with scissors or a craft knife.

2 Cut a rectangle of cream-colored cardstock to cover each side of the box, including the top of the box and its sides. Each rectangle should be just slightly smaller than the side it will cover: Glue each rectangle in place, centering it over the side it's covering.

3 For the sides of the box bottom, cut two rectangles of white paper for the long sides and two rectangles of white paper for the short ends. The rectangles should be slightly smaller than the cardstock rectangles.

4 For the top of the box, cut one rectangle of white paper slightly smaller that the cardstock rectangle.

5 For the sides of the box top, cut two rectangles of white paper for the long sides and two rectangles for the ends. The rectangles should be slightly smaller than the cardstock rectangle.

6 Use the large background stamp to stamp all the rectangles for the sides of the bottom of the box and for the top of the box. Use the border stamp to stamp the narrow rectangles for the sides of the top of the box.

7 Before gluing each stamped paper rectangle to the cardstock, try positioning it over the cardstock rectangle. You may find that you want more of a cardsotck border. Cut the stamped rectangles accordingly, then glue them in place over the cardstock rectangle.

8 Stamp three or four bow focal stamps. Cut them out and glue to three or four sides of the bottom of the box. Since one end of our box has a label holder, we used three bows.

9 Stamp and cut out six wreath focal stamps.

10 Use the craft knife to cut around the central motif of two of the wreath stamps. Set aside. Then use the craft knife to cut the borders from two of the wreath stamps. And set aside

11 Position and glue the two uncut wreath stamps on the top of the box in positions of your choice.

12 Use your scissors to cut small pieces of the double-sided poster tape. Position and stick the tape around the borders of the two wreaths glued to the top of the box. Position the cut-out border over the tape and gently press to adhere. Do the same with the cut-out centers.

13 Decorate the box as you will with lengths of ribbon to highlight the placement of the stampings.

Best
Wishes

An *Invitation*

Congratulations!

*To
From*

Designer: Chris Rankin

Scrapbook Pocket Page

Capture time in a scrapbook pocket page. You can keep memories safely and beautifully with this design. The pocket invites the reader to find the photo of the letter writer and recipient many years later—friends forever with fond memories of the lives they shared.

Materials and Tools

Burgundy paper
Small sea sponge
Acrylic paint in metallic gold and
   black
Paper plates
Pocket-watch rubber stamp
Black stamp pad
Black card stock
Embossing paste
Scissors
Sewing machine (optional)
Glue (optional)
Decorative silk leaf

Designer Tip

If you use markers instead of an ink pad, you can apply different colors to specific parts of the stamp's image. If the marker's ink dries too fast, hold the stamp's inked image close to your mouth and breathe on it several times—you should be able to get a few more stampings.

What To Do

1 Place a small amount of the metallic gold paint on a paper plate. Dip the sea sponge in the paint, then dab it on the burgundy paper to create a sponge-painted, textured background. Allow to dry.

2 With the pocket-watch stamp and black ink pad, stamp the watch in an allover pattern on the burgundy and gold paper. Allow to dry.

3 Mix the embossing paste with the black paint, using the pocket watch stamp, gently stamp the black cardstock in an allover design and allow to dry.

4 To make the pocket, cut the burgundy paper slightly less than half the size of the black cardstock. Use a sewing machine to topstitch the pocket to the cardstock, allowing for a ¼-inch seam. If you don't have a sewing machine, you can handstitch the pocket, or you can glue the pocket in place

5 Position the memorabilia in the pocket as desired and glue if necessary. Tuck the decorative leaf in place for the final touch.

Designer: Chris Rankin

Reverse Stencil Album Cover

The cover of your scrapbook album can carry as much design interest as the pages you create for the inside. It's a great way to personalize an album as a keepsake or to make one to give away. First, use your scrapbooking skills to establish a theme for the album, then use a reverse stencil technique to make your custom background paper.

Materials and Tools

Album
Paper
Stencils
Paper plates
Splatter brush
Acrylic paint in black
Deckle edge decorative
Scissors
Photo copies of photos and memorabilia
Rubber stamp
Brown or sepia ink pad
Charms

What To Do

1 Choose your album and cover paper. Used here is a spiral bound album with a black cover. To go with the aged theme and sepia tone photographs, a brown paper was selected.

2 Position stencils of your choice on the paper. Place some black paint on a paper plate. Dip the bristles of the splatter brush in the paint. To prevent big drops of paint from falling on your paper, tap the brush a few times on the edge of the plate to remove any excess paint.

3 Position the brush over the paper. Using your thumb, run your thumb lengthwise over the bristles. You control the splatters by the amount of pressure you use

as you press and release the bristles. You may want to do a few samples before you begin. Reload the brush as necessary. You may need to reposition the stencils as you work. Continue until the paper is covered in an overall pattern. Allow to dry.

4 Carefully cut the edges of the stenciled paper using the deckle-edge scissors. Cut the length of the paper to the length of the album cover. Position and glue in place. You may want to place a heavy book over the album while the glue dries.

5 To get the uniform aged look of the photographs and memorabilia, take them to a copy shop and have them copied in sepia tones. To give them more body, glue the copied photos and memorabilia on manilla cardstock. Stamp your motif on manilla cardstock. Glue the corner holders to the photo and stamped motif.

6 Position the photograph, memorabilia, and stamped motif in a layout that is pleasing to you. Glue them to the stenciled papers. For interest, add charms of your choice.

POST CARD

CORRESPONDENCE   ADDRESS

Designer: Chris Rankin

HEAT EMBOSSED VELVET AZALEA BLOSSOM PILLOW

Here's a stamping technique that doesn't involve ink. Using little more than a stamp and a dry iron, you can turn an ordinary velvet pillow into something extraordinary. You can work with a purchased slipcover pillow or with fabric yardage.

MATERIALS AND TOOLS

Broad-surface rubber or foam stamp with a simple design
Spray bottle with clean water
Ironing board
Pillow with removable rayon/acetate velvet slipcover or
  fabric yardage (avoid nylon velvet)

Dry iron
Test scrap of rayon/acetate velvet (optional)
Well-lit, well-ventilated room

WHAT TO DO

1 Remove the slip cover from the pillow and turn it inside out, setting the inner foam aside for later.

2 You'll use the ironing board as your work surface for the following steps. Place it in a well-lit area, as it can be hard to see the embossing in poor light. Also, make sure the room is well-ventilated—the synthetic fibers in the fabric may fume slightly when heated. Make sure your iron is dry and turn it on to its highest setting (cotton-silk).

3 To test the stamp and fabric, find the most inconspicuous spot on the pillow cover (or use a piece of scrap velvet, if available), and place it nap side down onto the stamp's face. Lightly mist the fabric with water—don't saturate it. Press the fully heated iron onto the moistened fabric for 20 to 30 seconds to test the amount of time needed to emboss with your particular fabric and stamp design. For best results, try to use a part of the iron without steam vents.

4 Once you've determined the correct amount of time, continue embossing the entire pillow case in a pattern that is pleasing to you.

5 When you've finished embossing the pillow case, simply turn it right side out, and replace the foam insert.

394

Designer: Susan McBride

STAMPING GALLERY

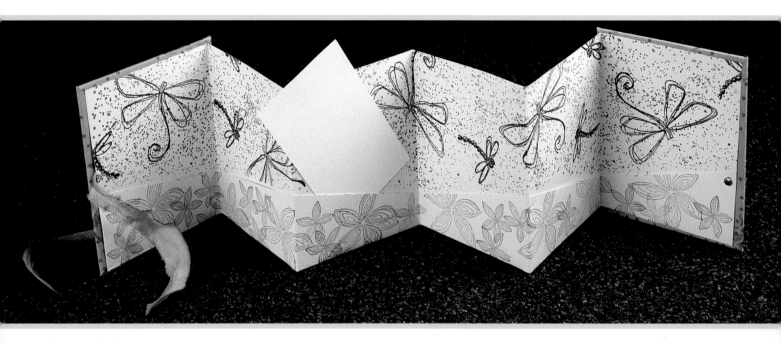

Above: Stamped motifs can be embellished as simply or elaborately as you like. Here, stamped dragonflies were jazzed up with colorful stones. Designer: Chris Rankin

Right: Monochromatic stamping creates a subtle, elegant look, both on paper and fabric. Designer: Karen Timm

Opposite page, top: A handmade accordion book provides ample surface area to play with your favorite stamps. Designer: Lynn B. Krucke

Right: Create your own gift wrap with colorful Happy Birthday stamps. Continue the theme on cards, place settings, and thank-you notes. Designer: Chris Rankin

Bottom right: Scrapbooking pages are all the rage, and stamping is a great way to add color and pattern to pages. Designer: Chris Rankin

Bottom left: Transform a simple wood box into a storage area for seeds. You can also stamp small envelopes and fill them with your own garden seeds for a special, home grown gift. Designer: Traci Neil-Taylor

CLAY CRAFTS

Finally—a middle ground between child's play and high art!
Sure, bread dough is easy (and safe enough) for kids, but as
the projects in this chapter demonstrate, it's a material with
plenty of possibilities for crafty adults, as well. Polymer clay,
too, has come into its own as a serious medium with nearly
endless artistic applications.

POLYMER CLAY

Polymer clay continues to increase in popularity as crafters realize its potential for stunning jewelry, home decor items, and even small sculptures. Polymer clay can be found in an incredible array of colors, and it can be stamped, sculpted, embedded, painted, sanded, and even drilled!

MATERIALS AND TOOLS

POLYMER CLAY
Each brand has its own unique pre-baking malleability and postbaking strength and flexibility. Experiment with different types to discover your favorite.

PASTA MACHINE
Pasta machines allow you to form even layers of clay with little effort. For safety's sake, do not use the same pasta machine for cooking and crafting.

ACRYLIC ROD, BRAYER, AND ROLLING PIN
Use instead of or in addition to pasta machine. Acrylic is best, rubber second. Avoid wood products — they leave grain marks and can be difficult to clean.

CUTTING BLADE
Many craft stores have cutting blades sold specifically for polymer clay crafters. Look for a blade that's 4 to 5 inches (10 to 12 cm) long. Wallpaper scraper blades will work, but razor blades are too short.

CRAFT KNIFE
Best for cutting tight curves and angles or intricate detail.

WORK SURFACE
Ceramic tiles are handy and can be used as a baking surface, too.

BAKING TRAY OR TILE
Put a piece of paper on the baking surface to prevent a shiny spot on the clay where it touches the tile.

OVEN
A dedicated oven is best; if not possible, make a "tent" of aluminum foil to go over the baking tray.

OVEN THERMOMETER
Oven thermometers are often inaccurate, so purchase one in a kitchen store.

SHAPE CUTTERS
Small cookie cutters or canapé cutters can be used to cut fun shapes for a variety of projects.

NEEDLE TOOL OR KNITTING NEEDLE
For piercing holes in beads.

SCULPTING TOOLS
Specialty tools are available, or you can use found objects such as a golf tee, a chair caning peg, cuticle pusher, crochet hook, etc. Or make your own from polymer clay.

TEXTURE
Commercially made texture sheets are available, but you can use window screen, lace, plastic embroidery canvas, textured wallpaper, etc. Always use a mold release to prevent sticking.

MOLD RELEASE
Water, nonaerosol auto interior vinyl protectant, or cornstarch.

WET/DRY SANDPAPER
Find this in the auto supply store. Never skip grits, and keep it wet to avoid breathing polymer dust and to prevent scratching.

BUFFING WHEEL
Use a jeweler's buffing wheel or a bench grinder to add shine.

BUFFING WHEEL SAFETY

* *Tie back long hair.*
* *Remove bracelets and necklaces.*
* *Don't wear loose sleeves.*
* *Wear eye protection.*
* *Wear a dust mask to avoid breathing cotton fibers.*
* *Hold the polymer clay piece on the underside of the wheel so that when it's snatched from your fingertips, it flies away from you.*
* *Make sure there are no children, pets, or breakables nearby.*
* *Keep the polymer clay moving constantly—holding it in one place will allow the friction to begin to melt the clay.*

BASIC TECHNIQUES

MAKING THE CLAY WORKABLE

Conditioning or kneading makes hard clay more malleable. Even soft-from-the-package clay should be conditioned to mix the plasticizer throughout the polymer clay. Unconditioned clay may break easily after baking.

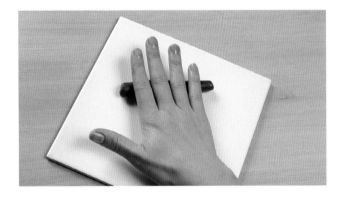

1 Condition clay by hand by squeezing a one-ounce block into a ball. Roll it into a snake shape, fold it back on itself, and roll it out again. Repeat until the clay stretches when it's pulled apart. Try not to incorporate air bubbles. Alternatively, clay can be conditioned with a pasta machine by cutting slabs just a little thicker than the thickest pasta machine setting, and rolling them through the machine. Fold in half and repeat, as many times as needed for the clay to stretch instead of break when pulled. Never feed clay into the machine fold-side-up, or you'll trap air and create bubbles.

2 If your clay is very soft and sticky, it will need to be leached to remove some of the plasticizers. To do this, roll it into a sheet and place it between two sheets of paper. Some of the plasticizer will leach onto the paper after a couple of hours. Repeat until the clay loses its stickiness, then condition it as described in Step 1.

DESIGNER TIP

Colored sand, rubber stamp embossing powders, dried spices, even potting soil can be physically mixed into polymer clay to create many interesting effects. They're especially useful in creating certain faux stones. Mix in enough of the inclusion to show, but not so much that it affects the integrity of the clay body. Be aware that cutting clay with inclusions in it will dull your blade faster, so you may want to dedicate one blade specifically to this technique.

BAKING

Polymer clay is picky! No matter how long you bake it, it won't fuse properly at too low a temperature, and the resulting pieces may be weak and easily broken. Too high a temperature and it burns. Learn your oven and its idiosyncrasies.

Although toaster oven temperatures are frequently inaccurate and their heating elements can easily burn the clay, they can still do a good job of baking polymer clay. Place a small ceramic tile in the toaster oven as a heat sink to help maintain an even temperature, and make a "tent" of aluminum foil to protect your projects from the heating elements. Be sure to ventilate well, especially if you burn the clay!

If a dedicated oven is not possible, you should clean your oven after baking polymer clay. Wipe with a little baking soda on a damp sponge, then wipe clean with a wet rag.

Polymer clay can be baked as many times as you want with no adverse effects. It doesn't shrink when baked, but it may be necessary to support some objects during baking to prevent sagging. Use polyester fiberfill or a wadded-up cotton cloth.

Do not microwave polymer clay!

SAFETY AND CLEANUP

Polymer clay is certified nontoxic, but there are a few commonsense safety tips you should be aware of.

* Polymer clay is not edible, and projects made from it should not be used for eating or drinking. Also, any kitchen tools used for polymer crafting should never return to the kitchen.

* Never use it for an ashtray or incense burner.

* Bake the clay in a well-ventilated room. If you burn the clay, open the windows and turn on a fan.

* Don't snack while working with polymer clay to avoid ingesting it.

* Wash your hands well after using polymer clay, then rub hand lotion into your hands and rub it off with a terry cloth rag. Use cold water, soap, and a nail brush to remove all residue.

BASIC TECHNIQUES

MAKING MOLDS

Molds can be made from seashells, buttons, beads, charms, and any number of other items.

1 To make a mold, wad up a piece of polymer clay that is larger than the object you want to make a mold of. Use strong clay; if you're using scrap, mix it thoroughly until it's all one color.

2 Set the clay on a piece of waxed paper on your work surface and cover with another piece of waxed paper. Flatten slightly and evenly by pressing with a flat object such as a jar lid. Remove the top piece of waxed paper and apply mold release generously directly to the clay.

4 Peel the waxed paper from the back of the mold and place the mold on your baking sheet. Bake at the manufacturer's recommended temperature for an hour. The longer baking time ensures a stronger mold.

5 To use the mold, apply a mold release directly to the mold and tamp out the excess. Roll polymer clay into a cone shape, place the point of the cone into the center of the mold, and press.

3 Press the object into the clay using a straight downward motion. Don't twist or turn the object. Then pull the object straight out.

6 While the polymer is still in the mold, cut excess clay from the back side with a polymer clay cutting blade.

ADDING TEXTURE

Texturing creates visual interest and hides fingerprints. Window screen, fabric, rubber stamps, textured wallpaper, textured leather, lace, plastic needlepoint canvas, and many other items are great for adding texture.

1 Apply a spritz of water from a spray bottle directly to the clay, or use a soft brush to apply cornstarch to serve as a mold release. Mica powders will act as their own mold release as well as add color to the texture.

2 If the clay and texture together aren't too thick, roll them through the pasta machine for deep, even texturing.

BLENDING CLAY

This technique, known as a Skinner Blend, lets you create subtle blends of color.

1 Roll two colors of polymer clay into sheets at the thickest setting of your pasta machine. Cut each diagonally, and set half of each aside. Fit the two remaining triangles next to each other.

2 Fold this sheet in half, bottom to top, and run it through the pasta machine. Repeat this many times, always folding from bottom to top.

3 After 20 or so passes through the pasta machine, the colors will have subtly blended from one to the other. You can experiment with more than two colors of triangle shapes. Just be sure to fold the clay and insert it into the pasta machine rollers in the same direction each time.

BASIC TECHNIQUES

SANDING AND BUFFING

A deep, lustrous shine can be created on your polymer pieces with elbow grease instead of varnish.

1 Use wet/dry sandpaper in the very fine grits that are available at auto parts stores. You can go as low as 320 grit to smooth lumps, but it's usually sufficient to start at 400 grit.

2 Keep the paper and the object wet, but constant immersion is not necessary. Use a bowl of water and frequently dip the paper and polymer to rinse them.

3 Don't skip grits, and sand each grit perpendicular to the previous one. For a soft sheen, buff by hand on a piece of soft denim or other cloth.

4 For a shine, use a cotton buffing wheel. A jeweler's buffing wheel is ideal, but a bench grinder with a cotton wheel attached will work well too. For small objects, you can use an electric hand-held rotary tool but use caution since the small wheel can easily gouge the clay.

CANEWORKING

A glass working technique that has been adapted to polymer clay, caneworking is sometimes referred to as mille-fiori , which translates to "a thousand flowers." A cane is a tube or log of polymer clay that has an image or pattern running through the length of it, and as slices are removed from the cane, the image is revealed. Caned patterns can be very complex, but even simple ones can be very effective elements of a project. Thick cane slices can be pierced to create beads, and thin slices can be used in a variety of ways for decoration.

Jelly-roll Cane. Roll out rectangular sheets of two colors of polymer clay and place one on top of the other, being careful not to trap air bubbles between the sheets. Starting at one of the shorter ends, roll the polymer clay into a tube.
Try varying the look of this simple cane by using more than two colors or by using sheets of differing thicknesses.

Bull's-eye Cane. Roll one color of polymer clay into a short log. Roll out a sheet of a contrasting color and trim the edges neatly. Place the log onto the sheet and roll it up. Trim the sheet so that the edges butt against each other when the log is completely wrapped.
Add as many rings of color as you'd like. Vary the thicknesses for added interest.

Striped Cane. Roll two or more contrasting colors of polymer clay into sheets and stack them. Cut the stack in half and place one half on top of the other. Repeat until you have the number of stripes you want.

Roll your brayer or acrylic rod over the stack as you layer it, to press out air bubbles and to compress the layers.

Again, varying the thicknesses of the sheets can result in interesting effects.

Checkerboard Cane. Roll two thick sheets of contrasting colors of polymer clay. Stack one on the other and trim the edges. Use your cutting blade to cut the stack into strips, then flip over every other strip. Cut the resulting stack in half and place one half on top of the other.

Slicing Canes. Remove slices from your cane with a polymer clay cutting blade. If the cane squishes or smears, the clay may be warm from working with it, and you'll get better results if you allow it to rest for a few hours or even overnight.

Wipe the blade on an alcohol-dampened paper towel to keep it clean between slices. Rotate the cane a quarter turn between each slice to keep it even.

Reducing Canes. Reducing canes refers to making the diameter of the cane smaller. You can reduce the entire cane you've made, or cut off portions and reduce each to a different diameter.

Roll a circular cane on your work surface, applying even pressure with your hands over the entire length of the cane. Roll it slowly and carefully to minimize distortion.

To reduce a square or rectangular cane, roll over it with your brayer or acrylic rod, flipping the cane over occasionally to make sure the pressure is applied evenly. Allow canes to rest and cool after reducing them.

Shaping Canes. You can reshape a cane by squeezing carefully with your fingers. For instance, turn a round bull's eye cane into a triangle by pinching the top slightly and pressing down at the same time. Flip it onto its side and repeat on each of the other sides. Smooth the sides with your fingertip or with your brayer.

STORAGE

Properly stored polymer clay will last indefinitely. Store your leftover clay away from heat and direct sunlight. Cover with waxed paper or keep it in a covered container to keep out dust and animal hair. Conditioned polymer clay may require brief kneading to get it to a workable state if it's been stored a while. Old canes can usually be brought back to a workable condition with careful warming and slight pressure.

ACCORDION BOOK

This book has the appeal of an ancient tablet and the durability of polymer clay, making it a wonderful gift for a writer or journal enthusiast. It's also a gorgeous embellishment for an Asian-inspired home or office. High-quality (often handmade) papers are sold in large sheets at art-supply stores.

MATERIALS AND TOOLS

Polymer clay, 2 ounces each black and maroon
Pasta machine, acrylic roller, or brayer
Wax paper
Gold-colored mica powder
Rubber stamp with Asian symbols or design
Asian coin or coin stamp
Art paper
Bone folder
Baking sheet or tile
Polymer clay cutting blade
Baby wipe or damp paper towel
Wet/dry sandpaper, 600 grit
Craft glue

WHAT TO DO

1 Roll the maroon polymer clay into a sheet of medium thickness (about ¹⁄₁₆ to ⅛ inch or 1.5 mm to 3 mm) on the pasta machine and place sheet on a piece of wax paper. You can also use an acrylic roller or a brayer to flatten clay.

2 Use your fingers to rub gold-colored mica powder on one side of the clay, covering the entire surface.

Position the rubber stamp onto the clay and firmly press over the entire surface to indent. Remove the stamp and set the stamped maroon clay aside. (The clay will "cool" as it sits, making the edges tear nicely.)

3 Roll the black polymer clay into the same thickness as the maroon sheet (see Step 1). Apply mica powder to the center of the black sheet, and press the Asian coin or coin stamp firmly into the clay to indent. Remove the coin or stamp and set the black sheet aside.

4 Crease and tear the art paper into a long strip that measures 51 x 4½ inches (130 x 11.25 cm); you may need to piece together several pages, depending on the size of your paper. Fold the paper back and forth (accordion style) into 3-inch (7.5 cm) sections. Crease the fold with a bone folder or your fingernail, then set aside.

5 Tear the maroon sheet into a rectangle that is roughly ½ inch (13 mm) larger than the size of folded paper. Hold the sheet on the work surface with one hand, grasp a corner with the other hand, and pull the clay forward to tear. (If the clay begins to stretch instead of tear, it is too warm; let it sit longer.)

Dip your finger in the gold mica powder and apply powder to the torn edges of the clay. Set the cover on your baking sheet or tile with the stamped side facing up.

6 Use a polymer clay cutting blade to cut the black clay into a rectangle that is slightly larger than the size of the folded paper and

Designer: Irene Semanchuk Dean

place on the baking sheet with the stamped side facing up. Use a baby wipe or a damp paper towel to remove any excess powder from the surface of each cover. Bake covers at the manufacturer's recommended temperature for 30 minutes and allow to cool completely.

7 Use wet 600-grit sandpaper to scuff away any remaining gold powder from the raised surfaces of the red clay. Wet the sandpaper, not the clay—the powder can get washed away if clay is immersed in water. Sand around the coin on the black sheet as well, if needed.

8 Glue one end page of the accordion to the inside of one clay cover and press firmly until dry. Repeat on other side of paper with other cover.

FAUX-MALACHITE SWITCH PLATES

Do your switch plates make a statement? These do! Once you get the bug, you will discover a host of faux stone surfaces can be created with polymer clay. Try also shaping objects out of the faux-malachite clay and attaching to the surface of the switch plate.

MATERIALS AND TOOLS

Polymer clay: green, black, and white
Pasta machine, acrylic roller, or brayer
Plastic or metal switch plates
Heat-resistant PVA glue
Wax paper

Craft knife
Pencil or golf tee
Wet/dry sandpaper, 400 through 1000 grit
Buffing wheel (optional) or soft cloth

WHAT TO DO

1 Coat the switch plate with a thin coating of heat-resistant PVA glue; allow to completely dry.

2 Mix the clay to create three shades of green: set aside some green straight from the package, mix three parts green and one part white to make a lighter shade of green, and mix six parts green and one part black to make a darker shade of green.

3 Roll each shade of green into a snake shape. Twist the three snakes together and roll into a log on the work surface. Fold, roll, and twist clay repeatedly until you have a log with a pleasing, random variegated pattern. (Be careful not to incorporate air bubbles into the clay as you work.)

4 Flatten the log with the palm of your hand until it is thin enough to roll through the pasta machine. Roll clay through the pasta machine on the thickest setting, rotate 90 degrees, then roll it through again at a slightly thinner setting. Alternative method: Roll the clay with a brayer or an acrylic roller, flipping the clay over occasionally. Roll in every direction to get the clay as even in thickness as possible.

5 When the clay is between 1/16 inch (1.5 mm) and 1/8 inch (3 mm) in thickness, determine which side of the clay has the most appealing design. Lay the sheet of clay onto the switch plate and cover with a piece of wax paper.

6 Working from the center outward, smooth the clay against the switch plate with your fingers or a brayer. If necessary, lift and replace sections of clay to eliminate air bubbles. Smooth the clay around the edges of the switch plate, and trim the excess clay from the edges with a craft knife.

7 Cut out the switch holes with a craft knife. Use a pencil or a golf tee to make screw holes.

8 Bake at the manufacturer's recommended temperature for 20 minutes. Allow to cool completely.

9 Beginning with 400-grit sandpaper and working up to 1000-grit, wet-sand the clay. Buff on a cotton buffing wheel or with a soft cloth. (See page 406 for sanding and buffing instructions.)

Designer: Irene Semanchuk Dean

FESTIVE CANDLESTICKS

Part of the appeal of these dramatic candlesticks comes from the fact that each is slightly different, while all share the same color scheme.

MATERIALS AND TOOLS

About 6 oz. (170 g) of polymer clay per candlestick, 2-inch diameter (50 mm) metal washer, fiberglass-reinforced tubing 6–8 inches (15–20 cm) long and ⅜ inch (1 cm) in diameter, copper plumbing pipe cap, electric drill, head pins, cyanoacrylate glue, small decorative beads (purchased or your own)

WHAT TO DO

BUILDING THE COMPONENTS

1 To make the base, form a ball of scrap polymer clay about 1½ inches (4 cm) in diameter and cover it with a very thin layer of solid-colored clay or a mosaic of cane slices.

2 Center the ball on a heavy metal washer, pressing down to cover the washer and create a mound shape about 1-inch (2.5 cm) high. The washer will be visible on the bottom; use it as a design element or cover it with clay as desired.

3 Using scrap clay, make a second ball somewhat smaller than the first. This will become the decorative element midway up the stem, so decorate it accordingly.

4 Arrow shaft tubing, a fiberglass-reinforced material, makes an effective stem because it is light and strong, and the clay adheres well to it. A wooden dowel can be substituted, but the clay won't adhere as well. Cover the tubing with a thin sheet of clay, making a butt joint and smoothing the seam carefully.

5 A candle, copper pipe cap, or mold of an existing candle holder can be used to form the candle cup. Cut a circle of clay ¼ inch (6 mm) thick, using your form to establish the diameter. From a sheet at least ⅛- inch (3 mm) thick, cut a strip of clay ½–¾ inch (1.5–2 cm) wide and bend it around your form to make a cylinder. (Apply some talcum powder on the form to make it release easily.)

6 Without removing the form, make a butt joint and smooth the seam of the clay cylinder. Then attach the circle of clay to the bottom edge of the cylinder, carefully smoothing the seam. While the cup is still supported by the form, decorate it however you choose. You can also shape the candle cup or give it a zigzag top edge, but you must maintain enough thickness and height to support a candle.

7 After removing the form from the candle cup, bake all of the components as instructed by the clay manufacturer.

ASSEMBLY

1 Measure the outside dimension of your stem, then mark the center of the other three pieces with a circle slightly smaller than the size of the stem. In the base, drill a hole about ¾ inch (18 mm) deep. Drill all the way through the decorative ball; then drill into the bottom of the candle cup without drilling through it.

2 Slide the decorative ball onto the stem and anchor it in place with rings of clay around the top and bottom. Place the bottom of the stem into the base and use another ring of clay to hold the two pieces together and hide the seam. If the stem wobbles in the base, fill any gaps with clay to secure it. Fill the top of the stem with a pea-sized ball of clay before placing the cap on the stem; then secure the cap with another ring of clay. Add more decoration—textures, cane slices, and the like—and bake the candlestick as directed.

3 After baking, drill several tiny holes down into the center of the candle cup through the pea of clay that was added. Into these holes, apply head pins coated with a couple of drops of glue. These provide some extra reinforcement to the union of the candle and stem.

4 Add finishing touches by drilling holes in various parts of the candlestick. Thread beads onto head pins that have been cut slightly longer than the depth of the holes; then apply glue to the pins and insert them into the holes. Press until the beads are flush against the surface of the clay.

Designer: Sarah Shriver

MOLDED KNOBS

Does your kitchen need a splash of color and originality? Personalize your cabinets and drawers with these great handmade polymer-clay knobs. And there's no end to the found objects you can use to create design motifs.

MATERIALS AND TOOLS

Wooden cabinet knobs
Heat-resistant PVA glue
Polymer clay in color of your choice,
 ½ ounce for each knob
Craft knife
Pasta machine, brayer, or acrylic
 roller
Wax paper
Sandpaper
1½-inch (4 cm) circle cutter
Mold made with a found object
 (see page 404)
Baking sheet or tile
Acrylic paint in color of your choice
Cyanoacrylate glue (optional)

DESIGNER TIP

When gluing onto baked polymer clay, always wipe the clay and the piece you're gluing to it with an alcohol-dampened paper towel or cotton ball. This will remove any oils or residue that would interfere with the glue bond.

WHAT TO DO

1 Use your fingers to coat the cabinet knob with a thin, even layer of PVA glue. Allow to dry completely.

2 Roll out a sheet of polymer clay that is long enough to wrap around the base of the knob. (The clay should not cover the top of the knob, but should be just wide enough to extend over the top edge.) Cut one end of the clay straight across with a craft knife then press the clay end into the base of the knob.

3 Wrap the clay around base of the knob, pressing firmly against the base as you wrap. Trim the clay with a craft knife where it overlaps and smooth the seam with your fingertips. Smooth clay against the top of the knob and slightly over edge, then trim away any excess clay. Set knob aside.

4 Roll a sheet of polymer clay on a pasta machine, brayer, or acrylic roller and position on a piece of wax paper.

5 Spray or wipe water (this serves as a mold release) onto the clay, then texture the clay sheet by pressing sandpaper into the clay until an

impression is made. Use the cutter to make a circle from the clay.

6 Center the circle on top of the knob and press clay firmly in the center to adhere. (Don't worry about marring the texture, as the molded object will cover any marks.) Press the rest of the circle of clay onto the knob, then texture with the sandpaper to cover any fingerprints (see Step 5). The circle should overlap the clay that has been wrapped around the base of the knob (see Step 3).

7 Create a molded object (see page 404). Center the molded object on the textured area of the knob. Press as firmly as possible without marring the surface of the molded object. Bake knob for 30 minutes at the manufacturer's recommended temperature. Allow to cool completely.

8 When knob is cool, apply acrylic paint with your fingertips, pushing the paint into every crevice. Wipe thoroughly with a paper towel to remove most of paint, leaving paint only in the recessed areas. When paint has dried, bake knob for 10 minutes at 200°F (93°C) to set paint. If the molded objects do not attach to the knob properly, secure with cyanoacrylate glue.

Designer: Irene Semanchuk Dean

THREE-LEGGED BOWL

This little bowl—perfect for a ledge or small nook—is adorned with an assortment of decorations that speak to the carefree attitude of the artist.

MATERIALS AND TOOLS

Polymer clay, 1 ounce each blue and purple, ½ ounce black, and small amounts of other contrasting colors
Pasta machine
Wax paper
Small shape cutters (optional)
Ripple blade or handheld crinkle French fry cutter (optional)

Cane slices (optional)
Acrylic rod or brayer
Texturing material (such as plastic embroidery canvas, lace, or window screen)
Craft knife
Oven-safe bowl
Cyanoacrylate glue (optional)

WHAT TO DO

1 Create a Skinner blend (see page 405) from the blue and purple clay. Roll clay out, using the thickest setting on a pasta machine. Place the clay on a piece of wax paper.

2 Create one or more Skinner blends from the other contrasting colors and roll them on a very thin setting on the pasta machine. Place these pieces on a separate piece of wax paper.

3 From the smaller blended sheets, cut a variety of shapes and stripes, using shape cutters and the ripple blade cutter, if desired. Position these randomly over the surface of the blue/purple blended piece of clay. Add thin cane slices as well, if desired (see pages 406 and 407 for how to make cane slices).

4 When you're happy with the design, lay a piece of wax paper over the clay and roll gently with a rod or brayer to press the embellishments into the background clay. Flip the sheet of clay to the other side, decorate, and roll, just as you did with the first side.

5 Position the clay sheet, with the top facing down, on a piece of wax paper. Spray or wipe water (this serves as a mold release) onto the polymer clay sheet, then position the textured material on top. Roll over the textured material to create an impression in the clay. Gently dab away excess water with a paper towel.

6 Cut a large circular shape from the clay, using a craft knife. Smooth the cut edges of the bowl gently with your fingertips. (Don't worry about cutting the shape

exactly round.) Set the excess clay aside and peel off the wax paper.

7 Turn an oven-safe bowl upside-down, and center the clay bowl (textured side up) on the oven-safe bowl. Use your fingers to work with the clay bowl until the curves along the outside rim are somewhat evenly shaped. Bake for 30 minutes, following the manufacturer's instructions, then allow to cool.

8 When the clay bowl is completely cooled (but still on the oven-safe bowl), add the feet. To make the feet, roll three equal-sized balls from black polymer clay and decorate with small pieces of colored clay. Position the balls so that they are evenly spaced on the underside of the clay bowl, then press them onto the clay.

9 Lay a piece of wax paper on the balls (now the feet of the bowl) and turn the clay bowl right side up on the work surface. If the bowl does not sit evenly, gently press down where necessary to level.

10 Turn the clay bowl back onto the oven-safe bowl, remove the wax paper, and bake again for 20 minutes. After the bowl has cooled, the feet can be secured with cyanoacrylate glue.

Safety Note: Do not put anything edible on or inside of polymer clay.

Designer: Irene Semanchuk Dean

CANEWORKED BEADS

The variety you get from one cane is truly amazing! Once you create your canes, you can use them in almost limitless ways. They make wonderful beads, and can be worked into different shapes and sizes.

MATERIALS AND TOOLS

Polymer clay, in colors to coordinate with your canes
Polymer clay canes
Needle tool
Steel weaving needle, knitting needle, or bamboo skewer
Polymer clay cutting blade
Shape cutters
Waxed paper

WHAT TO DO

CANE-SLICE BEADS

For sliced beads, cut thick slices (³⁄₁₆ to ⅛ inch) from your canes. Hold a slice between the finger and thumb of one hand, and insert the needle tool into the side of the slice. Press gently but firmly, rotating the needle tool in your fingers as you press it through the clay. When you see the tip of the tool appearing on the other side of the slide, withdraw the needle tool and re-pierce from the other side, which will ensure that the holes are neat.

SHAPED BEADS

1 To create beads of exactly the same size, roll a piece of polymer clay into a sheet. Cut numerous shapes from the sheet, and roll each into a bead in the palms of your hands. Using the same shape cut from the same sheet will result in uniformly-sized beads. By combining two or more shapes, you can also use this technique to make beads of graduated sizes.

2 Cut thin slices from your polymer clay canes and arrange them on the solid color bead shapes. Depending on your cane patterns and your desired outcome, the cane slices can overlap, or they might look better butted against each other. Roll gently in the palms of your hands to smooth the cane slices into the clay. Keep an eye on what you're doing, so you don't roll too much and distort the pattern.

3 Pierce as described in Cane-Slice Beads. Bake the beads on a nest of fiberfill or on wires suspended across a box or frame (see page 403).

TUBE BEADS

1 Roll a sheet of polymer clay to a medium thickness on your pasta machine. Cut many slices from your canes and apply them to the surface of the clay sheet. When the sheet is covered, place a piece of waxed paper on top and gently roll over the sheet to adhere all the slices.

2 Roll the sheet through the pasta machine on a setting one notch thicker than the sheet (the cane

(continues on page 420)

418

Designer: Irene Semanchuk Dean

slices have made the sheet thicker!). Set the pasta machine one notch thinner, turn the sheet 90°, and roll it through the pasta machine again, then set aside.

3 Roll a piece of scrap clay the size of a walnut in the palms of your hands. Pierce it with a long weaving needle, knitting needle, or bamboo skewer and leave the piercing tool in place. Roll this with the palm of your hand on your work surface to elongate the scrap clay. Roll slowly and gently so the hole doesn't become too enlarged. If it does, squeeze it together around the skewer. Roll until the scrap clay has formed a long tube of even thickness.

4 Cut a straight edge on your sheet of cane-decorated clay and turn the sheet right side down. Set the tube of scrap clay, still on the skewer, on the sheet of clay at the edge. Roll the sheet of clay around the pen, and trim the sheet so the edges meet but don't overlap. Roll the tube on your work surface to smooth it.

5 Fold a piece of paper into an accordion shape, place the tube in one of the folds, and bake for 30 minutes at manufacturer's recommended temperature. Alternatively, you could suspend the skewer across a box or frame.

6 When the clay has finished baking, remove the skewer from the tube of clay. Do this while the clay is still warm, but not so hot that you burn yourself. Use your cutting blade to cut the tube into bead lengths, using quick, straight, downward motions. You can allow the clay to cool completely, but it's more difficult to achieve clean, straight cuts.

DESIGNER TIP

Make buttons to match your jewelry! The stronger brands of polymer clay will withstand machine washing. Poke holes through the buttons for thread or use cyanoacrylate glue to attach plastic shanks to the polymer clay after baking. Turn the garment inside out and air dry. Do not dry clean.

POLYMER CLAY CHRISTMAS DECORATIONS

Although these precious little Christmas decorations are simple to make, they are sure to become treasured holiday ornaments.

MATERIALS AND TOOLS

Polymer clay, red and green
Pasta machine
Polymer clay cutting blade
Eye pins
Silver or gold lacquer pen
Cyanoacrylate glue (optional)
Decorative cording
Extruder

WHAT TO DO

TO MAKE GIFT PACKAGES

1 Roll red or green polymer clay through a pasta machine on the thickest setting. Make a slab of clay that is approximately ¼ inch (6 mm) thick by folding over the sheet of polymer clay, taking care not to trap air bubbles between layers. Cut clay into squares or rectangles in the desired dimensions with the polymer clay cutting blade.

2 To make ribbons, roll polymer clay in a contrasting color through the pasta machine on a medium setting. With the cutting blade, cut ⅛-inch-wide (3 mm) strips.

3 Position clay strips so that they cross on the front of the squares or rectangles. Loop strips of clay and arrange loops and strips in the centers of the clay packages to form bows (see photograph).

Designer: Tracy Hildebrand

4 Insert an eye pin in the center of one side of each package for a hanger.

5 Bake clay gift packages according to the clay manufacturer's instructions.

6 When clay has cooled completely, embellish with a metallic lacquer pen.

7 Apply a small dot of cyanoacrylate glue to the area where the eye pin is inserted into the clay. String cording through eye pin and tie.

TO MAKE THE WREATH

1 Using your hands, roll green polymer clay into a long cylinder that is about the diameter of the pencil. Cut cylinder into a 4¼-inch (36 cm) length. Form a circle with the length of clay and smooth clay where ends meet.

2 Squeeze green clay through an extruder on the "angel hair" setting. Cut the resulting clay into ¼-inch (6 mm) pieces and apply pieces in a random pattern to simulate the texture of greenery.

3 Make a clay bow from red clay as described above (Steps 2 and 3) and position bow on wreath. Roll tiny pieces of red clay into balls and attach to wreath (see photograph).

4 Follow Steps 4 through 7 to finish wreath.

Above: The intricate patterns of nature can be reproduced beautifully in polymer clay. Glass beads, telephone and brass wire, and glitter were also used in this grasshopper. Designer: Joyce Fritz

Right: A unique wall piece was created by gluing squares of polymer clay that had been stamped with a design to a large floor tile. Faux grout was created with rolled logs of clay and pressed between the tiles, and finally the clay was painted. Designer: Anna Riddle

Opposite page, top left: Polymer projects can do more than just look pretty. These colorful dominos play just like the traditional variety. Designer: Liz Mitchell

Opposite page, top right: Transform simple ink pens into glimmering keepsakes by covering them with black clay and variegated gold and copper leaf. Designer: Irene Semanchuk Dean

Opposite page, bottom left: Grace your favorite clothing with one-of-a-kind, customized buttons molded and baked over button backings. Designers: Steven Ford and David Forlano

Opposite page, bottom right: Wondering what to do with all of those polymer canes you made in a burst of creative energy? Merge them into interesting shapes, then cut mirrors to suit your new polymer frames. Designer: Bridget Albano

BREAD DOUGH

Dough craft is an ancient domestic art. On record since the beginnings of Western civilization, bread dough ornaments and devotional tributes decorate households around the world. Wherever there is grain and salt, people have used their hands and hearths to create fairy tale figures, religious subjects, and seasonal symbols. Crafting with bread dough (or "salt dough")—flour, salt, and water—provides both handsome ornaments and the joy of participating in a craft has lasted for generations. (For a modern alternative, see page 427.)

MATERIALS AND TOOLS

FLOUR
Choose all-purpose flour, not self-rising. Best results are obtained with flour that requires as little water as possible to make a strong, flexible dough.

SALT
A fine-textured salt blends well and forms the smoothest surface. Many experts recommend noniodized, non-flouridated table salt.

ADDITIVES AND ENHANCEMENTS
Wallpaper paste can increase salt dough firmness, and is important if you plan to air dry your pieces. Cornstarch or a small amount of vegetable oil or glycerin can improve flexibility.

TOOLS AND CRAFTING SUPPLIES
Scissors, modeling tools, paintbrushes, polyurethane varnish, a plastic ruler, paper clips, florial wire, wire cutters, pliers, household glue, and a pocket comb are all helpful.

KITCHEN SUPPLIES
Your kitchen probably already contains many of the supplies you'll need: mixing bowls, measuring cups, a container for clear water, cookie sheets, cooking oil, cake decorating tips, cookie or biscuit cutters, a small sieve or strainer, small knife, rolling pin, a cheese grater with several options for fineness, a garlic press, a potato ricer, and table forks. Aluminum foil, drinking straws, black peppercorns, cloves, and toothpicks are also helpful.

OPTIONAL INSPIRATIONS
Dried flowers, nuts and seeds, shells, pebbles, glass forms, ribbons, raffia, and moss are just a few possibilities.

BASIC TECHNIQUES

BASIC TECHNIQUES

Salt dough behaves best in a cool room, i.e., 70°F or below. Rinse your hands with cool water frequently to prevent over-warming of the dough. Keep dough covered when you are not using it.

PREPARING THE DOUGH

Salt dough must be kneaded until it is perfectly smooth and flexible. A sturdy hand-mixer, or a food processor fitted with a dough attachment saves time and effort. Be sure not to overheat your equipment with large batches.

Try to make only as much dough as you can work with at one time; fresh dough handles easily and stays moist longer. If you want to store it, however, seal out air and keep it in a cool place (not the refrigerator).

RECIPES

Basic proportions for your dough:

4 cups all-purpose flour

1 cup salt

1½ cup water

Different flours add variety in color and weight. Adjust the basic recipe for the browning tones of rye flour by preparing a large batch in combination:

3 cups all-purpose flour

1 cup rye flour

2 cups salt

1½ cups water

Having more dough on hand will help you adjust to rye flour's heavier weight in your models.

For more elasticity, or if you prefer to air dry your pieces, add 2 tablespoons of premixed wallpaper paste to a regular recipe Reduce water to ½ cup.

To make a finer salt dough for delicate modeling, combine:

2 cups flour

1 cup salt

100 g cornstarch

¾ cup water

Make a firm salt dough for textured models:

2 cups flour

2 cups salt

½ cup water

For even more firmness, as when you are making tiles or other flat pieces, add 2 tablespoons of wallpaper paste to this mixture.

426

MODELING

Begin modeling on a layer of aluminum foil or a cookie sheet that you have oiled and brushed lightly with water. This smooths the back of the model, eliminates air bubbles, and, as you will place the foil or pan directly in the oven, you won't risk distorting the piece by moving it. Avoid nonstick pans that have a slightly textured surface; cover them with aluminum foil if necessary.

Many projects have multiple parts to be attached after modeling. Join the freshest parts of a piece by brushing the surfaces with water, taking care not to spread moisture farther as it will stain the dough. If one part is dry, or if you are repairing a break in an unvarnished, dry piece, use a bread dough adhesive to connect them: add water to scraps of fresh dough and stir it until it forms a paste. Dried bits of dough can be powdered in a mortar and then mixed with water. Once pieces are dry, smooth with sandpaper as necessary. Painted and varnished pieces must be connected or repaired with wood glue, epoxy or fast-drying household glue.

AIR-DRY CLAY ALTERNATIVE

If you are in a modern hurry, air-dry clay will produce similar results in less time. There's no dough to make, and there's no baking; completed projects air-dry in about 24 hours.

These pliable, ready-made clays come in a variety of colors. For additional hues, you can knead two or more colors together or mix acrylic paint into the clay. After it has dried, it can be sanded and painted with acrylic paints.

Essentially the same tools and techniques are used to work salt dough and air-dry clay. While the family cooking utensils are often used for salt dough, it's probably wise to dedicate a separate set of those tools for clay. Since clay is somewhat denser than dough, an inexpensive plastic extruder works better than the garlic presses and cake-icing bags beloved by dough-crafters.

BASIC TECHNIQUES

To build basic models, practice the following steps until you feel confident enough to proceed to more complicated forms.

Frames and plaques: Add wallpaper paste or cornstarch, if you need to, to increase firmness. Roll dough at least ½-inch (12 mm) thick on the baking surface. Cut edges straight or use a modeling tool, such as a crimper. For a frame effect on a round or oval base, roll a dough rope, moisten it, and nestle it to the base, smoothing out points of connection. For squared edges, lightly define the rope as it turns the corners, and smooth the connection. Alternatively, cut the rope into four appropriate lengths (bevel the ends if you wish) and connect them at the corners.

Braids and wreaths: Roll oblongs of dough with closed fingers and flat hands into ropes of equal length. Begin braids by crossing ropes at their centers and twisting them away toward the ends. Place the ropes under each other as you braid to the left; place them over each other as you work toward the right. Bring the braids together before you, and cut the ends diagonally to match (undercut one, and overcut the other to fit). Press them together and blend carefully to eliminate "seams."

Three-dimensional objects: Save energy and time by removing weight and moisture from certain kinds of models. For hollow forms, bake pieces for two hours, or until the outer layer is dried through about the thickness of an onion layer. Core out the interior, leaving about ½ inch of the outer wall. Or create support forms with coated cardboard or aluminum foil. Aluminum foil also makes excellent "upholstery" for thick models. Simply wad it into the shape you want, coat it with ½ inch of bread dough, and proceed to ornament or baking. The foil can be removed from open forms or left inside, as you wish.

WELCOME GIFTS

Baskets and bowls are wonderful vehicles for treats, special soaps, jewelry, potpourri, nuts and fruit, or bread. Trim them with modeled braid or rope, cascading blossoms, a few pieces of luscious fruit, leaves, stars and moons, baby trinkets, or very personal mementos for a friend.

Reproduction: layer salt dough around your own vases and bowls, lightly coated with oil, or line the inside of a favorite pot or bowl if that is easier.

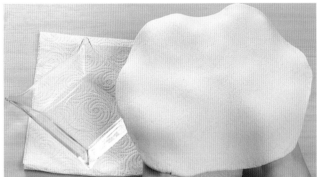

PATTERNS AND TEXTURES

Toothpicks, tweezers, fork tines, and patterned buttons are just the beginning; nearly anything with points or a pattern can be used to add texture and dimension to salt dough creations. A basket may sport plaits or a herringbone weave, repeated florals can trim out a plaque, picture frames gain depth from leaf-and-twig patterns, and fanciful figures can be enhanced by randomly stamped stars, moons, and clouds. Clove stalks become stems for cherries or apples; press stem in and star out and they are the blossom end of a pear or a kumquat. Black peppercorns are very effective as eyes for small people and animals.

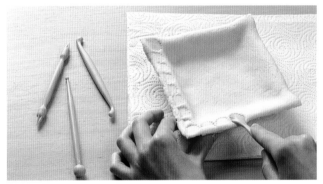

Two tools in particular are extremely handy for producing special effects; create fine lengths of "hair" by pressing dough through a strainer; thicker, curlier strands are possible with a garlic press. Form a halo of waving locks around a face, or pass a knife over the plate of the garlic press to cut pelts of sheep's wool.

BASIC TECHNIQUES

DRYING AND BAKING

You can dry your models in the open air, bake them in electric, gas, or convection ovens, or heat them through in a microwave unit. Consider whether you want most to save time or heating expense as you plan. Air-drying costs nothing and can take days to weeks to complete. Baking salt dough involves simple adjustments to take into account the rate and amount of water loss as your models dry. Electric ovens do the job in hours, depending upon the temperature setting; gas stoves provide natural evaporation and take half the time. Convection speeds surface drying; extra time is required to finish baking the interior. A microwave oven can be most efficient if the heating process is carefully monitored.

AIR-DRYING

Air drying is a convenient option to baking. This is the best method for very thin, flat creations since it reduces cracking. Adding wallpaper paste to your recipe will firm the dough.

Plan on a day of drying time for every 1/16 inch (1.5 mm) of dough thickness. A practical choice for a large, thick model might be to place it near—not on—a radiator or heating element for a day, or in a very warm, dry room. An air-dried project can be finished in the oven if you start at a low temperature setting, to prevent over heating of a still-moist interior. Watch for a pocked or curved under surface, caused by moisture loss; dampen it and "spackle" with salt dough paste to smooth.

OVEN BAKING

Electric: Set temperature at 300°F and allow one hour per quarter-inch thickness of the model. Thus, a 1½-inch (4 cm) piece will bake in about six hours. Tap on the surface; if it returns a thick, dull sound, raise the temperature every 20 minutes to 200°, then 250°, then 300°, or until the model sounds like hardened clay when tapped. Note: Begin baking colored dough at 150°, and limit temperatures to 250°, to avoid changes in shade.

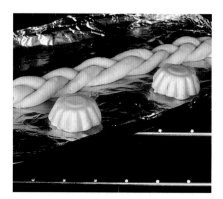

Convection: Set temperature at 170°. Bread dough models may require 12 hours to heat through. If further baking is needed, raise the temperature 25° every half hour, up to 250°. Watch for browning; cover with aluminum foil to preserve color.

Gas: The natural moisture content in gas results in an even evaporation of water, reducing drying time substantially. Set temperature at 225°F and leave the oven door open for an hour (taking precautions, of course, for the safety of children and pets). Prick any bubbles in the dough, and leave the door halfway open for the second hour. Then close the door until the project is finished.

Microwave: This method is great for impatient bakers, including eager children. Position your bread dough piece on an ungreased plate and use the "defrost," or lowest, setting, for five minutes at a time. Open the door after each session for several minutes to allow steam to escape. As the model dries, reduce cooking time and monitor carefully, watching for bubbles. Experiment to learn how various dough and model weights affect cooking time in your oven.

If you don't plan to paint or varnish your work right away, store it in a dry, airtight container.

COLOR

Dough may be colored in batches or in small quantities, if you don't want to paint later. Use food coloring if lightfastness is not a concern. Gouache (thick watercolor in tubes) or other liquid paints may be kneaded into dough by adding color to the center of a small section, folding it over, and working it through. Try dissolved coffee, cocoa, paprika, and other spices for natural hues.

Painting, while requiring practice, can add wonderful dimension to bread dough pieces. Use good-quality artist's brushes in a range of sizes and shapes, from very fine to broad. Remove rough edges from a baked piece to be painted with a knife or sandpaper. Polish it with a smooth, dry brush. For bright, clean color, apply a primer coat first, and allow it to dry.

Acrylics, watercolors, gouaches, and inks all take well to baked salt dough. Acrylic craft paint is glue based, so brushes must be kept wet during use and then washed out carefully. Watercolors lend a translucence that can be as light or deep as you desire. Gouaches are dense and cover surfaces well. Gold and silver paints in gouache or acrylic form can be applied before baking. Poster paints may be affected by the salt in the dough, taking on a greenish cast. Enamel paints are solvent based and therefore unsuitable for use by children and in unventilated rooms. They must be thinned with solvent and spray varnished to avoid ruining the color. Gold and silver enamels, applied after baking, are bright and lustrous and may be worth the extra effort required.

Simple, rustic effects can be achieved with natural glazes. To create a salt glaze, brush them lightly with saltwater several times in the last half hour of baking, if the temperature is above 250°, to make a tawny surface with a soft shine. A salt glaze can look deeper with a final application, during high-heat baking, of milk and water or egg yolk and water. Create a high-gloss look at the same heat with a mixture of corn syrup and water.

It takes practice to achieve the fetching beauty of painted models in a manual. Make a few extra decorations—an apple, shoes, leaves, a rosebud, a moon—each time you mold and bake. Practice using different paints and inks, experiment with shading, and try low- and high-gloss varnishes to view their effects. Always keep notes on techniques that work for you.

NATURAL MATERIALS

Grasses, pods, seeds, and flowers that dry well add texture and dimension to your work. Try incorporating yarrow, statice, or thistle in graceful groups or as single stems. Gild them with paint spray before gluing into place, or leave the natural color. A spritz of hair spray will intensify colors; spray varnish is enduring. Clean models with a hair dryer on a low, cool setting.

VARNISH

This step brightens and illuminates colors and preserves models from settling dust. Varnish also protects against moisture, which is drawn in and held by salt. Choose from wood varnish, which will add a yellow cast, or marine varnishes or polyurethane, which are transparent and bright. Both matte and glossy formulas are available.

If possible, select a varnish from the line of paints you are using. Place your completely dry creation facedown on a pillow covered with plain plastic or parchment paper, to protect delicate work. Varnish the back of the model first, in two or three coats, allowing four hours' drying time for each coat. Apply them carefully; keep the liquid from trickling underneath and spoiling the front. Clean the brush with mineral spirits between each application.

MOUNTING AND HANGING MODELS

Press coated paper clips, hairpins, or stub wire into dough before baking to serve as hangers for small pieces. Larger models can be safely mounted if you core out holes with a drinking straw before baking, and then use ribbon or wire to hang the piece after baking.

HOLIDAY ORNAMENTS

The accessories—hats and beards—are the fun feature in these ornaments. Think of favorite hats from sports, a wedding, a garden party, or an equestrian event, then make them in bread dough, adding as much detail as you wish.

MATERIALS AND TOOLS

Ingredients for 2 batches of bread dough (see page 426 for recipe)
Rolling pin
Liquid cake icing dye in red, royal blue, and green
Cutting board
Garlic press

Round toothpick or needle sculpting tool
Glass pony beads for eyes
Mini star cutter
Paper clips cut into **u**-shaped thirds with wire cutter
Foil-lined cookie sheet
Sealant

WHAT TO DO

1 Mix together one batch of bread dough, referring to the recipe on page 426, and color it with bright white liquid icing.

2 Mix together a second batch of bread dough. Divide it into four equal portions. Using the liquid icing dye, tint one portion red, one blue, and one green; leave the fourth portion untinted to serve as flesh-tone dough.

3 To make a face, form a 2-inch (5 cm) ball of flesh-tone dough. Place it on cutting board and use the palm of your hand to flatten it to a ⅓-inch (17 mm) thickness.

4 Place the pony beads about a third of the way down the face, using the toothpick or needle tool to pick them up and push them firmly into dough. Use the toothpick or needle tool to "draw" a smile. Repeat to make as many faces as you like.

TO MAKE THE HATS

For a Santa hat, make a 2-inch ball of red dough and shape it into a cone. Place it above the face and fold top of cone to the side.

For a cowboy hat, use red dough to make a 1¼ inch (32 cm) ball. Form a "peanut" shape with the ball, then place sideways above head.

For an Uncle Sam hat, roll a 6-inch (15 cm) cylinder of red and of white dough, just a little larger than ⅛ inch (3 mm) wide. Cut each cylinder into 1½-inch (4 cm) lengths. Press the cylinders together to form a red-and-white-striped cylinder 1½ inches long. Cut off uneven edges, then position it vertically on head.

5 Load your garlic press with white dough and squeeze out 2-inch (5 cm) lengths. For each length, use the needle tool to scrape the strings off and curl around the tool. Place one length at a time around your Santa's face, in desired way, to make his beard.

6 Form two long, thin teardrop shapes from the white dough to form the mustache. Place the fat sides together in middle of face, and curl the ends up on top of his beard. Use a small ball of flesh-colored dough to form a nose.

TO MAKE THE HAT RIMS

For the Santa hat, use a strip of white dough 3 inches (7.5 cm) long, ½ inch (13 cm) wide, and ¹⁄₁₆ inch (1.5 mm) thick. Make a ⅓-inch tassel from the white dough, then form tiny leaves from the green dough for a holly decoration.

For the cowboy hat brim, roll a 4-inch (10 cm) cylinder. Flatten with finger to ⅛ inch (3 mm) thick and ¾ inch (2 cm) wide. Place around head and curl up ends on each side. Use green dough to form tiny holly leaves on hat.

For Uncle Sam's hat brim, roll out a 3-inch (7.5) strip of blue dough, flatten to ¹⁄₁₆ inches (1.5 mm) thick, and place over hat. Cut out three stars from the white dough and press them onto the brim.

7 Press **u**-shaped paperclip pieces into the top of each hat for a

Designer: Bonnie Bone

hanger, then place them on a foil-lined cookie sheet and bake for approximately 2 to 3 hours. To test for doneness, remove from sheet and press very hard in thickest part of ornament. If it is still soft, put it back in the oven; continue testing every half hour until it is completely hard, then allow it to completely cool.

8 Glaze with your favorite sealant.

CLAY ALTERNATIVE

Replace the bread dough and liquid cake icing with air-dry clay in red, blue, green, white, and brown. (The white and brown are for flesh tones; mix the two in whatever proportions you like.) Replace the garlic press with a craft extruder. After forming the ornaments, allow them to air-dry for 24 hours.

ALL-AMERICAN APPLE PIE BASKET

Here's the next best thing to a real apple pie. You might consider a series: blueberry, peach, cherry, even blackberry. For best results, run your warm hands under cool water occasionally while you weave the lattice. For this project, salt dough is better than clay, since the look you want—baked dough— is exactly what saltdough is!

MATERIALS AND TOOLS

Ingredients for 2 batches of
  bread dough
Rolling pin
Cutting board
Liquid cake icing dye in red, white,
  and blue

Aluminum pie pan, any size
Sharp, nonserrated knife
Mini star cookie cutter
Small paintbrush
Sealant

WHAT TO DO

TO MAKE THE PIE

1 Mix together one batch of bread dough, referring to the recipe on page 426.

2 Roll the dough out to ¼-inch (6 mm) thickness on a lightly floured cutting board. Cut the dough into 1-inch-wide (2.5 cm) strips.

3 Lay the strips in the pie pan, alternating across length and width, weaving them as you would a pie crust. Depending on the size of the pan, try using four strips one direction, four strips the other, and one very long strip to go around the side of the pan, below the rim. Cut strips to fit over the rim of the pan.

4 With the palm of your hand, roll a long cylinder ½ inch (13 mm) wide. Place it on the rim and flatten slightly. Bake in a 300°F oven for one hour and let brown a bit. Allow to cool.

TO DECORATE THE BASKET

1 Mix together a second batch of bread dough and divide it into three equal portions. Tint one portion with bright red dye, one with bright white dye, and one with royal blue dye.

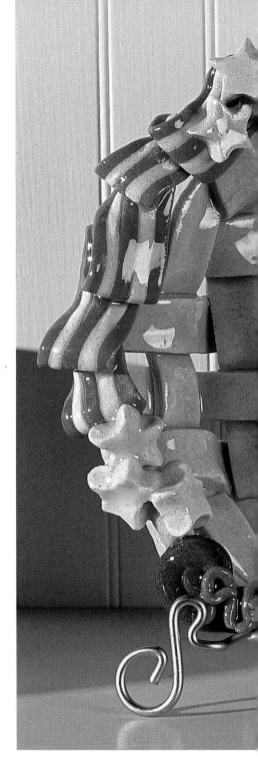

2 To form the ribbons, roll out three red and three white ⅛ inch-thick (3 mm) strips of dough about 9 inches (23 cm) long. Place the strips right next to each other so they touch, alternating the red and white. Press lightly to stick them together, then turn over to reveal a nice smooth side. Repeat to make a second ribbon.

434

Designer: Bonnie Bone

3 Brush the rim of the cooled basket with a bit of water so that dough will stick to it. Drape one ribbon gently down each side of basket, overlapping and folding every 1½ inches (4 cm).

4 Make 6-inch-long curlicues at top and bottom of the circle shape from the blue dough; flatten slightly.

5 Make ⅛-inch-wide (3 mm) ropes from the red dough, then use them to form the words "All American" at the top and "Apple Pie" at the bottom.

6 Cut out mini stars about ½ inch (12 mm) thick from the bright white dough and use them to fill in empty spaces on sides of basket.

7 Bake the basket at 250°F for two more hours, or until basket and decorations are hard to the touch when completely cool.

8 Glaze your basket with your favorite sealant.

PICTURE FRAME

Return photos of the event to the bride and groom in this special graphic frame, which may be decorated to resemble the actual cake, if you wish. Practice rolling and cutting petals for different flowers ahead of time.

MATERIALS AND TOOLS

Ingredients for 1½ batches of bread dough
Rolling pin
Liquid cake icing dye in bright white, light pink, dark pink, and green
Icing bag and #21 frosting tip
3- to 4-inch (7.5 to 10 cm) heart-shaped cookie cutter
Foil-lined cookie sheet
Small paintbrush
Stand-up frame backing (can be purchased at a framing store)
Craft knife
Glue gun

CLAY ALTERNATIVE

Replace the bread dough and liquid cake icing with air-dry clay in white, pink, and green. (If you want both a dark pink and a light pink, mix white clay into a portion of the pink.) Replace the icing bag with a craft extruder. After forming the frame, allow it to air-dry for a least 24 hours.

WHAT TO DO

1 Mix together one batch of bread dough, referring to the recipe on page 426. Divide the dough in half, then tint it with bright white icing dye.

2 Divide the remaining bread dough into three equal portions. Tint one portion light pink, one portion dark pink, and one portion green.

3 Mix together a half batch of bread dough, using only half the flour.

4 Roll out the bright white dough to a thickness of ⅓ inch (9 mm) and transfer it to a foil-lined cookie sheet. Use the template on page 516 to cut out the cake shape, then cut out a heart shape from the center of cake-shaped dough.

5 Roll two 2-inch (5 cm) balls of dough, one in light pink and one in dark pink. Next, roll each ball under the palm of your hand to make two 6-inch (15 cm) cylinders. Twist the two together to make a rope, then use the rope to line the inside of the heart-shaped dough.

6 Roll two 1-inch (2.5 cm) balls of dough, one in light pink and one in dark pink. Roll each ball into very long, thin cylinders, each about 10 inches (25 cm) long and ⅛ inch (3 mm) wide. Drape the light pink cylinder in a swag design across top, middle, and bottom tier of the cake, cutting them off at the edge of the heart shape and continuing them on the opposite side. Follow with a slightly longer swag of dark pink underneath.

7 Use a paintbrush and water to moisten each horizontal edge of the cake shape. Then, with your icing bag and tip, pipe the softer bright white dough made with less flour onto each of these edges in a zigzag pattern.

8 Make several leaves out of green dough by rolling ½-inch balls. Flatten one end of each ball with the thumb and index finger of one hand while pinching the other end with the thumb and index finger of the other hand. Attach two or three leaves at the top center swag, and some on the middle and lower tiers.

9 To make a flower, form a ½-inch ball of either shade of pink and roll it into a 1¼-inch (32 mm) cylinder. Flatten it with your finger, pressing slightly harder on one side than the other so that you end up with a long, thin wedge shape. Roll the flower up tightly from one end to the other, pressing slightly harder on the fatter edge

Designer: Bonnie Bone

this time to create a small rosebud
shape. Repeat to make multiple
flowers and place them at the top
of the leaf shapes in groups of two
or three.

10 Bake the frame at 250°F for
2 to 3 hours or until completely hard when cool, then finish
with a coat of sealant.

11 Use a craft knife to cut the
frame backing to fit the
finished bread dough frame, then
secure them together with a glue gun.

HOLIDAY WREATH

Richly textured and gleaming with color, this wreath has heirloom potential. Experiment with new surfaces, and handle the pressed dough tufts carefully to avoid clumping.

MATERIALS AND TOOLS

Ingredients for 2 batches of
  bread dough
Liquid cake icing dye in green, red,
  brown, yellow, and blue
Rolling pin
Mini Christmas cookie cutters, one
  a gingerbread man

Garlic press
Needle sculpting tool
Paper clip
Foil-lined cookie sheet
Nonserrated knife
Sealant

WHAT TO DO

1 Mix together one batch of bread dough, referring to the recipe on page 426. Tint the dough with green liquid icing dye.

2 Mix together a second batch of bread dough. Divide it in two equal portions. Tint one of the portions with red liquid icing dye. Next, divide the second half of the dough into three equal portions. Tint one portion brown, one yellow, and one royal blue.

3 Roll a green rope of about 18 to 20 inches (45 to 50 cm) long and ¾ inch (2 cm) wide. Arrange it in a circle in the middle of your cookie sheet. Allow at least 2 inches (5 cm) of room on all sides of sheet.

4 Load garlic press with green dough. Squeeze out tufts of dough about 2 inches long. Scrape off each tuft and casually place it in a random arrangement on the circle until the entire circle is covered and the wreath is of uniform width.

5 Flatten out a 4-inch (10 cm) ball of brown dough with a small roller or the back of a spatula to a thickness of ¼ inch (6 mm). Cut two gingerbread men out of the brown and decorate them with dough to resemble traditional gingerbread men cookies. Place one on each side of wreath.

6 To make the bow, roll two 2½ inch (6 cm) balls of red dough. Shape one into a cylinder and flatten it to a thickness of ⅛ inch, 1 inch (2.5 cm) wide, and 6 inches (15 cm) long. Place the rolled dough at the top of the wreath, gently overlapping the ends to form a graceful ribbon.

7 To continue forming the bow, shape the second ball into a cylinder about 5-inches (13 cm) long, and flatten to a thickness of ⅛ inch. Fold the ends over onto the center and pinch center to form a bow tie. Transfer the bow to the top of the ribbons, and gently press to stick. Roll out a ½-inch-long cylinder, flatten, and cover the pinched center of bow tie, using the needle tool to tuck the ends under the tie.

8 Make two to four small candy canes by rolling red and white ropes together (⅛ inch thick and 1½ inches long). Gently press the two lengths together, then twist them together. Press them onto the desired areas on the wreath and bend them into candy-cane shapes.

9 Cut mini stars or other Christmas shapes from the dough and place them randomly

CLAY ALTERNATIVE

Replace the bread dough and liquid cake icing with air-dry clay in green, red, brown, yellow, and blue. After forming the wreath, allow it to air-dry for at least 24 hours.

Designer: Bonnie Bone

on the wreath. If you don't have mini cutters, you can hand-form various shapes.

10 Roll tiny colored balls and place them randomly around the wreath to resemble lights.

11 Cut a large paper clip into thirds, pressing the largest piece into top of wreath as a hanger.

12 Bake wreath for 2 to 3 hours at 250°F. Cool completely. Test for doneness by pressing hard on the thickest part of the cooled wreath. If it is not completely hard, return to oven for another 30 minutes. Repeat until the piece is completely done. After it cools, glaze with a coat of sealant.

Above: Playful bunnies and colorful eggs embellish the grass around this spring basket. Designer: Bonnie Bone

Right: Bread dough photo frames can be customized for any occasion. This frame is the perfect way to mark a special birthday. Make the frame's base with the instructions on page 436, then embellish as desired. Designer: Bonnie Bone

Opposite page, top: The beauty is in the details of these timeless figures. Designer: Bonnie Bone

Opposite page, bottom: Always on the lookout for one-of-a-kind holiday gifts? These bread dough ornaments are simple and fun to make. Designer: Bonnie Bone

BREAD DOUGH GALLERY

FABRIC CRAFTS

With today's easy-to-use fabric paints and dyes,
the (cloth) world is your canvas! You don't have to be
Picasso to paint a T-shirt or Ringo Starr to appreciate
perennially popular tie-dye. Why settle for someone
else's patterns and designs when personalizing
everything from placemats to floorcloths is so easy?

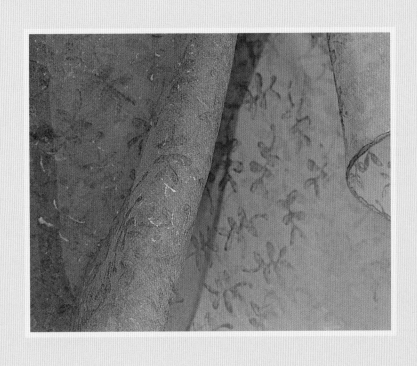

TIE-DYE

Tie-dyeing, also known as bound-resist dyeing, is one of the easiest ways to make your own clothing. Your design is accomplished by different methods of binding the cloth, then dipping it in colors you'd like to see together, or removing dye from colored T-shirts in a pattern of your choosing. The results can vary from high-energy, vibrant hues in wild combinations to a soft layering of complementary shades. The rewards are almost immediate, usually repeatable, and always fun.

MATERIALS AND TOOLS

SOMETHING TO DYE
The ordinary T-shirt is the most common tie-dyed item, but dresses, totes, socks, and even plain fabric yardage are also possibilities. Check the fiber content before you make a dyeing decision: cotton, rayon, hemp, and flax do hold dye, but wool, polyester, nylon, and other synthetic fibers do not.

DYE
Look for dyes labeled "fiber reactive" for bright, pure, lasting color. They come in powdered or liquid forms, and are activated by a dye fixer.

DYE FIXERS
Soda ash is the most common dye fixer. It's sold in powder form and is mildly caustic, so wear a dust mask and gloves when handling it.

DYE APPLICATORS
The most practical choice is often a simple squeeze bottle, but you can have a lot of fun and create an array of different effects with spray bottles, brushes, syringes, basters, and spoons.

BINDERS
Rubber bands are the most common binders; they're inexpensive and easy to find. Many professional tie-dyers recommend waxed string instead of rubber bands for increased control.

BUCKETS OR LARGE PANS
A bucket or pan is needed to mix the dye fixer solution and to soak the shirt. Purchase an inexpensive one and dedicate it to tie-dying projects.

RUBBER GLOVES
Fiber dyes are easily absorbed by skin, so always wear rubber gloves while tie-dying. Gloves are also a good idea when you're working with a dye fixer such as soda ash.

CANNING JARS
Dye concentrates can be stored in your refrigerator for up to two weeks.

BASIC TECHNIQUES

TIE-DYEING A SHIRT

Virtually all tie-dyed projects start with the same basic techniques. The unique patterns are created by the way you fold and secure the fabric.

1 Wash the shirt and lay it on a flat, protected surface, then spray it with a light misting of plain water.

2 Fold the shirt as directed in your pattern (see specific project instructions for tying instructions) and secure with rubber bands or waxed thread.

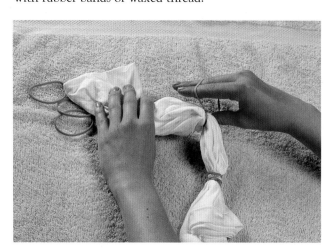

3 Fill a large bucket or pan three-fourths full of water, then add the appropriate amount of soda ash (1 cup per gallon of water), stirring well. Place the found shirt in the fixer bucket and allow to soak, undisturbed, for 20 minutes. (Your fixer solution can be reused if stored in a container.)

4 Wearing rubber gloves, remove the shirt from the fixer solution and place it on a layer of old towels. Squirt the dye onto the shirt as directed in your specific project instructions.

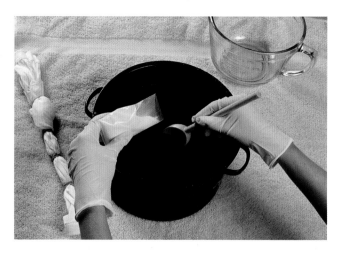

446

5 Wrap the shirt up in a sheet of clear plastic (or place it in a plastic bag) and leave undisturbed so the dye can set for 8–24 hours.

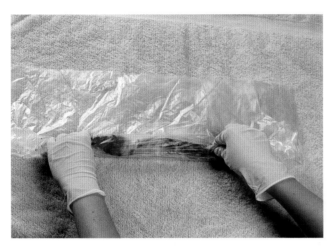

6 Remove shirt from plastic and rinse well, changing the water as needed. To finish, wash the shirt in the hottest water tolerated by your shirt's fiber content. Wash it separately until its wash water is clear after.

PREPARING DYE SOLUTIONS/CONCENTRATES

The way to prepare a dye solution varies, depending on the specific dye and how it's purchased.

◈ Read your product instructions carefully. Many tie-dye kits feature dye powder that already contains a premix solution. All you'll need to do is add water and mix well.

◈ If you're making your own premix solution, refer to the specific dye you've chosen. (Be sure it's labeled "fiber-reactive.") One common method is to mix a tablespoon of urea with a cup of hot water; then, after the mixture cools, add 2–5 tablespoons of dye. This mixture is now called a dye concentrate. Shake it vigorously to mix, and store any excess in the refrigerator. Note: Never mix dye concentrates or premixes directly with soda ash solution because the dye will be exhausted.

DECORATION

Screen printing, stamping, stenciling, and appliqué are a few methods you may wish to try to add even more character to a tie-dyed shirt. Once you've created a background pattern, study the shades within it. Would you like to capitalize on strong colors, or bring out one or two that are subtle? Stamp, stencil, or print dancing forms, flowers, or words onto a white piece of paper, cut them out, and hold them up to your shirt as you experiment.

PASTEL PILLOWCASE

A plain white pillowcase is tie-dyed in pastel and transformed into a lovely decorative accent. Either purchase a pillowcase or make your own—use the measurements from any standard case and make sure you use cotton fabric that will accept dye.

MATERIALS AND TOOLS

Cotton pillowcase
Waxed thread
Fabric-reactive dye concentrate
Nylon
1 cup salt

Glass canning jar
Dye fixer (washing soda, soda ash, or sal soda)
Enamel pot

WHAT TO DO

1 Wash and dry the pillowcase, and position on a flat work surface and straighten.

2 Fold the pillowcase lengthwise, accordion-pleat the fabric from the bottom to the top, then tie folded case tightly with waxed thread.

3 Mix ¼ teaspoon dye concentrate to 1 cup warm water (80°–100°F [27°–38°C]). Strain the dye liquid through two layers of nylon.

4 Mix 1 cup of salt in 1 gallon of water. Wet the pillowcase with the salt solution.

5 Pour the dye solution into a canning jar, then add the salt solution until the jar is about two-thirds full. Submerge the wet pillowcase in the jar, pushing the case down to the bottom of the jar. Put jar aside and do not disturb.

6 Dissolve ¼ cup dye fixer in 1 cup boiling water. Mix in ice cubes to bring the temperature down to 100°F (38°C). Remove the pillowcase from the jar, add dye-fixer solution to jar and stir, then put the pillowcase back in the jar. Allow pillowcase to sit in solution from between 1–24 hours.

7 Remove the pillowcase and rinse in cold water. Let stand in a tub of cold water for one hour. Wash case in cold water, then again in warm water, then again in hot water. Boil case for 10 minutes in an enamel pot that is not used for food. Wash case one final time, then dry and iron.

Designer: Caroline Manheimer

449

HEART T-SHIRT

A cheerful, tie-dyed heart pops nicely against a solid-colored background. Though a heart is easy to freehand, you can draw any shape—a star or a diamond, for example—on a piece of cardstock and cut the shape in half to create a template.

MATERIALS AND TOOLS

T-shirt
Washable marker
Waxed thread
Soda ash
Bucket
Old towels
Fiber-reactive dye concentrates
Scrap of fabric or paper towel
  (optional)
Rubber gloves
Squeeze bottle or other dye
  applicator
Eye dropper
Sheet of clear plastic or plastic bag

WHAT TO DO

1 Prepare the shirt, as described in the basics section (see page 446). Turn the shirt inside out and position on the work surface face up.

2 Fold shirt in half lengthwise, and draw a half-heart with a washable marker along the folded edge in the center of the shirt.

3 Beginning at the tip of the heart, make tight, ¼-inch (6 mm) folds along the marker line, so that the line becomes compact and straight as the shirt is folded.

4 Tie on the marked line tightly. Tie again ¼ to ½ inch (6 mm– 13 mm) below the heart line; this will create an outline area.

5 Prepare fixer solution with soda ash and water in a bucket, as described in the basics section (see page 446). Presoak shirt in the solution for 20 minutes. Remove shirt from solution and allow excess liquid to drain onto old towels.

6 Mix the dye concentrates. Choose any color combinations you find pleasing, though it's a good idea to experiment on a piece of scrap fabric or a paper towel.

7 Prepare the dye solutions, following the dye manufacturer's instructions. Experiment with dye/water combinations. Try 20 percent dye concentrate to 80 percent water for darker colors, and 5 percent dye concentrate to 95 percent water for lighter colors.

8 Wearing rubber gloves, first dye the heart up to the first tie. Allow dye to sit for five minutes, then squeeze excess dye out of the heart to prevent bleeding.

9 Next, dye the outside of the heart (the rest of the shirt) and the outline area in any color combination of your choice. Use colors that contrast nicely with the heart.

10 Use an eye dropper to apply color in the area between the ties to create the heart outline.

11 Turn the shirt to the other side, and repeat the dyeing process (see Steps 8–10, above).

12 Wrap the shirt in plastic, allow dye to set, then rinse and wash, as described in the basics section (see page 447).

Designer: True Tie Dye

ARROWHEAD T-SHIRT

A variety of interesting shapes can be created when tie-dyeing—it's just a matter of experimenting with tying and paint application. A clever designer has done the work for you here; simply use the template and follow the instructions to create this striking arrowhead motif.

MATERIALS AND TOOLS

T-shirt
Half-arrowhead stencil
Washable marker
Waxed thread
Soda ash
Bucket
Old towels
Fiber-reactive dye concentrates:
    dark green and/or dark blue, yel-
    low, and turquoise
Rubber gloves
Squeeze bottle
Sheet of plain paper
Sheet of clear plastic or plastic bag

DYE LAYERING

Once you have removed color from a shirt, you may proceed to adding dye to the bleached areas. Try re-tying the shirt after each process, adding the new color, rinsing the shirt thoroughly or laundering it, and adding fresh color to a shirt of two or three hues.

WHAT TO DO

1 Prepare the shirt, as described in the basics section (see page 446). Turn the shirt inside out and position on the work surface face up. Fold the sheet of paper in half and sketch a half arrowhead shape on the fold, referring to the photograph.

2 Fold shirt in half lengthwise, and position half-arrowhead stencil on the shirt 2–3 inches (5–7.5 cm) below the collar. Trace the stencil with a washable marker.

3 Draw a line to indicate where the yoke will be. Begin the line about 3 inches (7.5 cm) from the seam on the sleeve and bow the line toward the collar, then down, ending at the center of the shirt, 2–3 inches (5–7.5 cm) below the arrowhead shape (use photograph as a guide).

4 Beginning at the top of the arrowhead shape, make ¼-inch (6 mm) folds along the line, so that the line becomes straight as the shirt is folded.

5 Tie on the marked line tightly. Tie again about ¼ inch (6-mm) below the first tie.

6 Fold the yoke with ½-inch (13 cm) folds, just as you did with the arrowhead shape (see Step 4).

7 Tie on the line as you did above (see Step 5), then again ½ inch (1.3 cm) below this tie.

8 Prepare fixer solution with soda ash and water in a bucket, as described in the basics section (see page 446). Presoak shirt in the solution for 20 minutes. Remove shirt from solution and allow excess liquid to drain onto old towels.

9 Mix the dye concentrates. For a dark green color, either use 100 percent dark green concentrate or mix together 75 percent dark blue and 25 percent yellow. For a blue-green color, mix 75 percent turquoise and 25 percent yellow. For a yellow-green color, mix 75 percent yellow and 25 percent turquoise. (Feel free to experiment with color combinations.)

10 Prepare the dye solutions, following the dye manufacturer's instructions (see also basics section, page 447). For this shirt, you will need 2 shades each of the dark green and the blue-green colors; one shade should be very light and the other one darker (though still significantly lighter than the dye concentrate). To begin, try 20 percent dye concentrate to 80 per-

(continues on page 454)

Designer: True Tie Dye

cent water for the lighter color, and 5 percent dye concentrate to 95 percent water for the second shade.

11 Wearing rubber gloves, sprinkle droplets of each dye solution on the bottom of the shirt and on the inside of the arrowhead shape, beginning with the lightest shade and ending with the darkest. Since dark colors tend to overtake lighter colors as the dye spreads, be sparing with the darker shades.

12 Apply dark green dye to the yoke of the shirt with a squeeze bottle.

13 Turn the shirt to the other side, and repeat the dyeing process (see Steps 11 and 12, above).

14 Wrap the shirt in plastic, allow dye to set, then rinse and wash, as described in the basics section (see page 447).

PLAYING WITH COLOR

To make a lighter or pastel colored dye, experiment with mixing dilutions of your dye concentrate. A good starting point is 20% dye concentrate to 80% water for a strong dilution, and 5% dye concentrate to 95% water for a weak dilution.

VORTEX CARRYALL BAG

The swirling rainbow design on this bag is wonderfully dynamic and colorful and is the result of a surprisingly simple technique: twisting the bag into a spiral before dyeing.

MATERIALS AND TOOLS

Bag made from dyeable fabric
Fork
Waxed thread
Soda ash
Bucket
Old towels
Fiber-reactive dye concentrates: black, yellow, red, orange, blue, purple, green, and turquoise
Rubber gloves
Squeeze bottle or other dye applicator
Sheet of clear plastic or plastic bag

WHAT TO DO

1 Prepare the bag, as described in the basics section (see page 446). Turn the bag inside out and position on the work surface face up.

2 Place the tines of a fork against the bag where you would like the center of the spiral shape to be, then twist the fork clockwise several times, keeping the folds evenly sized as you twist. Remove the fork and hold the folds in place with the palm of your hand.

3 Wrap the rest of the bag around the twisted center (with your palm still in place), making sure to keep the folds relatively even all the way to the edge of the fabric. You should end up with a circular shape.

4 Tie across the diameter of the spiral with at least four ties, keeping the folds taut.

5 Prepare fixer solution with soda ash and water in a bucket, as described in the basics section (see page 446). Presoak bag in the solution for 20 minutes. Remove bag from solution and allow excess liquid to drain onto old towels.

6 Prepare the dye solutions, following the dye manufacturer's instructions (see also basics section, page 447).

7 Wearing rubber gloves, apply the dye with a squeeze bottle or other dye applicator. Begin by applying black to the underside of the spiral. Since dark colors will overtake lighter colors as the dye spreads, apply darker colors sparingly.

8 Beginning with the yellow dye solution, apply all six colors of dye in wedges evenly around the top (upper) side of the spiral, in the following order: red, orange, yellow, green, turquoise, blue, and purple. (This order prevents any colors from overlapping to make

Designer: True Tie Dye

brown.) You should end up with a design that resembles a pie graph. Note: Apply colors sparingly in the center, to prevent design from getting muddled.

9 Turn the bag to the other side, and repeat the dyeing process (see Steps 7 and 8, above), taking care to align color wedges with like-colored wedges on the opposite side.

10 Wrap the bag in plastic, allow dye to set, then rinse and wash, as described in the basics section (see page 447).

455

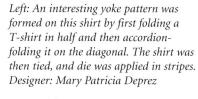

Left: An interesting yoke pattern was formed on this shirt by first folding a T-shirt in half and then accordion-folding it on the diagonal. The shirt was then tied, and die was applied in stripes.
Designer: Mary Patricia Deprez

Bottom left: Experiment with your favorite patterns on large pieces of fabric. The resulting yardage can be used as curtains, tablecloths, or sewing fabric.
Designer: True Tie Dye

Below: Sometimes just a small area of tie dye can be more dramatic than covering the entire surface area.
Designer: True Tie Dye

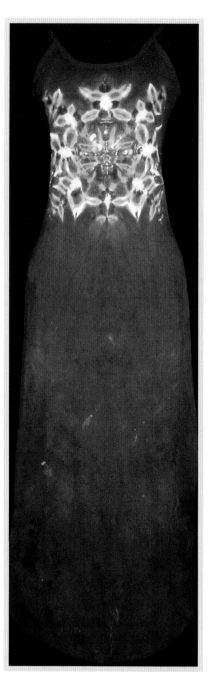

TIE-DYE GALLERY

Right: Instead of forming a swirl pattern in the center of the shirt, this designer chose to place it on the upper left side. Designer: Chris Rankin

Below: Cotton canvas is a great surface for exploring the intricacies of tie-dye patterns. Designer: True Tie Dye

PAINTING ON FABRIC

When it comes to decorating fabric with paint, it's like this: whatever you can do on paper, you can do on fabric. Here we've provided all you need to know about choosing the right paint and tools for your fabric-painting project, as well as some basic techniques to get you started. There's no reason to settle for boring fabric—just paint it!

MATERIALS AND TOOLS

FABRIC
Virtually any fabric can be painted, though you will need to choose paints that are appropriate for the type of fabric (see below). For example, some paints and dyes work better on synthetic fabrics; others are designed for natural fabrics. Remember that paints may bleed through fabric, so take care to protect your work surface.

FABRIC TRANSFER PAPER
If you don't feel comfortable sketching designs or patterns freehand, use fabric transfer paper. Look for it where fabric paints are sold.

FABRIC PAINTS
Also called textile paints, fabric paints are extremely versatile water-based paints that can be applied directly to fabric with a brush or a roller. Once the painted fabric is set by ironing on its wrong side or by placing it in the clothes dryer (see manufacturer's instructions), it can be washed repeatedly as you would any other fabric. Fabric paints are available in a number of forms, such as opaque, fluorescent, metallic, and glitter, as well as those designed specifically for certain fabrics (silk, for example), and certain processes, such as sun painting. In addition, you can mix fabric paint to achieve your own colors.

FABRIC MARKERS
There's a large color range of fabric markers available, including those with fine, medium, or wide tips. Markers are quite useful when designing freehand and when writing words, adding shading, or drawing details. Pens and markers that are not specifically designed for painting on fabric can be used; just make sure the label specifies that the ink is indelible on fabric. Fabric markers may require two or more coats to achieve the desired color saturation.

FABRIC TRANSFER CRAYONS
Particularly fun for the young-at-heart, fabric transfer crayons are much like the crayons you remember using as a kid. Sketch your design on plain white paper, then use the crayons to color in the design. Lay the paper with the painted side down, and iron the back side of the paper—the design will transfer to the fabric. Fabric transfer crayons work best on synthetic fabrics, though

using 50-50 cotton/synthetic blends will also result in a successful, albeit less vibrant, color transfer.

Pastel Dye Sticks

Though much like artist's pastels, these dye sticks are designed just for fabric. That being said, the results are very similar to ordinary pastels. Once you have applied the design, heat-set the pastels with an iron.

Dimensional Paints

These oft-criticized paints, puff paints as they are often called, can actually be a nice element in a whimsical fabric design, provided they are used with restraint to create accents or outlines. To apply, simply squeeze dimensional paint out of the applicator bottle that it comes in.

Paintbrushes

Any crafter knows that having a stock of paintbrushes in a variety of sizes is a good idea. Let the project dictate which brush to use; when working with bleach, for example, use an inexpensive brush that can be discarded when it begins to wear. Foam brushes work nicely for painting fabric, when you want to better control the amount of paint that is being distributed on the surface.

Stencils & Stamps

These can be used on fabric, just as you would on any other surface. Any material that repels paint can be used as a stencil—cardstock, cardboard, clear acetate, even wax paper, contact shelf paper, or masking tape can create interesting designs. Use a stenciling brush or a foam brush, and be sure to apply the paint in an up-and-down motion. Add a small amount of wallpaper paste powder to fabric paint if you are stamping on silk to prevent bleeding.

BASIC TECHNIQUES

PAINTING A DESIGN ON FABRIC

These are general guidelines for painting on fabric other than silk. You'll find that it's pretty foolproof, as long as you choose the right paint and take your time when planning and painting the design. You may want to practice on inexpensive fabric first.

1 Prepare the fabric. If you are using a washable fabric, it is a good idea to wash and dry the fabric (without fabric softener) to remove any sizing. Iron the fabric to remove any wrinkles and to create a smooth painting surface.

DESIGNER TIP

Always test paint on a spare piece of fabric before you begin any fabric-painting project. Simply brush some paint on the fabric and allow to dry. (This is also a good way to see what colors will look like once they dry.)

2 Gather together materials (paint, paintbrushes, water, and so forth) on a clean work surface. You may want to protect the work surface with craft or wax paper. Position the fabric with a piece of cardboard that has been covered in wax paper behind the area to be painted. (If you are stamping, you will need to lightly pad the cardboard with batting and cover the batting with wax paper.) Stretch the fabric taut and secure to the work surface with masking tape or tacks.

3 Choose a pattern and hold it against the fabric item you want to paint. If the size of the pattern doesn't suit the size of the item, enlarge or reduce it on a photocopier. Next, secure the transfer paper to your fabric item with tape or pins. Secure the pattern over the transfer paper, then lightly trace over it with a pen or stylus.

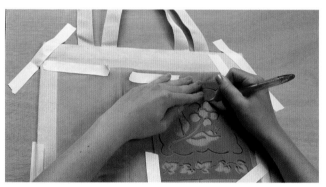

4 Paint the design, using paintbrushes, rollers, stamps, or any other painting tool. Allow to dry completely, according to the paint manufacturer's instructions. Remove any tape, outlines, or stencils. Once the fabric is dry, you may want to add details with a fine, dry brush. (Make sure there is very little paint on the brush—remember it's easy to add paint but not to remove it!)

5 Lay the painted fabric right side down on a towel, cover back side of fabric with a clean white cloth, and iron on a cotton setting for 5 to 10 minutes to set paint. Note: Follow paint manufacturer's instructions for setting paint. Wash the fabric and iron again.

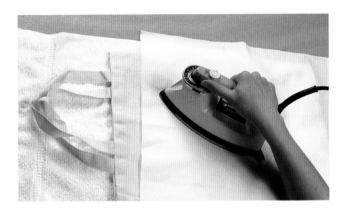

DESIGNER TIP

When working with fabric, experiment with scrunching, sponging, stenciling, stippling, splattering, and splashing, and any other technique you can think of. Stamping also works nicely—whether you use the plethora of rubber stamps available or make your own from cardboard or foam or a found object, such as a leaf. Choose stamps that are simple in design to avoid blurring on fabric.

PAINTING ON SILK

When working with silk, it is best to use paints that are specifically designed for silk, though regular fabric paints can also be used if the borders of the design are enclosed with masking tape or resist outliner paste.

1. Prepare the silk. It's a good idea to finish the silk edges with a zigzag stitch or to otherwise bind the edges (masking tape works well) before mounting the fabric on the frame.

2. Attach the silk to the frame. Stretch the silk taut with the fabric grain straight. If you are using a needlepoint hoop, simply position silk in the hoop so that the area to be painted is centered within the middle area. If using a frame, use pins to secure the silk every 2 inches (5 cm). When silk is mounted, run your hand over the surface of the silk to make sure there are no dips.

3. Plan the design, then sketch the design on the silk. If you are using resist outliner paste, trace over the sketch with the outliner in smooth, continuous lines, and allow outliner paste to dry thoroughly. After painting the design, set the paint as directed by the manufacturer's instructions.

FLORAL SCARF

Wearing this beautiful hand-stamped scarf is sheer pleasure; telling admiring friends that you made it yourself is the bonus.

MATERIALS AND TOOLS

Solid-color silk or rayon scarf (or one with a graduated tone, such as the scarf shown here)
Straight pins
Old towel or blanket
Large rectangular stamp

Fabric paint in colors of your choice (blues, greens, and white were used for this project)
Brayer
Sheet of glass (clean glass from an old picture frame works well)

WHAT TO DO

1 Iron the scarf, then use straight pins to secure the edges of the scarf flat to the old towel or blanket. Place the pinned scarf on a flat, firm work surface.

2 The design shown was created by applying layers of color with a large rectangular stamp. Choose your first color of fabric paint and pour a small amount onto the sheet of glass. Roll your brayer across the paint until it's evenly coated and then use it to ink the stamp, being careful not to overload the stamp with paint.

3 Stamp across the scarf, overlapping the design slightly at the edges, and reinking the stamp with the brayer for each impression. Don't worry about aligning the stamp perfectly each time—slight variations in the pattern are part of the charm of this handmade item.

4 Let the first layer of stamped color dry thoroughly, then repeat Step 3 with another color, positioning the stamp so some of the first layer of color still shows through. Keep adding layers of color (remembering to allow each color to dry thoroughly before moving on) until you've achieved the desired effect.

5 Refer to the fabric paint's instructions when your scarf needs to be cleaned.

Designer: Susan McBride

FLOWERY JACKET AND SHOES

Delight a little friend with an adorable hand-painted gift. This designer incorporated the v-shaped front seams on the jacket and the stitching on the shoes into her design; try to consider the lines and construction of your items as well.

MATERIALS AND TOOLS

Denim jacket and canvas shoes
Iron (optional)
Old towel or cloth
Chalk or pastel (optional)
Palette or clear white dish
2 small paintbrushes (with pointed ends)
Fabric paints: white, red, yellow, green, and dark blue

WHAT TO DO

TO PAINT THE JACKET

1 Wash and iron the jacket front, then place it on a flat work surface with an old towel or cloth inside the jacket to absorb any bleeding paint.

2 Lightly sketch the design onto the jacket with a piece of chalk or a pastel, using the pattern on page 516 as a guide. Do not include too much detail, as the chalk or pastel will repel the paint. Since fabric paints can be painted over many times, you can also sketch the design with a darker color of paint.

3 Mix the fabric paints on a palette or dish. Blending the paints, rather than using the colors straight from the tube, creates a far more interesting color palette. You will also want to thin the paints slightly with water.

4 Begin by painting the flower petals, using a pointed paintbrush. Load the brush with paint, then rest the brush against the fabric. Carefully remove the brush, leaving a petal-like imprint. Allow the paint to dry, then apply another layer of paint to build color intensity. Apply as many coats of paint as necessary to achieve the desired look.

5 Next, paint the stems and curled greenery. Create additional interest and contrast by applying dark blue and green paint around the flowers and stems (see photograph). Swirl and blend with the paintbrush as you paint; this will work the paint into the denim and create a softer effect.

6 Once the design has been painted, it's time to add the final details. Apply small dots in the centers of the flowers with white, yellow, and green paint. Define the petals by painting dark blue lines around the edges, and add dots of green paint randomly throughout the design.

TO PAINT THE SHOES

1 Using the stitching on the shoe as a guide, paint the toe and heel areas with two coats of bright green paint.

2 Paint a red flower on each toe and allow paint to dry. Fill in painted flowers with orange and yellow accents.

3 With green paint, add dots (in a random pattern) and a swirl on each side of the flower.

Designer: Susan McBride

SUN- AND FABRIC-PAINTED T-SHIRT

Regular fabric paints serve as highlights over psychedelic sun paints to create a look worthy of a designer boutique. Even the pickiest (and coolest) teen would wear this hip tee—but you may want to save it for yourself, instead!

MATERIALS AND TOOLS

Long-sleeved, 100 percent cotton T-shirt
Washing machine and iron
Flat, waterproof board (a piece of cardboard or plywood wrapped in a plastic garbage bag works well)

Sun printing fabric paints in red and yellow
Mixing containers for sun paints
Masking tape
Spray bottle filled with clean water
Foam brush

Handful of straw or dried grass
3–4 pressed flowers
Sunshine
Waxed paper
Fabric paints in green and red
2 fine-tipped paintbrushes

WHAT TO DO

1 Start by washing, drying, and ironing the T-shirt to remove any sizing.

2 Prepare a waterproof work surface for sun painting—simply wrap a piece of cardboard or plywood in a plastic garbage bag. Insert the garbage-bag-wrapped board inside the T-shirt, with the shirt's front (the side to be painted) stretched flat over one face of the board.

3 Following the manufacturer's instructions, mix your sun printing fabric paints. For the project shown, the designer mixed one container of yellow paint; then she created her own shade of orange by blending yellow and red paints together. (Mix the undiluted paints to achieve the desired color before adding water.) To achieve the intensity of color shown in the project, mix three parts water to one part paint. For more subtle hues, add more water. For greater intensity, use less water.

4 Sun printing paints tend to creep over fabrics, but for this project, you'll want to keep them confined to a roughly rectangular area centered on the T-shirt's front. To do this, use masking tape to outline the borders of the area you plan to paint. (Resist outliner paste will do the same job, but you'll need to apply it several hours before you plan to paint the shirt. Follow the manufacturer's instructions.)

5 Spray the rectangle of shirt defined by the masking tape with clean water until it is thoroughly wet. Smooth the wet fabric over the board to remove any wrinkles and to make the fabric stick to the board.

6 Using a foam brush, apply a coat of yellow paint to the wet fabric. (When working with sun paint, it's a good idea to start with the lightest color and finish with the darkest color.) You may paint the whole area, or leave patches white.

7 Using the same brush, dab the orange paint over about two-thirds of the rectangle, filling in any white spaces you may have left in Step 6, and leaving the upper, right third of the square yellow to suggest an afternoon sun in a summer sky.

8 Working quickly before the paint dries, arrange several strands of straw or dry grass over the yellow, upper right hand corner of the rectangle. (These grass strands will print a pattern reminiscent of sunrays). Arrange the flowers in a cluster in one of the lower corners of the square.

(continues on page 468)

9 Carefully move the shirt (still on the board) to a sunny, wind-free spot outside and let it dry in the sunshine until the shapes of the flowers and grass have printed on the shirt. (Check their progress by lifting a corner of a flower periodically.) When you're happy with the intensity of the print, remove the flowers and grass.

10 Make sure the fabric paints are completely dry before removing the board from inside the T-shirt; otherwise, the paint may seep through to the back of the T-shirt. Remove the masking tape. Stretch the dry T-shirt over an ironing board with the board between the shirt's front and back and set the paint by ironing it for about 3 minutes.

11 Determine which areas of your newly sun-painted shirt you'd like to accent with fabric paints. In the project shown, the designer highlighted the petals on several of the flowers with red paint; then she painted creeping vines around the flowers with green paint. You may want to sketch your design very lightly on the shirt with a pencil before you actually start painting.

12 When you're ready to start painting, stretch the T-shirt over the board as before. Then mix the fabric paints, following the manufacturer's instructions and paint your design, using fine-tipped paintbrushes and a dry-brush technique.

13 Allow your pattern to dry. Then set the paint as directed by the manufacturer.

PAINTED CURTAIN

Want window treatments that match just right? Try decorating them with the same paint that's on the walls! For an even more monochromatic and subtle look, the off-white fabric used for these curtains is very similar in hue to the paint, though this is a matter of preference—fabric in a contrasting color would also look great.

MATERIALS AND TOOLS

Fabric or purchased curtain
Iron
Freezer paper or purchased stencil
Tape

Foam paint roller
Acrylic interior house paint,
  or fabric paint of your choice
Clean cloth

WHAT TO DO

1 Either purchase a curtain or make your own from the fabric of your choice. Wash and iron the curtain.

2 The stencil for this project was made from freezer paper, though you can also use a commercial stencil. To make the stencil, cut wavy lines or any other design into the freezer paper, position paper on the fabric, then iron over the paper (with the shiny side of the paper facing down). Secure the paper or stencil, if necessary, with tape.

3 Spread the fabric onto a padded work surface and secure to the surface with tape, as needed.

4 Use a dense foam roller to carefully apply the latex paint to the stenciled areas of the curtain.

5 Allow curtain to dry thoroughly, then remove the freezer paper or stencil. Cover the painted areas of the curtain with a clean cloth, then iron.

Designer: Caroline Manheimer

MY DOG SPOT FLOORCLOTH

Why not add fun as well as function to your pet's area? This adorable floorcloth is sure to please faithful mate and doting master alike. Place it in an entryway or put it underneath your dog's bowls.

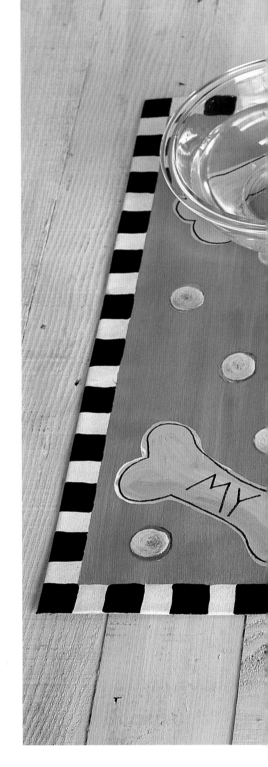

MATERIALS AND TOOLS

Canvas
Scissors
Primer
Paintbrush
Contact cement
Painter's tape
Craft paints in assorted colors

Matte medium or paint conditioner
Foam brushes
Scrap canvas or cardboard
Pencil
Laundry marker
Sponge pouncer (optional)
Acrylic varnish

WHAT TO DO

1 Cut the canvas to the desired dimensions, then use a paintbrush to apply several coats of primer. Allow canvas to dry thoroughly.

2 Mark a ½-inch (1.3 cm) to 1-inch (2.5 cm) hem, fold under, and secure hem to the underside of the canvas with contact cement.

3 Place painter's tape all around the top (right) side of the floorcloth, several inches in from the outside edge. Thin blue craft paint with a small amount of matte medium or paint conditioner, then use a

foam brush to apply this mixture to floorcloth (inside the taped area) to create a background. Allow to dry thoroughly.

4 Using the photo as a guide, cut dog and bones shapes from scrap canvas or cardboard. Referring to the photograph for placement, position templates on the floorcloth and trace with a pencil. Paint shapes with green and yellow craft paint. Allow to dry.

5 Trace around dog and bones with a laundry marker and draw words, if desired (see photograph).

Paint spots with red and blue paint, using a sponge pouncer. For a more interesting effect, use two tones of color and spin the pouncer slightly.

6 Remove painter's tape and paint checks around the edge of the floorcloth with a foam brush.

470

7 Finish the painted surface with acrylic varnish; apply as many coats as needed to achieve a smooth finish.

8 Flatten the floorcloth by placing it underneath a heavy object or by ironing the underside on low heat.

Designer: Kathy Cooper

LACE-PAINTED T-SHIRT

A piece of cotton lace or a doily can be used to print an exquisite (and quite intricate) design on a black T-shirt. Alternatively, dark paint can be used on a light-colored shirt. One word of advice: It's a good idea to practice on colored paper until you feel comfortable enough to print on the shirt.

MATERIALS AND TOOLS

Black or dark-colored T-shirt
Iron
Cardboard
Old plate or palette paper
White acrylic paint
Palette knife
Piece of lace or doily (3–6 inches [7.5–15cm wide])
Colored paper (optional)
Round #0 paintbrush
Clean cloth

DESIGNER TIP

For a totally different look, use a less intricate piece of lace and multiple colors of paint. The lace can be used like a stamp to create a random, all-over design, or to form a border design.

WHAT TO DO

1 Wash, dry, and iron the T-shirt. Place a piece of cardboard underneath the front of the shirt and position on a flat work surface, as described in Step 2 of the fabric-painting basics section (see page 460).

2 On a plate or piece of palette paper, mix the white paint with a small amount of water, using a palette knife (or other similar tool) to blend. Make sure the plate or paper is covered evenly with about 1/8 inch (3 mm) of paint.

3 Lay the lace or doily into the paint. Pat the lace gently with your hands, allowing the paint to saturate the lace thoroughly.

4 Practice imprinting the lace onto a piece of colored paper, if desired. When you feel comfortable with the process, saturate the lace with paint again (see Step 3), then lay the lace onto the shirt and pat each section firmly against the fabric. (To prevent smearing the image, take care not to move the lace.)

5 Carefully lift the lace from the shirt. (Wash the lace immediately to remove paint.) Allow the shirt to dry at least four hours, then touch up the design, as needed, with the #0 paintbrush.

6 Allow the shirt to dry overnight. Cover the painted areas of the T-shirt with a clean cloth, then iron.

SUNNY SUN-PAINTED PLACE MATS

Sun paints are a special kind of fabric dye that "fix" with help from the rays of the sun (or the light of a heat lamp). Objects placed on fabric treated with sun paint block the sun's rays, essentially printing their shapes right onto your project. These gorgeous place mats are just one example of possible sun-painting projects. Why not make a set of napkins and a tablecloth to match? The sky—or in this case, the sun—is the limit!

MATERIALS AND TOOLS

White place mats made from 100 percent cotton cloth (see Step 1)
Iron
Sheet of rigid plastic or cardboard wrapped with a plastic bag
Foam brushes or foam roller (choose applicators made from dense foam)
Sun paints

Plastic containers or shallow trays for mixing and holding paints
Spray bottle filled with clean water
Several large, whole leaves or paper cutouts of leaves
Stones
Bright, sunny day

WHAT TO DO

1 Choose white place mats made from 100 percent cotton cloth that has been specially prepared for dyeing—look for cloth that's labeled PFD. Wash the place mats to remove any sizing, then dry and iron them.

2 Prepare a flat, waterproof surface for painting and sunning the place mats. A sheet of rigid plastic or a square of cardboard wrapped in a plastic bag are both good options.

3 Following the manufacturer's instructions, mix the sun paints in plastic containers or shallow trays. The place mats in the project photo are painted with intense, vibrant colors. To replicate this look, use two parts water for every one part of paint. For subtler, pastel hues, add more water.

4 Stretch the place mats flat on the work surface you prepared in Step 2. Spray them liberally with water from the spray bottle and smooth them flat with your hand.

The wet mats should stick to the surface and remain flat.

5 Load the foam brush or roller with sun paint and stroke or roll it onto the place mats, saturating them completely with color.

6 Working quickly (so the paint doesn't dry), arrange the leaves

Designer: Caroline Manheimer

or other objects on the place mats in attractive patterns. Press the leaves flat, making them stick to the moist cloth.

7 Place the entire work surface, place mats and all, in a sunny spot. Try to find a location that isn't too windy. (Our designer sunned these place mats in the back of her pickup truck!) If breezes are unavoidable, you can place small stones on top of the leaves or other objects to hold them in place, but be aware that the shapes of the stones may print on your fabric, too.

8 Allow the place mats to sun for 15 minutes to an hour. Check the printing progress by lifting an edge of one of the leaves. When the pattern has printed to your satisfaction and the place mats are dry, iron them for 3–4 minutes each to set the paint. After ironing, the place mats should be color proof. Wash them (with like colors) before setting them on your table for diners to admire.

PAINTING ON FABRIC GALLERY

Left: Garden leaves were pressed flat and then used as patterns to embellish sheer curtains. Designer: Travis Waldren

Opposite page, top left: Feather and seed stamps were combined with random brush strokes to create a light, airy scarf. Designer: Judi Kauffman

Opposite page, top right: Transform a simple cotton robe with stems of rose buds and blooms. Designer: Joyce Cusick

Opposite page, bottom: Create a custom floorcloth for your porch or dining room floor with a combination of masking, stenciling, and freehand painting. Designer: Kathy Cooper

BEAD CRAFTS

Warning: Beading is addictive! Pick out some beauties for yourself—bead and wire jewelry couldn't be hotter! And choose some for your home, too. Everything's better with beads!

BEAD JEWELRY

Because of the fabulous beads and luxurious wire available these days, crafters everywhere are taking up jewelry making (and never looking back). And once you start twisting and looping and bending and stringing, you'll understand why.

MATERIALS AND TOOLS

BEADS
Rest assured that, whatever your preferences with regard to color, shape, and style, you will find beads you like—and in abundance! Beads are often sized and sold in millimeters; the number indicates the diameter. Seed beads are sold in numbered sizes, with the smallest beads having the highest numbers. Look for glass beads, polymer clay beads (see page 418 for instructions on how to make your own), ceramic beads, and metal beads.

WIRE
Wire is both decorative and functional in jewelry making. There is quite a selection of wire out there, in many colors and types of metals, as well as in a variety of gauges and shapes (including square, twisted, and flat). When choosing wire, make sure the wire will fit through the bead hole and that it is strong enough to support your chosen beads. Inexpensive alloy wires are available and are ideal for everyday wear and for practice designs. Colored plastic wire is a fun option for whimsical designs.

FINDINGS
Findings are the metal accessories used in jewelry making, including clasps, ear wires and posts, pin backings, head pins, eye pins, and jump rings. Though there are a variety of findings available commercially, it is often quite easy to make your own with a pair of pliers.

JIGS
Jigs are hole-drilled boards with pegs that are designed to hold and loop wire to create wire pattern links. Although not essential, jigs are useful when making more elaborate jewelry that has multiple links in the same shape. Consult jewelry-making books for jig patterns or experiment with a variety of jig peg configurations to create unique wire patterns.

WIRE CUTTERS & FILES
Making wire jewelry requires a good pair of wire cutters, preferably a small pair with pointed ends. A fine metal file should be used to smooth the edges of cut wire ends.

PLIERS
Round-nose, needle-nose, and flat-nose pliers are probably the most common, but many other types are also available. Choose pliers with a smooth inside edge, so as not to damage wire.

STRINGING MATERIAL
Beading cord or thread, tigertail wire, or monofilament all work well when stringing beads to make necklaces and bracelets, though note that the findings used to secure the ends will vary according to the material used.

BASIC TECHNIQUES

When you have a number of especially interesting beads, sometimes a great necklace or bracelet need only be a matter of stringing, attaching findings to secure beads, and finishing with a clasp. A variety of spacers can be purchased that make beads go farther and that can create visual and textural interest of their own.

1 Determine the length of the final necklace or bracelet, add 5 inches (12.5 cm), then cut beading cord or thread, tigertail jewelry wire, or monofilament to this length.

2 Determine the sequence of the beads and any spacers, then thread the beads and spacers onto the beading cord, tigertail wire, or monofilament.

3 If you are using beading cord, use bead tips to secure beads. Thread a bead tip onto one end of the cord, with the hook part of the bead tip facing away from the last bead. Tie a double knot, then tighten the knot into the cup of the bead tip. Secure the knot with a dab of craft glue. Trim excess cord, then use needle-nose pliers

to connect the hook of the bead tip to the clasp finding. Repeat on the other end of the cord with another bead tip and the opposite end of the clasp.

4 If you are using tigertail or monofilament (neither of which can hold a knot securely), you will need to use crimp beads. Thread a crimp bead onto the end of the cord, then thread the tigertail or monofilament through one end of the clasp finding and back through the crimp bead in the opposite direction. Pull the strand so that the crimp and clasp are close together and tighten (flatten) the crimp with needle-nose pliers. Repeat on the other end of the cord with another crimp bead and the opposite end of the clasp.

DESIGNER TIP

Want a matching necklace and earring set? Nothing could be easier, especially if you are making a necklace from jig links or bead links. Simply make two extra links and attach to ear wires with jump rings.

MAKING A SIMPLE BEAD & WIRE NECKLACE OR BRACELET

Here we've provided easy instructions for making a basic bead and wire necklace or bracelet by constructing and connecting links. Once you're comfortable working with the tools and materials, gradually try your hand at more difficult designs and invest in a few tools—you'll be surprised how quickly you will master the techniques.

1 Determine how much wire is required for each wire link, and how many links you will need, then cut the wire accordingly. Decide what shape you want the wire links to be. If you will be using a jig, set it up in the desired configuration. Of course, you can shape the links by hand or with pliers.

2 To create the jig link, make a loop on the end of a length of wire with round-nose pliers, and attach it to the first jig peg, then loop the wire around the rest of the pegs, as desired or as specified in the jig pattern. Repeat this step with the remainder of the wire lengths. Optional: Use a jewelry hammer or a soft mallet covered in a cloth to flatten wire links, if desired; this increases the stability of the links and gives a distinctive look.

3 To create beaded links, determine how much wire will be needed for each link as well as how many links you will need, then cut the wire into appropriately sized lengths.

4 Make a loop about ⅛-inch (3 mm) from the end of a wire length, slide on a bead (or several beads), then make a second loop that rests against the bead. You may wrap the wire around the base of the loop several times, for added security and visual interest. Trim off any excess wire. Repeat this process to create as many beaded links as needed.

5 Assemble the links. There are several options for connecting links: attach the loops of the links directly to each other, make your own findings by bending wire into shapes (figure-eight shapes are commonly used), or use jump rings. For jump rings, use pliers (two pairs work best) to open the jump ring from side to side (not straight apart, as this weakens the metal).

BASIC TECHNIQUES

6 Connect the clasp finding to the ends of the neck-lace or bracelet, using jump rings or any other applicable finding. Clasp findings are readily available anywhere jewelry supplies are sold; they can also be made, either by hand or on a jig.

7 Trim excess wire and file any exposed wire ends.

DESIGNER TIP

Although plastic-coated wires are fun to work with, some may contain lead. Make sure you verify that anything you purchase is certified lead-free.

USING FINDINGS

Often, the best way to attach one piece to another is with simple, manufactured clasps, jump rings, and bead tips. Your local craft supplier will carry these and many other findings.

1 To make jewelry, you'll need to attach the perma-nently closed loop of a clasp to one end of your beaded strand and create a loop of some sort at the other end for the clasp to clasp on to. You have a number of options at both ends of the strand, including jump rings (Step 2), bead tips (Step 3), and crimp beads (see Working with Flexible Beading Wire on page 498).

2 Jump rings are handy little circles of wire that are split along their circumference. They're perfect for attaching clasps and for fastening the end of a strand of beads in a clasp-friendly fashion. To fasten the end of a beaded strand, pull your needle and thread (or wire) through a closed jump ring, wrapping the thread twice. Push the needle back through several beads, knot the thread, pull it through a few more beads and knot again. Coat the knots in glue and trim the end of the thread.

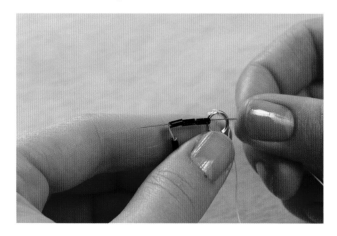

3 To attach a clasp, "open" the ring: Using two pairs of pliers, twist the split ends in opposite directions, rather than pulling them apart and enlarging the circle (doing so will weaken the metal). Slip the clasp on to the jump ring, then twist the ring closed.

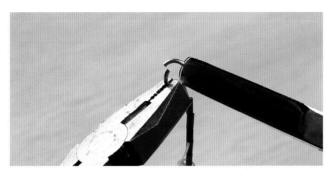

4 Bead tips, special beads that will hold and hide knots at the ends of strands, offer another good way to fasten a strand and attach a clasp. To attach one, push your needle and thread through the bead tip with the open hook facing outward. Knot the end of the thread twice, tuck the knots into the bead tip's cup, and coat them with fast-drying bead glue. Trim the thread tail close, slip the clasp onto the bead tip's open hook, and use chain-nose pliers to press the hook closed.

SIMPLE BEADED NECKLACE

Vibrantly blue and green, these gorgeous beads are striped and solid; smooth and raised; triangular, oval, round, and square. What could they possibly require other than a few silver spacers and a single strand of wire to hold them together? No complex technique need apply.

MATERIALS AND TOOLS

33-inch (13 cm) length of tigertail wire
Small/medium/large glass beads in various sizes and shapes
Small silver spacer beads

2–3 crimp beads
Clasp finding
Needle-nose pliers
3 head pins
Wire cutters

This all black-and-white variation is crisply stunning. The pattern is rhythmic: three small crystal beads (black, clear, black); a striped bead held by two silver spacers; then three small crystals again. A handsome square toggle clasp finishes it off.

WHAT TO DO

1 String the beads in any order you like, so that the necklace seems balanced and interesting. In most cases, the designer used one silver spacer between every two glass beads, but she occasionally broke that pattern, for variety. Sometimes two glass beads are adjacent to each other; sometimes there are two or even three spacers on each side of a single glass bead.

2 Thread one end of the tigertail through a crimp bead, then through one half of the clasp and back through the crimp bead, forming a loop around the clasp. Slide the crimp bead tight up against the clasp and flatten the crimp bead with needle-nose pliers. Trim the tigertail and thread the cut end back through a few beads.

3 Finish the other end of the necklace with the other crimp bead and the other half of the clasp. (Adding a second crimp bead is sometimes helpful in finishing the second end of the necklace.)

4 Thread three to five beads on a head pin. With the pliers, loop the head pin around the circle half of the clasp, so that the beads are tight against the clasp. Trim the excess head pin with wire cutters. Repeat with the two remaining head pins.

Designer: Joann Pearson

Designer: Tracy Hildebrand

THREE-STRAND BEADED NECKLACE

You can make this project a hundred times—and have a hundred totally different necklaces. It's just a matter of varying the color, style, and arrangement of the beads. So think of the beading cord as a blank canvas and have fun!

MATERIALS AND TOOLS

16-inch (40.5 cm) length of
   flexible wire
Wire cutters
Round-nose pliers
78-inch (2 m) length of
   beading cord
Scissors
Jeweler's cement

2 silver cones, ⅝ to ¾-inch long
   (13–18 mm)
Clasp finding
File or sandpaper
Seed beads
Small/medium glass beads
Sterling silver beads

WHAT TO DO

1 Cut the wire into two 8-inch (20 cm) lengths. Use the round-nose pliers to bend a loop at one end of one length of wire, then wrap the end of wire around the base of the loop to secure.

2 Cut the beading cord into three 26-inch (66 cm) lengths. Tie the three strands of beading cord securely to the wire loop with a double knot. Trim the ends and glue the knot with jeweler's cement. Note: Vary the length of the cord, as needed.

3 Thread the opposite end of the wire (the end that didn't get looped in Step 1) through a silver cone so that the knot and the loop are inside the cone.

4 With round-nose pliers, grasp the wire close to the narrow end of the cone and bend the wire away from you at a 45° angle, over the tips of the pliers, then back toward you to create an eye loop.

5 Slide one side of the clasp finding onto the wire eye loop, then wrap the end of the wire around the base of the loop several times to secure. Clip off excess wire and smooth rough wire edges with a file or sandpaper.

6 Beginning with the seed beads, string beads onto each strand of cord randomly or in a pattern of your choice. Position the largest beads near the center of the cord for balance.

7 Once each strand has been completely beaded, repeat Steps 1 through 5, above, to attach the opposite end of the clasp finding to the other side of necklace.

489

GOOD-MOOD NECKLACE

Designed to be worn close to the neckline (but not as a choker), this necklace features simple wire links that don't require a jig to make. It's the charming glass beads in a fun assortment of colors that make the visual statement—this one is sure to brighten even the most difficult day. These materials make a 14-inch (35 cm) strand, though of course you should vary the length (by varying the number of links) as needed.

MATERIALS AND TOOLS

64-inch (1.6 m) length of 16-gauge
   sterling silver wire
Wire cutters
Antique finish (optional)
32 glass beads, 12 mm
Round-nose pliers
33 jump rings, 5 mm
Clasp finding
File

WHAT TO DO

1 Cut thirty-two 2-inch (5 cm) lengths from the sterling silver wire. Apply antique finish to the wire and jump rings, if desired.

2 Slide a bead onto one of the pieces of wire, then use round-nose pliers to make a loop at each end. Make sure the loops face inward toward each other.

3 Bend the looped wire ends upward around the bead with your thumb and fingers, referring to the photo as a guide.

4 Connect bead links with jump rings. See Step 5 of basic instructions (page 483) for how to use jump rings.

5 Attach clasp finding to the links on each end of the necklace, using jump rings or any other applicable finding. File any exposed wire ends.

Designer: Mami Laher

491

SILVER AND BLUE NECKLACE & EARRINGS

Flexible beading wire is used to connect wire links and beads so that the two elements appear to be intertwined. The result is an intriguing design that looks deceivingly complicated.

MATERIALS AND TOOLS

20-gauge silver wire, 72 inches (1.8 m) for necklace and 18 inches (45.5 cm) for earrings
Wire cutters
Jig and pegs
Nylon jaw pliers

Crimping pliers
Flexible beading wire, 48 inches (1.2 m) for necklace and 28 inches (71 cm) for earrings
3-inch (7.5 cm) curb link chain
44 beads, 4 mm

192 silver seed beads
Silver hook or other clasp finding
Head pin
Ear posts or ear wires with jump rings

WHAT TO DO

1 To make the necklace, cut silver wire into eight 9-inch (22.5 cm) lengths. Set up the jig as shown (see pattern, page 516).

2 Following the jig pattern, loop the wire lengths around the pegs, making sure you loop the wire around the four outer pegs twice. (This necklace is made with eight wire links; change the number of links, if necessary, to alter the length of the necklace.) Make sure the wire loops are lined up and symmetrical, then flatten links with nylon jaw pliers.

3 Use crimping pliers to crimp two 24-inch (61 cm) strands of flexible beading wire to the last link of the curb link chain. Thread three 4 mm beads on the two strands of beading wire, then feed ends of the beading wire upward through the end loops of a wire link.

4 Continue to assemble the necklace as follows: Thread six seed beads on each strand of cord, then thread both strands through a 4 mm bead. Separate strands again and thread six seed beads on each strand. Feed strands downward through end loops on the wire link. With strands together again, thread three 4 mm beads, then separate strands and feed ends through another wire link, as in Step 3. Continue to string beads and wire links until all eight links have been used or until the desired necklace length is achieved.

5 When all the links and beads are in place, crimp the strands of beading wire to a silver hook or other clasp finding. String three 4 mm beads on a head pin and attach head pin to the curb link chain (on the opposite end of the necklace).

6 For the earrings, make two wire links, as described in Step 1. Cut four 7-inch (17.5 cm) strands of flexible beading wire. Center one 4 mm bead on two strands of the wire, then thread the strands upward through the end loops of one wire link so that bead rests between the two end loops. Thread beads as in necklace (see Step 4), ending with one 4 mm bead. Crimp ends of beading wire to an ear post or other earring finding, using a jump ring, if necessary. Repeat this process to make another earring.

Designer: Lilli Brennan

BEAD JEWELRY GALLERY

Right: Ethnic beads and charms look great when interspersed with smaller glass and metal beads. Designer: Jana Hunt Newton

Below: Glass beads make the perfect accessory for creative bent wire shapes. Designer: Betty Bacon

Bottom: This pair of bead and chain necklaces illustrates how beautifully different shapes of beads can be combined. Designer: Kimberley Adams

Left: Beaded watches can be created using the same basic beading techniques used in making necklaces. Designer: Chris Rankin

Below, left: These energetic bead people are made from simple beads and scrap wire. They look like they're dancing when you wear them! Designer: Susan Kinney

Below: A triangle clasp finding (made from simple bent wire) creates an ideal way to secure three separate strands of beads together. Designer: Leslie Bruntsch

495

HOME BEADING

Once upon a time, beads had serious jobs to do, serving as currency and even rudimentary calculators. Today, however, beads have one primary purpose—to pretty things up. Turn a plain-Jane bottle into a shimmering centerpiece with a twist of wire and a handful of sparkling beads. Add a romantic glow to your bedroom with a sumptuous beaded lampshade. Once you get started, you'll find dozens of everyday items that could benefit.

MATERIALS AND TOOLS

BEADS
Whatever your taste, you'll find beads to suit. See page 498 for more details.

COMPARTMENTALIZED TRAY
Keep your beads and other supplies organized in a compartmentalized tray, such as a kitchen-drawer utensil holder.

STRINGING MATERIAL
Sure, beads look pretty organized in a tidy tray, but to put them to work, you'll need to string them onto something. Several options are described below.

DECORATIVE CORD
Hemp, leather, elastic, waxed linen, and rattail (a supple cord with a satin finish) are all good choices for beading.

BEAD THREAD
Available in silk and nylon, bead thread comes in various thickness and colors and is used for sewing projects.

BEAD CORD
Similar to monofilament, beading cord won't decay within a year the way its fishing-line cousin will.

FLEXIBLE BEADING WIRE
A little stronger and a little less ductile than bead cord, beading wire is good for jewelry that features large beads.

WIRE
Wire is more a partner to beads than a supporting cast member. See pages 498 and 499 for more information about wire.

FAST-DRYING BEAD GLUE OR BEAD CEMENT
Make sure knots in cord and thread stay in place by coating them with bead glue.

BEADING OR APPLIQUÉ NEEDLES
Best for working with very small beads, these needles are numbered according to size (the larger the number, the slimmer the needle).

TWISTED WIRE NEEDLES
Use these big-eyed needles with all but the smallest beads and most intricate patterns. (The eye closes as it passes through a bead, but can be opened again with an awl or pin.)

BEESWAX OR THREAD CONDITIONER
Coat the ends of thread in beeswax to
make threading needles easier.

FINDINGS
Crimp beads and jump rings, clasps
and earring posts are essential components for every beader.

PLIERS
Round-nose pliers are good for gripping wire, and chain-nose pliers are
good for shaping it.

WIRE CUTTERS AND WIRE FILE
Choose diagonal cutters that will
allow you to snip ends in tight
spaces. File cuts smooth with a
wire file.

BASIC TECHNIQUES

KNOW THY BEADS

Shopping for beads can induce an adult bout of "kid in a candy store" syndrome. Stave off impulse buys by getting to know what's available before you're confronted with aisles full of tempting choices.

If you can string it onto a bit of thread, cord, or wire, it's a bead. Within this definition, the choices are seemingly infinite! There are, however, a few basic rules and categories that will help you keep the options straight. Beads, particularly handmade and specialty beads, come in endless shapes, but the image on previous page shows nine of the styles you'll see again and again. Beads are made from all kinds of materials, including glass, wood, ceramic, polymer clay, bone, plastic, semi-precious stone, metal, pearl, faux pearl, and shell. Most are measured in millimeters (mm) and can range in size from less than 2 mm in diameter to 24 mm and larger. Seed beads—small glass pellets—are sized according to their own numbering system: The smaller the number, the larger the seed bead.

TYING THE KNOT

Before you string your first bead in to place, figure out how you're going to keep it there. Unless you're working with wire or tigertail (see Working with Flexible Beading Wire, above right), a simple knot should suffice.

You can fasten the ends of cords, thread, and other "binding" materials with any kind of knot you'd like. Whatever knot you choose, though, if you want it to stay tied, secure it with a drop or two of fast-drying bead glue or, in a pinch, clear nail polish. (Avoid ordinary craft glue: It won't penetrate the knot thoroughly.) Although bead glue comes in a tube with a nifty applicator tip, use a toothpick or the tip of a straight pin to apply the glue to your knots; those nifty tips are notoriously sloppy. As its name implies, fast-drying bead glue should set in just a few minutes.

WORKING WITH FLEXIBLE BEADING WIRE

More flexible than standard wire and stronger than nylon beading thread, beading wire is perfect for supporting larger beads in projects that need to be sturdy, but should still have some flip—wind chimes, for instance!

There are several different varieties of flexible beading wire on the market. The most common is tigertail, a tiny steel cable that's encased in nylon. It comes in a variety of diameters, all of which are stiff enough to use without a needle. Because tigertail is so stiff, it's prone to kinks and won't drape well with smaller beads. It's also difficult to knot. Instead, use crimp beads to secure the ends of tigertail and other flexible beading wires: To fasten a string of beads, push the end of the wire through a crimp bead. To add a clasp to the end of the strand, slip the wire through its hole, then slip the wire back through the crimp bead. Use chain-nose pliers to flatten the crimp bead, then tuck the loose end of the wire into a bead.

WORKING WITH WIRE

Wire can be twisted, twirled, wrapped, and looped to hold beads in place while becoming part of a project's overall design.

Wire comes in a variety of metals and diameters, which are given by gauge number. Craft stores stock daintier wire, appropriate for delicate projects; your local hardware store will have spools of thicker wire for heavier-duty work. Thicker wires (particularly annealed steel or common black wire) can be a little oily; you may want to wipe them clean with a soft cloth before you start your project. You'll be able to shape many wire forms with just your fingers, but pliers make the job easier. If you plan to do much wirework, consider investing in a pair of chain-nose pliers and a pair of round-nose pliers.

To attach a strand of beaded wire to almost anything else, make a loop at the top of the wire. Working with chain-nose pliers, make a right-angle bend in the wire, leaving enough room between the bend and the uppermost bead for several wraps of wire. Switch to round-nose pliers and use them to grasp the right-angle bend. With your other hand, wrap the wire around the upper jaw of the pliers. Reposition the pliers so the bottom jaw is inserted in the circle of wire you just formed. If necessary, adjust the circle so that it's centered over the beads. Holding the pliers with one hand, use your other hand to wrap the circle's tail around the bead-supporting portion of the wire for several turns, until just above the uppermost bead. Trim the tail close and tuck it against the main wire.

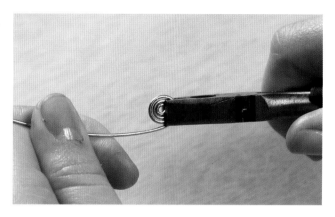

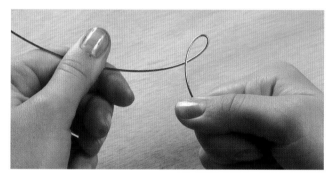

Easy to make, a wire spiral will keep beads in place and look pretty, too. Start by bending the end of your wire into a loop using round-nose pliers. Grasp the loop by its flat surface in the jaws of your chain-nose pliers. Use your fingers to coil the wire around the loop several times to form a spiral. Adjust the spiral so it's centered on the wire, and, if necessary, tap it flat with a hammer. For a more finished look, you can flatten not only the spiral shape, but the wire itself. Simply place the spiral on an anvil or another very hard surface that won't chip or yield, and gently tap the wire flat with a ball peen hammer.

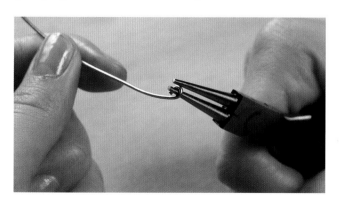

MAKING BEADED FRINGE

Shimmering along the hem of a curtain, the edge of a lampshade, or any other border, easy-to-make beaded fringe will add pizzazz to all the rooms in your home.

Thread your needle with nylon beading thread, using beeswax or thread conditioner, if necessary. At the edge of the piece you're adorning with fringe, take a small stitch to anchor the thread. Add beads to create the pattern and length of fringe you want. The last bead on the strand will act as a "stopper," holding the other beads in place. Using the image at bottom right as a guide, take the needle and thread back through all the beads in the strand (except the stopper bead), exiting at the top. Anchor the fringe in place with a stitch at the edge of the piece. For a variation, use a loop of beads as a stopper.

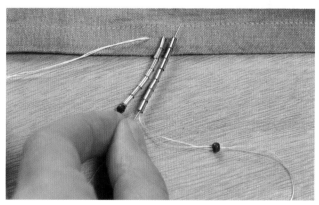

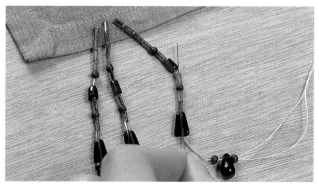

ALWAYS-IN-BLOOM BEADED BOUQUET

Everyone loves flowers—especially when they're guaranteed never to wilt! Made from beads and wire, these versatile blossoms have an endearing charm. They're easy to make, too, so you'll be able to "grow" dozens of them to give away, with plenty left over to brighten your home, too.

MATERIALS AND TOOLS

26-gauge floral wire
Seed beads, in the colors of your choice (Because you'll be stringing many small beads of the same color at one time, it's easiest to buy your beads on the hank and simply thread them directly from the hank to the wire.)

Wire cutters
Wired wooden floral stakes
Green floral tape
Scissors

WHAT TO DO

1 Each flower is made from several rows of beaded loops of wire, with each loop (or compound loop—see Steps 6 and 7) forming a petal or a leaf. You'll make each row of petals or leaves from one continuous strand of wire, stringing a set number of beads before twisting the wire to form a loop, cutting the wire from the coil only after you've completed the entire row. When you've made enough rows of petals and leaves to form a flower, you'll twist the ends of their wires together and fasten them to a floral stake with green floral tape.

2 In the flowers shown, the two rows of petals that form the two lower layers (the layers farthest from the flower's center) and the petals that form the center "ball" are made with a simple, single-loop technique: Each loop is formed from a single loop of beaded wire, as described in Step 3.

3 Start by stringing several feet of beads on the wire. (You'll get a feel for how much wire is required to make a row of petals as you work.) Slide forward 15 to 20 beads to about 6 inches (15 cm) from the end of the wire. Bend the beaded wire into a loop. Then twist the base of the loop once, insert your forefinger into the V formed by the wire at the bottom of the loop, and—using your other hand—twist the loop away from yourself twice. String the same number of beads onto the wire, threading them to about $1/16$ inch (1.5 mm) from the base of the first loop. Bend and twist the beaded wire as before. Repeat until you've made 10 petals. Cut the looped wire from the coil.

4 Repeat Step 3 to make a second row of petals, this one consisting of eight 20–25-bead loops. For the "ball" of petals at the flower's center, make three more rows: five 5-bead loops, six 9-bead loops, and seven 11-bead loops. Set the rows of beads aside while you make the compound petals and leaves.

6 The leaves and the third row of petals are made using a wrap-around-loop technique, which creates a compound—or multi-loop—petal or leaf. For the petals, start by stringing 14–16 beads onto the wire, threading them to about 6 inches from the main coil. Form a loop from the beaded wire, just as you did in Step 3. Next, string 24–26 beads onto the wire, threading them to $1/16$ inch of the base of the first loop. Instead of twisting this beaded length into a separate loop, bend it around the first loop; then twist the wire around itself twice at the base of the first loop.

7 To add the next petal, string 14–16 beads onto the wire, stringing them to about $3^1/2$ inches

(9 cm) or the amount of wire required to form the first petal from the petal you just finished. Bend the beaded wire into a loop, twist it twice, and add the second loop as in Step 6. Make eight of these two-layer compound loops to form a row of petals.

8 To make the leaves, use the wraparound-loop technique described in Steps 6 and 7. Each leaf in the project shown consists of a 36-bead loop, a 40-bead loop, and a 44-bead loop. You'll need two of these three-layer, compound loops to make a set of leaves for each flower.

9 Gather your rows of petals together, arranging them so that the shortest row of the smallest petals is at the center, above the other rows, and the longest row of the largest petals forms the lowest rung on the flowers. (You'll add the leaves in Step 10.) Twist the wires together at the base of the flower. Trim the excess wire, leaving a 2-inch tail.

10 Attach to the floral stake by wrapping the stake's wire around twisted flower wire. Then begin wrapping the stake with the floral tape, working from the bottom up. About 1 inch from the base of the petals, add the leaves, securing them in place with the floral tape. When you've finished wrapping the stake and attaching the leaves, trim the floral tape and smooth the cut end flat against the base of the flower.

Designer: Melanie Gidley

Designer: Melanie Gidley

BEADED CEILING-FAN CHAINS

Turn a boring old ball-chain fan pull into a snazzy centerpiece with an artful collection of glass or wooden beads. Instant pop!

MATERIALS AND TOOLS

Blasé ceiling-fan chain in need of beaded pizzazz
20-gauge wire
Wire cutters
Ball-chain connectors (available at hardware and jewelry stores)
Assorted beads
Needle-nose pliers

WHAT TO DO

1 Determine how long you'd like the beaded portion of your fan chain to be. If you'd like to hold the beads in place with coil of wire, cut a piece of wire 3 inches longer than the planned length of the pull, and proceed to Step 2. If you'd like to use a bead as a stopper, cut the piece of wire twice as long as the intended pull, plus 3 inches (7.5 cm), and proceed to Step 3.

2 Referring to Working with Wire on page 499 and using your needle-nose pliers, form a coil from about 1 inch (2.5 cm) of one end of the wire. This coil will act as a bead stopper, so make sure it's large enough to hold the first bead you string in place.

3 String the "stopper bead" to the middle of the wire. Fold the wire in half around the bead, then twist the two halves of the wire around each other to their ends, creating a double thickness of wire. Note: Make sure the remaining beads have holes large enough to accommodate the wire when it's twisted together.

4 String the beads onto the wire, stopping about ½ inch (13 mm) from the end of the wire. Trim any excess wire.

5 Use your needle-nose pliers to bend the ½-inch end into a "knot" or ball that will fit inside the ball-chain connector. Insert the knot into one end of the ball-chain connector.

6 Squeeze the ball-chain connector closed around the knotted end of the wire with your pliers. Then attach the other end of the ball chain-connector to your ceiling fan's chain.

BAUBLE-BEADED SWIZZLE STICKS

Sophisticated—yet playful!—these snazzy swizzle sticks will add a capricious twist to your grown-up drinks.

MATERIALS AND TOOLS

20-gauge stainless steel wire, 15-inch (38 cm) piece for each swizzle stick
Wire cutters
Clean cloth
Smooth-jawed, flat-nosed pliers
Eye pins, one for each swizzle stick (see Step 2.)
Colorful glass beads, one for each swizzle stick
Assortment of smaller beads in neutral colors
Assortment of gold- or silver-toned accent beads
Bench vice or locking-jaw pliers
Pencil or small dowel rod
Wire file

WHAT TO DO

1 Cut a 15-inch length of wire. Wire that's straight off the spool can be a little greasy, so take a moment to wipe it clean with a piece of cloth. Then measure and mark its center.

2 An eye pin is a type of jewelry finding. It looks like a straight pin, minus the pointy end and with a reclosable loop where the pinhead would be. If you can't find eye pins at a jewelry-supply store or through an Internet retailer, you can make your own from straight pins: Simply snip off the sharp end and, after you've added your beads, use needle-nose pliers to twist it into a small loop to hold the beads in place. As long as the end bead's hole is small enough, the pinhead will hold it in place.

3 String one of the colored glass beads onto the eye pin, followed by a gold or silver accent bead and one of the small, neutral-colored beads. Bend the end of the pin into a loop to hold the beads in place. (If you're using a straight pin that you've converted to an eye pin, string the beads in the opposite order, starting with the neutral-colored bead, and bending the snipped end into a loop after you've added the glass bead.) Set the beaded eye pin aside.

4 String beads onto the 15-inch length of wire. These beads will end up as a loop at the top of your swizzle stick, with the beaded eye pin as a bauble in the center, so string your beads in a symmetrical pattern. The projects shown, for instance, are strung as follows: four small neutral beads, one gold accent bead, two larger neutral beads, one gold accent bead, four small neutral beads. Make sure the two center beads (the larger neutral beads, in the project shown) are exactly on either side of the centerline that you marked in Step 1.

5 Bend the wire in half, trapping the beads in the U of the bend, with the two center beads falling to either side of the centerline. Then use the pliers to open the loop on the eye pin just slightly and slip the bauble into place, between the two center beads. Squeeze the loop closed again.

6 To twist the two sides of the wire together, start by gripping the loose ends in a bench vice or locking-jaw pliers. Then insert a pencil or a dowel in the U of the bend.

7 If you're working with a bench vice, pull the wire taut using the dowel, then wind the dowel like a clock to twist the two sides of the wire together. If you're working with locking-jaw pliers, you may want to ask someone to hold the pliers steady for you while you twist with the dowel. Otherwise, hold the pliers in one hand and the dowel in the other, keeping the wire taut between the two while you twist.

8 Snip any excess from the ends of the wire and file them smooth. Then pour and stir, baby!

Designer: Melanie Gidley

BEADED NAPKIN RING

Napkin rings dress up any table, and beaded ones add a splash of color and style. This one is made with memory wire—a wonderful material that always "remembers" to return to its coiled shape, no matter how it's stretched or straightened. These colorful accessories are so quick and easy to make that you can whip up new ones to complement any table setting.

MATERIALS AND TOOLS

24-inch (60 cm) length of steel
  memory wire in 2-inch (5 cm)
  coils
Round-nose pliers
Wire cutters
Medium beads

WHAT TO DO

1 Using the round-nose pliers, make a small loop in one end of the wire, to prevent the beads from sliding off.

2 String the beads on the wire, varying shapes, colors, and sizes to suit your taste. Remember that the beads will fall next to the ones strung on either side and the ones on adjacent coils.

3 When the napkin ring is as full as you want it to be, cut the wire, leaving about ½ inch (13 mm) of extra wire.

4 With the pliers, form a small loop in the end of the wire, trimming off any excess as necessary.

Designer: Carol Taylor

BEADED "HARDWARE" FOR DRAWERS AND CABINETS

Why settle for the same old drawer handles and cabinet pulls everyone else has? Customize your dresser drawers and kitchen cabinets with one-of-a-kind beaded hardware.

MATERIALS AND TOOLS

Screwdriver or power drill
16-gauge wire
Wire cutters
Screw eyes of a length to fit your drawer or cabinet, see Step 2 (You'll need 2 screw eyes for each handle and 1 for each pull)
Needle-nose pliers
Wire file
Nuts and washers to fit the screw eyes

WHAT TO DO

1 Start by removing the existing hardware from the drawer or cabinet, using either a hand-held screwdriver or a power drill.

2 Take a look at the screws you just removed—you'll need screw eyes of the same length and approximately the same diameter. If your screw eyes are larger in diameter, you may need to drill bigger holes in your drawer or cabinet to accommodate them.

3 Determine how much wire you'll need for each handle or pull. For handles, drape or bend a length of wire (without cutting it) between the two screw holes in the drawer, trying different lengths until you've found one that suits you; then cut a length 4 inches (10 cm) longer than you'd like your handle to be. For cabinet pulls, cut the wire 3 inches (7.5 cm) longer than you'd like the finished project to be.

4 If you're making cabinet pulls, skip ahead to Step 7.

5 To make a drawer pull, thread about 2 inches (5 cm) of one end of the wire through one of the screw eyes. Grasp the 2-inch end with your needle-nose pliers, bend it into a loose loop around the screw eye, leaving enough space for the screw eye to swing freely, and wrap the wire end around the main body of the wire several times. Trim any excess wire and file the end smooth.

6 Thread your beads onto the wire as desired, leaving the final 2 inches free. Thread this end through the second eyebolt and secure it as in Step 5. See Step 10 for installation.

7 To make a cabinet pull, start by forming a coil from 1 inch of one end of the wire. (Refer to Working with Wire on page 499.) This coil will act as a bead stopper, so make sure it's large enough to hold the first bead you string in place.

8 String your beads onto the length of wire, leaving the final 2 inches free.

9 Thread the last 2 inches of the wire through the screw eye. Grasp the 2-inch end with your needle-nose pliers, bend it into a loose loop around the screw eye, leaving enough space for the screw eye to swing freely; and wrap the wire end around the main body of the wire several times. Trim any excess wire and file the end smooth.

10 To install your new beaded hardware, simply insert the screw eyes into the holes vacated by the old hardware. If necessary, widen the holes to fit the screw eyes, using a power drill. Secure each screw eye with a washer and a nut.

Designer: Melanie Gidley

HOME BEADING GALLERY

Right: Always on the lookout for fun, inexpensive gifts to make? These beaded bottle toppers can be made to custom-match your favorite someone's dishware. Designer: Susan Rind

Below: Transform an ordinary ceiling fan or lamp pull with just a few minutes and some great beads. Designer: Kelly Lightner

Bottom: Bead your own fringe for a lampshade or window curtain. Designer: Sandi Abel

Opposite page, bottom: For special occasions or everyday pleasure, decorate your serving utensils with wrapped wire and beads. Designer: Susan Rind

Opposite page, top left: Add designer touches to finials and curtain rods with colorful beads and wire. Designer: Susan Rind

Opposite page, top right: Spend your next rainy afternoon decorating your favorite stemware and creating party picks. Designer: Susan Rind

511

Alphabet Stool

(see page 64)

Keepsake Box

(see page 66)

Wood Buttons

(see page 58)

Tidal Bowl

(see page 63)

TEMPLATES

Wine Goblets

(see page 24)

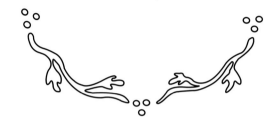

Painted Doors

(see page 27)

Fanciful Bottles

(see page 23)

Carved Candle

(see page 163)

Picture Frame

(see page 437)

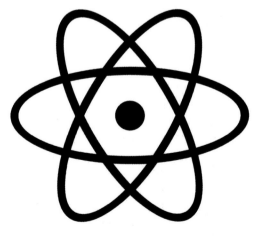

Jacket & Shoes

(see page 465)

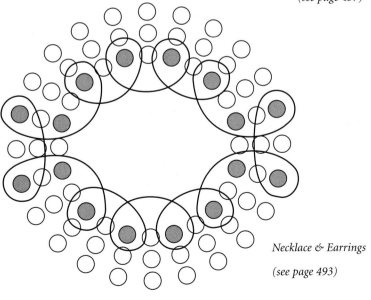

Necklace & Earrings

(see page 493)

Atomic Clocks

(see page 78)

CRAFT GLUES

If a crafter had to choose only two items to take to a desert island, chances are she or he would take a pair of scissors and their favorite all purpose glue or adhesive. Glue is an indispensable tool for a crafter; it's difficult (but not impossible) to imagine doing craft projects without it.

We use the terms glue and adhesive interchangeably because they both serve the same purpose—they bond two surfaces together. Technically, the only difference is in their composition. Glues are created from organic matter; adhesives are created with synthetic materials.

A smart crafter should always read the label on a glue or adhesive for recommended applications—especially when using a glue you're not familiar with. While you're reading the label, keep two questions in mind. Are your surfaces porous, semi-porous, or non-porous? This will give you an idea which type of glue to use. Next, ask yourself whether you want a strong, long-lasting bond or a temporary bond? Once you know the answer to these questions you can determine if the glue you're considering is right for the job.

WHITE GLUES

White glues are one of two of the most commonly used types of glues for crafting. They're readily found in most households and school rooms. These all-purpose glues are (usually) water soluble, dry clear, and are somewhat flexible. They can be used on almost all surfaces from paper to ceramics and fabric to some plastics. They're not recommended for use on metals or anything that will come in contact with water. Many—if not most—white glues are PVA glues (polyvinyl acetate adhesive). You can find many different brands with consistencies that range from thin to thick. In general, these glues can be thinned with water as desired.

HOT GLUE

Hot glue is the other frequently used glue for crafting. Most crafters would be loathe to give up their hot glue. (Alas, most desert islands don't have electrical connections!) Hot glue bonds quickly, can be used on both porous and non-porous surfaces, and works especially well for bonding uneven surfaces to each other. The only drawback to hot glue is that the bond is not good for structural uses that will be subjected to stress. In other words, don't try to build a chair with hot glue. Glue guns and glue pots heat the glue sticks for application. Hot glue sticks have temperature ranges from cool to hot; they can be found in different colors and with glitter imbedded in the sticks for special effects.

CYANOACRYLATE GLUES

These are the wonder glues of the modern world. Adjectives like super or crazy usually mean the glue is a cyanoacrylate glue. Just a drop (literally!) will usually do the trick. They are fast bonding, clear, and strong. Surfaces must fit tightly in order for these glues to work well. Their power is wasted on paper crafts and they may not work well with some plastics. Reading the label (the second commandment) is extremely important before you use this type of glue.

INDUSTRIAL STRENGTH ADHESIVES

Two-part epoxies, jewelry glues, silicone glues, china glues, multipurpose cements, and contact adhesives all fall into this category. They all offer a strong bond for hard to glue materials such as metals, ceramics, rubber, fiberglass, plastics, and glass. They dry clear and can sometimes be used as sealants as well. They should all be used with plenty of ventilation and by carefully following the manufacturer's instructions.

SPRAY ADHESIVES

These adhesives are great for covering large, flat surfaces such as papers and fabrics. Use them in well-ventilated areas with your work area covered to protect from overspray. They are repositionable, but the bond can be made more permanent by coating both surfaces to be joined, allowing them to become tacky or dry before joining. Just follow the manufacturer's recommendations.

WOOD GLUES

Wood glues are generally divided into two types: AR (aliphatic resin) and polyurethane glues. AR adhesives are the common yellow wood glues that are for interior use. Polyurethane glues are fine for both interior and exterior uses.

Here are 10 handy commandments to live by.
1. Identify the glue you think you need for the job.
2. Read the label carefully.
3. Make sure the surfaces to be bonded are clean and dry.
4. Know the working and drying time of your adhesive.
5. Apply adhesives in a well-ventilated area.
6. Test-bond the materials with the adhesive, if possible.
7. Use an even coat of adhesive.
8. Avoid contact with the skin or eyes.
9. Remove excess adhesive as quickly as possible.
10. Keep all containers firmly closed so the adhesive won't dry out.

LARGE, LOOPED BOW

MATERIALS AND TOOLS

3 yards (2.7m) wire-edge ribbon,
   2½ inches (6.4 cm) wide
Floral wire

WHAT TO DO

1 Make a loop on one end of the ribbon, leaving a tail equal to the length of the first loop. Keeping the ribbon pinched firmly between your thumb and forefinger, gather in the sides of the ribbon at the base of the loop.

2 Make a second loop of ribbon equal in size to the first loop. Place it on the opposite side of your thumb. Twist the ribbon as needed to keep the right side showing. Firmly pinch the ribbon between your thumb and forefinger as you gather the sides at the base of the loop.

3 Continue making equal-size loops until you have a total of six, all gathered between your thumb and forefinger.

4 Twisting the ribbon to show the right side, create a smaller loop on top of the first loop made in Step 1.

5 Make five or more smaller loops, placing one on top of each larger loop, until you have a total of six small loops.

6 Leave a tail on the ribbon equal to that left in Step 1.

7 Wrap the floral wire around the center of the bow, bringing the ends of the wire behind the bow. Firmly twist the free ends of the wire to secure the bow.

8 Make a fork cut in each ribbon tail.

◆ To make a fork cut, fold the ribbon in half lengthwise; then diagonally cut the end of the ribbon from the corner points to the folded edge.

GIFT PACKAGE BOW

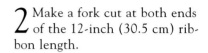
MATERIALS AND TOOLS

1½ yards (1.4 m) wire-edge ribbon,
   2½ inches (6.4 cm) wide
Floral wire

WHAT TO DO

1 Cut one piece of the wire-edge ribbon at each of the following four lengths: 18 inches (45.7 cm), 16 inches (40.6 cm), 12 inches (30.5 cm), and 7 inches (17.8 cm).

2 Make a fork cut at both ends of the 12-inch (30.5 cm) ribbon length.

3 Make a single large loop out of the 18-inch (45.7 cm) piece of ribbon, overlapping the ends approximately 1½ inches (3.8 cm).

4 Center the seam of the looped ribbon on top of the 12-inch (30.5 cm) length of ribbon.

5 Make a single large loop out of the 16-inch (40.6 cm) piece of ribbon, overlapping the ends approximately 1½ inches (3.8 cm). Center the seam of this looped ribbon on top of the looped 18-inch (45.7 cm) ribbon.

6 Make a small loop with the 7-inch (17.8 cm) piece of ribbon, overlapping the ends, and place it in the center of the 16-inch (40.6 cm) looped ribbon.

7 Insert a piece of floral wire through the center loop, bringing both ends of the wire to the back of the bow. Tightly twist the wire to secure the bow.

519

Picture Framing Made Easy

If you've gone to the trouble of making a great-looking project, you'll probably want to display it in proper style. In many cases, that means framing it. A good frame—one that will protect and enhance your work, in addition to displaying it—consists of six parts, plus rubber or felt bumpers to protect your wall and hardware for hanging the whole frame package.

Frame

The moulding, usually wood or metal, that holds the whole package together, forming a decorative and protective support for the picture or other work of art. You can purchase a pre-made frame in a number of standard sizes, order a custom frame, or cut your own from purchased wooden moulding. Regardless of which option you choose, pay special attention to the frame or frame moulding's rabbet; this is the grove that runs all along the inside edge of the back of the moulding and into which the glazing, mat, artwork, mounting, and backboard fit. (See page 523.) Thus, the rabbet must be deep enough to fit all of these components.

Glazing

The sheet of glass or acrylic that protects the artwork. Pre-made frames often come with glazing (as well as a backboard) already in place. You can cut your own glass glazing (it should have the same dimensions as the mat—see below), but leave acrylic cutting to professional framers. Both glass and acrylic are available with filters to protect your artwork from UV rays and with enhancements that will reduce glare and reflections (ask your glass dealer or frame shop for recommendations). Acrylic is lighter and stronger than glass (both big advantages), but scratches much more easily. Regardless of whether glazing is made from glass or acrylic, the artwork, once installed, should never lay flat against it; otherwise, the work may become vulnerable to moisture or mold.

Mat

This is the "frame inside the frame." Usually made from a special kind of cardboard, mat board has a paper front, a core, and paper backing. The mat's window (the portion through which the artwork shows) should be cut at a 45-degree bevel to prevent a shadow from falling on the framed artwork. Mat board is available in an endless array of colors to complement or accent your artwork. To select

a color, keep these tips in mind: To make sure that the artwork remains the focus, choose a mat that has the same or similar color as the predominant color in the work. A medium or pale-toned mat will make a photo stand out. Steer away from white mat board for watercolors, and skip mat board altogether for oil paintings.

A mat's primary function, however, is to act as a spacer between the glazing and the art, creating a small airspace that will prevent moisture and mold from attacking your work. So the type of mat board you choose is just as important as its color. Standard mat board should only be used with pieces that aren't terribly valuable to you; it contains naturally occurring acid that will eventually degrade your work. For more important pieces, use neutralized mat, which has a much lower acid content; or, for pieces you'd like to last a lifetime and longer, use rag mat or museum board, which is made from cotton and is 100 percent acid-free.

You'll find plenty of pre-cut mats with standard-size windows at frame shops and craft suppliers, but sometimes you'll want a mat color or window size that isn't readily available. (Unless you want to custom order a frame— a pricey proposition—try to stick to mats with outside dimensions that fit standard size frames, even when you're cutting your own mat from scratch.) Here's how to calculate window size and the necessary outside dimensions for a custom-cut mat.

Calculating Dimensions

1 Start by determining how large the window should be. First, measure your artwork. Let's say it's a collage that measures 5 x 7 inches. The mat should overlap the piece just slightly to hold it in place; an overlap of 1/8 inch on sides, top, and bottom is standard. Therefore, the mat window should be 1/4 inch smaller than the artwork along both its dimensions. (1/8 inch at the top plus 1/8 inch at the bottom equals 1/4 inch. The calculation is the same for the sides.) So, the window should be 4¾ x 6¾ inches.

2 Next, determine how wide you'd like the mat's borders to be. A good rule of thumb is to make the borders at least twice as wide as the frame moulding. For frames that are larger than 20 x 24 inches, however, the borders should be at least three times as wide as the moulding. Say you've selected a frame with ¾-inch-thick moulding; the mat border should be at least 1½ inches wide. Borders that are cut equally at top and bottom actually appear to be larger on top; to offset this natural optical illusion, make the bottom border a bit wider than the top— we'll add ⅛ inch to the bottom and subtract the same amount from the top. Thus, the border for our mat would be 1½ inches wide at either side, 1⁷⁄₁₆ inches wide at the top, and 1⅜ inch at the bottom.

3 Finally, determine the outside dimensions of the mat board. Simply add the dimensions of the window to the size of the border. For the mat's width, add the window's 4¾ inches to the border's 1½ inch at either side (3 inches all together) for a total of 7¾ inches. For the mat's length, add the window's 6¾ inches to the border's 1⁷⁄₁₆ inches at the top and 1⅜ inches at the bottom (3 inches all together) for a total of 9¾ inches. Thus, in an ideal world, your mat's outside dimensions would be 7¾ x 9¾ inches. Ours, however, is not an ideal world. Because frames come in standard sizes, you'll probably want to adjust your mat's dimensions to fit a standard frame size (otherwise, you'll spend a fortune custom ordering a frame). Round your mat up or down to the nearest standard frame size. In this case, that would be 8 x 10 inches, and you'd simply have to add ½ inch to both the length and width dimensions of the outside dimensions of your mat (the window size will not be affected).

You may either hand these dimensions to your local frame shop (or your favorite online retailer) and let them do the work, or you can cut the mat board yourself, either from a full sheet (which measures 32 x 40 inches) or a standard-cut sheet without a window. (If you choose the latter option, you'll only have to cut the window.) Here's how to cut mat board:

MATERIALS AND TOOLS

Mat board
Sharp pencil
Metal straightedge with a nonskid cork or rubber base
Triangle or protractor
Self-healing cutting mat
Mat knife
Mat cutter (This tool, made for cutting windows, creates a perfect, 45-degree beveled edge.)
Craft knife
Replacement blades for the tools listed above
Burnishing tool

CUTTING A MAT BOARD

1 Start by finding a stable, well-lit work surface that will be at waist-height to you while you're standing. (For maximum leverage and perspective, you should always cut mat board while standing up.)

2 Start by transferring the outside dimensions of your mat to the mat board, using the pencil and straight edge and starting at one corner to take advantage of the existing right angle. Use the triangle or protractor to make sure your right angle is exactly 90 degrees. Before you cut, check your measurements a second time. (The old woodworking axiom holds true here, too: Measure twice, cut once.)

3 Place the marked mat board on top of the self-healing cutting mat. Then cut the mat, using the straight edge to guide your mat knife.

4 Transfer the window dimensions to the board. Check to make sure the angles are 90 degrees and double check your measurements. Working with the mat cutter and your straightedge, cut the window, turning the board clockwise after cutting each edge so that you're always pulling the blade toward yourself. If the cutter becomes difficult to pull, its blade has probably become dull; replace it with a sharp one.

5 After you've made all the cuts, ideally, the window will fall right out. But, it probably won't—in which case, carefully cut any sticking portions with your craft knife. When the window does fall out, trim any nicks or undercut corners with the craft knife. Use the burnishing tool to smooth over any over cuts.

MOUNT BOARD

The stiff backing to which the artwork is attached, preventing ripples or wrinkles in the piece. Any kind of stiff, lightweight material can act as a mount board, including foam core, corrugated cardboard, or self-adhesive mount board. No matter what kind of material you choose, however, make sure it's acid-free to prevent damage to your artwork. The mount board should be the same size as the mat and can be cut the same way. The mount board and the mat are hinged together at their top edges; then the artwork is attached to the mount board. Here's how:

MATERIALS AND TOOLS

Mat
Mount board
Acid-free artist's tape or white linen tape
Mounting strips or corners
Scissors
Pencil

CUTTING A MOUNT BOARD

1 Butt together the top edges of the mat and the mount board, making sure the mat is placed face down on your work surface and the mount board is face up. Leaving about 1 inch at either end free, tape the edges together with acid-free artist's tape or white linen tape. The two pieces of board should fold like a

card that opens from the bottom, rather than the side. Close the "card" to make sure its edges are even; if they're not, adjust the mat and mount board until they're properly aligned.

2 Position the artwork on the mount board, folding the mat over it to make sure it's positioned properly. Mark the artwork's position on the mount board with a pencil. Then, following the manufacturer's instructions, attach the mounting corners or strips to the mount board, just a little beyond the artwork's position.

3 Following the manufacturer's instructions, secure the artwork in the mounting corners or strips. And close the mat over the mounting board. Your work is now ready to be placed in the frame.

BACK BOARD

The rigid backside of the frame package that protects the artwork from behind. The back board should be made from an acid-free, lightweight material that will resist warping—corrugated cardboard, foam core, and mat board are all good choices. Cut to the same size (and using the same technique) as the mat and mounting board, the back board is held in place with the brads or glazier points in the frame.

DUST COVER

The final layer on the frame package, the dust cover seals out dust and insects. Acid-free, brown craft paper is the most common choice of materials. After you've installed the glaze, the mat, artwork, mounting board, and back board inside the frame, run a bead of glue along the back of the frame. Spread the glue evenly with a damp sponge; then cover the back of the frame with the craft paper. Use a craft knife and a ruler to trim the paper to fit. When the glue has dried, you may install the hanging hardware and, if desired, attach self-adhesive protective bumpers to the bottom corners of the frame.

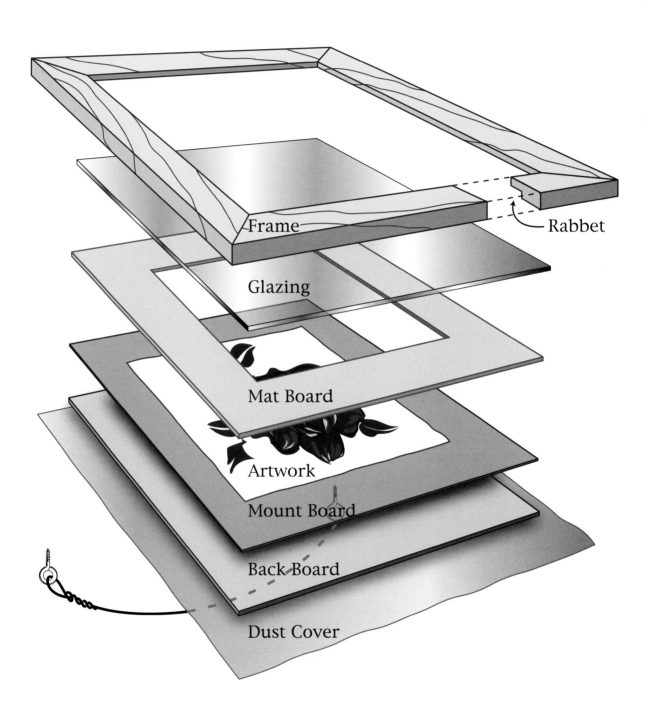

Frame

Rabbet

Glazing

Mat Board

Artwork

Mount Board

Back Board

Dust Cover

The ABCs of
Custom Lettering

Custom lettering was once the sole province of dedicated monks, many of whom spent their entire lives painstakingly illuminating religious texts. Today, of course, the art is accessible even to beginning crafters. And far from taking an entire lifetime, lettering a scrapbook or photo album can be accomplished in mere hours, thanks to such modern tools as specialty pens, tracing paper, and computer software. The following tips should have you setting pen to page (or fingertip to keyboard) in no time.

Fonts

For today's crafter, finding a font may prove far less difficult than picking one. Visit your local library and you'll find at least half a dozen books full of interesting custom alphabets, complete with instructions for recreating them. Prefer a more automated approach? A quick search of the Internet will turn up plenty of software packed with pre-designed fonts to print from your computer, as well as several that promise to transform your handwriting—no matter how messy and illegible—into a neat, readable, and yet entirely personal font. Alphabet stencils, rubber stamps, and stickers offer still more options.

To choose a font, consider your project. If you're creating a scrapbook of a friend's wedding, an elegant font embellished with serifs (those wispy lines added to the tops and bottoms of letters) would be appropriate. A bold, blocky font would work well for lettering a photo album documenting your son's high school sports accomplishments. Shadowed fonts look good with projects that have a sunshine motif. You get the idea.

Consider the lettering's function, too. Funky, chunky block letters make great titles—but might be a bit much for narrative text. For extensive, explanatory lettering, choose a font that's easy to read, but still appropriate for the project and the topic.

Getting It Straight

If you're hand lettering a project (as opposed to lettering with the aid of a computer), keeping your letters straight and evenly spaced can be a challenge, but one that's easy to overcome with the right tools, practice, and patience.

Arm yourself with a pencil, a good eraser, a ruler, lined paper, and tracing paper. Then start by deciding what you'd like to say in a given space. How many letters will it take? How can you break up phrases to make them fit? Sketch potential designs on scrap paper. When you're happy with a configuration, write the letters on lined paper; then transfer them to tracing paper, and finally to your project. Even if you're using stencils, stickers, or stamps, take time to plot your design on scrap paper before committing it to your precious project.

If you're more confident of your skills, you can lightly draw the letters directly on your project with a pencil—don't be too proud to make guidelines using a pencil and ruler first, though! Then take a good look at your penciled drawing before making it permanent with a pen. Make changes to your design now, while you can still undo mistakes with an eraser.

Adding Ink

Uncapping your pen should be the final step (not the first) in your lettering projects. By the time you're ready to use ink, your entire design should be sketched or traced on your project in pencil.

If you do much lettering, you'll probably want to invest in specialty dual-tipped pens; one end has a fine tip that's perfect for outlining, the other is equipped with a broader tip for filling space. Choose a fine-tipped black marker to outline letters and give them weight; colors tend to weaken text when used for outlining—save them for filling in and highlighting letters.

When you're ready to start adding weight and color to your letters, first, take a deep breath and relax. Make sure the entire tip of your pen is in full contact with the page and, whenever possible, write using a pulling motion rather than a pushing motion. Keep an eye on where your hand rests; a misplaced palm can smudge your freshly inked text. On the topic of smudging, if you're using more than one color, make sure to let the first color dry completely before adding a second or third; and allow all the ink plenty of time to dry before erasing any pencil lines that might still be showing.

OTHER IDEAS

◆ You can make letters from all kinds of stuff—old cards, magazines, photos that didn't turn out well, scraps of pretty fabric. If it's got an interesting pattern, color, or texture on it, it'll make a great letter. Simply trace the letters you want onto the material and cut them out. For a more precise look, use stencils to guide your tracings.

◆ Make three-dimensional letters by cutting them from foam core or heavy card stock. Use a sharp craft knife to cut thicker materials.

◆ Highlight your custom letters with well-placed specialty punches—tiny stars around photos of a senior prom or wee hearts dancing among honeymoon keepsakes.

◆ If you find a font that you love, but that's simply over the top—say, letters made entirely from intricately twining vines—use the font for initial letters only. All of the charm, none of the confusion.

CONTRIBUTING DESIGNERS

WILL ALBRECHT enjoys building and painting practical furniture, as well as marine biology and videography. He lives in Clyde, North Carolina.

BONNIE BONE has been making and selling her bread dough Christmas ornaments for 28 years—since she was 12 years old! For the past 15 years, her charming handmade ornaments have been sold in Macy's West department stores. They may also be purchased online at www.bonniesbuddies.com. Bonnie lives in Claremont, California with her husband Mike and her two sons, Andy and Matt.

LILLI BRENNAN has enjoyed a lifelong passion for jewelry. After experimenting with several forms of jewelry making, she has devoted her attention over the past several years to various wire working techniques. Lilli specializes in creating custom links using WigJigs, commercially available jigs made expressly for delicate wire work. Lilli lives in Stroudsburg, Pennsylvania and can be reached via email at wireandbeads@aol.com.

PAMELA BROWN has owned and operated Mountain Lights, a candle and lighting store in Asheville, North Carolina, since 1997. She leads candlemaking classes in her shop and has taught at John Campbell Folk School, as well. Pamela encourages everyone to reuse their leftover wax; her store even features a "recycled wax" bin, where customers may drop off their leavings, which are then given to novice candlemakers.

KATHY COOPER first discovered a love for creating floorcloths when she made one for her kitchen. Today she is a nationally recognized artist, a frequent guest on television, and the author of two best-selling books, The Complete Book of Floorcloths (Lark Books, 2002) and *The Weekend Crafter: Painting Floorcloths* (Lark Books, 1999). For a complete resource list or to learn more about floorcloths, visit her website at www.kathycooperfloorcloths.com.

JOYCE CUSICK is a painter and lace collector living in Dunnellon, Florida. She is the author of *Crafting with Lace*.

IRENE SEMANCHUK DEAN has been working with polymer clay for more than 10 years. Irene is the author of *The Weekend Crafter: Polymer Clay* (Lark Books, 2000), Kids' Crafts: Polymer Clay (Lark Books, 2003), and *Faux Surfaces in Polymer Clay* (Lark Books, 2003). She sells her work at local craft fairs, through stores and galleries, and on her website, www.good-night-irene.com.

MELANIE GIDLEY (melgidley@aol.com) is a multi-media artist whose passions include mosaic and beadwork. She has been crafting in Asheville, NC for the past eleven years and is the coordinator of the West Asheville Holiday Art and Gift Show. When she dies she would like her casket to be filled with seed beads.

CYNTHIA GILLOOLY is a former floral shop owner who now devotes her time to gardening and cultivating specialty orchids. She lives in Alexander, North Carolina.

SUSAN GREENELSH is a decorative painter and illustrator living in Waynesville, North Carolina. She believes painting and crafting are the best form of entertainment, and that the feeling of accomplishment that comes from completing things is very exciting.

CATHERINE HAM divides her time between homes in Austria and Greece. She is never without her knitting bag when traveling, and finds it starts conversations in the most unusual places. Catherine is the author of *25 Gorgeous Sweaters for the Brand-New Knitter* (Lark Books, 2000) and *Weekend Crafter Knitting: 20 Simple & Stylish Wearables for Beginners* (Lark Books, 2003).

TRACY HILDEBRAND is a glass beadmaker and jewely artist. She makes her home in Asheville, NC and is represented by galleries throughout the southeast.

DANA IRWIN has been an art director at Lark Books for 15 years. She spends her free time as an artist and freelance illustrator and a vegetable gardener of sorts. She also dabbles in puppet making, and has a family of three dogs and two cats.

MICHELLE KEENAN lives in Asheville, North Carolina. She is a fundraiser, freelance writer, and "specialist" in hodgepodge and ragammuffin chic. Michelle may be reached via email at michellekeenan@yahoo.com.

HEIDI KRONEN worked with interior designers for more than 10 years. It was during this time that she discovered a tremendous demand in the stencil market for unique, one-of-a-kind interior decorative stencils. To meet this demand, Heidi created a new line of exquisite stencils available online at www.RevelationStencils.com.

LYNN KRUCKE is an instructor and designer who works with a variety of media, including rubber stamps and paper arts, polymer clay, beads and wire, and fabric and fiber arts. Her favorite projects incorporate one or more of these techniques, and her designs have been included in a number of books and magazines. Lynn lives in Summerville, South Carolina and can be contacted via email at lkrucke@bellsouth.net.

MAMI LAHER is a jewelry designer and artist who seeks innovation in creative expression. Although wire and beads have been her favorite media for the past five years, she has been experimenting with silver clay recently. She also enjoys painting with watercolors and has an affinity for flowers, abstract, as well as real. Mami earned a B.A in sociology in

1984. To contact Mami or to view her work, visit her website at www.mamibeads.com.

DIANA LIGHT lives and works in the Blue Ridge Mountains of North Carolina. After earning her B.F.A. in painting and print-making, she extended her expertise to etching and painting fine glass objects. She has contributed to numerous Lark books and is the coauthor of Lark's *The Weekend Crafter: Etching Glass*.

SONJA LEE is a fabric surface-design artist who earned a B.A. in studio art from Saint Olaf College in Northfield, Minnesota. She is the co-owner of Friends Fabric Art in Lowell, Massachusetts, a creative place for anyone to dye, paint, or use other fun supplies to decorate clothing, household items, and fabric. Sonja can be reached via email at Sonja@FriendsFabricArt.com. For more information about Friends Fabric Art, call the store at (978) 458-4200 or visit www.friendsfabricart.com.

MARTHE LE VAN's painter-mom introduced her to the joys of framing at an early age. She garnered pocket money assembling metal frames and attaching hanging wires. This innocent task proved pivotal in Marthe's professional pursuits as a curator, exhibition manager, and craft designer. Marthe has created projects for several Lark publications, including *The Decorated Frame, Simple Glass Crafts, and Creative Tabletop Fountains*.

CAROLINE MANHEIMER began tie-dyeing her own curtains in the 60s. She continued to dye fabric and take art classes, even in the midst of a library career and raising a family. Since 1998, Caroline has been making quilts and dyeing cloth using increasingly complex surface design techniques. In 1999, she was juried into the Southern Highlands Craft Guild and the following year into the Piedmont Craftsmen, Inc.

SUSAN MCBRIDE is an illustrator and rubber stamp artist who enjoys gardening and spending time with her daughter. She resides in Asheville, North Carolina.

JOAN K. MORRIS's artistic endeavors have led her down many successful creative paths. A childhood interest in sewing turned into professional costuming for motion pictures. After studying ceramics, Joan ran her own clay wind chime business for 15 years. Since 1993, Joan's Asheville, North Carolina, coffee house, Vincent's Ear, has provided a vital meeting place for all varieties of artists and thinkers.

LEE PARTIN is a high school educator, as well as an art and pottery instructor for a junior college. She is an artist in a variety of media, including glass, pottery, and . . . fireworks! (Lee is a licensed pyrotechnician.) In addition to these creative endeavors, she is an accomplished shell builder, having recently been named as one of the top ten shell builders in the country. In fact, she was recently invited to shoot in the PGI All Stars. Of all her artistic interests, however, Lee enjoys fiber arts the most, particularly spinning, weaving, and dye work.

DYAN MAI PETERSON is an internationally known gourd artist and basketmaker. She lives in Asheville, NC with her husband, furniture maker Gary Peterson. dyanmai.peterson@verizon.net and www.thedecoratedgourd.com.

TANYA SAVAGE studied stained glass and glass mosaic in Raleigh, North Carolina. She found her niche working with glass tesserae and, over the past five years, has developed her own unique style of mosaic. Tanya creates glass mosaic stepping stones, tables, mirrors, and decorative wall hangings. She teaches mosaic classes in her studio, emphasizing the use of glass, tile, broken china, and found objects. Tanya and her husband are the co-owners of "space. an art gallery," which is located in Waynesville, North Carolina and serves as the exclusive outlet for Tanya's artwork.

TERRY TAYLOR lends his creative spirit full time to Lark Books, and, in his spare time, glues pastes, and otherwise assembles works of art using a wide range of media from old CDs to broken china. His current interests include metal jewelry, and his work has been exhibed in many galleries and in many publications.

TRUE TIE DYE started creating and selling tie dye in Colorado in 1995. Today, the company's line—which include t-shirts, ladies tops and dresses, children's clothing, and tapestries, all made from a variety of cotton and rayon fabrics—may be purchased online from anywhere in the world at www.truetiedye.com. Wholesale inquires are welcome, and the company can be contacted via email at info@truetiedye.com.

NICOLE TUGGLE combines bookbinding techniques with her passion for mail art to create unique letters, fine art, and gift items. Visit her website at: www.sigilation.com.

BONNIE WILBER lives in Ripon, Wisconsin. Her hobby is making beautiful handmade soaps, most of which she gives away to family and friends. She can be reached by phone at (920) 748 7127.

TRACIA L. WILLIAMS is a product developer and industry consultant for the craft and creative industry. She lives in sunny Orlando Florida with her four children and her business partner/husband, Chris. Tracia enjoys mixed media art, beading, paper crafting, and painting.

SHANNON YOKELEY grew up in the mountains of Western North Carolina. She did her first artwork, a mural on the wall of her mother's daycare, at the age of six. Woodburning has been a hobby she's enjoyed for many years, along with horse-back riding, painting, and frequenting the local flea markets for the odd piece of art.

INDEX

SUBJECT INDEX

A
Album, photograph, 393
Arrangements, 310-313, 318, 501

B
Bath bars, 285
Bottles
  Etched, 37, 46
  Painted, 23
Bouquets
  Dried flower, 298
Bowls
  Gilded, 110
  Polymer, 417
  Woodburned, 63
Boxes
  Gilded, 108
  Scented, 286
  Stamped, 388
  Woodburned, 66
Buttons, woodburned, 58

C
Candles
  Beeswax, 216
  Carved, 163
  Decorated, 164, 167
  Gel, 176-185
  Gilded, 115
  Layered, 215
  Painted, 160
  Pyramid, 219
  Soy, 212
  Tapers, 220, 221
Candlesticks
  Painted, 88
  Polymer, 413
Cards
  Accordion folded, 356-359
  Eyelet, 352-355
  Heritage, 348-351
  Kids, 347, 348
  Layered, 360, 361
Ceiling fan pulls, 503
Clocks
  Antiqued, 74
  Decoupaged, 80

  Painted, 77
  Polymer clay, 78
Curtains, 469

F
Finials, wood finished, 95
Floorcloths, 470
Frames, photo
  Bread dough, 437
  Faux finished, 142
  Gilded, 113
  Stenciled, 126
Furniture
  Crackled, 91
  Decoupaged, 334
  Distressed, 97
  Etched, 27
  Painted, 44, 149

G
Garlands, 301
Gourds, woodburned, 61

L
Lamp shades, 131
Lanterns, 41

M
Magnets, 330
Mirrors, 43

N
Napkin rings, 506
Necklaces, 486-493

O
Ornaments, holiday, 421, 433

P
Pillows
  Silk flower, 316
  Stamped, 395
Placemats, 475
Potpourri, 278

R
Room dividers, stenciled, 133

S

Sachets, 280-283

Scarves, 463

Shelves, faux finished, 144

Soap

    Melt and pour, 232-235

    Cold process, 236-247

Stools, woodburned, 64

Switchplates

    Faux finished, 147

    Polymer, 411

Swizzle sticks, 505

T

Topiary, dried rose, 295

Tray, mosaic, 264

T-shirts, 450, 453, 467, 473

V

Vases, sponged, 141

W

Wreaths

    Dried, 302

    Bread dough, 439

TECHNIQUE INDEX

Bead jewelry

How-to, 482-485

Materials and tools, 480

Projects, 486-493

Bread dough

How-to, 426-431

Materials and tools, 424

Projects, 432-439

Candlescaping

How-to, 190-193

Materials and tools, 188, 189

Projects, 194-203

Candlemaking

How-to, 208-211

Materials and tools, 206, 207

Projects, 212-221

Card making

How-to, 342-345

Materials and tools, 340

Projects, 346-361

Clock making

How-to, 72, 73

Materials and tools, 70

Projects, 74-81

Decorating Candles

How-to, 156-159

Materials and tools, 154

Projects, 160-167

Decoupage

How-to, 326-327

Materials and tools, 324

Projects, 328-337

Dried Flowers

How-to, 292-293

Materials and tools, 290

Projects, 294-303

Faux finishing

How-to, 138, 139

Materials and tools, 136

Projects, 140-149

Gel Candles

How-to, 172-175

Materials and tools, 170

Projects, 176-185

Gilding

How-to, 104-107

Materials and tools, 102

Projects, 108-115

Glass etching

How-to, 32-35

Materials and tools, 30

Projects, 36-47

Glass painting

How-to, 14-17

Materials and tools, 12

Projects, 18-27

Home beading

How-to, 498, 499

Materials and tools, 496, 497

Projects, 500-509

Mosaics

How-to, 252-257

Materials and tools, 250

Projects, 258-267

Painting on Fabric

How-to, 460, 461

Materials and tools, 458, 459

Projects, 462-475

Polymer clay

How-to, 402-407

Materials and tools, 400

Projects, 408-421

Sachets and potpourris

How-to, 274-277

Materials and tools, 272, 273

Projects, 278-287

Scrapbooking

How-to, 366-369

Materials and tools, 364-365

Projects, 370-373

Silk flowers

How-to, 308-309

Materials and tools, 306, 307

Projects, 310-318

Soap making

How-to, 226-231

Materials and tools, 224, 225

Projects, 232-247

Stamping

How-to, 384-387

Materials and tools, 382-383

Projects, 386-395

Stenciling

How-to, 120-125

Materials and tools, 118

Projects, 126-133

Tie-Dye

How-to, 446, 447

Materials and tools, 444

Projects, 448-455

Woodburning

How-to, 54-57

Materials and tools, 52

Projects, 58-67

Wood finishing

How-to, 86, 87

Materials and tools, 84

Projects, 88-97

ACKNOWLEDGMENTS

Thanks and gratitude need to be extended to the many people who contributed to this book.

Rob Pulleyn for his creative energy and guidance

Emma Marschall for hand modeling with grace and good humor

Pamela Brown, Irene Semanchuk Dean, Susan Greenelsh, Lee Partin, and Tina Poston for technical advice

Jackie Dobirnska, Margaret Murphey, Wes Albrecht, and Celia Naranjo for modeling projects

Mission Productions, Ltd. in Hong Kong for their professionalism and dedication to quality

Carol Taylor, Chris Bryant, Celia Naranjo, Terry Taylor, Shannon Yokeley, Marthe Le Van, Laura Gabris, Evan Krokowski, and Paige Gilchrist for saving the day at moment zero

Rosemary Kast, Jessy Mauney, and Jeff Hamilton for helping out in countless ways

Earth Guild in Asheville, North Carolina, for lending materials

Deborah Morgenthal and Todd Kaderabek for support

Julie Brown for proofreading

Susan McBride for lending us her garden

Sandra Stambaugh, Dwayne Shell, Richard Hasselberg, and Keith Wright for gallery photography

. . . and the dozens of cherished colleagues who kept us laughing, loaned us props, and brought chocolate.

I N D E X